The Mother Wave

Theorizing, Enacting, and Representing Matricentric Feminism

Edited by Andrea O'Reilly and Fiona Joy Green

DEMETER

The Mother Wave
Theorizing, Enacting, and Representing Matricentric Feminism
Edited by Andrea O'Reilly and Fiona Joy Green

Demeter Press
PO Box 197
Coe Hill, Ontario
Canada
K0L 1P0
Tel: 289-383-0134
Email: info@demeterpress.org
Website: www.demeterpress.org

Demeter Press logo based on the sculpture "Demeter" by Maria-Luise Bodirsky
www.keramik-atelier.bodirsky.de

Printed and Bound in Canada

Cover design: Michelle Pirovich
Typesetting: Michelle Pirovich
Proof reading: Jena Woodhouse

Library and Archives Canada Cataloguing in Publication
Title: The mother wave: theorizing, enacting, and representing matricentric feminism / edited by Andrea O'Reilly and Fiona Joy Green.
Names: O'Reilly, Andrea, 1961- editor. | Green, Fiona J., editor.
Description: Includes bibliographical references.
Identifiers: Canadiana 20240412753 | ISBN 9781772585056 (softcover)
Subjects: LCSH: Feminism. | LCSH: Motherhood.
Classification: LCC HQ1233.M68 2024 | DDC 305.42—dc23

Funded by the Government of Canada | Canada

The publisher gratefully acknowledges the support of the Government of Canada

For Marie Porter, AM, PhD
(4 November 1939 – 2 June 2023)

Profoundly dedicated mother, friend, feminist and mentor.

Marie's fierce love for family, friends and mothers propelled her to be a ground-breaking and extremely successful disability advocate, matricentric feminist, maternal scholar, educator, and researcher.

As the mother of three boys, and the primary care giver for one who was severely physically disabled, she was instrumental in the establishment of several organisations. Marie's experience of ensuring that Anthony lived many good decades beyond his given life expectancy of one year, informed her prominent involvement in the establishment of Friends of Brain Injured Children, the Mamre Association (Brisbane's longest-serving not-for-profit disability support providers respite care for parents of disabled people) and NIRAN Inc (permanent residential accommodation for severely disabled adults).

When forced to resign as a teacher in 1962, due to the marriage bar, Marie returned to University and over time completed her PhD. Passionate about mothering, Dr. Porter organized the inaugural course on motherhood at the University of Queensland. In 2005, she founded the Australian Motherhood Initiative for Research and Community Involvement (AMIRCI), which consists of a network of scholars, writers, activists, policy makers, educators, artists and practitioners whose work explores the experience of women as mothers, mothering and motherhood. She presided over multiple international conferences held in Australia, and published many articles and books addressing mothers at the margins and the transformative power of mothers and mothering.

Dr Porter was made a Member of the Order of Australia (AM) in 2018.

We are deeply saddened by her passing and are so much more enriched by her life. We are emboldened by her tenacity to act upon her passionate love and commitment of social change.

We dedicate this collection, which addresses the ways in which matricentric feminism is theorized, represented and enacted, to her memory and to her legacy.

Contents

Introduction

Andrea O'Reilly and Fiona Joy Green

Matricentric feminism begins with the conviction that mothering matters and is central to the lives of those who identify as mothers. In saying this, we are not suggesting that mothering is all that matters or that it matters the most; rather, any understanding of mothers' lives is incomplete without considering how becoming and being a mother shape that mother's sense of self and how they see and live in the world. When we use the term "mothers," we refer to individuals who engage in motherwork or, as Sara Ruddick theorized, maternal practice. Such a term is not limited to biological mothers or cisgender women but to anyone who does the work of mothering as a central part of their life. As noted by Michigan State University's Women*s Student Services website, "Gender is one part of our identities, and there is more to gender than the binary" (quoted in Willey, 78). In her chapter in this collection, Nicole Willey sees the power and need for this understanding: "Opening up our language, spaces, and scholarship—indeed our feminism—to a 'both-and' type of inclusion will support all mothers" (66). For individuals who are mothers, mothering is a significant if not a defining dimension of their lives, and, arguably, maternity matters more than gender.

Matricentric feminism seeks to make motherhood the business of feminism by positioning mothers' needs and concerns as the starting point for a theory and politics on and for the empowerment of mothers and women. This repositioning is not to suggest that matricentric feminism should replace traditional feminist thought; rather, it is to emphasize that the category of mother is distinct from the category of woman and that many of the problems mothers face—social, economic, political, cultural, psychological, and so forth—are specific to mothers' role and identity as mothers. "Matricentric feminism," as Zaje Harrell explains in her chapter in this collection, "holds the cogent position that motherhood is a common and encompassing experience for the majority of women. This makes it relevant to feminism, as many of the social limitations women face are rooted in their status as mothers" (Harrell, 46). Moreover, as Patrice DiQuinzio emphasizes: "To the extent that mothering in all its diverse forms remains an important aspect of women's lives and that decisions about whether, when, and how to mother continue to face almost all women, feminism cannot claim to give an adequate account of women's lives and to represent women's needs and interests if it ignores the issue of mothering" ("Mothering and Feminism" 545). Indeed, as Eva Feder Kitty emphasizes, "Most women care for their dependents at some point", and for many women, "this occupies the better part of their lives" (qtd. in Stephens 141). Moreover, as Zaje Harrell notes in her chapter in this collection, "84.3 per cent of women between forty and forty-nine in the United States have had at least one biological child" (45). However, as Harrell continues, "the experience of mothering has not received proportionate scholarly attention" (45). More specifically, as Lucy Jones notes in her recent book *Matrescence: On the Metamorphosis of Pregnancy, Childbirth and Motherhood*: "[Motherhood] is a major female experience where feminism has failed" (202). Indeed, as Andrea O'Reilly argues in her book *Matricentric Feminism: Theory, Activism, Practice*, motherhood is the unfinished business of feminism. Mothers are oppressed under patriarchy as women and as mothers. Consequently, mothers need a matricentric mode of feminism organized around their particular identity and work as mothers. Thus, mother-centred feminism is needed because mothers—arguably more so than women in general—remain disempowered despite sixty years of feminism.

In the call for papers for this collection, we invited contributors to share how they view this wave of matricentric feminism in micro and macro ways and to explore the impact and influence of matricentric feminism on families and children, culture, art/literature, social media, public policy, education, workplace practices, and so forth. We were delighted to receive a range of submissions touching on many of these areas through personal reflections, scholarly essays, memoirs, creative nonfiction, poetry, and photography. As a result, this collection investigates how scholars and activists are developing theories, enactments, and representations of matricentric feminism. In her book *Mothers: An Essay on Love and Cruelty,* Jaqueline Rose argues that "Mothers ... are the original subversives, never what they seem or are meant to be" (18). However, as Rose continues, "Despite the evidence, the acuity and rage of mothers, somehow continue to be one of the best-kept secrets of our times" (18). This collection aims to render visible the perception and power of matricentric feminism as it is theorized, enacted, and represented to realize and enact the subversive potential of mothers and their contributions to feminist theory and activism. In this introduction, we explain our use of the mother wave metaphor, provide an overview of matricentric feminism, and introduce the sections and chapters of the collection.

Matricentric Feminism as the Mother Wave: Riding the Wave Rather Than Waving It Off

We are aware that the term "wave" attracts criticism by some for, among other reasons, being selected and defined by the media, being dismissive of the multiplicity and difference among feminists and feminisms, focussing upon particular interests and groups of feminists, and for pushing and celebrating specific feminists as icons of that moment and wave (Hemmings; Laughlin et al.; Springer). Yet we chose to use the concept because the waves of feminism do not represent, nor reflect, the entire history of feminism but rather are "ascribed to moments that seem particularly inflamed and intense" (Chamberlain 7). Like Prudence Chamberlain, we believe the "surging and forcefulness connoted by the wave speaks to periods of affective intensity, prompting increased action, within feminism" (6). We understand, as Chamberlain notes, that rather than "conflating the wave with a particular generation, or attributing it to the inevitability of progress, surges are formulated through a range of interdependencies. The wave is a moment in which discourse, effect, context, and affect all converge, creating an adaptable and evolving energised period of concerted activism" (8). By moving away from the divisive perspective of the wave narrative and rejecting waves as connoting generational difference and chronological separation of the new replacing the old, we come to understand that "waves are not predictable, uniform or monolithic" but rather are "capable of multiplicity and diversity" (Chamberlain 22).

Oceanic waves do not begin from a definitive starting point or have an endpoint; rather, each wave is connected to the entire ocean. Waves carry energy from the environment around them, such as the energy caused by earthquakes, volcano eruptions, landslides, and wind. Oceans are full of cross-currents and eddies with surges of water that carry energy forces in the form of waves from one moment to another, drawing energy to sustain their movement until the wave breaks. We believe it is possible to refute both the linearity and generational limitations of the waves of feminism because chronological order does not preclude a crossing of temporalities (Chamberlain 30). Understanding feminist waves as part of a larger body recognizes that they emerge from within a considerably broader body of historical and contemporary feminist work and that they are in a "stronger conversation with one another than a linear interpretation may allow" (Chamberlain 30). Furthermore, feminist waves can encourage and support internal personal and feminist dialogue central to engaging with disagreements among feminists and others to make visible and work with those folx marginalized within and outside feminist movements.

Matricentric feminism is the mother wave in the feminist ocean. Like a wave that rises to minimally swell or break through the calm of a body of water, matricentric feminism brings to the surface the undercurrents of feminism, mothering, and motherhood, which have gone unnoticed. And like a wave, matricentric feminism forcefully arcs away from normative mothering and feminist practices and smashes through patriarchal beliefs about mothering, motherhood, and feminism. Rather than separating itself from other feminisms, as has been practiced by some in previous feminist waves, the mother wave of matricentric feminism invites conversations with others and offers a praxis of feminism that aims to coexist, overlap, and intersect with others.

Contributors in this collection use water metaphors when speaking about their reflections and understandings of matricentric feminism; such words as "water," "waves," "rivers," and "deltas" appear in some of the chapters. These authors clearly understand how the past informs the present and the future, and they are not wedded to a single silo of ideas, movements, or understandings. As Abigail Palko notes in her chapter in this collection: "For the mother wave to be successful, we need to have messy conversations about the maternal Möbius strip of judging mothers and mothers speaking, and then we might find beauty in the chaos" (170).

Matricentric Feminism: Possibilities, Challenges, and Controversies

Possibilities

In this collection, we use the term "matricentric" to define and describe a mother-centred mode of feminism. Feminist literary critic Elaine Showalter uses the term "gynocentric" to signify a woman-centred perspective; similarly, we use "matricentric" to convey a mother-centred perspective. The choice to use the word "matricentric" over "maternal" and to use the term "matricentric feminism" instead of "maternal feminism" is to distinguish a mother-focused feminism from maternalism. Judith Stadman Tucker argues that maternalism "conforms to the dominant ideology of motherhood and emphasizes the importance of maternal well-being to the health and safety of children." (2) "Maternalism," she continues, "overlaps with what has been called 'difference feminism'—particularly the idea that women are 'naturally' or intuitively more empathic, less exploitative, and more closely attuned to relational ambience than men" (2). Likewise, Rachel V. Kutz-Flamenbaum, writing in *The Encyclopedia of Motherhood*, says:

> Maternalism, like paternalism, is an ideology and philosophy. It asserts that "mother knows best" and that women, as a group, maintain a set of ideas, beliefs or experiences that reflect their motherly knowledge and motherly strengths. Maternalism suggests that women are (and should be) the moral conscience of humanity and asserts women's legitimate investment in political affairs through this emphasis. (712)

Patrice DiQuinzio further elaborates that maternalist politics "refers to political activism and political movements that invoke motherhood as the basis of women's agency" ("The Politics of the Mothers Movement" 58).

A matricentric perspective is not to be confused with a maternalist one. Although some perspectives in matricentric feminism may be considered maternalist, they are largely limited to the activism of certain motherhood organizations. Moreover, matricentric feminism understands motherhood to be socially and historically constructed and positions mothering more as a practice than an identity. Central to matricentric feminist theory is also a critique of the maternalist stance that positions maternity as basic to and the basis of female identity; it also challenges the assumption that maternity is natural to women (i.e., all women naturally know how to mother) and that the work of mothering is driven by instinct rather than intelligence and developed by habit rather than skill. Although matricentric feminism does hold a mother-centred perspective, it does not advance a maternalist argument or agenda. Thus, matricentric feminism marks the crucial difference between a focus on mothers and a politics of maternalism.

When discussing matricentric feminism, we draw on the concept of a matrifocal narrative, particularly as it has been developed in maternal literary theory. In her introduction to *The Mother/Daughter Plot*, Marianne Hirsch queries why in Sophocles's *Oedipus Rex* is the voice of Jocasta, Oedipus's mother, missing. She connects this narrative silence to a larger literary lacuna: "In asking where the story of Jocasta is in the story of Oedipus, I am asking not only where the stories of women are in men's plots, but where the stories of mothers are in the plots of sons and daughters" (4). She concludes that "Clearly, to know Jocasta's maternal story ... we would have to begin with the mother" (5). Drawing on Hirsh, Brenda O. Daly and Maureen T. Reddy emphasize in *Narrating Maternity* that even of the limited number of fictional or theoretical texts that do "begin with the mother in her own right, from her own perspective ... [they] seldom hold fast to a maternal perspective; further when texts do maintain this perspective, readers and critics tend to suppress the centrality of mothering" (2–3). Daly and Reddy have coined the term "daughter-centricity" to describe the perspective in which less is learned about "what it is like to mother than about what it is like to be mothered, even when the author has had both experiences" (2).

Within the last three decades, as motherhood studies has emerged as a distinct and established academic discipline, this daughter-centricity has been countered and corrected in fiction and theory. Indeed, a central aim of motherhood studies is to articulate and theorize "the voice of the mother"—that is, to analyze becoming and being a mother from the perspective and subjectivity of mothers themselves. Adrienne Rich concludes *Of Woman Born* with these words: "The words are being spoken now, are being written down, the taboos are being broken, the masks of motherhood are cracking through" (239). Whether such "unmasking" (Maushart) is conveyed through a sociological study of mothers or in a popular motherhood memoir, feminist writers and scholars endeavour to unmask motherhood by documenting the lived reality of mothering. In so doing, they counter the daughter-centricity, described by Daly and Reddy above, to create and compose what O'Reilly has termed a "matrifocal narrative."

Our use of the term "matrifocal" is drawn from Miriam Johnson's discussion of matrifocality in *Strong Mothers, Weak Wives*:

> [Matrifocal societies] tend to have greater gender equality because of the power of a maternal paradigm. In these societies, regardless of the particular type of kinship system, women play roles of cultural and social significance and define themselves less as wives than as mothers.... Matrifocality however, does not refer to domestic maternal dominance so much as it does to the relative cultural prestige of the image of the mother, a role that is culturally elaborated and valued. Mothers are also structurally central in that the mother as a status has some degree of control over the kin unit's economic resources and is critically involved in kin-related decision making processes. It is not the absence of males (males may be quite present) but the centrality of women as mothers and sisters that makes a society matrifocal. (226)

A matrifocal narrative, borrowing from Johnson's terminology above, is one in which a mother plays a role of cultural and social significance and in which motherhood is thematically elaborated and valued and is structurally central to the plot. In other words—and to draw on the work of Daly and Reddy—matrifocal narratives "begin with the mother in her own right, from her own perspective," and they "hold fast to a maternal perspective" (2–3). In addition, a matrifocal reading attends to and accentuates the maternal theme in any given text.

As matricentric feminism is matrifocal in its focus, it is multi- and interdisciplinary in its perspective. Matricentric feminist theory draws from many academic disciplines—including anthropology, history, literary studies, sociology, philosophy, psychology, sexuality studies, and women's studies—as well as from the established schools of academic feminism. Indeed, far from being an island on its own, matricentric feminism is informed by traditional schools of academic feminism and its most prominent theorists: womanist and African American feminism (e.g., bell hooks and Patricia Hill Collins), liberal feminism (e.g., Ann

Crittenden), psychoanalytic feminism (e.g., Nancy Chodorow and Jessica Benjamin), queer-lesbian feminism (e.g., Baba Copper), cultural-difference feminism (e.g., Adrienne Rich), socialist feminism (e.g., Mary O'Brien), and third-wave feminism (e.g., Ariel Gore). For example, matricentric feminism is informed by the African American feminist commitment to the epistemological importance of lived experience while also being informed by third-wave feminism's commitment to intersectional analyses.

We are frequently asked what matricentric feminism is. As a new and emergent feminism, it is difficult to define matricentric feminism other than to say that it is explicitly matrifocal in its perspective and emphasis—it begins with the mother and takes seriously the work of mothering—and that it is multidisciplinary and multitheoretical in its perspective. Below, we gesture towards a possible definition by listing what we see as the central and governing principles and aims of matricentric feminism:

- asserts that the topics of mothers, mothering, and motherhood are deserving of serious and sustained scholarly inquiry;
- regards mothering as work that is important and valuable to society and emphasizes that the essential task of mothering is not, and should not be, the sole responsibility and duty of mothers;
- contests, challenges, and counters the patriarchal oppressive institution of motherhood and seeks to imagine and implement a maternal identity and practice that is empowering to mothers;
- seeks to correct the child centredness that defines much of the scholarship and activism on motherhood and seeks to develop research and activism from the experience and the perspective of mothers;
- commits to social change and social justice and regards mothering as a socially engaged enterprise and a site of power, wherein mothers can and do create social change through childrearing and activism;
- understands mothering and motherhood to be culturally determined and variable and is committed to exploring the diversity of maternal experience across race, class, gender, culture, ethnicity, sexuality, ability, age, and geographical location; and
- endeavours to establish maternal theory and motherhood studies as autonomous, independent, and legitimate scholarly disciplines.

The above list is only partial and provisional. Since the publication of the first edition of *Matricentric Feminism* in 2016, numerous scholars, writers, and activists across diverse perspectives and disciplines have taken up matricentric feminism to explore topics as varied as literature, film, art, photography, public policy, politics, incarceration, critical disability, health, violence against women, and activism, to name but a few. Two journals have published special double issues on matricentric feminism: the Australian journal *Hecate* (2019) and *The Journal of the Motherhood Initiative* (2019). Indeed, a Google search of the term "matricentric feminism" reveals eleven thousand entries. This scholarship recognizes the need for a distinctive feminism for and about mothers, and it explores mothers' particular needs, experiences, and desires, which continue to be marginalized as compared to nonmothers. It is our hope that this collection builds upon this emergent scholarship to deliver and impart new understandings and uses of a feminism in which, to paraphrase writer and activist Marilyn Waring, mothers and mothering count.

The Disavowal of Mothering in Academic Feminism

Matricentric feminism, however, has yet to be incorporated into the field of academic feminism. In making this claim, we are not saying no feminist scholarship on motherhood exists but rather that matricentric feminism remains peripheral to academic feminism. Over the last two-plus decades as motherhood researchers and publishers, we have heard countless stories from motherhood scholars about how their work has been ignored, dismissed, invalidated, or trivialized by academic feminists; how the women's studies conferences they attend have few, if any papers, on motherhood; how motherhood is seldom a topic of discussion in women's studies classrooms and rarely included in academic feminist textbooks; and how articles on motherhood or reviews of motherhood books are all but absent in the leading women's studies journals. Andrea O'Reilly's 2016 study of the place of motherhood over the previous ten years in academic contexts, such as National Women's Studies Association conference panels, in top feminist journals—such as *Signs*, *Frontiers*, *Women's Studies Quarterly*, *Feminist Studies*, and *Gender and Society*—and in gender and women's studies textbooks and syllabi confirmed this anecdotal evidence, finding that only 1 per cent to less than 3 per cent of the content is devoted to the topic of motherhood (*Matricentric Feminism*).

Given that 80 per cent of women become mothers in their lifetime, there is an evident disconnect between the minimal representation of motherhood in academic feminism and the actual lives of most women.

A demand for a theory and practice based on a specific identity of women is hardly an innovative or radical claim. Over the last fifty years, many groups of women have argued that mainstream feminism—largely understood to be liberal feminism—has not adequately represented their perspectives or needs. Women of colour, for example, have advocated that feminism address the intersectionality of their oppression as racialized women, a feminism now known as womanism; women from the Global South have called for the development of a theory of global feminism; and queer, lesbian, bi, and trans women have supported the growth of queer feminist theory and activism. Likewise, the development of third-wave feminism in the 1990s grew out of young women's sense of alienation from the aims of second-wave feminism. When such women demanded a feminist theory of their own, the larger mainstream feminist movement acknowledged, albeit often reluctantly, that such women had been excluded from the more established canon of feminist thought. Feminist theory was subsequently revised to include these different positions and perspectives within feminism. Most introductions to women's studies textbooks or courses now include chapters or units on socialist feminism, global feminism, queer feminism, third-wave feminism, and womanism, and these perspectives and topics are well represented at women's studies conferences and in women's studies journals.

However, as mothers began to call for feminism for and about mothers over the last decade or so—what Andrea O'Reilly has defined as matricentric feminism—and to ask for its inclusion in academic feminism, their calls were not met with the same respect or recognition. More often than not, their claims were dismissed, trivialized, disparaged, and ridiculed: Why would mothers need such a mother-centred feminist perspective? The question implies that mothers do not have needs or concerns separate from their larger identity as women. It troubles us deeply that feminists can understand the intersectionality of gendered oppression when it comes to race, class, gender, sexuality, and geographical location but not so for maternity. Yet, we argue—and we suspect most mothers would agree—that maternity needs to be likewise understood in terms of intersectional theory. The category of mother is distinct from the category of woman; many of the problems mothers face—social, economic, political, cultural, and psychological—are specific to their work and identity as mothers. Mothers, in other words, do not live simply as women but as mother-women, just as Black women do not live only as women but as racialized women. Moreover, mothers' oppression and resistance under patriarchy are shaped by their maternal identity, just as Black women's oppression and resistance are shaped by their racialized identity. Thus, mothers need a feminism of their own—one that positions mothers' concerns as the starting point for empowerment. For us, this seems self-evident. Why then is maternity not seen as a subject position and, hence, not theorized with other subject positions in terms of the intersectionality of gendered oppression and resistance? Why do we not recognize mothers' specific perspectives as we do for other women, whether they are queer, working class, racialized, and so forth? Why do mothers and mothering not count or matter? The second edition of *Matricentric Feminism: Theory, Activism, and Practice* (2021) considers three reasons for what O'Reilly terms the disavowal and disappearance of motherhood in academic feminism: confusing mothering with motherhood, the conflation of matricentric feminism with maternalism and gender essentialism, and the cultural ascendancy of postmaternal thinking.

In the introduction of this collection, we briefly examine four central concerns of matricentric feminism: the specific political import and intent of racialized women's motherwork, the radical queering of empowered mothering, the real and prevalent oppressions of motherwork, and, finally, the foregrounding of mothers and mothering in feminism. This discussion considers these concerns with attention to the use of the words "mothers" and "mothering" in matricentric feminism. Overall, we argue that matricentric feminism affords a gender-neutral understanding of motherwork in its positioning of mothering as a verb and allows for an appreciation of how motherwork is deeply gendered and how this may be challenged and changed through empowered mothering. Thus, matricentric feminism, we argue, moves beyond gender towards resistant and inclusive mothering.

Why Mothers and Mothering?

In matricentric feminism, the term "mother" refers to any individual who engages in motherwork; it is not limited to cisgender women; rather, it includes anyone who takes upon the work of mothering as a central part of their life. Building upon Sara Ruddick's concept of maternal practice, matricentric feminism positions the word "mother" as a verb, as something one does—a practice. For Ruddick, as Sarah LaChance Adams notes, "It is the practice of mothering that makes one a mother, not a biological or social imperative [and] therefore, the title of 'mother' is not strictly limited to biological mothers, or even women" (727). She continues: "Maternal commitment is voluntary and conscious; it is not inevitable, nor is it dictated by nature" (727). Repositioning mother from a noun to a verb degenders mothering and divests care of biology to dislodge the gender essentialism grounding and structuring normative motherhood.

However, despite this degendering of mothering in matricentric feminism, some have argued that the term still excludes trans and nonbinary folx and have called for more inclusive language to replace the words "mothers" and "mothering" with "parents" and "parenting." Indeed, as Sarah Ratchford comments, "As a gender-nonconforming person, I feel left out of the parenting discussion. It's time we became more inclusive in our language." In the introduction to their book, *The Liminal Chrysalis: Imagining Reproduction and Parenting Futures beyond the Binary*, H. Kori Doty and A. J. Lowik posit that "Trans and non-binary people, of all identities and expressions, are framed as the exception, even as aberrational" (16). Here, we want to take up these concerns to consider how to navigate, negotiate, and create inclusive language while recognizing that for many mothers and in particular contexts, mothering is a culturally and politically determined concept that still has significance and consequence. In this discussion, we contend that replacing the word "mothering" with "parenting" is particularly problematic for racialized women because it dilutes the specific political import and intention of their motherwork and denies the significance of maternal identity for reproductive justice. Furthermore, the word "parenting" does not effectively convey the radical queering of empowered mothering. Using the term "parents"—that is, conflating mothers with fathers—is often also disingenuous if not dangerous because it deflects, disguises, and denies the real and prevalent gendered oppressions of motherwork. Moreover, switching to the term "parenting" makes mothering invisible as it is practised and researched. However, as we make these arguments, we also recognize how problematic the terms "mothers" and "mothering" are for trans and nonbinary individuals. Overall, we seek to explore how to achieve inclusion without exclusion by positioning mothering as a verb while acknowledging the gendered oppressions of motherwork.

"Deeply Political": The Specific Meanings and Practices of Racialized Women's Motherwork

"Black motherhood," in the words of Dani McClain, is "deeply political" (4). In *We Live for the We: The Political Power of Black Motherhood*, McClain writes the following: "Our job as Black mothers is to keep pushing the liberation ball down the court. Our obligation is to leave the world better for [our children] and to ensure that they are equipped with the tools that they need to fight.... Black mothering is a political project, and our mission—should we choose to accept it—is nothing short of revolutionary" (201). Chapter one of *Matricentric Feminism* explores how the Black maternal practices of other/community mothering, social activism, and nurturance as resistance render Black mothering profoundly political and public in contrast to the dictates of normative motherhood discussed above. Patricia Hill Collins uses the term "motherwork" to refer to what is usually meant by nurturance, love, or mothering generally ("Shifting the Center"). Collins's word choice is significant because it foregrounds mothering as labour and calls attention to how mothering is socially and politically motivated and experienced in African American culture. Her emphasis is on how the concerns of what she calls "racial ethnic mothers" differ from those in the dominant culture. She identifies the goals of "racial ethnic mothers" as the following: keeping the children born to you; supporting the physical survival of those children; teaching the children resistance and how to survive in a racist world; providing those children their racial-cultural history and identity; and practising a social activism and communal mothering on behalf of all the community's children. Collins argues that this construction of mothering as social activism empowers Black women because motherhood operates, in her words, as "a symbol of power" ("The Meaning of Motherhood" 51).

Motherhood is likewise a site of empowerment and resistance for Indigenous mothers. Indigenous scholar Jennifer Brant argues that Indigenous cultures possess a matriarchal worldview, which holds women in high esteem and honours them as powerful for their ability to give life to the community in a physical and spiritual sense (112). Indigenous scholars and activists Dawn Memee Lavell-Harvard and Jeanette Corbiere Lavell emphasize the following: "The historical persistence of our cultural difference generation after generation (despite the best assimilative efforts of both church and state) is a sign of our strength and our resistance.

That we have historically and continually mothered in a way that is 'different' from the dominant culture, is not only empowering for our women, but is potentially empowering for all women" (3). Indeed, as Amber Kinser comments, "In Indigenous cultures, women's traditional roles have long been recognized and celebrated as powerful" (6). Moreover, as Kim Anderson explains, family in Indigenous culture "can be a site of resistance and renewal" (762), which is similar to hooks's theory of homeplace for African American mothers. Thus, similar to Black mothers, Indigenous mothers achieve power and worth precisely through their politically and socially valued motherwork. Indigenous and Black mothers must also assert and retain a maternal identity for reproductive justice. The realities of past sterilization as well as higher maternal mortality rates for racialized women show that they often cannot even become mothers; moreover, the histories of slavery for Black women and residential schooling for Indigenous women, along with the disproportionate numbers of their children in foster care, mean that these mothers are often not permitted to mother the children born to them.

To become and be a mother as a Black and Indigenous woman is, thus, a radical act of defiance and resistance, as it defies and disrupts the cultural denial and disparagement of racialized women's motherwork and motherlove in resisting and surviving the colonial project of genocide. Commenting on the enslaved mother Sethe in her novel *Beloved*, Toni Morrison asserts as follows: "Sethe's claim is an unheard-of outrageous claim for a slave woman to make; for what Sethe is claiming is the right and responsibility to say something about what happens to [her children]" (qtd. in Danille Taylor-Guthrie 252). We suggest that similar to the character of Sethe, in claiming the identity of mother, racialized women assert the rights and responsibilities accorded to white mothers: They demand that they, not others, will determine the fate of their children. Thus, for racialized women, the words "mother" and "mothering" must be retained and preserved; to replace them with "parents" and "parenting" erases the specific and radical political intent and import of racialized women's motherwork and disregards, if not discounts, how claiming and holding a maternal identity is a necessary act of survival and resistance for Black and Indigenous women. The challenge, therefore, is to determine how to include the meanings and practices of parenting for trans and nonbinary folx without excluding those of racialized women.

Queering Motherhood: Enactments of Empowered Mothering

The term "empowered mothering" is used in matricentric feminism because it is overwhelmingly women who are oppressed by normative motherhood and who engage in various strategies to challenge and change normative motherhood. In enacting empowered mothering, these outlaw mothers, we argue, queer motherhood. Queering, as Margaret Gibson explains in the introduction to her book *Queering Motherhood: Narrative and Theoretical Approaches*, "makes the things we otherwise take for granted suddenly unpredictable, uncooperative, and unexpected" (1). Thus, Gibson emphasizes: "To queer motherhood is to re-think, re-shape ... [normative] motherhood" (12), particularly its ideological mandates of essentialization, normalization, naturalization, and biologicalization. Black families in their practices of other/communal mothering and extended kin "challenge heteronormative ideas of family," and, thus, we must "name the specific ways that the queerness of family can benefit those involved" (McClain 60). Feminist mothers likewise queer mothering in their practices of coparenting and political activism as do lesbian mothers through same-sex parenting.

We suggest that the social location of the mother or parent determines what strategy they will use in their resistance to normative motherhood; their modes of resistance will never be complete or include all mothers, nor can they. Young mothers may challenge the ageism of normative motherhood, which limits the age parameters of when a woman should become a mother, whereas feminist mothers may insist upon the political dimension in their childrearing and through public activism. Racialized mothers may resist normative family configurations through communal-other-mothering, fictive kin, and extended families, whereas queer, trans, and nonbinary mothers may do so through comothering or nonconforming gender identities and relationships. Ultimately, the strategies chosen by any marginalized group of mothers and parents—whether they be Indigenous, trans, nonbinary young, or racialized—need to be acknowledged and respected while remembering their inherent limitations for other marginalized mothers. We also argue that they all queer motherhood and, in so doing, show that not all parents are women or that there is one correct way to create a family. Queering motherhood also means that the desire and ability to mother is not innate to one sex or gender and that kinship is not only defined by blood. Queering motherhood makes possible the identities and practices needed for empowered modes of mothering—a multitude of maternal identities, diverse family formations, and a variety of motherhood practices. To queer motherhood is, thus, to empower mothers and parents.

Gendered Oppressions of Motherwork

As we must retain the words "mothers" and "mothering" to respect the specific political import and intent of racialized women's motherwork and to acknowledge the diverse resistant practices that queer normative motherhood, we must also do so to emphasize the lived gendered oppressions of motherwork. To conflate mothers with fathers in the word "parents" disguises, deflects, and denies how carework is emphatically and unequivocally gendered in patriarchal societies. Michelle Hughes Miller elaborates:

> Neutral language is often used to erase gendered, racialized, classed differences among individuals. The goal is often purportedly equality or inclusion, but that is rarely the outcome we see. Instead, that erasure of specificity is important and dangerous. In the case of the use of parenting versus mothering, while the actions of mothering could be performed by anyone (Ruddick), they are overwhelmingly performed by women. Parenting and caregiving as neutral concepts both presume that anyone can do and everyone does do these tasks when data are clear: everyone does not do these tasks, and certainly not to the extent that those who identify as women do. Thus, the problem with neutral language is its negation of the motherwork that women actually engage in, often to the detriment of their other labor, such as paid work, and their leisure time, and sometimes their physical and mental well-being.

Indeed, fathers are not oppressed by an institution of fatherhood as mothers are by the institution of motherhood.

In contemporary patriarchal culture, normative motherhood defines mothering as natural to women and essential to their being, positions mothers as the central caregivers of their biological children and assumes that children require full-time mothering. Good mothers are nurturing, altruistic, patient, devoted, loving, and selfless; they always put the needs of their children before their own and are available to them whenever needed. And should mothers work outside the home, their children rather than their employment should be at the centre of their life. Good mothers are the primary caregivers of their children, and the care potentially provided by others is viewed as inferior and deficient. Feminist scholars rightly argue that normative motherhood is disempowering if not oppressive for a multitude of reasons, including the individualization and devaluation of mother-work, the endless tasks of privatized mothering, the incompatibility of wage work and motherwork, and the impossible standards of idealized motherhood. Moreover, all statistics and studies confirm that mothers do the bulk of motherwork and often, as Hughes Miller notes above, to the detriment of their employment, leisure, and wellbeing. Hence, it is mothers not fathers who are restrained and regulated by normative discourses and practices of care labour. To imply otherwise through the term "parents" is not only disingenuous and specious but also potentially injurious.

The recent pandemic reveals and confirms the necessity of using the words "mothers" and "mothering" so that the very real and prevalent gendered effects of COVID-19 do not disappear through the concept of parenting. In 2021, we published *Mothers, Mothering, and COVID-19: Dispatches from a Pandemic*. Arguably, we could have used "parents" and "parenting" in the title, but to do so would have been disingenuous and erroneous because it is mothers, not fathers, who have been most affected by the pandemic; mothers, not fathers, have been forced to do the necessary and arduous carework to sustain their families and communities. Mothers, not fathers, have done the bulk of domestic labour, childcare, and elder care. With the implementation of social isolation and pandemic protocols, the burden of their carework increased exponentially in both time and concern, as mothers were running households with little or no support, under close to impossible conditions, while also often engaged in wage labour. One Canadian study reports that men spent an average of thirty-three hours of caregiving per week before the pandemic and forty-six hours during the pandemic. Women spent an average of sixty-eight hours before the pandemic and ninety-five hours during it (Gregory). The pandemic has particularly compounded the "third shift"—the emotional and intellectual labour of motherwork. Such labour also mirrors what philosopher Sara Ruddick has termed "maternal thinking": the organizing, remembering, anticipating, worrying, and planning that mothers take on for their families. During COVID-19, many mothers worked in what may be termed the "fourth shift"—that is, the homeschooling of their children. A *New York Times* survey found that 80 per cent of mothers said they were picking up most of the responsibility for homeschooling, whereas only 3 per cent of women said that men were doing more (Daniel). Indeed, as Sara Petersen notes in her July 2020 *YahooStyle,* article: "The burden of unpaid labor in the home has always fallen disproportionally on mothers, but the pandemic has shone a glaring neon light into a situation that has always been impossible." Despite the cataclysmic upheavals of the pandemic, one fact remains unchanged: Motherwork remains invisible, devalued, and taken for granted. Indeed, as Andrea Flynn observes: "The coronavirus has laid bare many divisions in our society. And, like any serious crisis does, it has elevated the extent to which structural sexism permeates our lives: impacting the gendered division of labor within the home and also shaping what is possible for women, and particularly mothers, in the public sphere." We conclude the introduction to the *Mothers, Mothering, and COVID-19* book writing: "Many feminist and social justice researchers and activists see the COVID-19 crisis as opening space for a coalition movement for workplace justice and for reevaluating carework as an essential part of an economic agenda. This collection dispatches the maternal visions and voices for this necessary and long-overdue conversation on, and action towards, empowered social change" (29). However, we emphasize here that these necessary conversations and actions towards empowered social change are only possible with the words "mothers" and "mothering" as well as a matricentric focus, which recognizes and supports the crucial work mothers have done as frontline workers to keep families functioning throughout the pandemic and beyond.

Foregrounding Mothers and Mothering in Feminism

Finally, we argue that as the words "parents" and "parent" disguise the real and prevalent gendered oppressions of carework; they also render invisible motherhood as it is experienced and studied. When words are eliminated, so too are the concepts they refer to. In chapter four of *Matricentric Feminism,* O'Reilly explores matricentric feminism in relation to feminist theory and women's studies or what may be termed "academic feminism." Matricentric feminism as noted above and explored fully in *Matricentric Feminism* understands motherhood to be socially and historically constructed by imperialist, white supremacist, and capitalist patriarchy and positions mothering as a practice and not as a fixed, stable, and essentialist identity. Thus, although matricentric feminism does hold a matrifocal perspective and insists that mothering does matter, it does not advance a gender-essential argument or agenda.

However, matricentric feminism—in its focus on the gendered experience of mothering (and the related ones of pregnancy, childbirth, and breastfeeding)—does force us to address the thorny issue of gender differences. Feminist theory, with the notable exception of cultural-difference feminism, positions gender difference as central to, if not the cause of, women's oppression. Liberal feminists advocate what has been called "sameness feminism," wherein women become more like men. Radical-libertarian feminists promote androgyny, and poststructuralist feminists seek to destabilize and deconstruct gender difference altogether. Indeed, as Niamh Moore notes, "Challenging biological determinism and other essentialisms has been a crucial policy strategy for feminists" (qtd. in Stephens 141). Thus, because feminists are uncomfortable with anything underscoring gender differences and suggesting essentialism (i.e., cisgender men are naturally this way, and cisgender women are naturally this way), motherhood becomes problematic, as it more than anything else marks binary gender differences. And because gender differences are seen as structuring and maintaining male dominance, many feminists seek to downplay and disavow anything that marks these differences—the main one, of course, being motherhood. For many feminists, to call attention to women's specific gendered subjectivity as mothers is to subscribe to an essentialist viewpoint—acknowledging and affirming what is seen as marking and maintaining gender differences and, hence, the oppression of women. As Julie Stephens writes in *Confronting Postmaternal Thinking*: "The primary focus of the second -wave feminist movement has been one long struggle against essentialism, whether this be biological, cultural or ideological. This makes any discussion linking women and care, or mothering and nurturing, particularly troubling" (10). Consequently, as Stephens goes on to argue, "Any activism done in the name of the maternal will be unsettling, particularly for those who perceive feminism as primarily a struggle against essentialism" (141). Indeed, as Tatjana Takseva emphasizes,

"Within the mainstream feminist paradigm, the absence of the maternal bespeaks the perspective that the feminist empowerment project is essentially incompatible with the social and personal entanglements arising out of the maternal role" (29).

We agree that gender is constructed in the West by colonial and imperialist white supremacist heteronormative capitalist patriarchy and that sex does not equal gender. As Simone de Beauvoir once said, "One is not born a woman but made one" (70-71). Thus, people cannot define themselves or limit their lives to what is socially constructed by gender. However, we likewise believe that feminists should not disavow motherhood or erase it through parenting language to facilitate this destabilizing of gender. We believe it is possible to simultaneously argue that both gender and motherhood are constructed and that mothering matters and is often integral to a mother's sense of self and her/their experience of the world. In our view, the apprehension over gender differences, identities, and expressions is the elephant in the room of academic feminism; it has shut down necessary and needed conversations about important—and, yes, gendered—dimensions of women's lives: menstruation, pregnancy, childbirth, breastfeeding, and mothering. Some mothers are finding that they can no longer talk about their reproductive identities and experiences without being called essentialist.

Yet maternal scholars do not reduce women's sense of self to motherhood, nor do they say that this is what makes a woman or that motherhood is more important than other variables that constitute the self. They say only that motherhood matters and is central and integral to understanding the lives of anyone who identifies as a mother. Indeed, although matricentric feminism does create a space for women to talk about and theorize mothering, as it is both embodied and practised, it does not limit discussions of mothering to embodiment or the maternal practices of cisgender women. Rather, the terms "mother" and "mothering" in matricentric feminism refer to any individual who engages in motherwork and includes anyone who takes on the work of mothering as a central part of their life. However, without these terms, the concept of motherhood may be completely erased through the word "parenting." Indeed, as the research on mothers and COVID-19 shows and confirms, mothers and mothering must be foregrounded to understand maternal oppression and reach appropriate responses.

Inclusion without Exclusion

Nonetheless, we understand that words do matter and that many trans and nonbinary individuals regard the words "mothers" and "mothering" as exclusionary. So, the challenge is how do we include trans and nonbinary practices of parenting without excluding those of mothers. How can we use the terms "parenting" and "parents" without erasing the specific meanings of motherwork for racialized women, minimizing the radical queering of empowered mothering, deflecting the very real gendered oppressions of motherwork, and making invisible mothering both as it is practised and researched? We suggest that in everyday conversations and circumstances, the words "parenting" and "parents" should be used as well as in most legal, educational, and medical contexts. However, in the specific context of racialized women, empowered mothering, gendered resistance, and the oppressions of motherwork (as lived and studied), the words "mothers" and "mothering" must be retained. Gemma Bath argues the following: "Removing the entirety of gendered language is a long road because it's so entrenched. But creating a more inclusive, non-binary and respectful dialogue with what we *do* have available to us doesn't have to be." She continues: "There's always going to be a level of push back from those who don't think the way we speak should change. But we're always inventing new words: think 'clickbait,' 'selfies' and 'podcasts.'" Although we agree with Bath that we should be inventing new words for inclusivity, we also suggest that normative words can be reclaimed and reconstituted to become resistant and potentially inclusive. Words such as "queer," "slut," and "breeder" have been reclaimed and have become transgressive and so too can the words "mothers" and "mothering." Matricentric feminism recuperates the word "mothering" by positioning it as a verb and divesting it of biology, thus making it both resistant and inclusive. Speaking about inclusive language, Bath writes, "The more we see gender-neutral terms front and centre, the more they will become normalized." And we would add that the more we position mothering as a transgressive verb, the more it will include all parents. To borrow from Bath's words, both strategies "are important because we have a responsibility in 2021 to make everyone in our society feel seen, heard and understood." As Nicole Willey notes in her chapter in this collection, "Language matters, and so holding onto and naming mothers while including others should be our goal" (66). She further argues: "I like the idea that we can continue to use the word 'mother' while simultaneously recognizing that our previous binaries and definitions do not always work for everyone" (79).

By positioning mothering as a verb, matricentric feminism allows for gender neutrality. In its understanding of maternal oppression and resistance, the term likewise provides needed gendered analyses, ultimately moving matricentric feminism beyond gender. In its explicit and emphatic matrifocal perspective, matricentric feminism is concerned with anyone who identifies as a mother, practises mothering, or both. In this, matricentric feminism is certainly a feminism for trans and nonbinary individuals who take up nongendered practices of mothering. Moving beyond gender, matricentric feminism delivers resistant and inclusive maternal identities and practices for all who seek empowered social change.

The collection is divided into three sections: Theorizing Matricentric Feminism, Enacting Matricentric Feminism, and Representing Matricentric Feminism.

Section One: Theorizing Matricentric Feminism

The first section explores the role and importance of matricentric feminism, different understandings of matricentric feminist theory, and the nexus of matricentric feminist theory and praxis. In the opening chapter, "This Love Is Revolutionary: Mothering as Resistance to Oppressive Systems," Zaje A. T. Harrell explores the role of revolutionary love in a conversation with O'Reilly's work on matricentric feminism. Harrell interrogates the mothering experience in the context of racialized oppression and examines Black and colonized mothers' experiences of nurturing as resistance. The work offers a guiding framework for proceeding with inclusive and contextual matricentric feminism based on a liberatory love ethic.

In the following chapter, "The Case for Radical Inclusion in Mothering Studies: Matricentric Feminism Can and Should Take on Genderism," Nicole L. Willey explores how mothering studies could be more inclusive through the expansion of the definition and operationalization of the definition of matricentric feminism to include genderism. Willey argues that this additional layer of inclusion in our language, spaces, scholarship, and advocacy is not only the right thing to do but will also allow for a stronger coalition of people working to help all families, children, and mothers.

The third chapter, "The Mother Wave and the Italian Matricentric River Delta" by Veronica Frigeni, explores Italian feminism from a matricentric standpoint to argue that Italian matricentric feminism exists in the shape of a river delta that emerges from the interaction of sexual difference and queer feminism and which challenges the country's cultural and socioeconomic antimaternal context. Repositioning motherhood as an essential concern for Italian feminists, the chapter engages theory and fiction, reading Maria Rosa Cutrufelli's novel *L'isola delle madri* (2020) as a potential mother-centred and counter-narrative of mothering.

Chapter four, "Centring the Voices of Caribbean Mothers: Making the Case for a Matricentric Feminist Theorizing" by Daniele Bobb, explores the applicability of a matricentric feminist lens to an analysis of mothers' experiences. Bobb argues that motherhood is a complex and dense site of simultaneous contradictory and supportive discourses on relations of power and maternal experiences.

Chapter five, "Out of Praxis, Theory: Being and Becoming a Matricentric Feminist" by Michelann Parr, explores a hopeful nexus of matricentric feminist theory and praxis, paying particular attention to where the personal, political, and pedagogical merge in acts of resistance and empowerment. Experimenting with potentiality, repetition, and resolution, she plays with fragments (e.g., poems, short essays, and reflections) and writes fragmentarily. Using a paired-ABC structure in multiples of one hundred words, Parr weaves together seemingly unrelated concepts as she honours matricentric feminism and the work of m/others past, present, and future. Moving from intent through reality, commitment, and meditation, she resolves theory and praxis as reciprocal and relational processes: One cannot exist without the other.

In the sixth chapter, "Mother's Speaking: Towards an Ethics of Maternal Monstrosity," Abigail Palko blends autoethnographic reflections and scholarly analysis of the interplay between Sara Ruddick's philosophy of maternal peace politics and Jude Doyle's explication of the monster figure. Palko explores the ways rhetoric about maternal monstrosity reflects limitations imposed on mothers to argue that one of matricentric feminism's great, as-yet-unfinished, tasks is the development of an ethos of maternal voice that supports mothers' self-expression without harming their children.

The final chapter of section one, "Choosing Matricentric Feminism in an Era of Choice Feminism: A Way Forward" by Katie B. Garner, argues that while many feminisms coexist in the United States (US), choice feminism, which relies on basic neoliberal and capitalist tenets to encourage women to be self-sufficient via their engagement with waged work, is the most visible. Capitalism, however, permits no room for carework, including mothering. US feminism thus needs to incorporate matricentric feminism better so that mothers can effectively advocate for equitable support from businesses, their governments, and their male partners.

Section Two: Enacting

The second section of the book shares examples of how matricentric feminism is enacted in various ways, whether in business, work-family balance, teaching, or self-love. Chapter eight, "The Theory and Praxis of Matricentric Feminism in the Lives of Motherhood Studies Certification Course Participants" by Sophie Brock, explores her own experiences of how she drew on matricentric feminism in her journey of single mothering and creating a business of teaching an online motherhood studies course to mother-supporting professionals and practitioners. Brock uses interviews with fourteen course graduates to explore how participants' learning of motherhood informed their own mothering experiences and careers and culminated in the development of their matricentric feminist praxis. The chapter concludes that through matricentric feminist education and learning, mothers can claim new relationships with feminism and position their mothering as a site of activism and power.

Chapter nine, "I Am Becoming My Mother: Conjuring Black Motherhood on Our Own Terms" by Sheree Mack, uses a Black matrilineage lens to explore Black motherhood and mothering; it conjures history, memories, and stories to widen representation within matricentric feminism and centres diversity, difference, and becoming through radical self-love.

Chapter ten, "Black Mothers' Responses to Systems of Oppression: Navigating Work, Family, and Self-Actualization" by Nicole Dezrea Jenkins, uses an intersectional analysis of race and gender to explore how Black women conceptualize motherhood and navigate work-family balance. Drawing on two years of participant observation, ethnography, and unstructured interviews conducted in a Black, immigrant, and women -owned and operated hair salon in the Southern US, the chapter highlights the experiences and problems faced by Black women navigating US institutions. Jenkins argues that within child-friendly working environments, Black women employ strategies for work-family balance based on their conceptualizations of good mothering practices by leveraging the established community present in salons and collectively sharing responsibilities for childcare to highlight the real and prevalent oppression of motherwork as well as the racial queering of empowered mothering in matricentric feminist theory.

Chapter eleven, "Using Matricentric Feminist Research to Create Space for Mothers on Campus" by Alexis Carrion and Andrea DeKeseredy, explores the concepts maintaining the academic maternal wall and how the ongoing neoliberalization of universities exacerbates it. The authors share their experiences as researchers applying matricentric feminism and maternal theory to their research in a field that often does not recognize it. The scholars conclude by arguing the reasons for including matricentric feminism in their work and discuss the use of public feminist sociology to reach nonacademic audiences while engaging in matricentric activism.

The final chapter of the section, chapter twelve, "Without a Village: Motherhood, Child Care, and COVID-19—A Research Journey" by Bailey Higgins, draws upon the experiences mothers shared with her about changes to motherhood during the early stages of the COVID-19 pandemic and to their motherwork as they navigated the childcare system to accommodate their children's childcare needs. The chapter highlights the necessity for matricentric feminism in understanding innovative ways to address the challenges of engaging in motherwork that mothers face both within and outside of systemic changes to childcare related to the global health crisis.

Section Three: Representing

The third and final section of the book focusses on the importance of representing matricentric feminism in two main ways: within research and scholarly disciplines and within literature, artistic production of images, and performance art. Nevertheless, each contributor in this section illustrates the influential prevalence and power of matricentric feminism. In the opening chapter, chapter thirteen, "Towards a Literary Theory and Criticism of Matricritics: 'Begin with the Mother in Her Own Fight' to Deliver 'New Meanings of Motherhood' and 'Transform Maternal Thinking Itself,'" Andrea O'Reilly proposes a literary theory of matricritics for a reading of maternal narratives and establishing a matrilineal tradition in women's contemporary fiction. This theory is developed from two of the central principles of O'Reilly's theory of matricentric feminism—challenging child-centredness and countering normative motherhood—and employs Olivia Heal's theory of maternal poetics along with Elaine Showalter's concept of gynocritics and a female literary tradition. The chapter then explores how matricritics may function as literary criticism by discussing O'Reilly's current study on the maternal in post-2010 women's fiction and memoir. More specifically, the chapter shows how matricritics in its excavations of matrifocal narratives and their unmasking of motherhood allows for and enacts critique of normative motherhood to make possible a change to this institution.

Chapter fourteen, "Swimming against Plato—Rachel Cusk's *Outline*" by Else Werring, argues that Cusk's novel *Outline* is a work of matricentric feminism, urging us to remember our motherline. Werring depicts Cusk's narrator Faye as a feminist mother in a state of "dereliction" (Luce Irigaray's term for feminine homelessness under patriarchy), who is propelled to time travel to the "matricidal" beginnings of literature and philosophy. On her journey, Faye discovers how the past lingers in our present. Through investigating the link between maternity and temporality, *Outline* criticizes the lack of attention to the mother in contemporary feminism and pushes Faye into "digging up her liquid ground" (Irigaray) in a bid to elbow out some space for an embodied maternal subjectivity that is nevertheless deessentialized.

The following chapter, chapter fifteen, "Matricentric Feminism and Non-Normative Migrant Mothering in Recent Contemporary Fiction from Spain and the United States" by Carolina Toscano, explores three matrifocal contemporary novels written by transnational authors to argue that these novels studied as cultural artifacts reflect the growing "wave of matricentric feminism" that is being enacted through examples of nonnormative feminist mothering.

Chapter sixteen, "Matricentric Art: A Philosophy of Maternal Work Through the Act of Creativity" authored by Anna Hennessey, uses

Andrea O'Reilly's theory of matricentric feminism to examine how a rise in the artistic production of images related to mothering in the twenty-first century correlates with the emergence of new models of feminism and a philosophy of maternal work through the act of creativity. This matricentric art, claims Hennessey, has created a visual space for collective understandings that mothering in all its forms is a means of empowerment for many from around the globe.

In chapter seventeen, "Commoning the Maternal: Matricentric Feminism and Motherworks Festival," Jodie Hawkes and Pete Phillips (Search Party) reflect on their performance *Playing Kate: Disruptions and Confrontations* at Motherworks festival at Cambridge Junction. The authors address the absence of class in the field of maternal performance and argue that the "Playing Kate" persona performs as an act of commoning, a distinct category of O'Reilly's queering that foregrounds class as a means to disrupt normative mothering.

Chapter eighteen, "The Last American Housewife" by Martha Joy Rose, provides an autoethnographic account of the evolution of the motherhood movement, highlighting its successes and setbacks. Drawing on personal experiences, academic scholarship, and visual media, Rose demonstrates the continued relevance of matricentric feminism as a means of advancing women's rights and promoting gender equality while arguing for the creation of new parameters of thought, identity, and action, which must be encouraged through continual reassertion of feminist arguments in a world informed by patriarchal structures. She calls for new language and fresh matricentric feminist approaches to inform contemporary activism in ways that move beyond opposition and are more collaboratively constructed.

In the final chapter of the collection, chapter nineteen, "Riding the Wave Rather than Waving Off: The Academic Study of Religions and Matricentric Feminism," Florence Pasche Guignard and Pascale Engelmajer explore the effects of maternal theory and matricentric feminism in the academic study of religions. They show how collaborative endeavours carved out a space for the study of mothers and mothering in religious studies, a topic long neglected in a field that mostly ignores women's experiences as mothers.

Conclusion

Rafia Zakaria's concludes her brilliant book *Against White Feminism,* writing: "I see too many women of colour turning away from feminism. In some cases, they are saying goodbye to mainstream white feminism in order to build more specialized movements: Muslim feminisms, Black feminisms, and queer feminisms" (209–10). Zakaria continues:

> These smaller groups have a powerful role to play, but we also need to create a space where different tribes can work together on issues that affect us all—and vitally, where they can lend one another equally ardent support for issues that do not affect us all. Communities must remain free to have their own specialized groups, but that need not reduce their capacity or potential for coming together to create a potent and transformative mainstream feminist politics. (210)

Building upon Zakaria's argument, we suggest that many mothers have likewise turned away from mainstream feminism to build their own movement of matricentric feminism. And with Zakaria, we also argue that while specialized feminisms like matricentric feminism are certainly necessary, we also need to create a space wherein we can work together to create a truly inclusive feminist politic. Indeed, as Samira Kawash emphasizes:

> Feminist theorists, scholars, and writers, as well as feminist mother activists, have a lot to say to each other, and a lot to learn from each other, about motherhood. Motherhood studies needs the perspectives and commitments of feminism as well as the institutional resources that feminism and women's studies have accumulated over the past four decades. At the same time, feminism cannot possibly hope to remain relevant without acknowledging motherhood in all its contradictions and complexities. (986–987)

In this introduction, we discussed the disavowal of motherhood in academic feminism. However, despite this disavowal, we do have a feminist theory and movement of our own as evidenced by the chapters of this collection. Yet matricentric feminism must be more than acknowledged as a legitimate, viable, and independent school of feminist thought;

it must be integrated into mainstream academic feminism. But how do we accomplish this? We need more women doing motherhood scholarship and more mother professors in academe. We demand that matricentric feminism have a chapter of its own as do other schools of feminism theory —queer, global, womanist, third wave—in our feminist theory readers, that introduction to women's/gender studies courses and textbooks include sections on motherhood, that women's journals and conferences include more papers on motherhood, and that more books on motherhood are reviewed. We must continuously challenge the conflation of mothering with motherhood within academic feminism as well as counter the association of matricentric feminism with gender essentialism. Decisively and urgently, we must interrupt the received narrative of academic feminism, in particular its normalization of the genderless and autonomous subject, to foreground the centrality of the reproductive identities and lives of mothers and the importance of care in our larger culture. Indeed, as Ann Marie Slaughter comments, "The bottom-line message is that we are never going to get gender equality between men and women unless we value the work of care as much as we value paid work. That's the unfinished business" (qtd. in McCarthy). Finally, and most importantly, we must demand that matricentric feminists be recognized and respected as the feminists that they are and that their feminism, that of matricentric feminism, have a room of its own in the larger home of academic feminism.

Works Cited

Anderson, Kim. "Giving Life to the People: An Indigenous Ideology of Motherhood." *Maternal Theory: Essential Readings*. Edited by Andrea O'Reilly. Demeter Press, 2007, pp. 761–81.

Bath, Gemma. "An Australian University Has Offered New Words for 'Mother' and 'Father'; This Is Why It Matters." *MamaMia*, 16 Feb. 2021, www.mamamia.com.au/gender-neutral-terms-mother-father/. Accessed 28 June 2024.

Brant, Jennifer. "Indigenous Mothering: Birthing the Nation from Resistance to Revolution." *Routledge Companion to Motherhood*. Edited by Lynn O'Brien Hallstein, Andrea O'Reilly and Melinda Vandenbeld Giles. Routledge Press, 2019, pp. 11–121.

Chamberlain, Prudence. *The Feminist Fourth Wave: Affective Temporality.* Palgrave Macmillan, 2017.

Collins, Patricia Hill. "Shifting the Center: Race, Class, and Feminist Theorizing about Motherhood." *Mothering: Ideology, Experience, and Agency.* Edited by Evelyn Nakano Glenn et al. Routledge, 1994, pp. 45–65.

Collins, Patricia Hill. "The Meaning of Motherhood in Black Culture and Black Mother-Daughter Relationships." *Double Stitch: Black Women Write About Mothers and Daughters.* Edited by Patricia Bell-Scott, et al. Harper Perennial, 1993, pp. 42–60.

Crittenden, Ann. *The Price of Motherhood: Why the Most Important Job in the World Is Still the Least Valued.* Henry Holt and Company, 2001.

Daly, Brenda O., and Maureen T. Reddy, eds. *Narrating Mothers: Theorizing Maternal Subjectivities.* University of Tennessee Press, 1991.

Daniel, Zoe. "How Coronavirus Has Changed the Roles in the Family Home." *ABC News*, 13 May 2020, www.abc.net.au/news/2020-05-13/coronavirus-has-changed-roles-in-family-home/12239542?fbclid=IwAR1PRqB8h_4M0XGbu1zpGjUN5Zg89IXHavtHyRAC0trw4AVmckwG9DPyhVM. Accessed 28 June 2024.

De Beauvoir, Simone. *The Second Sex.* Translated by Constance Borde and Sheila Malovany-Chevallier, Vintage, 2011.

DiQuinzio, Patrice. "Mothering and Feminism: Essential Mothering and the Dilemma of Difference." *Maternal Theory.* Edited by Andrea O'Reilly. Demeter, 2007, pp. 542–55.

DiQuinzio, Patrice. "The Politics of the Mothers' Movement in the United States: Possibilities and Pitfalls." *Journal of the Association for Research on Mothering*, vol. 8, no. 1–2, 2006, pp. 55–71.

Doty, H. Kori, and A. J. Lowik. *The Liminal Chrysalis: Imagining Reproduction and Parenting Futures Beyond the Binary.* Demeter Press, 2022.

Douglas, Susan J., and Meredith Michaels. *The Mommy Myth: The Idealization of Motherhood and How It Has Undermined Women.* Free Press, 2004.

Flynn, Andrea. "The 'All-Consuming' Emotional Labor Caused by Coronavirus—And Shouldered by Women." *Ms.*, 31 Mar. 2020, msmagazine.com/2020/03/31/op-ed-the-all-consuming-emotional

-labor-caused-by-coronavirus-and-disproportionately-shouldered-by-women/. Accessed 28 June 2024.

Gibson, Margaret, ed. *Queering Motherhood: Narrative and Theoretical Perspectives*. Demeter Press, 2014.

Gregory, Laurel. "Mothers Taking on 'Shocking' Number of Hours Caring for Children during Pandemic: Study." *Global News*, 20 Oct. 2020, globalnews.ca/news/7408226/mothers-hours-child-care-pandemic-study/. Accessed 28 June 2024.

Hemmings, Clare. *Why Stories Matter: The Political Grammar of Feminist Theory*. Duke University Press, 2011.

Hewitt, Nancy A. "Feminist Frequencies: Regenerating the Wave Metaphor." *Feminist Studies*, vol. 38, no. 3, 2012, pp. 658–680.

Hirsch, Marianne. *The Mother/Daughter Plot: Narrative, Psychoanalysis, Feminism*. Indiana University Press, 1989.

hooks, bell. *Yearning: Race, Gender, and Cultural Politics*. South End, 1990.

Johnson, Miriam. *Strong Mothers, Weak Wives: The Search for Gender Equality*. University of California Press, 1988.

Jones, Lucy. *Matrescence: On the Metamorphosis of Pregnancy, Childbirth and Motherhood*. Allen Lane, 2023.

Kawash, Samira. "New Directions in Motherhood Studies." *Signs*, vol. 36, no. 4, 2011, pp. 969–1003.

Kinser, Amber E., editor. *Mothering in the Third Wave*. Demeter Press, 2008.

Kutz-Flamenbaum, Rachel V. "Maternalism." *Encyclopedia of Motherhood*. Edited by Andrea O'Reilly. Sage Press, 2010, pp. 712–16.

Laughlin, Kathleen A., et al. "Is it Time to Jump Ship? Historians Rethink the Waves Metaphor." *Feminist Formations*, vol. 22, no. 1, 2010, pp. 76–135.

LaChance, Sarah Adam. "Maternal Thinking." *The Encyclopedia of Motherhood*. Edited by Andrea O'Reilly. Sage Press, 2010, pp. 726–27.

Lavell-Harvard, Dawn Memee, and Jeanette Corbiere Lavell, editors. *Until Our Hearts Are on the Ground: Aboriginal Mothering, Oppression, Resistance and Rebirth*. Demeter Press, 2006.

Maushart, Susan. *The Mask of Motherhood: How Becoming a Mother Changes Everything and Why We Pretend It Doesn't*. Penguin Books, 2000.

McCarthy, Ellen. "Why Neither Men nor Women Can 'Have It All.'" *The Toronto Star,* 30 Aug. 2016, http://torontostar.newspaperdirect.com/epaper/viewer.aspx. Accessed 11 Sept. 2016.

McClain, Dani. *We Live for the We: The Political Power of Black Motherhood.* Bold Type Books, 2019.

Miller Hughes, Michelle. "Email correspondence." February 2021.

O'Reilly, Andrea, and Fiona Joy Green. *Mothers. Mothering, and COVID-19: Dispatches from a Pandemic.* Demeter Press, 2021.

O'Reilly, Andrea. *Matricentric Feminism: Theory, Identity, Practice.* 2nd ed. Demeter Press, 2021.

Petersen, Sara. "After the Pandemic, We'll Finally Have to Address the Impossible State of Motherhood." *YahooStyle,* 24 June 2020, ca.style.yahoo.com/pandemic-ll-finally-address-impossible-193034 205.html. Accessed 28 June 2024.

Ratchford, Sarah. "The Way We Talk about Motherhood Is Deeply Alienating." *Today's Parent,* 2018, www.todaysparent.com/family/family-life/the-way-we-talk-about-motherhood-is-deeply-alien ating/. Accessed 28 June 2024.

Rich, Adrienne. *Of Woman Born: Motherhood as Experience and Institution.* 2nd ed. W. W. Norton, 1986.

Rose, Jacqueline. *Mothers: An Essay on Love and Cruelty.* Farrar, Straus, and Giroux, 2018.

Ruddick, Sara. *Maternal Thinking: Toward a Politics of Peace.* Beacon Press, 1989.

Showalter, Elaine. "Toward a Feminist Poetics." *The New Feminist Criticism: Essays on Women, Literature and Theory.* Edited by Elaine Showalter. Pantheon Books, 1986, pp. 125–43.

Springer, Kimberly "Third Wave Black Feminism?" *Signs,* vol. 27, no. 4, 2002, pp. 1059–1082.

Stephens, Julie. *Confronting Postmaternal Thinking: Feminism, Memory, and Care.* Columbia University Press, 2011.

Takseva, Tatjana. "One Is Not Born but Rather Becomes a Mother: Claiming the Maternal in Women and Gender Studies." *Journal of the Motherhood Initiative,* vol. 10, no. 1–2, 2019, pp. 27-44.

Taylor-Guthrie, Danille. *Conversations with Toni Morrison*. Mississippi University Press, 1994.

Tucker, Judith Stadtman. "Motherhood and its Discontents: The Political and Ideological Grounding of the 21st Century Mothers' Movement." Motherhood and Feminism Conference, Association for Research on Mothering, Toronto, Ontario, 2004.

Waring, Marilyn. *If Women Counted: A New Feminist Economics*. Harper and Row, 1988.

Zakaria, Rafia. *Against White Feminism: Notes on Disruption*. W. W. Norton & Company, 2021.

Section I.

Theorizing Matricentric Feminism

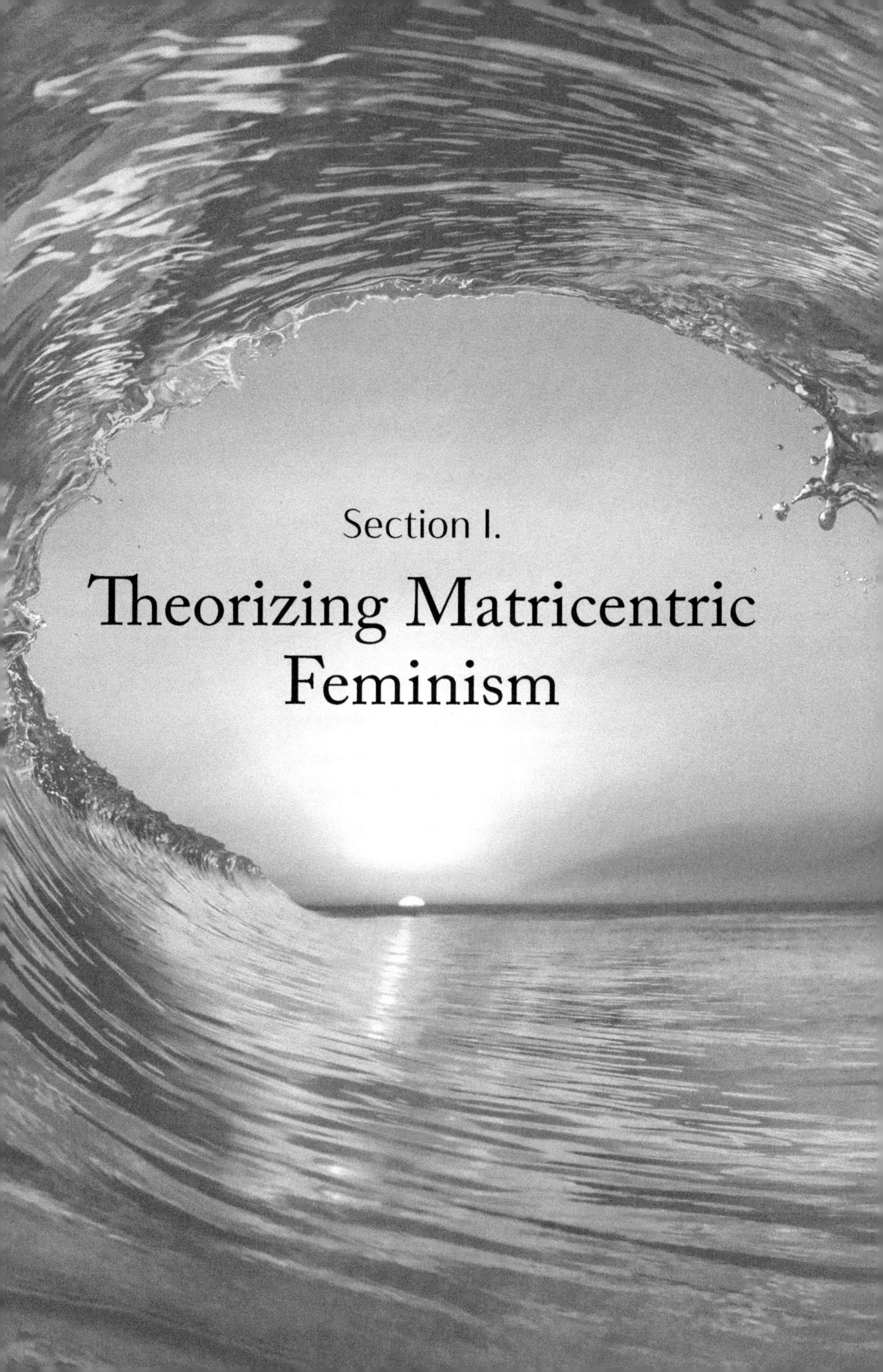

1.

This Love Is Revolutionary: Mothering as Resistance to Oppressive Systems

Zaje A. T. Harrell

Introduction

Feminism is an expansive liberatory social movement, which has improved women's lived experiences and provided them greater visibility, legal rights, and material gains (Cott). It has also laid the foundation for analyzing gender oppression. Feminist scholarship examines why patriarchal power persists, requiring taking seriously women's lived experiences. According to the Centers for Disease Control and Prevention (CDC), 84.3 per cent of women between forty and forty-nine in the United States have had at least one biological child (Martinez and Daniel). The international data indicate that about 82 per cent of women between the same ages have had a child (United Nations). However, the experience of mothering has not received proportionate scholarly attention.

Andrea O'Reilly articulates this deficit in feminist scholarship by proposing mothering as central to a "theory and politics on and for women's empowerment" (14). She introduces matricentric feminism as a context for understanding the experience of mothering. For some, the centring of women as mothers seems to essentialize and go against feminist aims of gender equality (Harrell). It is important to stipulate that not all women want to or will become mothers and that biological essentialism is a problematic framing for the role of mothering. Yet it is the case that people engage in mothering practices, such as nurturing and caring for dependents, regardless of their gender and biological attachment to a child. Matricentric feminism holds the position that motherhood is a common and encompassing experience for most women, making it relevant to feminism, as many of the social limitations women face are rooted in their status as mothers (O'Reilly 15).

The matricentric feminist framework also "understands mothering and motherhood to be culturally determined and variable" (O'Reilly 18). It explores how mothering is informed by social identity categories. This chapter focusses on how aspects of identity and lived experiences are fused with the work of nurturing. To accomplish this, I examine ways to approach the experience of racialized women within a matricentric feminist framework. Experiences of racial oppression have affected mothering practices. Themes of trauma and resistance permeate the narratives of groups that have faced enslavement, colonization, and racism. I examine the role of love and mothering as evolved resistance to racial oppression.

Like mothering, love has received limited treatment in feminist scholarship. Love is an emotion of strong familial or romantic attachment; it is also the foundation for community building and social action. Black feminist scholar bell hooks produced a trilogy of books about love, primarily communal, familial, and romantic love: *All about Love; Salvation: Black People and Love,* and *Communion: The Female Search for Love.* In *Salvation* she calls for a return to a "love ethic" as a source of renewal for communal and political progressive change (hooks xxiv). A love ethic requires treating love seriously as a force for social good and connection. hooks uses her Black experience in a Southern community, in a patriarchal family, and as a seeker of interpersonal love to illuminate the ways that love informs the Black experience and has feminist relevance. This chapter explores these themes of love in conversation with O'Reilly's introductory work on matricentric feminism. Black and global majority feminist perspectives on love as a force for interpersonal and social good are integrated into a matricentric analysis.

In the following sections, I first underscore the need for a matricentric view within feminist thought and then introduce matricentric feminism and Black and global feminist thought as relevant standpoint epistemologies. The cultural context for matricentric feminism and a love ethic are then established. Next, I establish how love is central to understanding resistance among oppressed groups, particularly through the role of mothering. Examples of how oppressive forces have attempted to disrupt nurturing and cultural transition are also explored. Finally, the grounding questions for approaching matricentric feminism integrating a love ethic and racial/ethnic lived experience will be introduced. This work intends to offer a perspective on a culturally relevant matricentric framework and expand the understanding of love and resistance in feminist thought.

It Goes without Saying: Limitations in the Feminist Project

Western feminism has largely focussed on the goals of gender equality. The feminist movement has worked to restructure the social conditions limiting the ability of women to reach their full potential. This has largely been addressed for what I will describe here as inclusion and expansion. Inclusion has focussed on ways that women gain rights and power within society. The struggle for women's suffrage, fair access to education, and employment parity are all aspects of feminist inclusion. Inclusion in feminism assumes that the social structures limiting women require ameliorating through participation. This can conflict with the dismantling of patriarchal systems. For example, by including women in the electoral process, the political system is improved and made more democratic. Inclusion prioritizes participation and, in some cases, includes resource redistribution to benefit women. Thus, inclusion as a feminist goal aims to improve the functioning of Western society.

Within the liberal feminist framing, women are a socially cohesive class requiring redress through the established political structures (Cott 5; Mohanty, "Categories"). The framing of feminist priorities in this way points to a potential limitation of inclusion approaches. The question becomes: Are women indeed a socially cohesive class? Some feminists interested in social context would argue that women "cannot be defined as coherent interest groups" (Mohanty, "Categories" 7) because the variability in social position between women can create opposing interests when it comes to social change. When considering categories of women with shared interests, the sociopolitical meaning of these groups becomes important beyond gender (e.g., socioeconomic class, race/ethnicity, and age). For example, the term "women of colour" is used as a sociopolitical position that is inclusive of nonwhite women from a variety of backgrounds based largely upon encounters with racist oppression and colonialism (7).

Furthermore, the liberal feminist orientation does not offer a critical perspective on aspects of gender oppression not amenable to solutions of inclusion. The inclusion of women within systems from which they have been historically excluded will not remedy the oppressive and patriarchal nature of those systems. Rather, it has been argued that women will assume power within those oppressive systems without fundamentally reforming their exploitative nature. Feminist projects ignoring the relevance of multiple identities will fail to address the plight of the majority of women. Those who will be included will be those who are already close to structures of power. For this reason, forms of feminism focussing on inclusion within existing social structures are limited in their impact on social change.

Another way to consider the feminist project, both in scholarship and politics, is through expansion. Intersectional frameworks explore gender through race, class, and other social locations (Crenshaw). These are illustrative of the growth in the modern feminist project. Feminist thought beyond the Western paradigm also provides a framework for understanding how Indigenous practices and colonial forces have shaped women's experiences (Mohanty, "Under Western Eyes").

Focussing on dismantling barriers to women within high-status power positions (e.g., shattering the glass ceilings) has also led to a feminist politic that disproportionately addresses the needs of women privileged by race and class. Journalist Mikki Kendall takes the position in her book *Hood Feminism* that mainstream liberal feminism has ignored issues relevant to poor, working-class, and many women of colour, such as hunger, quality education, poverty, and reproductive justice. Kendall argues that these issues require prioritizing in the form of feminism expanded beyond markers of social privilege. Similarly, Rafia Zakaria's *Against White Feminism* takes an oppositional stand to what she calls "white feminism" and the subsequent objectification of Black and brown women. Zakaria points to the potential for white feminism to cause harm by carelessly using the global currency of white privilege to affect policies without understanding community needs. For example, she points to the desire of nongovernment organizations to impose the standards of white feminist values of empowerment in a global context without consulting the affected community (68).

Arguably, it is a limited understanding of women's lived experiences under patriarchy and the concomitant social actions that have led to feminist politics having a stifled effect on gender equality. Feminist psychologist Abigail Stewart argues that one way to apply feminist theory to research is to "look for what has been left out" (56). Thus, the question emerges: Where is motherhood within the scholarship and priorities of modern feminism? The following section will analyze motherhood from an epistemological standpoint and introduce matricentric feminism.

Taking a Stand for Mothering

Feminist critical theory is grounded in concerns over women's material reality and the accompanying knowledge production. Sandra Harding describes standpoint theory as one aligned approach to the "production of knowledge and practices of power" (1). Standpoint theory upsets the epistemological assertion that knowledge production is separate from the social context. The traditional idea of the objective "knower" is challenged by one's perspective. Standpoint theory reveals the androcentric bias within scholarly investigation—a bias towards patriarchal norms in which what is knowable is objectified. Even within feminist projects, this androcentric bias can exist where sexist norms and values have not been interrogated. As Sara Ruddick describes: "A standpoint is an engaged vision of the world opposed and superior to dominant ways of thinking.... Even now, the vision offered by a feminist standpoint reveals that dominant ways of knowing are ... 'partial and perverse'" (162–63).

Matricentric feminism focuses on nurturing as embodied and contextual as it seeks to produce relevant knowledge. This form of knowledge production offers a perspective on the experience of mothering as both a material condition and a lived experience. Centring the experience of mothers in feminist inquiry is a way to consider how mothering is connected to subordinate social power and how to address this aspect of patriarchy through feminist politics. Mothering is a serious point of intellectual inquiry and requires elevation as both epistemology and ontology.

A matricentric feminist framework requires examining biological differences and social dominance to understand motherhood. To this end, it is important to acknowledge that institutional motherhood, under patriarchy, remains a form of social control and oppression (Green; Rich). Evidence of this is the essentialization of the experience of motherhood as natural and rooted in femaleness and biology. O'Reilly also addresses biological essentialism in the study of motherhood by distinguishing the concept of maternalism from matricentric feminism. Maternalism focusses on an innate framing of the qualities of women as caring and empathetic; women are uniquely designed to carework. Matricentric feminism, in contrast, acknowledges that the category of mothering is socially constructed and tied to power structures. This framing is beneficial in understanding that mothering is a practice, culture, and time bound, which offers those who engage in it a particular societal lens (16). According to O'Reilly, "Much of second-wave feminism—in particular that of liberal and racial-libertarian feminism—views motherhood as a significant, if not determining, cause of women's oppression under patriarchy" (21). However, the institution of motherhood remains underinvestigated in feminist scholarship.

One answer to why motherhood has been diminished in modern feminist inquiry can be found in the longstanding tension between women's roles in the private and public spheres (Cott). Feminism is often solely envisioned as a political project in the public sphere of women's rights. The private domestic sphere is often considered the realm of "choice," where decisions made around family structures, division of labour, and childrearing make it a private matter outside the purview of politics. Critical theorists and social scientists have offered a material analysis of why the private sphere has been a more challenging area of feminist inquiry. Women do the majority of carework, which is largely invisible low-status labour. Capitalist patriarchy requires that women take this subordinate position in providing care for relations and dependents, which is largely uncompensated in the private sphere. Rather than illuminating these relationships of gender power, the relegation of women to nurturing and carework is largely framed as the territory of biological difference and individual choice. The complexities of gender oppression are ignored.

Matricentric feminism challenges the dominant paradigms of individualism and the private sphere in favour of adopting the positionality of mothering as a central unit of analysis. This framing takes on empowerment and agency as found through the experience of mothering, which is distinct from the sexist framing of maternalism. The idea of motherhood as static should also be challenged, as the expectations for nurturing shift generationally. For example, parents today spend more time with their children than forty years ago, even with greater workforce participation by mothers (Dotti and Treas). These shifts in the demands of mothering situate mothering in context and history.

As matricentric feminism is introduced, there remains less discussion of the nurturing aspects characterizing the mothering relationship (O'Reilly). Indeed, it is difficult to operationalize these dimensions of human relationships. However, matricentric feminism requires that we treat dimensions of attachment and care seriously. The following section argues for centring love in this analysis and explores how love is an impetus for community and social movements.

Love Is Essential

This chapter understands love as an emotion, a practice, and a guiding ethic. Love is key to a worthwhile human experience and a justice orientation (hooks xxi). The capacity to experience love opens a pathway to other positive emotional states and allows a person to act from a place of positive emotions (Garland et al.). This basic emotional reaction to positive states offers support for the assertion that it is love that allows us to build.

A feminist perspective requires examining love as an analysis of interpersonal dynamics and as relevant for communal social good. In *Salvation*, hooks details how Black intellectuals have treated love as a force in opposition to dehumanizing oppression. She makes a plea for the Black community: "To heal our wounded communities, which are diverse and multilayered, we must return to a love ethic, one that is exemplified by the combined forces of are, respect, knowledge, and responsibility" (4–5). This is the vision of love that can create community and undergird activism.

The role of love in social movements has been understood largely from a theological position in the American struggle for civil rights. The prominence of Christian ministers, most famously Dr. Martin Luther King Jr., offered a particularly Christian interpretation of the meaning of loving one's enemies and seeking a religiously based form of social justice. Black American theologian James Cone writes of King's commitment to nonviolent social changes as related to a Christian faith, but it also fits the love ethic as described by hooks: "King's faith that God is the movement depend on his commitment to justice and sustain him in his struggle ... reassuring him that love and nonviolence, despite the odds, would triumph over hate and violence" (125). The idea of love here is rooted in the spiritual mandate based upon the Black Christian social gospel. In the modern Western imagination, this version of love is the most salient as related to political action. Feminism, particularly matricentric feminism, requires a love ethic as well. To understand how love is relevant in matricentric studies, we can widen the aperture to examine love beyond a theological framing.

Theorists of social change have articulated how love is present in natural systems. Essential to the human experience is love and care for others. As argued by Ruddick, "This means that the material world, seen under the aspects of caring labor, is organized in terms of people's needs and pleasures of any animal or plant that is instrumental in human caring or is tended for its own sake" (163). The world is diverse and requires caring—a caring guided by the deep connections of sacrifice, commitment, pleasure, and grief, which define love. Writer and social justice facilitator Adrienne Maree Brown has eloquently framed the idea of love and community: "When we are engaged in acts of love, we humans are at our best and most resilient ... the love of children that makes us change our lives to meet their needs, the love of family that makes us drop everything to take care of them, the love of community, that makes us work tirelessly with broken hearts" (9).

If mothering is worthy of scholarship, the relational aspects of family life should be explored. Mothering is a social role experienced by the majority of women worldwide. It is through mothering that (most) human beings know love in their earliest stages of development (Chodorow). Failure to centre how love and care shape human relationships is informed by an androcentric bias in epistemology. The territory of emotional bonds and nurturing challenges the objective and detached knower. However, some areas of scholarship endeavour to better articulate the meaning of love. Within a feminist framework, Chodorow's psychoanalytic analysis of mothering offers a critical perspective on how women's oppression is rooted in the dynamics of mothering under patriarchy (Chodorow; Tong). Matricentric feminism is a feminism of relationships. It is a feminism that requires serious consideration of interconnectedness in a form not measured by achievement and power. It is feminism that requires us to consider the root of our primary relationships. However, in exploring love as an interpersonal and political force, we must also consider social forces and resistance.

Revolutionary Love

The language of revolution is often the language of war. We think of those who have fought for liberation from oppression, invasion, and tyrannical forces as being unified by an animating force that provides a counterforce to those that require submission. Women have suffered from the most violent aspects of systems of white supremacy while engaging in mothering practices. To introduce this as linked to matricentric feminism, I use the examples of Black (American) women's literature and feminist thought. I consider the tension existing between resistance and the need to build community. Forces of oppression disrupt community and connection, and nurturers, most often mothers, have a primary role in sustaining oppressed peoples. Where people face the forces of enslavement, colonization, and disruption of tradition and familial instability, the concepts of mothering and love become essential for the transmission of culture. Even in a state of bondage, love transmitted generationally is marked by themes of a different kind of revolution.

When taking on this project of analyzing matricentric feminism as informed by a perspective on racial oppression, I was drawn to Toni Morrison's masterpiece, *Beloved*. This novel is based on the true story of an enslaved woman, Margaret Garner. Garner escaped slavery but was recaptured under the fugitive slave law and was fated to be returned to plantation life. In an act of desperation, resistance, and sacrifice, she killed her daughter to spare her from returning to bondage. In the fictionalized version, Morrison's protagonist, Sethe also escaped slavery to Ohio, where she found her way, with her children, to the home of her mother-in-law, Baby Suggs, an "unchurched" preacher. In a famous scene, where Baby Suggs delivers a sermon to her community in a clearing, the subjects of grief, oppression, suffering, and love emerge. After leading the gathered audience in an emotional release of laughing, crying, and dancing, Baby Suggs instructs the crowd on the importance of loving themselves in their bodies in the face of oppression: "'Here,' she said, "in this here place, we flesh; flesh that weeps, laughs; flesh that dances on bare feet in the grass. Love it. Love it hard. Yonder they do not love your flesh. They despise it" (88).

Morrison provides a different type of revolutionary view—a feminist one that centres a framework for resistance. Those who have their humanity denied in interactions with the dominant white culture listen to this "grand" mother explain how to spiritually heal by embodying pleasure, sorrow, and the full range of emotions. This is the resistance to the dehumanization of racial oppression. In *Beloved*, the act of violence committed by Sethe against her children is horrific yet elicits sympathy in the reader. Rather than this seminal act dehumanizing Sethe, it offers a human perspective on the trauma of enslavement. The unfathomable experience of having children legally considered property is common in Black women's writing. In her poem, "Our Grandmothers," Maya Angelou, writes the chilling words: "She gathered her babies/their tears slick as oil on black faces, / their young eyes canvassing mornings of madness. / Momma, is Master going to sell you/from us tomorrow? ...Yes. / Unless the keeper of our lives/releases me from all commandments. Yes." This heartbreaking stanza underscores that violence, likely futile violence, is an option close to the minds of enslaved women. The themes of trauma, violence, loss, and love resonate throughout the narrative of how racism has affected Black family structures.

Barbara Omolade describes the experience of enslaved Black women who were exploited for labour, breeding, and nurturing: "She learned to use her darkness to create light, she would make the divided, white and black, external and internal world into wholeness...reaching out to help and for help and would gather around her children and kin to help them make the whole world livable. She would mother all the children, black and white" (375). Black women's experience under chattel slavery is an experience of nurturing in peril and having to extend care to Black and white children. This care extended to white children as a part of domestic labour offers a sense of intimacy rarely discussed in the analysis of Black love. The loving of one's enemy begins with the Black woman as nurturer of their future masters.

Much of hooks's writing focusses on the Black community as a place and the social context of oppression as gathered in lived experience, literature, and popular culture. Through this body of work, hooks asserts that the Black family and Black experience can offer an understanding of the depth of relationships that merits attention and study. In other words, Black love has a relevant voice in the discourse on social relationships. The loudness of Black love within hooks's analysis is not solely maternal; hooks experiences the multigenerational aspects of mothering as a daughter and caretaker for elders. She also considers love to inform an ethical position essential for community building. In the book *Yearning*, she argues love creates the space for social change:

> Historically, black women have resisted white supremacist domination by working to establish homeplace... It does not matter that sexism assigned them this role. It is more important that they took this conventional role and expanded it to include caring for one another, for children, for black men in ways that elevated our spirits, that kept us from despair, that taught some of us to be revolutionaries able to struggle for freedom. (385)

While addressing the circumstances of Black mothers, hooks does not offer a full analysis of motherhood within a matricentric framework. However, she does offer the idea of love as central to mothering.

As Cone argues concerning King's Christian love social gospel, hooks presents a feminist argument that resistance to oppression is rooted in love, connection, and culture. White supremacist capitalist patriarchy benefits from separation and exploitation; the aim of these systems is objectification and hierarchy without concern for the impact on the lower-status group. Taking responsibility for each other is antithetical to this oppressive worldview. The disruptive nature of these oppressive forces will be explored in the following section.

Where Love Is Lost

The hierarchies of Western civilization are marked by oppressive forces that impose a subordinate status upon the conquered. In contrast to the ecological connections of humans, plants, and animals in the natural world or the resilience of love within the human community, slavery and colonialism have created hierarchies unconcerned with love as an ethic. The white supremacy imposed on people of the global majority requires the disruption and exploitation of relationships within the oppressed group (Mohanty, "Under Western Eyes").

Marxist feminists have asserted that family life reproduces material relations and is bound by class. For example, Rosemarie Tong argues that "Monogamous marriage is a social institution that has nothing to do with love and everything to do with private property" (49). Thus, family structures for the bourgeois and proletariat classes serve capital. Within a capitalist system, the tasks associated with this caregiving are broken apart and commodified. It is a sociopolitical choice, rooted in white supremacist capitalist patriarchy, to situate caregivers, nurturers, and mothers in low-status roles. Those who do this work provide the essential labour for our human interconnectedness. There are also relevant intersections of identity that must be analyzed in mothering scholarship (Crenshaw). Racialized identities and experiences of oppression certainly inform mothering. For instance, the act of mothering or nurturing emerges among the racially oppressed as simultaneously an area of vulnerability and strength. Angela Davis interrogates the assumptions of mothering have been historically entangled with race: "European women in an increasingly obsolete domestic economy as the producers, nurturers, and rearers of children caused slave women to be valuated in accordance with their role as breeders ... the one presumed to capture the moral essence of womanness, while the other denied ... the very possibility of morality and thus also participation in this motherhood cult" (211). Thus, nurturing for Black women was removed from the idea of womanhood in contrast to evaluating mothering among privileged white women. Higher-status white women have long had help with the care of their children, employing women of colour and working-class women to take on the primary nurturing role (Cott; Omolade). Furthermore, elevating mothering as the primary role for women is a white middle-class privilege (Cott).

White supremacy, as a global force, has been the foundation of a racial caste system that interrupts the physical and psychological well-being of those who seek to live and thrive under its structures (Bulhan). The forces of colonialism and the global slave trade were both dehumanizing and broke apart cultural structures (Zakaria 142). Colonialism is marked by the separation of peoples from transmitting language, religious practices, and understanding of history to their offspring (Mohanty, "Under Western Eyes"). These racist practices exploit people of colour by destroying cultural foundations. They disrupt family relationships through the removal or sale of children and the imposition of foreign cultural norms on families in racially subordinate groups. This leads to a recording of relationships, notably mother to child. Mohanty makes the following point: "That women mother in a variety of societies is not as significant as the value attached to mothering in these societies. The distinction between the act of mothering and the status attached to it is a very important one" ("Under Western Eyes", 60). As colonial legal structures were imposed on traditional societies, there were ways that the family structures and female power were insufficiently addressed through Western justice models. For example, when colonial law was imposed upon the Bemba tribe in Zambia, women lost the ability to refuse their betrothed (60), which resulted in a loss of protection. Thus, women in the tribal society did not benefit from this shift in legal structures and became more socially vulnerable.

Racist systems have interrupted cultural transmission, nurturing, and the historically grounded mechanisms for community and family. However, the fact that oppressed people have endured white supremacy, including the undermining of family structures, demonstrates resistance and resilience. Survival within these frameworks of racial oppression requires an adaptation of mechanisms for care and community building.

Love as Resistance: Guiding Questions

Matricentric feminism takes mothering seriously. This chapter adds to that charge by including history, social context, and love in matricentric scholarship. The work of mothering fits within the concept of love as an interpersonal and community practice. Within a Western capitalist framework, considering mothering as this devalued form of labour allows the opportunity to centre marginalized women. However, it is also important to recognize the relevance of a love ethic, especially among racially marginalized mothers. Centring the present and historical experiences of racialized women who care and mother allows for the opportunity to further align resistance with matricentric feminist aims.

The next step is to integrate these concepts into scholarship. Returning to the idea of application, as introduced by Stewart, the following guiding questions offer perspective on approaching matricentric feminism with a cultural lens:

1) Where is love present in interpersonal relationships and community building? As has been articulated, love can be defined in multiple ways and at multiple levels of human relationships. A love framework should be included within matricentric work; it is a key dimension of nurturing and human thriving. This does not mean that all mothers have to be analyzed as "loving" caregivers. Rather, an analysis of mothering requires

that evidence of love within the culture and community be presented.

2) Is matricentric feminism inclusive of historical analysis and social condition? The matricentric framework offers space for a diverse understanding of mothering practices. However, the study of mothering needs to be grounded in the relevant historical context. This specifies for whom and under what conditions certain mothering practices have emerged, avoiding assumptions about a universal mothering experience.

3) Does matricentric feminism focus on justice for those who are most marginalized within society? The matricentric project should recognize the material concerns of those pushed to the margins. The need for resources and social remedies for mothers who parent under challenging conditions should be centred within the body of knowledge.

4) Does matricentric feminism focus on creating nonexploitative conditions for all families? A justice framework will focusses on how family life can reflect a love ethic rather than relations of exploitation. The reliance on the unpaid labour of mothers is a critical issue for women who must labour in the public and private spheres. The need for social structures supporting families, such as quality affordable childcare, can be articulated within a matricentric framework.

5) Does matricentric feminism focus on how love is a motivating force for resisting oppression? We build communities to thrive. When communities face threats, they always resist. Mothering within marginalized groups has provided a gateway to resistance and social action. The manifestation of love and nurturing as resistance should be highlighted in matricentric work.

These guiding questions are a reminder to consider racialized oppression and material deprivation as conditions for mothering. This framing also helps to integrate a love ethic, which is essential for social change. Social change is not an individual project, just as childrearing is not an individual project. Living in a community is a common feature of the human experience. Recognizing multiple identities and statuses allows for a more effective praxis of matricentric feminism.

Conclusion

Matricentric feminism removes mothers from the margins. The impact of colonialism, enslavement, and racial caste structures means that the social order reinforces the inferiority and invisibility of the oppressed (Bulhan). White supremacy in mothering scholarship can be challenged through culturally relevant approaches. Black feminist theory and standpoint praxis help to avoid the assumptions of mothering as a racially neutral activity. Matricentric feminism is a useful standpoint. It is critical to avoid a narrow focus on the most privileged categories of mothers. The matricentric project requires an assertion that love and nurturing deserve scholarly attention. Matricentric work must also critique the racial hierarchies evident in the social construction of motherhood. Not only do these aspects of the private sphere merit attention, but the impact of mothering as a social act should also be treated as a dimension of feminist work.

The ethics of community and love are essential for social change. Matricentric scholarship can remedy the past limitations of the feminist project, which have not prioritized mothering. If women's liberation is the work of feminism, we must explore this complicated territory of mothering, love, and community. Here, we will find evidence of what prepares societies for revolutionary change.

Dedication

For my beloved teacher, Beverly Guy Sheftall, and her beloved sister-friend, bell hooks—I wanted to write about Black mothering, and their work constantly reminds me that it is all and always love.

Works Cited

Angelou, Maya. "Our Grandmothers." *Afro Poets*, https://www.afropoets.net/mayaangelou25.html. Accessed 30 June 2024.

Brown, Adrienne Maree. *Emergent Strategy: Shaping Change, Changing Worlds*. AK Press, 2017.

Bulhan, Hussein. *Frantz Fanon and the Psychology of Oppression*. Plenum Press, 1985.

Cone, James. *Martine and Malcolm and America: A Dream or a Nightmare*. Orbis Books, 1993.

Cott, Nancy. *The Grounding of Modern Feminism.* Yale University Press, 1987.

Crenshaw, Kimberlé. "Demarginalizing the Intersection of Race and Sex: A Black Feminist Critique of Antidiscrimination Doctrine, Feminist Theory, and Antiracist Politics." *The University of Chicago Legal Forum*, vol. 1989, no. 1, pp. 139–67, https://chicagounbound.uchicago.edu/cgi/viewcontent.cgi?article=1052&context=uclf. Accessed 30 June 2024.

Davis, Angela. "Surrogates and Outcast Mothers: Racism and Reproductive Politics in the Nineties." *The Angela Y. Davis Reader.* Edited by Joy James. Blackwell, 1998, pp. 210–21.

Dotti, Giulia M., and Judith Treas. "Educational Gradients in Parents' Childcare Times Across Countries 1965–2012." *Journal of Marriage and Family*, vol. 78, no. 4, 2016, DOI. http://dx.doi.org/10.1111/jomf.12305.

Garland, Eric, et al. "Upward Spirals of Positive Emotions Counter Downward Spirals of Negativity: Insights from the Broaden-and-Build Theory and Affective Neuroscience on the Treatment of Emotion Dysfunctions and Deficits in Psychopathology." *Positive Clinical Psychology Clinical Psychology Review*, vol. 30, no. 7, 2010. pp. 849–64.

Green, Fiona. "Practicing Matricentric Feminist Mothering." *Journal of the Motherhood Initiative*, vol. 10, no. 1 & 2., 2019, pp. 83–99.

Harding, Sandra. "Introduction: Standpoint Theory as a Site of Political, Philosophic, and Scientific Debate." *The Feminist Standpoint Theory Reading Intellectual and Political Controversies.* Edited by Sandra Harding. Routledge, 2004, pp. 1–15.

Harrell, Zaje A. T. "I Am Never Sleeping with You Again: Reflections on Mothering, Community Building, and Unstable Allyship." *Coming into Being: Mothers on Finding and Realizing Feminism.* Edited by Andrea O'Reilly et al. Demeter Press, 2023, pp. 197–213.

hooks, bell. *All about Love: New Visions.* Perennial, 2000.

hooks, bell. *Communion: The Female Search for Love.* Perennial, 2003.

hooks, bell. "Homeplace a Site of Resistance." *Scribd*, https://www.scribd.com/doc/210061173/bell-hooks-homeplace-a-site-of-resistance#. Accessed 30 June 2024.

hooks, bell. *Salvation: Black People and Love.* William Morrow, 2001.

Kendall, Mikki. *Hood Feminism: Notes from the Women That a Movement Forgot*. Penguin Books, 2021.

Martinez, Gladys, and Daniels, Kimberly. "Fertility of Men and Women Aged 15–49 in the United States: National Survey of Family Growth 2015–2019." *National Health Statistics Report*, No. 179, 2023. pp. 2–21.

Mohanty, Chandra T. "Categories of Struggle: Third World Women and Politics of Feminism." *Third World Women and the Politics of Feminism*. Edited by Chandra T. Mohanty, et al. Indiana University Press, 1991, pp. 2–45.

Mohanty, Chandra T. "Under Western Eyes." *Third World Women and the Politics of Feminism*. Edited by Chadra T. Mohanty. Indiana University Press, 1991, pp. 51–80.

Morrison, Toni, *Beloved*. Plume, 1998.

Omolade, Barbara. *The Rising Song of African American Women*. Routledge, 1994.

O'Reilly, Andrea. "Matricentric Feminism: A Feminism for Mothers." *Journal of the Motherhood Initiative*, vol. 10, no. 1/2, 2019, pp. 13–26.

Rich, Adrienne. *Of Woman Born: Motherhood as Experience and Intuition*. 2nd ed. W. W. Norton, 1986.

Ruddick, Sara. "Maternal Thinking as a Feminist Standpoint." *The Feminist Standpoint Theory Reading Intellectual and Political Controversies*. Edited by Sandra Harding. Routledge, 2004. pp. 161–67.

Stewart, Abigail J. "Doing Personality Research: How Can Feminist Theories Help?" *The Gender and Psychology Reader*. Edited by Blythe Clinchy and Julie Norem. New York University Press, 1989. pp. 54–68.

Tong, Rosemarie. *Feminist Thought. A Comprehensive Introduction*. Westview Press. 1989.

United Nations. "Populations and Families." *United Nations*, https://worlds-women-2020-data-undesa.hub.arcgis.com/pages/population-and-families. Accessed 30 June 2024.

Zakaria, Rafia. *Against White Feminism*. W. W. Norton, 2021.

2.

The Case for Radical Inclusion in Mothering Studies: Matricentric Feminism Can and Should Take on Genderism

Nicole L. Willey

Mothering studies has promoted an empowered mothering that is intersectionally feminist. Lately, the push (and push back) around opening language and spaces to mothers who are not cisgender women or parents who are birthing but are not immediately seen as mothers has come to the forefront. This chapter is my effort to present the case for the radical inclusion of all who are mothers*[1] into mothering studies spaces, communities, scholarship, and advocacy. First, I will discuss the history of mothering studies and how we have arrived at our current conceptions of matricentric feminism. From there, I will look at the importance of extending the definition of matricentric feminism to include the fight against genderism, even when that means our language and spaces must accommodate those we do not automatically think of as mothers or as doing mothering work. This discussion of language expansion, along with ideas around queer theory and queering mothering, will be followed by an examination of how trans experiences can and should transform our mothering studies work. Matricentric feminism has led us towards powerful, intersectional work, and it is time to push past biological restrictions and binaries in our thinking. This will help us match our feminist parenting with our feminist scholarship.

Our History and the Need for Change

Around the time of the first Women's March in 2017 after Trump's election in the United States (US), Katha Pollitt noted that there is such a thing as "Too-Big-Tent-Feminism" (6) and that not all women's rights groups are the same. Women's choice and autonomy over their bodies must be nonnegotiable in feminism. In other words, focussing on women is not enough to be feminist; we need to strive for intersectionality and autonomy for all women*. Similarly, focussing on mothering and mothers* does not always mean the focus is feminist. Mothering studies scholars should be familiar with the history of the field—that it took writers like Adrienne Rich questioning patriarchal-informed motherhood to lead the way and that Nancy Chodorow was one of the first to point out that the reproduction of gender roles was socially constructed rather than natural. Jessie Bernard's 1974 writing was "the first publication to consider motherhood as a social institution rather than a natural fact" (qtd. in F. Green 37).

Those foremothers opened a pathway to discussing feminist mothering as oppositional to patriarchal motherhood. Mothering is an empowering process that "seeks to grant mothers agency, authority, authenticity, autonomy, and advocacy–activism denied to them in patriarchal motherhood" (O'Reilly, "Feminist Mothering" 44). Andrea O'Reilly, a touchstone for mother scholars, provides the following "open-ended definition of feminism" that has helped guide my understanding of matricentric feminism, which is:

> the recognition that most if not all cultures are patriarchal and that they give prominence, power, and privilege to men and the masculine; they depend on the oppression, if not disparagement, of women and the feminine. Feminists are committed to challenging and transforming this gender inequity in all of its manifestations: cultural, economic, political, philosophical, social, ideological, sexual, and so forth. As well, most feminisms (including my own) seek to dismantle other hierarchical binary systems, such as race (racism), sexuality (heterosexism), economics (classism), and ability (ableism)… . Feminist mothering, thus, seeks to transform both the patriarchal role of motherhood and that of childrearing. ("Feminist Mothering" 48–49)

Taking this definition to its logical conclusion, genderism (transphobia) should be added to the "so forth" that O'Reilly mentions. It is time for us as mother scholars to recognize that our feminist mothering work must include the further breaking down of yet another binary harmful to individuals' ability to live their fullest lives.

Sara Ruddick, another foremother, importantly recognizes the possibilities of extending the definition of mothering to anyone interested in doing the work: "Briefly, a mother is a person who takes on responsibility for children's lives and for whom providing child care is a significant part of her or his working life. I *mean* 'her or his.' Although most mothers have been and are women, mothering is potentially work for men and women" (49). In 1989, before a real reckoning in feminist studies, mothering studies, or our culture at large with the realities and dangers of genderism and transphobia, Ruddick rightfully placed the work of mothering in the hands of anyone who is responsible for childcare. Ruddick's ways of being and thinking are available to those engaged in the "protection, nurturance, and training [of children]—they are engaged in maternal practice ... [which] gives rise to a specific discipline of thought—a cluster of attitudes, beliefs, and values" called "maternal thinking" (O'Reilly, "Maternal Theory" 21). Taking Ruddick's admonition of allowing all to mother, together with O'Reilly's concern for breaking down harmful binaries, it means we must engage in further work to open up matricentric feminism. Fiona Joy Green is leading the way: "More recent feminist mothering focuses on understanding, troubling, and challenging binary gender categories, as well as being open to and supporting varied expressions of gender fluidity in children, family members, friends, and others in society" (41). This openness must become an automatic extension of how we engage with trans parents.

I have come to a revised and radically inclusive definition of matricentric feminism through my mothering work and its connection to matricentric feminism. Along the way, I found queer and trans voices that helped me see that the way forward for matricentric feminism, mothering studies, and family and societal structures is to open our spaces and scholarship to all mothers*. As I have written elsewhere:

> To move our mothering forward, we must move away from ideas that pigeonhole all of us into serving the status quo. Mothering, and allowing fathers and others to mother, toward connection and away from shame, humiliation, and gender straitjackets, will

> allow—finally—true family values, values that recognize the humanity and worth in everyone. ("Mothers and Sons" 324)

I am not arguing that we should call everyone a mother; many fathers (and others) will prefer masculine and nonbinary nomenclature for their mothering practice. What I am suggesting is that we cannot talk about mothering (or birthing) as though only women do it. Trans people should feel welcome in our mothering-advocacy spaces, and I hope that opening up our definition of matricentric feminism will ultimately convince mothering studies scholars, and eventually the general public, that erasing cisgender/biological mothers will not come to fruition. Opening up our language, spaces, and scholarship—indeed our feminism—to a "both-and" type of inclusion will support all mothers*. Therefore, I would like to focus on what can be gained by broadening our focus and inclusion in mothering studies work and activism. Lane Hollis recently shared this perspective on the trans parent memoir:

> In making pregnancy and parenthood more gender-neutral by using terms like 'gestational parenting' and 'chestfeeding,' as well as finding androgynous versions of Mom or Dad, all trans and nonbinary gestational parents are doing is carving out a space for themselves in the parenting sphere that has been historically dominated by cishet parents. No erasure or usurping of the parenting community is occurring whatsoever; if anything, queer parents of all orientations are the ones who have been erased for decades. (10)

Excluding trans people from mothering work is something we must fight against. Ensuring that mothers are still named while increasing the use of the types of terms Hollis uses above, along with other recommendations, will form a broader coalition of those doing mothering work. Language matters, so naming different kinds of mothers* should be our goal.

Matricentric feminism has always been intersectional; it is time for it to become completely intersectional by adding genderism to our lens. This means, somewhat paradoxically, that it must be part of the project of radical inclusion for all mothers*, which means sometimes deemphasizing the singular role of cisgender/biological mothers. Although it sometimes makes sense to continue to use the words "mother," "mothering," and "women" in spaces where it is an accurate description, we cannot fall prey to the fear of mothers being cancelled if we make our language more inclusive, along with our spaces. It is only through moving away from gender binaries that we will be able to experience the gains and possibilities our feminist parenting should enact. Our children, prepared by our feminist parenting, which is informed by a more expansive version of matricentric feminism, will continue to create in families, and ultimately in our communities and society at large, structures that refuse to reproduce gender roles based on stereotypes. Cisgender women may still be the majority of those who mother, and they will be less alone in the project of raising the next generation.

To state this another way, if matricentric feminism does not become part of the project of removing the conditions that reproduce our gender roles, and thus our oppression, we are in trouble and we are on the wrong side of justice. We can move forward without disregarding actual bodies —the bodies of women and others who mother—and we can do this as part of a more inclusive definition of matricentric feminism.

Part of what is at stake in redefining matricentric feminism is the idea that we think we already know what mothering means and what mothers do. We assume that mothering "implies ongoing care and nurturing of children" (Coltrane 4). Following the tenets of matricentric feminism, we hope that all mothers* can experience these actions as empowered and empowering, as they mother away from patriarchy. The problem is that for us to do this, we need to expect more, for instance, from fathers. Scott Coltrane notes that fathering "has typically implied an initial sex act and the financial obligation to pay" (4), even as we hope for more involved fathers and household partners.

Feminist women who mother in a heterosexual union usually hope for involved coparenting, even though mothers still carry the mental load and much of the actual labour of households and childrearing in these partnerships. There is plenty of popular press and anecdotal evidence given to the idea that fathers are not fulfilling their share of domestic and parenting labour, even when they wish to: "Most of the fathers in [in the study by Harrington et al.] aspire to share equally in caregiving with their spouse/partner, but often are unable to bring this desire to reality" (Ennis 275).

Matricentric feminism can help move the needle on family structures and help those, like Coltrane, who are working for "the potential of richer lives for men, more choices for women, and more gender equality in future generations" (4). We have seen that "change in fathering is occurring, and that diverse forms of fathers' involvement are an indication of the movement we have witnessed away from monolithic, stereotypical views of father involvement" (Devault et al. xii). But as our ideas of expanded roles for fathers, even the possibility of feminist fathering, have evolved, we know that many families are not in heterosexual partnerships, and we need to open our theories and spaces wide for everyone who is mothering while pushing even involved fathers towards more egalitarian parenting practices. In a perhaps surprising move, this project pushes us to use feminism and queer theory because we need to "brea[k] down gender binaries (queer theory) coupled with a commitment to overcoming inequities based on those hierarchical binaries (feminism)" (Willey, "Choose Your Own" 185) to find all mothers* through sharing a radically inclusive matricentric feminist ethos.

Language and Political Realities

What happens to mothering studies and matricentric feminism when we let all mothers* in? After US President Joe Biden's administration began to use "birthing people" in its maternal health guidance documents, Jessica Anderson, the Executive Director of Heritage Action, a conservative think tank, tweeted: "Biden's budget would literally erase the word 'mother' and replace it with the woke and watered-down term 'birthing people' in relation to maternal health. Why does Biden want to cancel mothers?" (qtd. in Fearnow par. 8). This issue of nomenclature has been in the headlines over the past year as conservatives have attacked inclusive language as part of their culture wars. It has been interesting to note that this polarization seems to be working at times in unexpected places. For mothering studies scholars, fighting for mothers and their embodied experience has been much of the battle. Mothers' ways of being, experiencing, and knowing are celebrated and trusted, as they should be. Therefore, some mothering scholars have gotten nervous about this seeming erasure.

It can be scary to have to open our valued words and definitions to be "sensitive to individual needs and as beneficial, kind, and inclusive.... Yet, this kindness has delivered unintended consequences that have serious implications for women and children" (Migdon par. 3). Emma

Green notes that this language, rather than being inclusive, can be seen by some as "exclusionary because it erases women and mothers as worthy categories of identity" (par. 2). In broadening the language around mothering, are we dehumanizing mothers? Does gender-inclusive language reduce women to their physiological processes and body parts? (Migdon par. 4).

Language changes can be difficult, but as a community of scholars, we can learn new ways of thinking and speaking about transgender inclusivity and mothering. In the same way that we cannot fathom leaving women of colour out of the field (whether we are inclusive enough in the area of race and ethnicity is certainly an important discussion, but it is understood that matricentric feminism must be intersectional around race, class, (dis)ability, and many other categories), we should not leave out people who are mothers* but who have different gender identities. Kinnon R. MacKinnon et al. note the following:

> Some might object that this nomenclature favours inclusivity over the experiences of the majority of pregnant people who are cisgender women. However, the term "pregnant person" does not discredit cisgender women; rather it opens the umbrella to cover everyone seeking obstetrical care. Language evolves and words matter. Providing comprehensive and accessible healthcare to all includes broadening gender-neutral and affirming language in obstetrics. (202)

Cisgender women will continue to be the majority of mothers but making the argument that the majority is the only group that should be included discredits our intersectional efforts. Minority voices (and bodies) must be included.

The National Institutes of Health (NIH) gives guidelines inside its gender-inclusive language guide for sometimes being more limited in language use: "Using more limited and specific language is sometimes important. For instance, if discussing a study that only involves cisgender women, gender-specific language (pregnant women) would be most accurate ... if the word *women* is preferable, but if transgender and nonbinary people are also referenced, phrasing like *women and other pregnant patients* can provide an inclusive alternative" (par. 9). In other words, we can and should demarcate the appropriate language choices for the appropriate space, and women do not have to be erased in this larger umbrella. The dangers of being noninclusive are much more harrowing than the perceived harm to mothers in changes and expansions to language. As Virginia Duan reminds us, these language changes—to this point largely seen in medical settings—are "not advocating for excising gendered terms entirely—they are merely *adding additional language* to include people who do not identify as women or are not in heterosexual relationships. The logic is to help normalize all different kinds of people who need perinatal care and make folks feel safe" (par. 5). My ability to be a cisgender, heterosexual, and partnered mother is not hurt by the additional language; no one's mothering identity is.

The New York Times published the article "G.O.P. Lawmakers Push a Growing Wave of Anti-Transgender Bills" on January 30, 2023. Such bills are appearing in a growing number of US states and globally. Removing medical care for youth in transition, closing drag shows, trying to make gender and sexuality discussions in academic settings illegal, and suggesting that athletes should have their genitals examined before being able to compete are all painful and harmful realities that trans people face. One argument I have read against inclusivity is that trans parents are a small minority and that society is somehow caving to this vocal minority. However, when a person's existence is being legislated away (no matter the size of the population affected), the alarm bells should be ringing, loudly. E. Green's interview with Louise Melling, deputy legal director of the ACLU and director of the Ruth Bader Ginsburg Center for Liberty, points out this danger: "When you think about the bills that passed this year, they try not only to attack, but almost obliterate transgender people. A total erasure from the language has huge consequences" (par. 1). Moreover, the number of transgender adults may be higher than realized. A 2016 study "found that as many as 1.4 million American adults (0.6%) identify as transgender" (Brooks par. 9). This likely means that in the US, more than two hundred thousand people who do not identify as female (or as a mother) could be giving birth (Brooks par. 9). Justin S. Brandt et al. have found that even with "increased visibility of transgender people, contemporary medical providers are largely unprepared to care for them" (17). This means that between .5 and 2 per cent of the American population may not even seek health care due to previous bad experiences, poverty, and discrimination (Brandt et al. 18).

The preponderance of cisgender mothers is real, but a majority alone does not mean they own mothering. Matricentric feminism must demand that we welcome all who mother and give birth, since "normativity is comfortable for those who can inhabit it" (Sara Ahmed qtd. in Mac Kinnon et al. 201). Cisnormativity—like heteronormativity, which matricentric feminists do not accept—"creates an environment of discomfort and systemic prejudice towards trans people" (MacKinnon et al. 201). The good news is that being inclusive in our language, scholarship, and spaces will not erase the majority of mothers who are cisgender women. As Melling says, "Nobody is stopped from speaking about her motherhood or the importance of that" but the project is to "open up space so that we no longer have the cultural expectation that women are caregivers" (qtd. in E. Green par. 37). In fact, holding onto cisgenderist language around mothering is part of the reason "gender stereotypes really do lock everybody into different kinds of roles" (Melling qtd. in E. Green par. 38). As Melling notes, the patriarchal structures and gender stereotypes that hurt women also hurt trans people too; they "hurt all of us by locking us into some kind of vision" (qtd. in E. Green par. 27). Including others in mothering frees all of us.

Furthermore, if genderism and cisnormativity hurt trans people who mother, these effects are compounded for those who are mothering as racialized trans people. Intersectional feminism reminds us, as does the medically informed multiple minority stress model, of the following: "[There is a] multiplicative impact of racism and transphobic violence experienced by Black transmasculine and gender diverse birthing persons. These vulnerabilities are linked to racism and transphobic violence simultaneously" (Gillette-Pierce par. 8). It should be everyone's goal to provide not only gender-inclusive medical spaces but also community spaces, educational spaces, academic realities, and advocacy spaces in which we can realize "the highest level of health for all people" (par. 12).

Breaking Down Binaries Helps Everyone Who Mothers

Creating a matricentric feminism that automatically includes the call to be inclusive and break down genderism will allow feminist mothers* to embrace more fully the work of inclusivity. Feminist mothers* should be "applying the values of non-oppression and non-domination in [our] relationship[s] with others" (Bartlett 23). We do this with our children already, but we should be doing our best to enact this in all of our spheres of influence. As Lynn Comerford et al. write: "Feminist parenting affects the political, economic, emotional, symbolic, and physical conditions of women's and men's [and everyone's] lives. To be a feminist parent is to confront and correct system gender inequalities and injustices associated with parenting children" (1). F. Green also offers a comprehensive list of the goals of what she calls "matroreform" and its four practices: (1) "creating alternative nonpatriarchal family formations; (2) teaching children how to think critically about the world; (3) creating respectful, nonhierarchical parent/child relationships; and (4) engaging in anti-sexist parenting and gender socialization practices" (39). Matroreform must become part of the project of creating authentic, nonsexist, nonracist, nonableist, nonclassist, and, indeed, nongenderist relationships and ways of thinking.

As feminist mothers* and parents, we should strive to create these ideals in our homes and communities. Mothering studies scholars should embrace these ideals as well. We can all recognize the myriad ways that mothers (in their homes, workplaces, and cultures at large) do not have the support they need. Courtney Megan Cahill's examination of maternity in constitutional law shows that part of the desire to keep the definition of mother monolithic is harmful and discriminatory; perhaps her greatest point is encapsulated here: "The ... objection—that reforming constitutional maternity could devalue women's reproductive labor—assumes that constitutional maternity values women's reproductive labor" (80). In other words, mothers are by and large not valued currently in the US; children and families are not prioritized, such as the lack of mandatory maternal/paternal leave, the lack of affordable and subsidized childcare or universal PreK, and the inability to provide all people in the US with healthcare. Indeed, Linda Rose Ennis notes the importance of creating a world in which mothering is more fully supported:

> We want equality for women and encourage them to be involved in the workforce for their family security as well as to justify having an equal education to men. However, we do not offer encouragement to anyone for raising children, neither to mothers or fathers. Why would anyone, other than those in a lesser financial position or who have bought into the expectations of intensive mothering, want to engage in an activity that isn't respected and doesn't offer remuneration? (277)

Joanna Frye further argues: "We must continue to work for the institutional changes that support parenting: paid parental leave that also takes into account the distinctive requirements of pregnancy, childbirth, and breastfeeding; universal free early childcare; and affordable after-school care for older children (28). Support in these areas would help all children, all parents, and all families. All mothers* and their allies should work together on these interrelated issues, and we should work towards all mothers* having access to safe healthcare.

Matricentric feminism should provide the guidance needed to become empowered mothers* and parents (because feminist men can and should learn from it as well) to "help our children learn strategies to move in the world with peace" (Willey, "Mothers and Sons" 317). Excluding anyone from this project enacts the types of exclusion and violence that we say we are against as mothering studies scholars and maternal feminists. As Comerford and colleagues write: "Feminist parents argue that one's gender, sexual orientation, marital status, or biological relationship does not determine parenting ability and they resist arguments that each could" (6). The radical inclusion of all mothers* must be part of our project, as we all suffer from living in a world in which we are "stratified by gender, race, class, nationality, sexuality, ability, as well as many other identity markers" (Comerford et al 6). These identities are set up to discriminate against feminist parents as they try to parent their children away from these oppressive systems. Furthermore, as O'Reilly notes, neoliberalism has downloaded caregiving responsibilities to mothers, who are now responsible for more with fewer resources, and they alleviate this anxiety by reproducing their class privilege and status (O'Reilly, "Maternal Theory" 27). This scarcity mindset is harmful in terms of economics, and it is also harmful in terms of who we include or exclude from our spaces. All mothers* work under these same constraints (although we may be affected differently), and our goal should be to work together for the betterment of all.

A related goal is to empower our mothering practices through "affirming maternal agency, authority, autonomy, authenticity, and activism, and by opening up new maternal practices and identities" (O'Reilly, "Maternal Theory" 31). Indeed, new ways of being a mother, or of being maternal, need to be taken seriously by matricentric feminism. Nancy Dowd notes as follows: "Good parenting is neither sex-specific nor sex-related. The attributes of good parenting are more strongly associated with mothering, but the connection is cultural, not biological" (8–9). Understanding there is nothing natural about good mothering allows us to learn and work together towards our expansive feminist goals. F. Green synthesizes prevalent ideas about feminist/empowered mothering and parenting here:

> By emphasizing their own agency, authority, authenticity, and autonomy as mothers, empowered mothers redefine motherhood through varied transformative practices. Empowered mothering is alive in nonpatriarchal family models; in community and othermothering; and in non-authoritative, anti-discriminatory, and anti-racist ways of parenting. As maternal activities, empowered mothers are mindful and deliberate in their approaches to mothering that counter those of mainstream society; they consciously redefine and actively engage in motherwork through which cultural, social, and political change can be made possible. (42)

Working against patriarchal ideals and mainstream culture, which are currently poised to roll back freedoms and rights for trans people—not to mention the right to bodily autonomy for all people who can get pregnant—means that we must open our theory to welcome all mothers*. When we lead the way with radical inclusion in empowered mothering practices, we allow for children who grow up with radical inclusion philosophies, expanded definitions of family, and the chance to unite those working against patriarchy for additional support for all mothers*, parents, caregivers, and children.

Using Queer and Trans Ways of Knowing

Part of what might be holding some back from including all parents under the umbrella of mothering and parenting could be the historic discomfort with queer theory. As I have explored elsewhere:

> It is no secret that feminism and queer theory are often at odds. For instance, some feminist theorists rely upon gender and sex definitions that reinforce binaries that queer theorists strive to break down, whereas, queer theorists sometimes prize private queer choices over the lived lives of women, even in some cases

> uncritically embracing sex positivity without accounting for real harm done to women through sexual violence. (Willey, "Choose Your Own Fathering" 185)

However, the queering of motherhood has been happening for at least as long as we have been studying it, so we should not feel uncomfortable with it. As F. Green has noted: "Ruddick 'queered motherhood' long ago by theorizing the gender flexibility of maternal thinking that takes place in the work of mothering, and which continues to inform an understanding of who mothers are and what mothering entails" (45). And, of course, queer theory and practice are an important part of allowing for transformation away from patriarchal gender roles and families. Heather Jackson notes that queer theory helps families build the world on their terms and are effectively "queering the world": "Queering the world involves resisting heteronormativity through sexuality, gender identities, and family structures. For example, the mothers I interviewed have queered their lives and families with their own identities by being feminists, single mothers, queer, and by questioning the gender binary" (96). The aforementioned concerns of queer theory at times leaving out women's realities can and should be ameliorated by the transformative possibilities present inside of the freedom queering mothering provides.

Radical inclusion of all interested mothers* under the umbrella of matricentric feminism may feel difficult at first because genderism may be the last frontier in what have been typically feminist battles. Riki Wilchins writes:

> It's because gender is not just a system of laws and practices but also a way of thinking and seeing that it has taken so long to come to the fore as a political issue. Yet unlike the struggles against homophobia, racism, and sexism, the struggle against genderism will not only be about gaining rights for an oppressed class of men and women. It will be about gaining equality for all men and women. And paradoxically, it will be about the rights of some of us to not be men or women. (14)

Feminists have long been trained to see that gender is a "*doing* rather than a being" (Wilchins 12). Being a woman, maybe especially for cisgender women who are also biological mothers, may feel like a being, like something we naturally are. But we constantly perform our gender inside and outside of prescribed gender roles, as Judith Butler famously proved in *Gender Trouble*. Although many feminist mothers are comfortable with pushing back against misogynistic cultural norms, we need to move further and allow for all who mother to be a part of our feminist process. Our bodies and experiences do give us access to knowledge, and part of that knowledge is the awareness that we do not fit precisely into the narrow moulds our society says mothers should fill. We similarly do not want to be the ones demanding queer and trans people fulfill only the roles we readily understand. Wilchins points out that patriarchy creates real pain:

> The feelings of shame, humiliation, and fear are not the result of personal failings. Nor are they the inadvertent side effects of a benign system of gender norms. Such feelings are the gender system itself at work: enjoining us in policing ourselves, reminding us of our place, shaming us into submission, and making our gender appear natural, seamless, and voluntary. (14)

We need to break away from arguments for gender roles and patriarchal norms that keep oppressed people, and everyone, in boxes. Indeed, not allowing trans parents into our lingual and actual communities is harmful and limiting. As Cahill notes, "We limit people's ability to become parents when we assume a biological difference" (83). Brandt et al. have found the following: "The reproductive desires of transgender men appear to be similar to those of cisgender individuals. Some transgender men will have highly desired pregnancies whereas others perceive pregnancy as necessary to start a family ... unintended pregnancies are also common, occurring in approximately 30% of transgender men in one study" (18). These experiences of pregnancy and childbirth can create "worsening gender dysphoria" for some trans men; for others, however, pregnancy "can be a remarkable introduction to fatherhood" (Brandt et al. 19). Brandt et al.'s work demonstrates that pregnancy and childbirth are not universal experiences, as mothering scholars already understand from our own examinations of mothering across various individuals, identity positions, geographical realities, and the like. Mothers and pregnant people in all these situations deserve our care and concern.

One way to show that care and concern is to follow caring health providers and NIH guidelines and use gender-neutral language, as in the phrase "pregnant people" used above. As Melling notes: "People are really committed to using gender-neutral language. Historically, people have been punished for deviating from gender norms. That includes women, that includes transgender people, that includes nonbinary people. I see commonality, not difference, in this struggle" (qtd. in E. Green par. 12). A. J. Lowik suggests that we should refer with specificity to body parts and body functions, without linking them to gender; it is a "process of unlearning and untying the binary linkages between bodies, identities, and behaviours" (211). We must strive to create language and spaces where parenting is not about biological sex because gendered language "fails to capture the diversity and fluidity of parents and families" (Lowik 212). Feminist mothering requires the ability to escape patriarchy; trans ways of thinking, practice, and language allow us as mothering scholars to fully embrace this nonoppressive way of being in our world. This accuracy and neutrality can at times feel dehumanizing, but I think it can be easily ameliorated by such constructions as "breast- and chestfeeding" and "mothers and pregnant people."

In particular, transfeminist theory can and should inform our matricentric feminism. Emi Koyama's *The Transfeminist Manifesto* theorizes and "embodies feminist coalition politics in which women from different backgrounds (including trans and non-trans) stand up for each other, because if we do not stand for each other, nobody will" (qtd. in F. Green 46). Protecting each other is necessary, and that happens incrementally through the cultural changes wrought by feminist parenting practices. Jake Pyne's study finds that "Trans parents ... preserved gender options for their children, expanded notions of biological possibilities, negotiated new identities, and role modeled authenticity and embodiment" (127). These are common goals for all feminist parents, and trans parents will often have transformative models of being in family and parenting relationships by necessity. We should learn from them. F. Green shows that combining a variety of theories and practices continues the difficult and powerful work of challenging patriarchy:

> As a result of integrating the theories of intersectionality, maternal thinking, and transfeminism, which trouble and contest gender essentialism in mothering identities and childcare practices, feminisms and feminist mothers are becoming more conscious of the ways in which mothers' lives today are more complex and diverse than ever before. Intersectionality, maternal thinking, and transfeminisms assist in the project of disrupting the gender

essentialism presupposed by patriarchal discourses of mothering and contest gender-essentialized norms of motherhood. (46)

If our matricentric feminism is not fully intersectional, it is not feminism. It is time for mothering scholars to move away from binary thinking. As Chodorow argued decades ago, "Women's mothering is one of the few universal and enduring elements of the sexual division of labor" (3). In releasing ourselves from gender norms, we can finally "reproduce" ourselves away from gender binaries, challenging these roles and these ways of being that keep many oppressed. We should not rely on the "myth of the natural mother ... [which] assumes that mothering requires no particular knowledge, skills, or education and as a further consequence, deserves no economic return" (Courtenay 223). Pretending that mothering is a "natural" skill set makes it hard for any mothers* to be truly valued, particularly economically. Removing the final -ism, genderism, from our matricentric feminist practice and scholarship is a step towards acknowledging that mothering should be a choice and that it takes skills that people can learn that provide real service to society. It will also allow us to be truly intersectional.

We can start by adding gender-neutral language, as suggested by various health entities, to our discussion of mothering functions. This expansion does not erase women's experiences; rather, a coalition against gender norms helps all oppressed mothers* and should be part of feminist parenting practice. Including, recognizing, and celebrating all mothers* will go a long way towards elevating the status of mothering as knowledge -based work that should be valued and supported, which will protect those who are currently oppressed and formalize our feminist parenting practice.

Endnotes

1. I am borrowing the asterisk from the Michigan State University's Women*s Student Services website. They write:

   We use an asterisk in Women*s Student Services to share that there is more to the story. Gender is one part of our identities, and there is more to gender than the binary. The movement for gender equity is work that everyone, regardless of gender, can and should do. We are made up of intersecting identities—including our gender—that shape our life experiences. ***All*** who are interested in supporting students in working toward an inclusive and equitable community are welcome. (par. 4)

I like the idea that we can continue to use the word mother while recognizing that our previous binaries and definitions do not always work for everyone.

2. Although most men who are caregivers/parents are called (and likely prefer) the term "father," my coedited collection *Feminist Fathering/ Fathering Feminists: New Definitions and Directions* explores how the word "father" can be used by many, even by those we would not normally think of as fathers. The collection interrogates falling back on names and roles just because they are there and finding ways to father and examples of fathering where we might not typically see them. This chapter focusses on the project of finding and including mothers by their choices and actions; it is not about including cisgender men who are comfortable with the term "father" under the umbrella of mothers*.

Works Cited

Astor, Maggie. "G.O.P. State Lawmakers Push a Growing Wave of Anti-Transgender Bills." *New York Times,* 30 Jan. 2023, https://www.nytimes.com/2023/01/25/us/politics/transgender-laws-republicans.html?smid=nytcore-ios-share&referringSource=articleShare. Accessed 30 June 2024.

Bartlett, Elizabeth Ann. "Feminist Parenting as the Practice of Non-Domination: Lessons from Adrienne Rich, Audre Lorde, Sara Ruddick, and Iris Marion Young." *Feminist Parenting.* Edited by Lynn Comerford et al. Demeter Press, 2016, pp. 23–37.

Brandt, Justin S., et al. "Transgender Men, Pregnancy, and the 'New' Advanced Paternal Age: A Review of the Literature." *Maturitas,* vol. 128, Oct. 2019, pp. 17–21. *EBSCOhost,* https://doi.org/10.1016/j.maturitas.2019.07.004.

Brooks, Heidi. "Exploring a Nonbinary Approach to Health: Holding Space for Inclusive and Expansive Language in Maternal and Child Health." *National Institute for Children's Health Quality,* 29 June 2021, https://www.nichq.org/insight/exploring-nonbinary-approach-health. Accessed 30 June 2024.

Butler, Judith. *Gender Trouble: Feminism and the Subversion of Identity.* Routledge, 1989.

Cahill, Courtney Megan. "The New Maternity." *Harvard Law Review,* vol. 133, no. 7, May 2020, pp. 2221–303, *EBSCOhost,* proxy.library.kent.edu/login?url=https://https://search.ebscohost.com/login.aspx?direct=true&db=aph&AN=143201302&site=ehost-live. Accessed 30 June 2024.

Chodorow, Nancy. *The Reproduction of Mothering: Psychoanalysis and the Sociology of Gender.* University of California Press, 1978.

Coltrane, Scott. *Family Man: Fatherhood, Housework, and Gender Equity.* Oxford University Press, 1996.

Comerford, Lynn, et al. "Introduction." *Feminist Parenting.* Edited by Lynn Comerford et al. Demeter Press, 2016, pp. 1–20.

Courtenay, Pamela. "Disability and the Price of Myths about Mothering." *Mothers and Sons: Centering Mother Knowledge.* Edited by Besi Brillian Muhonja and Wanda Thomas. Demeter Press, 2016, pp. 222–34.

Craig, Elaine. "Converging Feminist and Queer Legal Theories: Family Feuds and Family Ties." *Windsor Yearbook of Access to Justice,* vol. 28, no. 1, 2010, pp. 209–390.

Devault, Annie, et al., eds. *Fathering: Promoting Positive Fathering Involvement.* University of Toronto Press, 2015.

Dowd, Nancy, *Redefining Fatherhood.* New York University Press, 2000.

Duan, Virginia. "Chestfeeding, Co-Parent, Perinatal Ward—It's Time To Normalize These Birthing Terms." *Scary Mommy* 30 Mar. 2021, https://www.scarymommy.com/inclusive-terms-birth-breastfeeding. Accessed 30 June 2024.

Ennis, Linda Rose. "Mothering or Parenting?" *The Routledge Companion to Motherhood.* Edited by Lynn O'Brien Hallstein. Routledge, 2020, pp. 274–83.

Fearnow, Benjamin. "Biden Admin Replaces 'Mothers' with 'Birthing People' in Maternal Health Guidance." *Newsweek,* 7 June 2021, https://www.newsweek.com/biden-admin-replaces-mothers-birthing-people-maternal-health-guidance-1598343. Accessed 30 June 2024.

Frye, Joanne S. "Parental Thinking: What Does Gender Have to Do with It?" *Essential Breakthroughs: Conversations about Men, Mothers, and*

Mothering. Edited by Fiona Joy Green and Gary Lee Pelletier. Demeter Press, 2015, pp. 14–31.

Gillette-Pierce, Zahada. "Black Birthing Persons Matter–All of Them." *Harvard Medical School Primary Care Review*, 14 Apr. 2022, https://info.primarycare.hms.harvard.edu/review/black-birthing-persons-matter. Accessed 30 June 2024.

Green, Emma. "The Culture War over 'Pregnant People.'" *The Atlantic*, 17 Sept. 2021, https://www.theatlantic.com/politics/archive/2021/09/pregnant-people-gender-identity/620031/. Accessed 30 June 2024.

Green, Fiona Joy. "Feminist Mothering." *The Routledge Companion to Motherhood*. Edited by Lynn O'Brien Hallstein. Routledge, 2020, pp. 36–50.

Hollis, Lane. "Off the Beaten Binary: Transgender and Nonbinary Experiences with Pregnancy and Parenthood." Canvas Course, Senior Seminar, Professor Nicole L. Willey, 2023.

Jackson, Heather. "How Single, Queer, and Feminist Mothering Deconstruct Patriarchy, Gender, and the Nuclear Family." *Feminist Parenting*. Edited by Lynn Comerford et al. Demeter Press, 2016, pp. 94–110.

Lowik, A. J. "The Ties that Bind Are Broken: Trans* Breastfeeding Practices, Ungendering Body Parts, and Unsexing Parenting Roles." *Essential Breakthroughs: Conversations about Men, Mothers, and Mothering*. Edited by Fiona Joy Green and Gary Lee Pelletier. Demeter Press, 2015, pp. 205–21.

MacKinnon, Kinnon R., et al. "Recognizing and Renaming in Obstetrics: How Do We Take Better Care with Language?" *Obstetric Medicine*, vol. 14, no 4, pp. 201–03, https://doi.org/10.1177/1753495X211060191.

Migdon, Brooke. "Experts Warn Gender-Neutral Language Like 'Pregnant People' May Put Mothers at Risk." *Changing America*, 1 Feb. 2022, https://thehill.com/changing-america/respect/diversity-inclusion/592335-experts-warn-gender-neutral-language-like/. Accessed 30 June 2024.

O'Reilly, Andrea. "Feminist Mothering." *Feminist Parenting*. Edited by Lynn Comerford. Demeter Press, 2016, pp. 38–62.

O'Reilly, Andrea. "Maternal Theory: Patriarchal Motherhood and Empowered Mothering." *The Routledge Companion to Motherhood*.

Edited by Lynn O'Brien Hallstein. Routledge, 2020. pp. 19–35.

National Institutes of Health. "Inclusive and Gender-Neutral Language." *NIH*, https://www.nih.gov/nih-style-guide/inclusive-gender-neutral-language. Accessed 30 June 2024.

Pollitt, Katha. "Too-Big-Tent-Feminism." *The Nation*, 27 Mar. 2017, pp. 6+.

Pyne, Jake. "Complicating the Truth of Gender: Gender Literacy and the Possible Worlds of Trans Parenting." *Chasing Rainbows: Exploring Gender Fluid Parenting Practices*. Edited by Fiona Joy Green and May Friedman. Demeter Press, 2013, pp. 127–44.

Rich, Adrienne. *Of Woman Born: Motherhood as Experience and Institution*. Norton, 1976.

Ruddick, Sara. *Maternal Thinking: Toward a Politics of Peace*. Beacon Press, 1989.

Wilchins, Riki. "A Continuous Nonverbal Communication." *GenderQueer*. Edited by Joan Nestle, Clare Howell and Riki Wilchins. Alyson Books, 2002, pp. 11–17.

Willey, Nicole L. "Choose Your Own Fathering Style." *Feminist Fathering/Fathering Feminists: New Definitions and Directions*. Edited by Nicole L. Willey and Dan Friedman. Demeter Press, 2020, pp. 181–93.

Willey, Nicole L. "Fathering and Feminism: Notes Toward Understanding. *Feminist Fathering/Fathering Feminists: New Definitions and Directions*. Edited by Nicole L. Willey and Dan Friedman. Demeter Press, 2020, pp. 19–38.

Willey, Nicole L. "Mothers and Sons." *The Routledge Companion to Motherhood*. Edited by Lynn O'Brien Hallstein et al. Routledge, 2020, pp. 308–27.

Willey, Nicole L., and Dan Friedman, eds. *Feminist Fathering/Fathering Feminists: New Definitions and Directions*. Demeter Press, 2020.

Women*s Student Services, Michigan State University. "Learn More About W*SS," https://wss.msu.edu/about/index.html. Accessed 30 June 2024.

3.

The Mother Wave and the Italian Matricentric River Delta

Veronica Frigeni

Introduction

This chapter aims to explore Italian feminism about matricentric feminism.[1] To this end, it addresses the following question: Is there an Italian matricentric feminism? That is, is there a feminism that is both matricentric—allowing mothers "to move from motherhood to mothering and mother against motherhood" (O'Reilly, "That Is What Feminism Is" 192)—and is distinctively rooted in Italian feminist thought? In answering this question, this chapter argues that the mother wave takes the shape of a matricentric river delta in the Italian context. A river delta defines an ecosystem that forms when because of sediments and a decreasing speed, a river breaks from its singlestream as it approaches its mouth, and divides into smaller channels, creating new wetlands. Similarly, Italian matricentric feminism is a novel land, which emerges from the interaction of manifold feminist strands, flows and sediments.

To navigate the Italian matricentric delta, this chapter first engages with Italy's socioeconomic antimaternal structures and the still-dominant patriarchal mythology of motherhood. It then untangles the reasons why the question of motherhood has become controversial and marginalized, if not censored, within contemporary feminist discourses and practices. It looks at the legacy of Italian feminism's long-standing challenges to and resignification of maternity by interrogating the recent debate on reproductive technologies, which several Italian feminists have argued have eclipsed the figure of the mother, opening a deep fracture between sexual difference and queer approaches to motherhood. As a way out of this rift, I present a distinctive Italian matricentrism, rooted in both sexual difference and queer theories, that in its nuanced declinations understands mothering as an embodied sexual difference and as a relational practice, which turns the fragmentation of the mother's figure brought about by reproductive technologies into the empowering interconnectedness of different experiences and identities.

No scholars of Italian feminist thought have used the matricentric framework. This chapter is the first to propose and test the hypothesis that Italian feminist theories have developed unsystematic loci of reflection resonating with matricentrism and can be interrogated and developed from such a theoretical standpoint. In particular, I see in the late queer feminist writer and activist Michela Murgia the beginnings of the rootedness of the matricentric river delta in Italian feminist thought. Exploring the interconnections of queer motherhood and surrogacy from the perspective of the multiplication of maternal figures and bonds, and without negating the centrality of the gestational mother's body, I claim that Murgia pioneers a distinctively Italian matricentric theory. Lastly, this chapter argues that Italian matricentric feminisms need a mother-centred narrative that can account for the different forms and experiences of motherhood in today's context. It examines Maria Rosa Cutrufelli's novel *L'isola delle madri* (*The Island of Mothers*) alongside an interview with the writer and offers potential counternarratives of motherhood and significant commentaries on Italian matricentric feminism.[2]

Not a Country for Mothers

Italy is not a country for mothers. It has the lowest fertility rate in the world, with less than 1.[3] children per woman. The country also suffers from a huge fertility gap, the difference between fertility intentions and actual rates, as more than half of the population desires two children or more (Minello 1). In this socioeconomic "antimaternal context" (Bettaglio) women tend to postpone their reproductive decisions and increasingly become mothers in their forties, whereas the number of childless women who do not have children (but might in the future) and childfree women who do not want children in their life projects is increasing steadily. Nonetheless motherhood "remains fundamental to how Italian women, whether mothers or not, think about themselves" and how men have perceived them (Morris and Wilson 1).

Italy is also not a country for mothers due to structural and cultural reasons. It is worryingly stalled in the first phase of an incomplete gender revolution, which is a conceptual framework examining the asymmetries of men's and women's respective roles and explaining family changes in individuals' economic positions. This theory presupposes a two-phase process: In the first stage, women enter the labour market, collapsing the traditional distinction between men as the breadwinners and females as caregivers and destabilizing traditional family arrangements, which results in a tendency of low fertility. In the second phase, men increasingly engage in domestic activities and family care, which should lead to a new equilibrium and consequently to higher fertility rates (Goldscheider et al.).

Despite women's increased access to the job market in Italy, only half of the female population aged between fifteen and sixty and only 56 per cent of mothers are employed, while antimaternal conditions in the workplace and unequal gender division of domestic labour continue to exist (Minello). Thus, the country is still distant from transitioning to the second phase of the gender revolution.

Yet in Italy, women are subjugated by a strong myth of motherhood, which naturalizes unattainable ideals of perfection, to the extent to which "la parola 'donna' evoca l'idea di un destino femminile e un preciso sistema di aspettative" ("the word 'woman' evokes the idea of a female destiny and a specific system of expectations") (Bassano and Tiralongo 107).[3] Maternity is traditionally at the centre of Italian culture, yet it is a distorted mythology, since mothers have a strong symbolic authority within the domestic sphere but are powerless in public affairs. Despite the declining influence of the once-dominant Catholic Church, a central position in the Italian imaginary is still occupied by the trope, shaped by the religious icon of the Madonna and child, of maternal self-sacrifice and mothers as desexualized, almost sacred figures, intensively taking care of their sons (Bravo). This dominant symbolism of motherhood propounded by official discourses is inherently patriarchal and maternalist. First, it premises upon a "patriarchal oppressive institution of motherhood" that is "male defined and controlled" (O'Reilly, "Matricentric

Feminism" 22), which reinforces a patriarchal narrative that glorifies self-sacrificial mothers while devaluing maternal work. Second, this mythology "positions maternity as basic to and the basis of female identity" (O'Reilly, *Feminist Mothering* 22) so that women find themselves torn between their identity as women and mothers who are oppressed by traditional social norms and contemporary expectations.

Furthermore, Italian institutions across the political spectrum have historically been blind to recognizing and satisfying mothers' needs (Giorgio 3), and in the last decade, Italian politics has witnessed the affirmation of conservative and maternalist feminism (Arfini et al.). In 2016, Beatrice Lorenzin, the minister of health, received fierce backlash from feminist movements when she organized a Fertility Day, an awareness-raising day dedicated to sensitizing public opinion to the Italian falling birth rate and issues related to fertility. This initiative reinstated the cultural construction of maternity as essential to women's identity and self-fulfilment. Similarly, the recent appointment of Eugenia Roccella at the newly named Ministry of Family, Natality, and Equal Opportunity, by Italy's first female prime minister, Giorgia Meloni, has sparked controversies surrounding Roccella's antiabortion position and conservative essentialism.

Never Quite Done with the Mother

It is difficult nowadays to be taken seriously when reflecting on the seemingly obsolete question of the mother (Casarino and Righi 1). However, this is crucial for Italian feminists given that in a way, "We are never quite done with the mother" (Casarino and Righi 1–2). Mothering is "una delle radici portanti della complessa genealogia del femminismo" ("one of the supporting roots of the complex genealogy of feminism") (Ammirati 28). Since the 1970s, Italian feminism has deconstructed the patriarchal mysticism of motherhood based on the conflation of woman, family, reproduction, and nurturance, thus dismantling the idea of maternity as a natural and crucial aspect of women's self-realization. However, today's feminists encounter a symbolic vacuum, as they confront the lack of shared discourses and practices about mothering. In 2020, a special issue of the feminist journal *DWF* explored such issues within historical and contemporary Italian feminisms. Emerging was a widespread feeling of estrangement and discontent due to the question of the mother having been erased from collective feminist narratives. Today, Italian feminist mothers feel the suffocating pressure of "una doppia normatività: quella della società patriarcale ... e quella del femminismo" ("a dual normativity: that of patriarchal society... and that of feminism" (*DWF* 12). This disavowal of mothering is undeniably rooted in the matriphobic stance of second-wave feminism and uncovers how, even in contemporary feminism, there is a difficulty "nel riconoscere e nominare i mille modi per essere o non essere madre" ("in recognizing and naming the thousand ways of being or not being a mother") (*DWF* 10).

The question of the mother is strictly intertwined with the history of Italian feminist theories and practices. The feminist generation of the 1970s questions motherhood from the daughters' point of view: to them, motherhood is responsible for female subjugation and domestic oppression. They promote, in contrast, the discovery of women's sexuality and the radical critique of their socioeconomic oppression. Rejecting "women's prescriptive maternal role and deconstructing the traditional, religious and political constructions of maternity" appear as preconditions for overcoming female subordination in the patriarchal system (Prevedello 23). Fighting for the right to abortion (legalized in Italy in 1978), second-wave feminism freed women from the duty of being mothers, as they separated sexuality from reproduction. Additionally, feminists acknowledge how women's reproductive labour is exploited both biologically (motherhood) and socially (unwaged housework). This is why feminist groups, such as "Lotta Femminista" ("Feminist Struggle"), campaign for both abortion and domestic salary because "having motherhood recognized as socially valuable" and "countering ... the notion of the 'naturalness' of mothering" (Giorgio 7) can reframe reproductive labour as productive work.

In the 1980s and 1990s, the thought of sexual difference, developed by the community of women philosophers Diotima, founded at the University of Verona, gained prominence. Sexual difference feminism distances itself from the "practice of equality and equal rights which buys into the concepts of universal rights as defined by a male tradition" (Parati and West 19) and counters any attempt to erase sexual asymmetry between men and women, as the latter is perceived as potentially productive. Diotima values the symbolic figure of the mother, who gives birth to both life and language. It stresses the urgency of articulating a female symbolic order centred around the maternal figure, which allows for a "non-conflictual construction of meaning elaborated in a relationship between mothers and daughters" (Parati and West 19). The mother is defined as "non-metaphorical symbolic" (Muraro 19), since it refers to mothers and to those who engage in mothering as a practice. Accordingly, the mother is not to be conceived as static but as a relational concept, a primary triangular relation between mother, child, and language.

Moreover, the mother is symbolic to the extent to which she does not refer (exclusively) to a flesh-and-blood individual but expresses a dialogical, empowering alliance between women. Diotima emphasizes the need for a female genealogy that reinstates the authority of the mother; this translates, for example, into the practice of entrustment—a sort of "elective mother-daughter relationship" (Parati and West 19) within which a less experienced woman entrusts herself to an inspirational mentor who guides her in the exploration of potential social translation of her desires and projects. Although not all sexual difference theorists embrace entrustment (Cavarero and Restaino), it is part of a shared effort towards restructuring the patriarchal symbolic order.

At the turn of the millennium, seen as a period of dissatisfaction with and, at times, open hostility towards the legacy of feminism, several groups and generational collectives navigated the third wave of Italian feminism, understanding maternity as a problem first and foremost concerning ontological precariousness. Here, the question of the mother shifts from the urgency of controlling fertility to understanding whether there is any space (and time) left for it. From this perspective, the issue of insecure maternity links to the emerging debate on reproductive technologies so that being a mother also becomes a way to affirm one's own freedom and self-determination in procreative choices. Asking "se e come è avvenuto, dentro la politica del femminismo, il passaggio da un'idea statica ... di madre a una narrazione capace di rappresentare la pluralità di modi possibili di essere madre" ("whether and how the shift from a static idea ... of mothering to a narrative capable of representing the plurality of possible ways of being a mother has occurred within the politics of feminism") (Burchi and Martucci 89) reveals a void on the front of activism. Shared narratives on new mothering modes, particularly those assisted reproductive technologies (ARTs) make possible, are non-existent. Likewise, experiences of feminist mothering remain largely invisible, almost censored, in feminist discourses and praxes (Vianello).

Nonetheless, current feminist reflections on motherhood can be traced, though fragmentarily and indirectly, by looking at the debate on ARTs and surrogacy, which has ignited Italian feminists in the past few years and which, despite seemingly irreconcilable positions, reinstates the mother as the essential, albeit controversial, figure of Italian feminism.

Total Eclipse of the Mother

Through an interrogation of what has been happening in the last two decades of Italian feminism, in its various declensions, with regard to the question of motherhood, I examine how reproductive technologies are approached by the two major feminist paradigms in contemporary Italy: sexual difference and queer feminism. The former revolves around the group of Diotima, whereas the latter combines intersectional and queer feminism and has its leading collective in the organization "Non una di meno" ("Not One [Woman] Less" [NUDM]), a transnational and transfeminist movement. However, in the past decade, tension "has emerged between the two" (Bazzoni 51), largely ascribable to reciprocal over-simplifications and misinterpretations. Queer movements have critiqued sexual difference feminists as reiterating an outdated and essentialist conflict between the sexes, which, these movements argue, the idea of fluidity has superseded. However, this is a misconception, since sexual difference "constitutes the ontological condition of possibility of several other sexual differences" historically produced and based on "specific social, political, cultural and economic conditions" (Casarino and Righi 13). At the same time, queer theory has been partially misconstrued by difference feminists, being criticized as a normative project of blind indifference that "by erasing sexual differences, is complicit in reproducing the oppression of women" (Bazzoni 53). Queer theory is seen as harmful to feminist political action, since it obliterates difference and seemingly reinforces the disembodied and unencumbered notion of the liberal subject.

In 2015, preceding the Italian Senate's approval of the Law on Civil Partnership (Law 76/2016), feminists became involved in a heated debate about ARTs and surrogacy, which resulted in a divisive clash between "abolitionist" and "reformist" sides (Bandelli).[4] Surrogacy determines an epochal shift in articulating and resignifying the experience of motherhood, as it allegedly contributes to the "deconstruction of motherhood," whereby mothers are disassembled into "ovarian mothers who supply eggs, uterine mothers who give birth to children, and social mothers who raise them" (Stanworth 16). Gestational surrogacy in Italy is prohibited by Law 40 of 2004 on assisted reproduction (Italian Law 40/2004, n.40. Gazzetta Ufficiale n. 45, 24 February 2004). Nevertheless, it is estimated that every year, one hundred Italian women use surrogacy abroad to have babies, and some recent court verdicts acknowledge couples' parental status on children born to surrogate mothers, including same-sex partners' status (Bandelli 105).

The practice of ARTs elicits significant interrogatives. Who is the mother? Can there be more than one mother? What role does the female body play in being a mother? And how does this affect and make room for feminist mothering practices, which challenge institutionalized motherhood? Although public (and feminist) debates should engage these questions, they remain largely ignored. In particular, in "una sfera pubblica satura di parole ed immagini sull'origine della vita, la madre era ... oscurata" ("in a public sphere saturated with words and images about the origin of life, the mother was ... obscured") (Boccia 87). This results in the fact that "il discorso pubblico non ha offerto, e non offre, una rappresentazione appropriata della procreazione assistita, proprio perché nasconde la madre" ("public discourse has not offered, and does not offer, an appropriate representation of assisted reproduction, precisely because it hides the mother") (Boccia 87). Nonetheless, like in physical eclipses where the moon obscures the sun yet it continues to exist, the mother, though neglected and concealed, exists and resists. This is why thinkers of difference reassert the centrality of the mother who gives life, as "ancora l'esperienza umana è di nascere da donna" ("still the human experience is to be of woman born") (Boccia 94).

Adopting a prohibitionist stance, sexual difference feminism is premised upon the assumption that the female body cannot be detached from the biological act of giving birth, though not because of (potentially nonexistent) biological ties but because it is the first moment of an experience of (symbolic) mothering. Muraro's essay "L'anima del corpo" ("The Body's Soul") clearly articulates this position. In her reflection, Muraro reverses the roles of intentional and surrogate mothers, claiming that the gestational one is the real mother who symbolically renounces her position. Muraro posits some controversial points. For one, sexual difference originates within the maternal relationship, and the latter begins with and during pregnancy; thus, it is unacceptable to plan for its interruption without real necessities (such as, in the worst scenario, the mother's death). Another controversial claim is that maternal relationships can multiply without losing their uniqueness, insofar as the symbolic order of the mother commences with actual ones but expands to include symbolical mother figures. This means that to make a mother, it takes a flesh-and-bone woman, gestation, and a symbolic order valuing the relationship with the mother.

Accordingly, the symbolic order positions women in a maternal continuum, whereby the bond of the daughter with her mother, who gave her life and language, restores the one between the latter and her mother, and so forth, to create a genealogy that women must constantly rekindle by forming signifying relationships with other women. In the end, arguing that, unlike the maternal relation, the mother is replaceable, surrogacy is unacceptable for Muraro, since it breaks both the maternal relationship and the maternal continuum in which each mother-daughter kinship is situated. Recognizing the possibility of plural mother figures, Muraro is not conflating biological and social motherhood; more subtly, she implies that an essential part of the latter originates with and during gestation.

Other nuanced positions have emerged within the common stream of sexual difference feminism, creating bridges with nonabolitionist stances. Crucial, in this regard, is the contribution of feminist philosopher, activist, and politician Maria Luisa Boccia, who speaks of "grembo insostituibile" ("an irreplaceable womb")(97) to signify, provocatively, the fact that a woman can be replaced as a mother but not as a procreative uterus—a womb that is both physical and feminine-human as it situates the indissoluble intermingling of a woman's body and mind. This implies acknowledging that dependency is the original human condition: We all come to life through and thanks to a relationship, first and foremost corporeal, though not exclusively physical, with a woman. This embodied tie is the matrix of life; it cannot be dispossessed by technology and needs to find adequate symbolic representation. Sexual difference lies at the origin of human relationships as an embodied relationship with a womb. Still, at the same time, this singular, embodied bond with a woman does not make her a mother. Boccia exhorts finding a balance between the irreducibility of motherhood to gestation, on the one hand, and women's procreative power, on the other hand, to avoid the dual pitfalls of essentialism and falling prey to new forms of control over female reproduction. She counters the resurgent biological reductionism in the definition and meaning of motherhood put forth by abolitionist voices and argues that in stretching the distance between the body and the maternal role, the public discourse criticized by feminists obliterates the maternal body, reducing it to a reified uterus that matters solely as a temporary fetal container. That we still are "of woman born" has not found adequate representation in the surrogacy debate. The question becomes: does this make the gestational body a mother? Boccia thinks not. In the end, the answer to the eclipse of the mother is not a superimposition of the mother onto the pregnant woman. Rather, in a scenario that multiplies maternal subjectivities, the feminist endeavour must put all women at the centre of procreative relationships so that women's procreative potentiality is not devalued or commodified by exploiting technologies.

There is not a shared discourse on ARTs and surrogacy in reformist groups. In her comprehensive survey of the multifaceted anti-abolitionist positions, Eleonora Cirant identifies some common points: the non-coincidence of motherhood and gestation; the assumption that it is both illegal and useless to forbid a personal choice damaging no one while it is a collective objective to guarantee psychophysical wellness to gestational mothers and children; and surrogate mothers are not necessarily manipulated victims, making it important not to talk on their behalf but to talk with and to them. Similarly to sexual difference feminism, which foregrounds the importance of enacting relational practices among women, for queer feminists also "la via femminista alla Gpa passa certamente per la costruzione di relazioni, nel duplice senso di nuove relazioni e di relazioni nuove" ("the feminist path to surrogacy goes through the creation of relationships, in the dual sense of new and novel relationships" (54). This shared focus on relationality is all the more crucial given that also for antiprohibitionist strands, we are all of women born and leaving aside those cases in which humans are born without the consent of the birthing person, which falls beyond the scope of the debate: "si viene al mondo se—e solo se—una donna dice sì, anche quando quel 'sì' è in vece di altre donne"("You come into the world if—and only if—a woman says yes, even when that 'yes' is on behalf of other women" (Cirant 55). However, this maternal embodiment needs to be explored as a new signification of motherhood—that is, as a relational practice that cannot be reduced to biologism or to gestation.

In the light of the divisive feminist debate about ARTs and gestational surrogacy, the quest for an Italian matricentric feminism is thus reframed: Can this much-needed dialogue between abolitionist and reformist positions and between sexual difference and queer feminisms generate an Italian matricentric wave? If so, how is it distinctively rooted in the thought of embodied female subjectivities as inherently relational and open to queering motherhood? And how does it position itself concerning the current mothering experiences and representations?

The River Delta of Italian Matricentric Feminism

This chapter presents Italian matricentrism as an interpretative thesis, not as a systematic, theoretical perspective within Italian feminism. In exploring the reflections and debates on motherhood within Italian feminism and whether, how, and to what extent they suggest a matricentric approach, I argue that Italian matricentric feminism develops as a river delta, emerging from the interaction of multiple streams and sediments and linking remote flows. Italian matricentric feminism is inherently relational, as it puts diverse feminist strands in a mutually enriching relationship that needs to be constantly reworked and negotiated. Sexual difference and queer feminisms display some criticalities that can be mitigated solely when put into dialogue. The former, despite deconstructing the critique of essentialism by articulating difference as a category of potentiality, risks overemphasizing the role of gestation in mothering experiences and being insensitive to other maternal identities, positions, and perspectives. So the effort is conceptualizing empowering motherhood from the distinct perspective of sexual difference. Queer feminism, in contrast, risks overstating the positive consequences of self-determination and of naively embracing "choice feminism" (Hirschman), which might eventually converge with the affirmation of the unencumbered, neoliberal self.

Once these two paradigms are combined and reframed about the question of the mother, the Italian matricentric river delta uncovers how difference feminism, by promoting relational practices of maternal continuum and entrustment, grants actual and symbolic mothers "agency, authority, authenticity, autonomy and advocacy," which is "the central aim of maternal empowerment" (O'Reilly, "It Saved My Life" 186–89).

Dialoguing with queer perspectives, this praxis can be extended beyond female mothers, although they are necessary to this endeavour to include any mothering experience, which resonates with the symbolic order of the mother.

What needs to be stressed is that what I am originally calling Italian matricentric feminism does not overlap with sexual difference feminism, despite the latter's emphasis on practices and politics of relationships predicated on maternal authority. Rather, the Italian matricentric river delta, in its nuanced declinations, understands mothering as embodied sexual difference and as rooted in mutual relationships between maternal positionalities and figures, who are always unique, partial, and situated. Motherhood is conceptualized, therefore, as a relational practice, and the fragmentation of the mother's figure is positively turned into the empowering interconnectedness of different experiences and identities. Italian matricentric feminism takes the political and symbolic enterprise of sexual difference beyond the boundaries of deconstructing patriarchal frameworks and institutions, including motherhood. Indeed, it is a feminism for mothers whose subjectivity is inherently relational—as they are immersed in a network of exchanges with other embodied, sexed selves—and "internally differentiated"—as they are nonnormative, multilayered, and complex singularities (Braidotti 66).

Sexual difference feminism adds a specific nuance to matricentric values of agency, authority, authenticity, autonomy, and advocacy. Agency is "the ability to influence one's life, to have power to control one's life" (O'Brien-Hallstein 698). As such, it has always been crucial to Italian difference feminists, whose practices, such as entrustment, are simultaneously social and symbolic and therefore aim at changing political reality and restructuring the representational order. Recovering maternal agency demands and determines authority, which in Italian feminism is contrasted with the male hierarchical notion of power. The latter is conflictual and aimed at preserving the status quo, whereas authority is dialogical and informed by a significant relationship between women, which makes it possible to translate socially those women's desires that are not represented within the male symbolic order. Likewise, authenticity, defined as "independence of mind and the courage to stand up to dominant values" (Butterfield 701), underlies the feminist attempt to articulate a symbolic order of the mother, where women can be truthful to their desires. Finally, autonomy and advocacy can be linked to Italian difference feminism's endeavour to create significant relationships between women (genealogy and maternal continuum), whereby the collective political and social dimensions are always crucial to one's singular praxis.

Moreover, I argue that the Italian matricentric river delta embraces the view of empowering mothering as queering motherhood. Matricentric mothering queers motherhood to the extent to which it challenges and unsettles the latter's normative forms and ideological assumptions to include a plethora of counterpractices and modes of resistance. The matricentric approach to queering motherhood affords an original insight into the Italian feminist debate on ARTs and the question of the mother, since it puts forth the idea that the desire and capacity to mother is not gendered and defined by blood. By queering motherhood, mothering moves beyond gender. However, with difference feminism, the mother is and does at the same time, since her subjectivity is from the outset relational (i.e., there is no mother outside of a relationship). This relational experience of mothering can be extended to other symbolic and actual mothers (and potentially also men, trans, nonbinary individuals, and more broadly anyone who engages in motherwork). Still, it begins with symbolic work during pregnancy. Bearing a child is the first moment within a continuum of maternal work: the latter, while degendered, begins with(in) a female body. Opposing the "constructivist approach to sex identity" and gender feminism (Bandelli 118), sexual difference limits female sexed bodies to cisgender ones. However, through its cross-fertilization with queer theory, Italian mother-centred feminism gestures towards a more inclusive, intersectional understanding of the female body. The main challenge and the contribution of the Italian matricentric theory that I am proposing is, therefore, thinking of mothering as a relational practice that is both inclusive of and open to multiple, queer symbolic figures who take on this relationship as an essential part of their life. This entails understanding mothering as a practice that is, at the same time, necessarily derived from a primal relationship with a female body that can self-identify as female or woman, though not necessarily a cisgender one.

An attempt to reconcile the two perspectives, or rather develop Italian feminism from a queer standpoint, was recently advanced by the late writer and activist Michela Murgia. In particular, while never explicitly referring to or using the matricentric paradigm (in part because matricentric reference texts have not yet been translated into Italian), Murgia has made a significant contribution to the debate on surrogacy since 2015, and in the last months before her death (August 2023), she proposed a widely acclaimed and highly debated reflection on queer, empowering motherhood, starting from her own experience of "soul mother."

Italy has a history of practices that could be described as forms of queer mothering, including social mothering developed in the early twentieth century by first-wave feminists, such as novelist Sibilla Aleramo and educator Maria Montessori (Moretti), and communal mothering, such as the use of wet nurses, called "milk moms," particularly in rural areas. These practices were replaced by the nuclear family model following the economic boom of the 1960s (Saraceno). However, Murgia is the first writer, feminist, and queer activist to articulate a thinking of empowering mothering as queer and of queer mothering experiences as empowering for mothers. She is the first to use the terms "queer family" and "queer mothers" in the Italian context. Her ideas on the subject were published in a series of Instagram posts before her death in 2023 and in the book *Dare la vita* (*To Give Life*), published posthumously in January 2024.

Murgia belongs to the prosurrogacy front, demanding new regulations to remove this practice from the risk of capitalist commodification. Central to her reflection on the issue is the queer-informed assumption that surrogacy is exclusively about pregnancy and not about motherhood, which is something quite different and cannot be reduced to either a biological or a physical connection. Murgia objects to the contemporary developments of sexual difference feminisms, which she refers to as "femminismo del corpo" ("feminism of the body") (*God Save the Queer*) for positing difference solely on biological sex and developing an almost mystical view of motherhood and pregnancy. However, partially recasting the legacy of sexual difference feminism, Murgia recognizes how fundamental, even in surrogacy, is the woman's body, the female womb, which "non è un mero corpo attraversato" ("is not a mere transversed body") (*Dare la vita* 82). Indeed, Murgia claims for the gestational mother not only more substantial assistance but also the possibility of choosing to keep the child until after birth. The newborn is, in fact, "un dono, che può restare in mano alla sola persona che ha il diritto di considerarlo proprio fino a quando non rinunci spontaneamente a farlo" ("a gift that can remain in the hands of the one person who has the right to consider it her own until she voluntarily renounces it") (*Dare la vita* 82), and what the intended parents pay for is not a child but the time and risks of the gestational mother. This is why in her last novel *Tre ciotole. Rituali per un anno di crisi* (*Three Bowls. Rituals for a Year of Crisis*), Murgia speaks of "utero in affido" ("fostered womb") rather than "utero in affitto" ("rented womb") to emphasize that surrogacy can only be a beneficial, mothering experience if it is understood as a relational practice based on gift.

Murgia, however, draws on both the surrogacy debate and her own experience as a mother of four soul children to theorize a new form of queer motherhood based on "la generazione di volontà, la capacità non di ri-prodursi, banalmente animalesco o industriale, capitalista, consumistico, ma quella di moltiplicarsi" ("the generation of will, the capacity not to re-produce oneself, trivially animalistic or industrial, capitalist, consumerist, but to multiply oneself") (*Dare la vita* 58). In Murgia's lived experience and narrations, soul motherhood is the result of a mutual choice, one made jointly by the maternal figures and the other by the child's acceptance of the new mother. Similarly to what happens with surrogacy, soul motherhood is a freely chosen relationship, independent of bloodlines, that multiplies simultaneous maternal figures who enter into a queer relationship of solidarity and mutual care. Like soul motherhood, Murgia describes queer motherhood as a form of nonbiological, relational, degendered, but also activist motherhood. In particular, she argues that in the Italian context, claiming for queer motherhood is a radically political act, since it replaces the biological, essentializing dimension of normative motherhood, which, she denounces, "è la cosa più fascista che esista" ("is the most fascist thing that exists") (*Dare la vita* 57). Dismantling the patriarchal mandates of normative motherhood and kinships, Murgia throughout her work articulates an autobiographical and collective discourse that strengthens Italian feminism's long-standing oppositional discourse of motherhood, accounts for new mothering forms, and promotes transformative practices of motherhood.

It is no coincidence that Murgia was herself a writer because if a matricentric river delta lies behind the eclipse of the mother, new narratives are finally required to resignify cultural representations of motherhood and to articulate a symbolic order of the (queer) mother and of the diverse and new mothering experiences in today's Italy. To this end, I read Maria Rosa Cutrufelli's novel *L'isola delle madri* and her interview as crucial texts that "clear a space for the articulation of a counter-narrative of mothering ... imagining and implementing a view of mothering that is empowering to women" (O'Reilly, *Mother Outlaws* 12). Cutrufelli, a long-established feminist, recognizes how we—Italian feminists, women, and mothers—are moving from and within the field of sexual difference feminism, thus without denying the unavoidable presence of a female body and the significance of the maternal continuum. This can encourage unconventionally resistant and empowering praxes of mothering.

The Island of Mothers

L'isola delle madri is a dystopian novel set in the near future when the world is affected by a pandemic "disease of emptiness" (sterility). This malady, which is the outcome of present-day environmental crisis and climate change, forces people to use biotechnologies to procreate. As Cutrufelli admits in the interview, "Sicily, mythologically, is the island of mothers, the place where Demeter loses Persephone, where the division between mother and daughter takes place"; thus, the island captures the controversies of Italy's long-standing maternal mythology, as "the Sicilian matriarch personifies well the contradiction of the maternal, which has enormous symbolic power, and which is, however, nullified when it comes to deciding the common fate and collective affairs."

Nina narrates the story on her eighteenth birthday, and every chapter traces the figure of each of her four nonnormative mothers. Livia is an Italian professor of Greek literature and an influential scholar on the ancient myth of Demeter and Persephone; she is a sterile woman who decides to have a child through surrogacy in a fertility clinic in Sicily. Kateryna is the ovum mother, who lands on the island from an Eastern European country devastated by fratricidal wars and antinatalist extremists to work as a doctor at the fertility clinic. Mariama, Nina's "kangaroo mother," comes from a village in West Africa, from which slave ships used to depart, and who in her flight to Europe is captured and raped. Sara is Nina's gardener mother, or her "mother of the stories," as she calls her, who becomes director of the House of Maternity after years spent as a volunteer in devastated countries and eventually adopts Nina after Livia's deadly plane crash.

As Cutrufelli comments in the interview, the novel incorporates an awareness of intersectionality, as she did not choose the various "mothers" at random. In contrast, they reflect the current, worldwide division of the work of motherhood. The archaeologist, who is a Western intellectual, strongly desires to become a mother, a desire that today is confronted with serious and widespread problems of infertility. Kateryna, the biological mother, comes from Eastern Europe because, as is unfortunately the case in reality, people want children with white skin. The gestational mother is Black because the labour of pregnancy is seen just as labour, so often the surrogate mothers are Indian or at least from poor countries, from what used to be called the "third world."

The novel engages issues of motherhood within an isomorphic relationship between environmental crisis and women's—and men's—fertility. It is a narrative of the "Maternalocene," as it addresses the environmental issues of the Anthropocene from a distinctive maternal perspective (Avery 141). Not only is sterility the biggest pandemic, but it also shifts the question of the mother from asking who the mother is to interrogating what possible mothering experiences and roles are available. Read against the backdrop of the Italian debate on ARTs and surrogacy, the novel encourages a mild, critically aware, technophile approach (Onnis and Spinelli 9). However, the reader is presented with a society in which men are still in charge, so that, meaningfully, Sara's clinic is a branch of a multinational, BioCompany, established, owned, and managed by the leading (male) biologist Doctor Weaver. As Cutrufelli observes in the interview, her nuanced position comes from the fact that it has become "almost impossible in [Italian] feminism to talk about changes in the very idea of motherhood and about new forms of motherhood, to make it a fruitful confrontation of ideas. But if we do not discuss about what divides us, why and how it divides us, what else should we talk about? And then, is it a real division or a phantasmal one?"

Although narrated by the daughter, the novel has a distinctive matrifocal narrative. The many references to "the story of Demeter and Persephone gives priority to one role, namely, that of the mother, over that of the daughter. Yet, its fabric importantly suggests that daughter and mother are one and that their experiences both reciprocate and replicate each other" (Spitz 411). On the island, Livia visits Demeter's temple and attends a conference entitled "From Mother to mothers: a historical evolution," where her colleague Antonia posits questions that, for the reader, trigger a reflection on narratives and practices of motherhood:

"chi è una madre? Che cos'è una madre? perché, all'improvviso, è diventato così difficile definirla? ... da quando la maternità si è frantumata ... chi ha diritto al nome di madre? ... la Madre non si è già persa nelle madri?" ("who is a mother? what is a mother? why, all of a sudden, has it become so difficult to define her? ... since motherhood has been shattered ... who is entitled to the name Mother? ... hasn't the Mother already got lost in mothers?") (154–55). Livia, though, believes these are the wrong questions because one should ask first "cos'è la maternità. Questo evento che attraversa il corpo delle donne e va oltre. Che le possiede con una forza estranea eppure intima. Terribilmente intima, perché si nasce sempre in due. Sempre e comunque" ("what motherhood is. This event that goes through women's bodies and beyond. That possesses them with a force that is foreign and yet intimate. Terribly intimate because one is always born in two. Always and anyway") (213).

The mother-daughter reciprocity, key to Demeter's myth, resonates with sexual difference feminists' take on mothering as originally and radically relational. Similar to the newborn turtles that at the end of the novel run into the sea "a cercare le loro madri. La loro storia" ("seeking for their mothers. Their story") (229), Nina narrates her mothers' stories to rearrange the fragments of her origin, which does not coincide with her birth. Starting from her name, chosen by Livia, who gave Nina "un posto nel tempo e nello spazio. Una radice" ("a place in time and space. A root") (52), Nina realizes how she exists only thanks to Livia's desire: Kateryna's and Mariama's distinctive "yes" are on behalf of Livia's original acceptance. Tracing her mothers' threads connects her to a wider, female genealogy. This gesture aligns with sexual difference feminism's concepts of female genealogy and the symbolic order of the mother, and it is no coincidence that the only thing Nina knows about her anonymous genetic father is his medical records. Yet because of the multiplication of maternal figures, her genealogical tree "è cresciuto in maniera piuttosto arruffata" ("has grown rather dishevelled") (18).

Livia's desire sees a potential actualization only when she encounters Sara who, more of an expert in fertility and surrogacy, can guide her towards the realization of her project. This liaison enhances the practice of entrustment, as Livia, who already refused her sister's offer to be her gestational mother, entrusts herself to Sara. The centrality of the female body—which in the book appears either (mostly) as "faulted" or as the embodied symbol of women's procreative power—echoes the image of the irreplaceable womb. Meaningfully, for Cutrufelli, "That is still the universal experience: being of woman born." Yet she also thinks that the womb "is no longer irreplaceable, at least from the point of view of technology." However, she adds in her commentary, "the apprehension should not only be about the fact that, in this way, women are being dispossessed of their reproductive power (would that be so bad?)" but about the fact that women, "who are at the center of this upheaval that invests their bodies, their minds and their fantasies," need to think "without preconceptions about the transformations that have already taken place and may take place in the future."

Livia in her classes analyzes the myth of Orestes, the murderer of his mother, Clytemnestra. Reading his trial, she highlights how it stages a conflict between the primeval order of the mother, as the giver of life, and the new patriarchal order embodied by Athena, a father's child, born from Zeus' forehead. Yet Livia comments that despite Athena, or the new reproductive technologies, a woman's body is still necessary to have a child. Similarly, Doctor Weaver asserts that the artificial womb is useless and worries more about the shortage of fertile gametes.

At the same time, the novel illustrates alternative, queer, family configurations, specifically of communal mothering, as they represent a "republic of women" founded upon empowering alliances between women; mutually enriching relationships are the distinctive feature of these new mothering forms. As Sara keeps repeating, without relationships among all mother figures, surrogacy saves the species but not humanity. Significantly, Cutrufelli comments in the interview: "All these mothers stand in relation to each other, so the process that leads to the birth of a new human being somehow escapes the terrible condition of exploitation of one or the other and becomes a different way of living together and of weaving family knots."

Nonetheless, her representation of surrogacy is not naïve, as she exposes the social and political dimensions of reproduction and motherwork, alluding to the risk of unfair power relations embedded in the practice. This is why Mariama is granted citizenship rights on the island in exchange for the exploitation of her gestational body: this recognition shows "gratitudine. Il riconoscimento sociale di un debito che non potrà mai essere ripagato" ("gratitude. The social acknowledgment of a debt that cannot be paid back" (193) given that, as sexual difference feminism argues, pregnancy is a "condivision eprofonda e segreta di sé" ("deep and secret sharing of oneself") (193). The island of mothers is also an example of a "matrifocal community" (Chodorow), wherein women take on roles of mothers and sisters, rather than those of wives—Kateryna is a widow, and only Livia is married to Giacomo. Here, women's mutual friendships are crucial, and motherhood is not their defining role. Besides, it is a queer, empowering motherhood. Normative motherhood is deconstructed when sterility makes it impossible to maintain conventional family organizations and a traditional way to have children. Likewise, it no longer requires a nuclear family based on blood ties and is a shared and public practice. Finally, mothering experiences are highly politicized: They must comply with specific local policies, and they are at the centre of public clashes and even experience violent and physical turmoil. However, on this point, Viktor, one of Kateryna's colleagues in Eastern Europe, observes how motherhood has always been a troubled issue, an ideological war fought by governments, churches, political agendas, and societal expectations. In the past, abortion clinics were the enemies to be bombed; now, extremist religious movements attack fertility labs.

To conclude, *L'isola delle madri* can be read as the narration of new mothering modes and figures through the perspective of an Italian matricentric feminism. The novel combines sexual difference feminism's emphasis on genealogy, the irreplaceable womb and female alliances, with maternal praxes queering normative motherhood, and it promotes a distinctive, not disingenuous view of surrogacy as a potential site of power for mothers as long as it is based on empowering relations among all the mothers involved. As Cutrufelli remarks, the novel is a "hybrid from a feminist point of view" as it "metabolizes" different feminist experiences. Finally, in articulating new parental dynamics, an expanded experience of the motherline (Lowinsky) and feminist mothering practices, the novel makes a political statement, "essentially seeking an imaginary answer to this pressing topical question: can women humanize what has become a need that is often met in a nonhuman way?"

Conclusion

In today's Italy, motherhood is a troubled issue addressed with increasing popularity (Lazzari and Charnley). Nonetheless, there is a double yoke on mothering experiences and discourses: the still hegemonic, patriarchal one, exacerbated by the country's anti-maternal socioeconomic context, and the feminist one, as motherhood is, for many feminists, either an anachronistic issue to be marginalized or, especially in its newer forms, a taboo to be censored. Italy, therefore, lacks a proper feminist, mother-centred narrative capable of enhancing both its long-standing oppositional discourse of motherhood and positive reappropriation of the mother figure, accounting for new mothering experiences and forms, and promoting feminist theories and practices of motherhood. To fill this gap, this chapter repositions motherhood as an essential concern for Italian feminism. By doing so, it argues that an Italian matricentric feminism exists and resists behind the controversies, erasure, and reticence surrounding the question of the mother and that it needs to be voiced. In particular, this chapter demonstrates how adopting a matricentric feminist standpoint fruitfully opens a way out of the division between sexual difference and queer feminists' understanding of motherhood and, specifically, of their different approaches to reproductive technologies. Although to date no scholars of Italian feminist thought have used the matricentric framework, I suggest that Murgia's related reflections on surrogacy and queer motherhood pioneer a distinctively Italian matricentric position supporting my interpretative hypothesis.

Furthermore, I argue that Italian matricentric feminism takes the shape of a river delta, being inherently relational and hybrid—to use Cutrufelli's definition—since it mixes and uses different feminist perspectives on motherhood. In contextualizing Italian matricentric feminism, it becomes clear how theoretical reflection needs fiction: to share resisting and transformative feminist mothers' stories; to show potential connections and overlapping among differing feminisms; and to resignify cultural representations of motherhood; and to advocate for the symbolic and political order of the (queer) mother. Accordingly, navigating this delta, the chapter eventually, though provisionally, lands on the island of mothers, the eponymous place in Cutrufelli's novel, where, as the writer clarifies in her commentary/interview, different feminisms flow to negotiate a distinctive counternarrative of motherhood and where mothering gains meaning on symbolic and political levels.

Endnotes

1. Italian feminism was not and is not a monolithic theory; therefore, when used in its singular form, the term "feminism" is intrinsically plural.
2. Telephone interview with the author (Feb. 23, 2023).
3. Unless otherwise stated, all translations from Italian are mine.
4. A new debate is taking place just as I am finalizing the writing of this chapter, triggered by a circular of the Ministry of the Interior (Jan. 19, 2023) that forbids transcription of birth certificates of children born to same-sex couples.

Works Cited

Ammirati, Angela. "Il divenire madre tra continuum e discontinuum materno." *DWF*, vol. 3–4, 2020, pp. 28–33.

Arfini, Elia, et al. "Can Feminism Be Right? A Content Analysis of Discourses about Women by Female Italian Right-Wing Politicians." *Rassegna Italiana di Sociologia*, vol. 60, no. 4, 2019, pp. 693–719.

Bandelli, Daniela. *Sociological Debates on Gestational Surrogacy. Between Legitimation and International Abolition*. Springer, 2021.

Bassano, Giuditta, and Anna Tiralongo. "Mistica della maternità: nuove repressioni 'secondo natura'." *gender/sexuality/italy*, vol. 5, 2018, pp. 107–41.

Bazzoni, Alberica. "A View on Queer and Feminism in Italy: Conflicts and Alliances." *gender/sexuality/italy*, vol. 6, 2019, pp. 51–65.

Bettaglio, Marina. "Maternal Momoirs in Contemporary Italy." *Intervalla*, vol. 1, 2016, pp. 47–60.

Boccia, Maria Luisa. "Ancora si nasce da donna." *Diotima. L'ombra della madre*. Edited by Chiara Zamboni Robotti and Luisa Muraro Brunello, Liguori, 2007, pp. 87–100.

Braidotti, Rosi. *Nomadic Subjects: Embodiment and Sexual Difference in Contemporary Feminist Theory*. Columbia University Press, 2011.

Bravo, Anna. "La nuova Italia: Madri fra oppressione ed emancipazione." *Storia della maternità*. Edited by Marina D'Amelia, Laterza, 1997, pp. 138–83.

Burchi, Sandra, and Chiara Martucci. "Dalla madre alle madri? Riflessioni a briglia sciolta sui femminismi italiani dal duemila a oggi." *DWF*, vol. 3–4, 2020, pp. 88–106.

Butterfield, Elizabeth. "Maternal Authenticity." *Encyclopedia of Mothering*. Edited by Andrea O'Reilly. Sage Publications, 2010, pp. 700–01.

Casarino, Cesare, and Andrea Righi. *Another Mother. Diotima and the Symbolic Order of Italian Feminism*. University of Minnesota Press, 2018.

Cavarero, Adriana, and Franco Restaino. *Le filosofie femministe. Due secoli di battaglie teoriche e pratiche*. Mondadori, 2002.

Chodorow, Nancy. "Family Structure and Feminine Personality." *Woman, Culture and Society*. Edited by Michelle Z. Rosaldo and Louise Lamphere. Stanford University Press, 1974, pp. 43–66.

Cirant, Eleonora. "Ora che l'utero è mio, come lo gestisco? Femministe antiproibizioniste di fronte alla GPA." *Utero in affitto o gravidanza per altri? Voci a confronto*. Edited by Lidia Cirillo. Franco Angeli, 2017, pp. 45–60.

Cutrufelli, Maria Rosa. *L'isola delle madri*. Mondadori, 2020.

Giorgio, Adalgisa. "Motherhood and Work in Italy: A Socio-cultural Perspective." *The Journal of Romance Studies*, vol. 3, no. 1, 2016, pp. 1–21.

Goldscheider, Frances, et al. "The Gender Revolution: A Framework for Understanding Changing Family and Demographic Behavior." *Population and Development Review*, vol. 41, no. 2, 2015, pp. 207–39.

Hirschman, Linda. *Get To Work: A Manifesto for Women of the World*. Viking, 2006.

Lazzari, Laura, and Joy Charnley. "To Be or Not to Be a Mother: Choice, Refusal, Reluctance and Conflict." *Intervalla*, vol. 1, 2016, pp. 1–7.

Lowinsky, Naomi Ruth. *Stories from the Motherline: Reclaiming the Mother-Daughter Bond, Finding Our Feminine Souls*. Jeremy P. Tarcher Inc., 1992.

Minello, Alessandra. *Non è un paese per madri*. Laterza, 2022.

Moretti, Erica. "Beyond Biological Ties: Sibilla Aleramo, Maria Montessori, and the Construction of Social Motherhood." *Italian Culture*, vol. 32, no. 1, 2014, pp. 32–49.

Morris, Penelope, and Perry Willson. *La Mamma: Interrogating a National Stereotype*. Palgrave Macmillan, 2018.

Muraro, Luisa. *L'anima del corpo. Contro l'utero in affitto*. Brescia: La Scuola, 2016.

Muraro, Luisa. *The Symbolic Order of the Mother*. Translated by Francesca Novello. State University of New York Press, 2018.

Murgia, Michela. *God Save the Queer: Catechismo Femminista*. Turin: Einaudi, 2022.

Murgia, Michela. *Tre ciotole. Rituali per un anno di crisi*. Milan: Mondadori, 2023.

Murgia, Michela. *Dare la vita*. Rizzoli, 2024.

O'Brien Hallstein, Lynn. "Maternal Agency." *Encyclopedia of Mothering*. Edited by Andrea O'Reilly. Sage Publications, 2010, pp. 697–99.

Onnis, Ramona, and Manuela Spinelli. "Dalla Madre alle madri? Fra distopia, mito e realtà." *Narrativa*, vol. 43, 2021, pp. 1–18.

O'Reilly, Andrea. *Feminist Mothering*. State University of New York Press, 2008.

O'Reilly, Andrea. "'It Saved My Life:' The National Association of Mother Centres, Matricentric Pedagogy, and Maternal Empowerment." *Journal of the Motherhood Initiative*, vol. 4, no. 1, 2013, pp. 185–209.

O'Reilly, Andrea. "Matricentric Feminism: A Feminism for Mothers." *Journal of the Motherhood Initiative*, vol. 10, no. 1–2, 2019, pp. 13–26.

O'Reilly, Andrea. *Mother Outlaws: Theories and Practices of Empowered Mothering*. Women's Press, 2004.

Parati, Graziella, and Rebecca J. West. *Italian Feminist Theory and Practice: Equality and Sexual Difference*. Fairleigh Dickinson University Press, 2002.

Prevedello, Michela. "The Impossibility of Motherhood in Oriana Fallaci's *Lettera a un bambino mai nato*." *Intervalla*, vol. 1, 2016, pp. 22–34.

Saraceno, Chiara. "Trent'anni di storia della famiglia italiana." *Studi Storici*, vol. 20, no. 4, 1979, pp. 833–56.

Spitz, Ellen Handler. "Mothers and Daughters: Ancient and Modern Myths." *The Journal of Aesthetics and Art Criticism*, vol. 48, no. 4, 1990, pp. 411–20.

Stanworth, Michelle. *Reproductive Technologies: Gender, Motherhood, and Medicine*. University of Minnesota Press, 1987.

Vianello, Maddalena. *In fondo al desiderio. Dieci storie di procreazione assistita*. Fandango Libri, 2021.

4.

Centring the voices of Caribbean Mothers: Making the Case for a Matricentric Feminist Theorizing

Daniele Bobb

Introduction

My experience as a migrant mother in Barbados[1] sparked my interest in motherhood. In 2011, I was working and studying in Barbados when I confided in my coworker about the emotional challenges I was experiencing as a mother and wife, and she responded, "That's what mothers do; mothers are strong, take it one day at a time." This sounded eerily familiar to what I was told on my eighteenth birthday: "You are a woman now. You are strong." The problem was, that my challenges before becoming a mother and those after I became a mother, felt starkly different. My colleague's dismissive advice angered me because it was an inaccurate justification. I knew I was not the only woman experiencing this dissonance around mothering. I also knew I experienced situations differently as a mother. Thus, I embarked on my PhD research journey seeking to understand how women navigate motherhood and work.

In my review of the literature on Caribbean motherhood, I discovered that scholarly explorations of Caribbean mothers and motherhood are mostly subsumed within family studies, women studies, and literary scholarship (Barrow; Onuora; Otterbein; R.T. Smith). Motherhood is often conflated with womanhood, which masks maternal experiences and is framed around discourses, such as the self-sacrificing mother, which intersects childcare and gender role assumptions. What I realized then, and argue in this chapter, is that Caribbean motherhood is a heterogeneous experience that denaturalizes and deuniversalizes motherhood, centring mothers as the subject of investigation. Such an explanation is absent from most Caribbean research on motherhood, which is grounded in sociological theories on the family. In these early sociological Caribbean studies, the central subject of analysis is not the mother but rather the institution of the family. My PhD research in Barbados emerged from my personal experience as a mother and wife and my interest in how mothers are made invisible. The study aimed to do two things. First, it sought to observe and nuance how women recreate a distinct practice of mothering that contradicts, resists, and reinscribes homogenized and hegemonic conceptions of motherhood, mapping motherhood as complex and dense. Second, the research explores how the maternal subject is produced and reveals the points at which worker subjugation mobilizes to challenge maternal scripts folded into neoliberal practices.

My research demonstrates that the challenges mothers encounter are specific to their role as women and also as mothers (O'Reilly). For example, mothers' experiences of conducting house chores depend not only on the norms around who should complete the tasks but also on their paid employment, household size, and the cultural acceptability of hiring help and how such an act presents a type of mothering that is seen as bad or good. This chapter explores the applicability of a matricentric feminist lens to an analysis of mothers' experiences and argues that motherhood is a complex and dense site of simultaneous contradictory and supportive discourses on relations of power and maternal experiences.

In this chapter, the concept of "complexity of motherhood" refers to women's positioning and repositioning in multiple and often contradictory ways, shaped by and shaping motherhood. For example, the complexity of mothering emerges in the household and family structures. It is expected that a mother be present with her children or in the case of transnational mothering that a female figure be present in the household to care for the children. However, within the Caribbean family and household, birth mothers may reside in one household while a female relative in another household mothers their child. This does not mean that the birth mother does not mother her child; rather, it complicates the accepted meaning of "mother" as a woman who gives birth when it incorporates a naturalness within all women to mother.

Motherhood is not simply bad or good in a binary manner but operates intersectionally. The density of motherhood applied here involves the convergence and interplay of affective, social, cultural, economic, and gendered relations of power as mothers navigate their lives. My analysis of the complexity and density of motherhood uses matricentric feminist theorizing and strengthens the case for its recognition in the school of feminist thought. The subject "mother" remains central to a woman's identity.

In this chapter, I develop my argument in three ways. First, I examine the concept of gender and show how it informs mothers' relationships with people and affects their access to resources, status, and power, thus demonstrating how these interactions are different for women as mothers and laying the foundation for matricentric theorizing. Second, by exploring the literature on Caribbean motherhood, I demonstrate that broad sociological theories fail to capture mothers' experiences, as these theories were developed to analyze the family and cultural structures, not the mother. This advances the call to centre mothers in sociological and feminist theorizing. Finally, I engage maternal scripts/narratives with participants in my research on house chores and tropes of motherhood (i.e., ideal body and use of time) to demonstrate a form of matricentric analysis in which the mother is the central subject of analysis.

In 2014, I began collecting data through in-depth interviews with twenty-one Caribbean mothers engaged in paid work. The data collected led to my theorizing on the density and complexity of motherhood and mothering. The table below provides a demographic description of the mothers whose experiences I share in this chapter.

Table 1. Demographics of Mothers

Mothers	# of members in household	Age	Marital status	Number of children	Age of children (years)	Occupation	Education	Nationality
Charlize[2]	3	31	Common law	1	3	Chef	Secondary	Guyanese
Linda	4	36	Married	2	5, 7	Lawyer	Tertiary (degree and legal edu. cert.)	Barbadian
Kim	3	34	Married	1	2	Lawyer	Postgraduate	Trinidadian
Carly	3	33	Married	1	7	Nurse	Tertiary (nursing)	Vincentian
Rose	3	51	Single	2	18, 21	Clerk	Postgraduate (MSc.)	Barbadian
Vicky	4	49	Married	2	6, 9	Development specialist	Masters	Trinidadian

An interview guide with thirty-nine open and closed-ended questions was the primary tool for data collection. The interview schedule comprised twenty-five open-ended questions designed to generate sufficient information highlighting the women's experiences. This semistructured interview allowed me to have structure, probe when necessary, and maintain an informal conversation. It also allowed the participants to construct their lived experiences in their own words, which allowed for deeper analysis. Each interview was audiotaped with the participant's written consent and lasted between sixty and ninety minutes. This resulted in over five hundred pages of transcript.

Conceptualizing Gender towards an Understanding of the Complexity of Mothering

Feminism is the belief that people should be equal and afforded social, economic, and political equity (Tong). Historically, women have been othered and positioned as inferior and unequal to men. Women's experiences have been fraught with inequity because of oppression. A basic understanding of feminism refers to the awareness of gender oppression of women because of male dominance in ideology and practice. Part of this ideology rests in the definition of gender. Feminists agree that gender is socially constructed and refers to the social differences between being feminine, masculine, and nonbinary. However, Eudine Barriteau goes beyond this definition to conceptualize gender as a complex system. She argues that gender is a "complex system of personal and social relations of domination and power through which women and men are socially created and maintained and through which they gain access to, or are allocated status, power and material resources within society" (17).

Gender, therefore, masks unequal relations of power, which means that resources are not evenly distributed. One's identity—for example, racial, ethnic, sexual, religious, and maternal—defines their interaction with the state and society and access to material resources. Additionally, gender is always present in how we interact with each other and how we interact with institutions within the state and society. The experiences of mothers entail multiple identities and interactions. Kimberlé Crenshaw, a leading Black critical race theorist and lawyer, would refer to these experiences as intersectional. Crenshaw defines intersectionality as follows: "[It is] a lens through which you can see where power comes and collides, where it interlocks and intersects. It's not simply that there's a race problem here, a gender problem here, and a class or LBGTQ problem there. Many times, that framework erases what happens to people who are subject to all these things" (1). Thus, power operates simultaneously through multiple spheres and interactions. These experiences highlight that motherhood is not straightforward or universal, thereby requiring feminist theorizing that is mother centred. For example, the mothers in my study who hire house help do so reluctantly because they believe it is their womanly responsibility to clean the house. However, their schedules are too hectic to complete chores on time and they therefore opt to hire part-time help (two to three days per week) to complete specific chores, such as cleaning and laundry but not cooking or organizing cupboards, which are seen as too intimate or 'personal'. This labelling of chores is a means to justify the presumed digression from the gendered roles. Hiring help is seen to be an option based on one's class and income, indicating maternal practices were influenced not only by discourses but positionalities, such as class, career, and household structure. These intersecting positionalities operate differently for each mother. Charlize, a self-identified working-class Indo-Guyanese mother of one, brings this out more prominently. As a chef, she explains that sometimes she is so tired she does not want to cook: "But then if I want to starve myself, you got to think now 'bout the little one. So then now you will watch the little one and say I got to go again. *Got* to go and get up, light the stove, find something for him to eat."

Unlike Linda, who can afford to dine out, Charlize's financial situation is such that she cannot and must prepare her child's meal. Hence, their reaction to these expectations (which they both recognize as "unfair"), while different, stems from the differences in their living and financial circumstances and their access to material resources. These contrasting experiences are only exposed through an analytical approach that centres on mothers as the subjects of investigation.

Historicizing Motherhood: The Need for Matricentric Feminism

To make my case for matricentric feminist theorizing, I highlight the gaps in traditional scholarship on motherhood in the Caribbean. Sociological studies by such scholars as R. T. Smith, M. G. Smith, and Edith Clarke have masked the experiences of women, leading to explorations of motherhood that do not reflect mothers' relations with socioeconomic and political processes.

When motherhood is subsumed in research on the family, mothers' experiences are silenced, as there is an external gaze away from the individual experience to the collective and homogenous one of the family. In Smith's work on the Caribbean family, he labels lower-class households as "matrifocal"—that is, women in their combined roles of mother and wife are the focus. Smith does not historicize or interrogate the reproduction and production of the belief but rather generalizes it as a norm, arguing that men as husbands and fathers were marginal in Caribbean families. While men absented themselves, they were not marginalized.

Mothering is important in early anthropological studies on the family in the Caribbean, but it is rarely the focus of discussion outside the discourse on family types. These early scholars accept the generalization that a mother figure was a constant in West Indian families, whereas the father was often absent. Examining how the different family types operated meant that these scholars, too, subscribe to the traditional gendered identity of the mother. George Peter Murdock, an early Western sociologist, provides a definition of the family that became the basis of early anthropological studies in the Caribbean. He notes the following: "[The family is] a social group characterized by common residence, economic cooperation, and reproduction. It includes adults of both sexes, at least two of whom maintain a socially approved relationship, and one or more children, own or adopted, of the sexually cohabiting adults" (1). Comparing the structure of Caribbean families to this definition led early anthropologists, such as Smith, to label Caribbean families as abnormal. Such a negative depiction has silenced the experiences of mothers, homogenizing them as central to the family without any explanation of what that centrality looks like. Drawing on G. P. Murdock's framework, Smith's argument about the Caribbean's "abnormal" family types neglects to consider the histories and socioeconomic conditions of the societies. Rather, it is premised on the centrality of the nuclear family form within Anglo-American thought when, in reality, Caribbean families are characterized by both legal marriages and many other conjugal relationships (Rajack-Talley).

This nuclear family unit has sustained the patriarchal oppression of women, as men are regarded as breadwinners and heads of the household. Thus, in Murdock's nuclear family unit, gender ideologies construct women as subordinate and other. Mothering is defined within the confines of the nuclear family unit, limiting the diverse ways in which it presents itself in the Caribbean. This framing of motherhood, extracted from early studies on the Caribbean, misses the density and complexity of motherhood, such as the relation between the mother's self-identified class and marital status, as well as the attachments to unachievable ideals specifically around the ideas of marriage as an indicator of respect and reputation and how this ties into notions of good mothering. These discourses are culturally specific to the West with sociological theorizing around the family and roles within the family.

Like Smith, Edith Clarke's research focusses on the Afro-Caribbean rural family in Jamaica and posits a matrifocal family. She advances the idea of Caribbean women's strength and independence, one premised on the assumption that women create "the material of their lives only in relation to the real or imagined 'marginal' Caribbean male" (qtd. in Mohammed and Perkins 8). This reinforces women's subordinate position, suggesting that they can only be viewed in relation to men. Tracy Robinson argues that despite the advocacy for gender equality in the Caribbean, men "remain the paradigm of a citizen and in significant measure, women are included as citizens through their relationship to men" (232). Western sociological theories are premised on this paradigm. Even the incorporation of matrifocality is flawed.

Matrifocality is not only essentialist but also ambiguous, often being used to conveniently treat women as equal to men (e.g., as enslaved field labourers) or for women to be excluded from state assistance and access to material resources because it is seen as natural for them to do it all on their own (Barriteau; Robinson). Patricia Mohammed and Althea Perkins capture this ambiguity when they note that the categorization can be positive, as it confers "on Caribbean women a tradition which was antithetical to the received European ideology of the weak and dependent female character" (8–9). Yet it also suggests that if women are strong, resilient, and heads of households, then they can do everything without assistance, and when they are emotionally and financially unsupported, they will survive and manage; it also assumes women have power in decision making within households. This perspective brings mothers to the forefront, as women's identity became centred around their gendered maternal role. However, Mohammed and Perkins do not examine motherhood beyond the mothers' engagement with the state or family.

In her work *My Mother Who Fathered Me*, Clarke specifically focusses on the varying mating systems and how they affect the structure and processes of the family, which, in turn, shape communities. Like Smith, Clarke examines the socioeconomic conditions affecting the organization and household groups in Jamaica in the 1950s and 60s. While Smith and Clarke differ in the explanations they use, their focus on mothers is in relation to their position within the family structure and processes—not as the subject of investigation.

Clarke's analysis is informed by the discourse on family in the 1950s to 1960s, which was primarily based on European misunderstandings of the Caribbean family. She focusses on class, structure, and status of family, noting that women's role in postcolonial societies is both nurturing and instrumental. Clarke fails to adequately account for the power relations within families and presents motherhood as natural, with the sacrificial mother being the best kind. Clarke argues that it is the weakness of the father's role that explains the importance of the maternal figure in Jamaican households; women are, therefore, forced to work in poor unsanitary conditions for low wages to support their families, a breadwinner role that is usually male.

This introduces a motherhood that conforms to yet challenges Eurocentric norms. Unlike theorizing on the family, it is evident that Caribbean motherhood resists gender roles, as mothers are the breadwinners and caretakers in a patriarchal system. These theoretical approaches were unsettling for me during my studies, and thus, without knowing the name of my analytical approach, my research examined mothers' navigation and negotiation with the patriarchal system through matricentric feminist theorizing that captures the complexities of the experiences.

By centring the experiences of mothers in some of the early writings on women and the family in the Caribbean, I unpack gendered biases that align with sociological theories. For example, using the 1980s data from the Women in the Caribbean Project (WICP),[3] Olive Senior observes that "Although women today have greater options through education than their mothers and grandmothers ever dreamed of, the view persists that the real vocation for women is motherhood" (66). Senior illustrates the regulation of young girls' bodies: "In her constant exposure to conflict between what she is told and what she perceives around her, the young girl is also being subjected to strong pressures in a society which presents her with few alternatives to childbearing" (76).

Robinson argues that the unmarried mother is portrayed as a liberated female because of the image of her as a powerful matriarch who can accomplish anything. Her sacrificial action for her children is therefore how this matriarch maintains her femininity (250). The mother becomes instrumentalized as her value as a citizen is seen only through her production of children as valuable citizens. More interestingly, we see the conflation of womanhood with motherhood even as she demonstrates how one (motherhood) defines the other (womanhood). The same markers of femininity (e.g., unselfishness) are the same ones that define motherhood (e.g., sacrificing). This conflation subsumes the maternal experience as one of womanhood when, as espoused by matricentric feminism, it is distinct. To demonstrate, I apply this matricentric feminist analysis to interview transcripts on the theme of house chores in the following section.

A Matricentric Feminist Analysis of Maternal Scripts

The Caribbean's household and family structures reveal the complexity of motherhood. It is expected that a mother be present with her children or in the case of transnational mothering that a female figure be present in the household to care for the children (Crawford). However, within the exploration of Caribbean family and household dynamics, birth mothers may reside in one household while a female relative, namely a grandmother or an aunt, in another household mothers their child (Barrow; Brereton). This complicates the accepted meaning of "mother" as a woman who gives birth (Rich) when it incorporates a naturalness within all women to mother.

I explore the gendered practice of household chores to demonstrate a matricentric approach. They are seen as women's natural responsibility, but it is even more stark for mothers. Childcare and domestic chores merge as if the latter is a necessity of the former. However, I focus on the naturalizing of house chores as women's work, especially for mothers. Women continue to be divided on the notion of equality within the home concerning household chores (Bailey et al; Freeman).

Despite their educational achievements and sometimes personal conviction, a woman residing with a male partner can feel she has no choice but to take on the care of the household because of her partner's career. This feeling of being responsible for household chores is influenced by ideas of womanhood that arguably attract positive emotions of accomplishment and respect, which promote such behaviours that endorse the unequal division of labour. Linda, a thirty-six-year-old lawyer, wife, and mother of two commented: "I don't believe anyone should clean my family's mess but my family. I'm old school like that. I don't want no maid cleaning my house. That's madness!" This belief echoes notions of respectability in the Caribbean, where there is an expectation that respectable Caribbean women will take care of their home by themselves even if they are employed (Moses).

This ideology reproduces maternal behaviours that mothers would like to challenge but feel it is inherent to their gender role. This introduces into their intimate and public lives a state of "crisis ordinaries" (Berlant) where women themselves are attached to these domestic practices because they are optimistic about its ability to deliver the desired outcome (such as enjoying feelings of accomplishment, having a successful child, receiving respect for being a so-called good mother), even when it does not.

Nataly, a mother of three children, complains of her daily exhaustion from her job and household chores, but she believes that a child "needs a clean environment to grow and learn. It is mothers who have to do this because men can't clean properly." Carly, a thirty-three-year-old mother of one, explained that she is often tired from her job as a nurse, especially when she works the night shifts, because her days are expected to be spent cleaning rather than sleeping. Yet she argued, "My husband cannot clean like me ... when he cleans, I have to redo it so it can be properly clean." Carly's and Nataly's practice is a maternal gatekeeping that naturalizes household chores as feminine and maternal.

Negotiations between mothers and their family's expectations occur in an interconnected and simultaneous manner. Mothers are usually organized and strategic in their way (Crosby), which suggests that motherhood is not natural but a social experience requiring systematic investigation and matricentric feminist theorizing. My study highlighted that many women's lives were strictly organized within the home's care or social reproduction practices to allow for the demands of their careers. For example, Linda noted:

> I am not the perfect mother; I am not the perfect woman. The day that I am unable to cook, you will buy lunch, and I will not feel guilty. Because I just can't do it. I think everybody, every mother and especially working mothers, you have to find something that will work for you because society can put a lot of pressure, oh you need to stay home with the children, or you need to do this, or you need to do that. No! I need to work out for me and my family what's best for us because what's working in your household will not work in mine. You follow me? So, the day I am not able to clean, and you come at me, and you find my table with Arthur's schoolbooks, and you have a problem, don't come back. That's my personality because if I ain't able to clean, trust me, I ain't pulling out my hair worrying how much time or getting up at one in the morning to clean. You follow me? I am one of those mothers.

Linda challenges maternal expectations, arguing that every family is different and must work out a suitable routine for themselves rather than be restricted to what is outlined by society. Yet this perceived act of transgression continues to be framed within maternal discourses of doing what is best for the family. Although Linda's action can be described as transgressive, it simultaneously reinforces the naturalization of motherhood, which she attempts to challenge. This is why motherhood is complex; it is both contradictory and supportive.

To keep up with the demands of their lives, some mothers often "buy help." Of the families in my research, 25 per cent of the women navigate career and mothering by hiring help. Although the women do not have full-time help (forty hours per week), they engage in part-time help where someone cleans and does laundry approximately twice a week. Vicky, a self-identified upper-class mother and wife, explained it this way: "Well right now, because of the workload and the demand from the children and so, I have somebody that comes in once a week to help me with ironing, and they do a bit of cleaning, and that's about it." Another participant, Kim, a lawyer, wife, and mother added: "We have a cleaning lady who does the majority of the household chores so basically, it's left to take care of Dexter. And I guess it's to do a little washing up in between during the week which I would probably do."

Thus, the trend of hiring help was not greatly reflected in the sample of women interviewed in this study. Rather, the findings showed that there was a sharing of household chores between mother and father in at least nineteen out of twenty of the households where nuclear family units existed. However, a closer interrogation of the sharing reflects the negotiation of gendered power relations, which results in the continued unequal division of household work, as mothers complete most of the tasks, whereas fathers help by taking the children to the play park, washing the dishes, taking out the garbage, and doing other small tasks.

Some mothers practise maternal gatekeeping, as they see housework as their domain even when they receive outside help. As Kim explained: "I have a lady who comes in and cleans and cooks." Notice how she uses "I," suggesting that she sees the domestic chores as her responsibility. She further noted that she tries to do "a little cleaning up on weekends when the housekeeper is away." In the interview, she never mentions her husband engaging in any household chores, and in fact, Kim complained bitterly about the little time her husband spends with their son. Despite Kim's belief that she could not manage the chores of her home without help, in the Caribbean, there are paradoxical perceptions of "buying help." Although the practice suggests that one is financially able to afford it, thereby reflecting a middle- to upper-class status, the belief about motherhood suggests that for a mother to hire help is indicative of a failure to be a good mother.

Rose, the oldest participant in this study (fifty-one), called hiring help "shameful": "One thing my mother taught me is that a woman should always take care of her home, so, I don't want anybody cleaning my house for me. That is just shameful. As a mother, I have to set the right example for my children. I will clean my house myself." Rose's response suggests that cleaning one's home is even more important for mothers as they have children who are watching and learning from them.

Viewing hired help as the mother's help reinforces the notion that domestic activities are mothers' work and that they are responsible for overseeing the hired help. This is seen in the participants' responses to the question: Do you get help caring for your child?[4] Interestingly, many participants responded with a puzzled look. Their varying responses to the question suggest that hiring a nanny for childcare was frowned upon and even seen as unwomanly or a bad practice. Moreso, it was perceived as unmotherly because mothers are expected to provide intimate and emotional care for their children to ensure they become upright citizens, and any errors on their part threaten the outcome of the children.

This is observable even in the process of seeking household help, as the task is left to the mother (Bowman and Cole). Thus, the domestic sphere remains tied to the mother. Contrarily, in Carla Freeman's study, participants viewed having a maid as a sign of middle-class status and respectability. They saw it as necessary for the success of their business and one way of navigating the political economy and institution of motherhood. Hiring a nanny or housekeeper that permits them the required time in their business without sacrificing their family is a negotiation strategy employed by the mothers in Freeman's study. A matricentric analysis unpacks these diverse beliefs and practices of motherhood, which speak to the fluidity of motherhood based on intersecting aspects of class, time, and space.

Societal expectations for mothers inform new practices or modes of operations, in this case labour (i.e., paid help). The maternal practices enforce neoliberal notions and mastery of work-life balance. Neoliberal expectations (such as extracurricular activities for children and access to learning support) for mothers ignore economic inequalities and promote gender inequality, as mothers are the ones expected to multitask and balance. This negotiation is not necessary for men, as according to Freeman's work, the male participants did not identify the maid as a necessity for the success of their businesses as the women did.

Thus, hiring help is portrayed as a neoliberal maternal practice that has an affective component based on ideals of a good life and how it can be acquired. The desire to achieve the dream of doing it all, which is portrayed through the Western media as an indicator of being a good mother and woman (Rosebaum), has reinforced mothers' engagement in income earning activities while taking care of the home and children. The attachment of these desires to a set of positive emotions of accomplishment encourages certain behavioural practices, which reinforce and reproduce maternal activities that are aligned with neoliberal ideals and mask gendered inequalities.

The gendered norms that govern behaviours and attitudes require a persistent consciousness to undo and rectify. This is only possible if one understands how these norms shape the experiences of women, specifically mothers, based on their demographics, such as educational background, career, family structure, class, culture, and race. This is illustrated by Linda, a self-identified upper-middle-class mother of a preteen: "I think people put pressure on them [mothers], but you need to know. Umm, society put a lot of pressure on mothers; church put a lot of pressure on women, on wives, of who you are supposed to be." Linda is mostly a transnational mother who travels and resides for months at a time in different countries. Sometimes, Linda's daughter may live with her for a period in her country of residence. Still, Linda experiences and speaks of a "pressure on mothers." This pressure coerces women to construct their mothering within the expectations of motherhood, and thus the way they experience life is thwarted. I see this pressure as a form of disciplinary power (Foucault).

Kim, a married Trinidadian lawyer and mother of one, responded to the question "Do you think there is a lot of pressure on mothers" in the following way:

> Yeah, I think so! People expect you to do everything. Cause there's the pressure to be slim and trim and still exercising and taking care of your hair and your nails and all those kinds of things. Not for me personally cause my husband is into, very into natural things. I stop going to the hairdresser a while ago because I just can't afford it anymore. I just try to use the treadmill, but I just find myself putting on weight. It was a lot of stress for me. You're putting on weight, but you don't have the time to exercise. My husband is a coach and says, "Oh, you know, you really need to take care of yourself" but I find myself [saying] practically "How is that going to happen?" So, I find myself having to get up for quarter to five to go for a fifteen-minute run. And it's just unreasonable. I don't have to do that. I'm not doing that. That's just crazy, so I think there is pressure there. And then for people, I don't know how people clean house and stuff as well.... I just can't practically envision how you take care of a household much less you have other kids as well. You have to do your work. Plus, you have to be a wife and take care of your spouse, then somehow find time for yourself and your spirituality and all this thing. That's a lot of stress. I haven't even thought about the second child right now because I don't know how I would manage all of that.

Kim lists the expectations of beauty placed on the bodies of mothers after pregnancy as a set of stressors. Her narrative is rich and contradictory; it discusses her struggle with her beliefs, how she feels, and her husband's expectations. For instance, Kim says the stressful expectations do not affect her because her "husband is into, very into natural things." As a result, she stopped going to the hairdresser. However, her husband's comment made her focus on her weight and finding time to exercise. Although she claims she feels less pressure because her husband is into "natural things," she is invested in losing weight, however unreasonable, and becomes stressed when she cannot do so. Thus, she still engages in practices based on beauty standards and her husband's opinions.

Kim disciplines herself to femininity norms through technologies of the body and internalizes the resulting pressure. When Kim's husband is not pleased with her weight, she unwillingly engages in exercise activities to address the issue even though she wants to challenge her husband's opinion. Kim adheres to the belief that a wife should please her husband and thus she attempts to satisfy her husband's wishes even as she feels his expectations are unwarranted and unreasonable. Kim presents her husband as an additional stressor, as more work. Thus, the relationship is work itself. and it is related to the relationship she is having with her own body and her identity both as a woman and mother.

Thus, even when contradictory beliefs are present, they are mitigated by these gendered norms or expectations which support the ideal body image. Throughout our interview, Kim talked about her life story, which allowed her to understand how certain routines are unreasonable: "I don't have to do that. I'm not doing that. That's just crazy." However, her actions do not always cohere to these beliefs.

Merged with the pressures of the ideal body is the concept of time, which is an indicator of gender inequality. These pressures become self-regulatory and spill into other problems. Many women do not want any more children. This decision to have few children is often perceived as a result of women's equality and breaking of the glass ceiling (St. Bernard; Douglas and Michaels; Trotz and Peake;) and not the demands placed upon mothers by society. This has led to an aging population in Barbados according to the United States Census Bureau. Women are now negotiating motherhood by avoiding it. This socioeconomic issue requires research that captures the intersectionalities and complexities of the mother's experience. Hence, a matricentric feminist research approach would be most suitable.

Conclusion

This chapter demonstrates the use of a matricentric feminist approach to research Caribbean motherhood, which developed from my research project on motherhood and work in the twenty-first century. It analyzed interviews with Caribbean mothers for what was said and for the intersecting themes arising from their experiences (such as class and family type). The chapter also examined historical studies on the Caribbean family that reproduced norms about motherhood rather than treating mothers as subjects. Through interrogating these sociological and anthropological studies focussing on the family, I highlighted the gaps in the findings and critiqued the idea that the Caribbean family is dysfunctional because of its single-mother household structure. This critique was strengthened by contextualizing the sociological studies to show how socioeconomic circumstances led to maternal practices that did not conform to Caribbean families' realities, such as mothers being the caretakers and breadwinners. Subsuming this discussion on motherhood under a general analysis of women is limited, as it cannot capture the complexities of mothering or how women's maternal identity shifts their reality. These experiences require a feminist theorizing that centres on the mother.

A matricentric feminist approach examines the maternal practices and relations that reproduce families and societies. It deepens and broadens understandings of institutional (such as the family) operations. Thus, ideas of motherhood can be challenged to reflect maternal realities. For instance, the belief of the mother as a self-sacrificing, child-focused being emerges from family-centred research framed within theories that do not focus on the mother as a subject. A matricentric analysis of Smith's conclusion on the Caribbean family structure reveals that mothers are the primary and often sole caretakers of children and that women's subordination to men is tied to their domestic position as mothers, which excludes them from political citizenry. Matricentric feminism advances mothers' experiences as unique and centres their experiences on theorizing about their lives rather than trying to explain mothering using sociological theories on the family.

Endnotes

1. Barbados is a small island of 167 square miles situated in the Eastern Caribbean and is located at 13°10' north of the equator.
2. Pseudonyms were used to protect the identity of the mothers and their children.
3. The Women in the Caribbean Project (WICP), which was conducted across fourteen Caribbean countries between 1979 and 1982, was an attempt to explore the experiences of Caribbean women. It provided information on women's social reproductive roles in society and their contribution to economic development.
4. As discussed earlier, childcare for these mothers involved taking care of the domestic sphere.

Works Cited

Anderson, Patricia. "Women in the Caribbean (Part 1)." *Social and Economic Studies*, vol. 35, no. 2, 1986, pp. 291–325.

Arnold, Elaine. *Working with Families of African Caribbean Origin: Understanding Issues around Immigration and Attachment*. Jessica Kingsley Publishers, 2012.

Bailey, Wilma, et al. "Parenting and Socialisation in Caribbean Family Systems," *Caribbean Dialogue*, April 2017, https://journals.sta.uwi.edu/ojs/index.php/cd/article/view/88.

Barriteau, Eudine. "Theorizing Gender Systems and the Project of Modernity in the Twentieth-Century Caribbean." *Rethinking Caribbean Difference*. Edited by Patricia Mohammed. Routledge, 1998, pp. 186–210.

Barrow, Christine. "Men, Women and the Family in the Caribbean: A Review." *Gender in Caribbean Development*. Edited by Patricia Mohammed and Catherine Shepherd. UWI Press, 1988, pp. 149–163.

Berlant, Lauren. *Cruel Optimism*. Duke University Press, 2011.

Blake, Judith. *Family Structure in Jamaica: The Social Context of Reproduction*. The Free Press of Glencoe, Inc, 1961.

Bowman, John R., and Alyson M. Cole. "Do Working Mothers Oppress Other Women? The Swedish "Maid Debate" and the Welfare State Politics of Gender Equality," *Signs: Journal of Women in Culture and*

Society, vol. 35, no. 1, 2009, pp. 157–84.

Brereton, Bridget. "Gendered Testimonies: Autobiographies, Diaries and Letters by Women as Sources for Caribbean History." *Feminist Review,* vol. 59, no. 1, 1998, pp. 143–63.

Chamberlain, Mary. *Family Love in the Diaspora: Migration and the Anglo-Caribbean Experience.* Transaction Publishers, 2009.

Clarke, Edith. *My Mother Who Fathered Me.* George Allen & Unwin, 1966.

Crawford, Charmaine. "The Continuity of Global Crossings: African-Caribbean Women and Transnational Motherhood." *Journal of the Motherhood Initiative for Research and Community Involvement,* vol. 2, no. 2, 2011, pp. 9–25.

Crenshaw, Kimberlé. "Kimberlé Crenshaw on Intersectionality, More than Two Decades Later." *Colombia,* 2017, https://www.law.columbia.edu/news/archive/kimberle-crenshaw-intersectionality-more-two-decades-later. Accessed 3 July 2024.

Crosby, Faye. *Juggling: The Unexpected Advantages of Balancing Career and Home for Women and Their Families.* MacMillan Inc, 1991.

Douglas, Susan, and Meredith Michaels. *The Mommy Myth: The Idealization of Motherhood and How It Has Undermined Women.* Free Press, 2004.

Foucault, Michel. *Discipline and Punish: The Birth of the Prison.* Translated by Alan Sheridan, Vintage Books, 1977.

Freeman, Carla. *Entrepreneurial Selves: Neoliberal Respectability and the Making of a Caribbean Middle Class.* Duke University Press, 2014.

Mohammed, Patricia, and Althea Perkins. *Caribbean Women at the Crossroads: The Paradox of Motherhood among Women of Barbados, St. Lucia and Dominica.* Canoe Press, University of the West Indies, 1999.

Moses, Yolanda. "Female Status, the Family and Male Dominance in the West Indian Community." *Caribbean Sociology: Introductory Readings.* Edited by Christine Barrow and Rhoda Reddock. Ian Randle Publishers, 2001, pp. 427–35.

Murdock, G. P. *Social Structure.* Macmillan, 1949.

O'Reilly, Andrea. *Matricentric Feminism: Theory, Activism, Practice.* Demeter Press, 2016.

Rajack-Talley, Theresa-Ann. "A Feminist Review of the Idea of Africa in Caribbean Family Studies." *Feminist Africa,* vol. 7, 2007, pp. 32–48.

Reddock, Rhoda, and Yvonne Bobb-Smith. *Reconciling Work and Family: Issues and Policies in Trinidad and Tobago.* Conditions of Work and Employment Series No. 18, ILO, 2008.

Robinson, Tracy. "Beyond the Bill of Rights: Sexing the Citizen." *Confronting Power, Theorizing Gender: Interdisciplinary Perspectives in the Caribbean.* Edited by Eudine Barriteau. University of the West Indies Press, 2003, pp. 231–61.

Senior, Olive. *Working Miracles: Women's Lives in the English-Speaking Caribbean.* Institute of Social and Economic Research (Eastern Caribbean), 1991.

Smith, M. G. *West Indian Family Structure.* University of Washington Press, 1962.

Smith, R. T. *The Matrifocal Family: Power, Pluralism and Politics.* Routledge, 1996.

Smith, R. T. *The Negro Family in British Guiana: Family Structure and Social Status in the Villages.* Routledge & Kegan Paul Ltd, 1956.

Trotz, D. Alissa, and Linda Peake. "Work, Family and Organising: An Overview of the Contemporary Economic, Social and Political Roles of Women in Guyana." *Social and Economic Studies,* vol. 50, no. 2 (June 1, 2001), pp. 67–101.

Turner, Sasha. *Contested Bodies: Pregnancy, Childrearing, and Slavery in Jamaica.* University of Pennsylvania Press, 2017.

US Department of Commerce Bureau of the Census Center for International Research. "Ageing Trends: Barbados." US Government, 2017.

5.

Out of Praxis, Theory: Being and Becoming a Matricentric Feminist

Michelann Parr

The Intent (400)

Matricentric feminism (O'Reilly): Theory that picks up where feminism left off. Praxis where m/othering is personal, political, and pedagogical. M/otherworlds (McDermott) that honour the needs, lived experiences, and concerns of m/others. Site of Resistance. Empowerment. Hope. Homeplace.

M/other: A concept that reminds us that, as m/others, we need to treat ourselves as we would others entering our home. Radical guest mentality that affords us the same dignity, respect, care, and kindness as we do others. A word far more expansive than mother. A creation of time, space, knowing, doing, failing, resisting, theory, and praxis. Deep knowing and reconciliation that often emerge long after children are grown and return as guests in your home. Way of being that is part of all we know and do from the very first moment we arrive in this m/otherworld.

I have dabbled in feminism throughout my m/otherlife. Today, I reach for a hopeful nexus of matricentric feminist theory and praxis where the personal, political, and pedagogical merge in acts of resistance and empowerment, if indeed that is possible. I desire to connect with my inner matricentric feminist in a performative way to "produce new 'identifications' [that] may therefore be understood as a maternal, ethical act ... [that] involves among other things a challenge to traditional masculine notions of knowledge production, which have rested on a conception of the self as contained and rational" (Jeremiah 30).

In this chapter, I experiment with potentiality, repetition, and resolution (Elias, *Clowns*) as I write fragments (poems, short essays, and reflections) and write fragmentarily, ultimately settling into five movements that frame my exploration of a matricentric feminist self: "The Intent," "The Reality," "The Commitment," "The Meditation," and "The At-One-Ment." The meditation unfolds through a paired ABC structure (Carlin and Walker) in one-hundred-word multiples (Berlant and Stewart) where I play with the juxtaposition of seemingly unrelated concepts whose very openness makes the wide space of researching matricentric theory and praxis the meaning (Elias, *Fragments*).

At the risk of being reductive, I am a white, cisgender, able-bodied, Canadian mother of three, chosen mother, daughter, nana to two, and eldest sister of four. I am a M/otherScholar, and I recognize the blending of personal, political, and professional identities and the integration of personal and scholarly pursuits (Spradley et al.). I unapologetically reject seeing myself as contained and rational; I will always choose the freedom of being and becoming.

Little did I know.

The Reality (300)

As I sit nestled deep in the embrace of winter, I recognize the need to not only imagine matricentric feminism in the ivory tower of academia but also to theorize in a way that reaches those who need it most: those who mother every day, whose ordinary celebrations and struggles inform our work, who continue to be oppressed under patriarchy and are unable to fight for their rights (O'Reilly), and for whom the world of academia is inaccessible. I wonder how to capture the complexity of this inner work of becoming a matricentric feminist—the living, experiencing, practising, and interrogating that will inevitably give way to theorizing.

Months later, on the eve of the summer solstice, my bare hands are buried deep in the earth. I nurture roots and watch guard as yet another creature munches on what promised to be a summer blossom. I come to terms with what is holding me back: Matricentric feminism, like a garden, is a wide-open space with room to make a big mistake; the flip side, of course, is that it comes with limitless opportunities to grow.

Early summer, 'twas the night before this chapter was due. In the early morning, my phone rang. My mother was stirring in a two-story house with little light: Her fall down a flight of stairs resulted in a back compression fracture, two broken wrists requiring surgery, and ten weeks of convalescing. Sometimes, things that go bump in the night are truly terrifying. Honouring my mother, I temporarily retreat into performative harmony (Fivush), which may or may not be at odds with matricentric feminism.

As I am in m/othering, I am overwhelmed by the tasks before me: full-time teaching and care of my grandchildren and aging parents. Writing is yet again on hold.

But not forgotten.

The Commitment (400)

I call on Clarissa Pinkola Estés whose work helps me to see in the dark. I follow the path of Mother Night: "the quintessential medial woman, the woman who can walk in two worlds ... 'the one who knows' and who reveals solid ways of living and unleashing creative life in both worlds" (*Mothernight*).

I glance down at a recent tattoo: "Be still and know."

And so I am.

I resign to walk in both worlds as the one who practises and the one who theorizes.

I reach for a muse that is akin to "one's breath, one's arm, one's hips, one's eyes ... always there, waiting to spring into action if only we lay out an empty space. Seed goes first to the places which are most empty" (Estés, *Mothernight*).

I try to shake off the overacculturation (Estés, *Mothernight*) that comes with being an intensive m/other, daughter, nana, and scholar.

I accept that there is nothing predictable about life, and that to produce anything of value, I must travel the bridge from resolve to acceptance and learn to embrace the multiple opportunities, setbacks, and turns in the plot that life offers (Griffith).

I sneak away to (re)claim the gift of time, knowing that to care for others, I must first care for myself. This brings me to contemplation, to deep walks within myself.

Still, the words, like tears, refuse to fall.

And so, I ask for an extension for the chapter but not for life.

I begin to piece together the scraps and fragments of theory and praxis. I will myself to write in fragments, in times I gift myself: in early morning silences, in late night solitudes, in mid-day reprieves.

I attempt to begin at the beginning with "artist" but go instead where the "zephyr" moves me. I accept that moving from A to Z is never a sequential, logical, and rational journey, but is instead a traditional and slightly outdated construct; that is only how we sing the alphabet. I settle in and allow words and experiences to find their way into my consciousness, urging myself to be open to alternative ways of viewing the world and this matricentric feminist life I claim for myself. As I move through my days, I take note of the emptiest spaces, channel my energy, and sow seeds.

I come to understand that how I do one thing is how I do everything.

The Meditation (100)

What follows is an intention of sorts, a love song to myself, an anthem, a call to action, and a glimpse into the workings of my mind, body, and soul as I inhabited this space of possibility, creation, and destruction. I invite you to journey with me; feel free to begin at the beginning or jump into the midst as I did. Go wherever the wave carries you. I have resisted the urge to contain letters in a rational order and have allowed each paired sequence to emerge in this chapter in the same way they showed up in my consciousness.

Artist and Activist (100)

I am.
Artist.

I celebrate magic. I acknowledge miracles. I embrace mystery.
I reach for creativity, openness, and possibility.
I piece together
    moments and experiences
    hopes and dreams
    realities and potentialities.

I am.
Activist.

I shed what is not mine to carry. I sift through the mess.
I (re)claim skills, tools, and sacred feminine energy.
I grow through
    optimism and self-determination
    willingness to try and fail
    independence and interdependence.

I am.
M/other. Daughter. Nana.

I am one of many.
I contribute to a collective voice.
I imagine
    borders and boundaries
    butterflies and chameleons
    shared m/othering and honest dialogue.

I breathe.

(Re)Birth and Breathwork (200)

Conscious breathwork interrupts pain signals to our brains, releases much-needed just-in-time pain-relieving hormones, and preserves our oxygen supply. Maternal breathwork signals that contractions are beginning, intensifying, and ending. Each new inhale and exhale brings me closer to matricentric feminism, no matter how terrified and unprepared I might feel.

> Inhale: You were made for this.
> Exhale: Ride the wave.

Over and over and over again, I breathe, I push, and I deliver.
I resist the urge to hold my breath.

Much of m/othering is focussing on what is right in front of us, willing ourselves messages of comfort, empowerment, and hope.

Inhale: M/othering is intense.
Exhale: You've got this.

Inhale: I'm not sure where to begin.
Exhale: Start where you are.

Breathwork (re)centres and grounds my m/othering self in my body when I struggle to reframe my ordinary pain as positive, productive, and manageable, when I fail to release the shackles of patriarchal motherhood.

Inhale: Where do I go from here?
Exhale: Be. Here. Now.

Inhale: I am not perfect.
Exhale: I am perfectly human.

I am still, and I know: this too shall pass.

when a mother
somewhere
forgives herself
for being human,

earth
exhales
a little.

—breeze (Waheed)

Pause and Potential (100)

I lean into the pregnant pause that allows me to engage with the potential of (re)imagining matricentric feminism, rehearsing with words what I would like to embody in my practice. I fear that the desire to theorize at this moment defies the seeming potential of my need to articulate unclear ideas in the name of progress. Is that not, after all, my choice? This "style in the making, style in the breaking" (Elias, *Fragments* 42) is what I reach for, which renders me yet again uncertain and more than a little fragmented.

Perhaps, that is the point after all...

Searching and Sacred (300)

I am open to the truth that things, especially m/othering, can be made sacred by the attention we grant them (Haupt), when we will ourselves to be silent, struggle, and surrender to all that is, all that can be, and all that is not.

I think of the just-right shoes I searched for over the years: the pretty, the sensible, the practical, the outrageous, the sparkly, the overstated, the unwearable. I even tried the shoes other mothers wore, learning to judge softly and imagine walking in their moccasins (Lathrup). Finding that not a single pair fit just right, I cast away pretense, illusion, and discomfort. I release the blindfold on my soul. Barefoot and soul bared, I feel the earth beneath my feet. I walk mindfully. I pay attention in unexpected ways. I allow myself to feel everything, giving "rise to a gait of ease and grace" (Kaupf 56) in how I embody and enact m/othering. Inviting matricentric feminism into my consciousness, I accept the challenge of rocky terrain that is past, present, and future m/othering; the instability of grade that is my life's intensity; the sensory involvement in my inner and outer worlds; and the awareness of my unique landscape as m/other, daughter, nana, scholar.

I begin to recognize the lies, deficiencies, and failures I internalized as a mother as a function of time and place.

I (re)awaken my heart and mind, I find the courage to stand my ground, plant my feet, I (un)earth the sacred within, knowing that this is work that only I can do.

I find comfort in silence, solitude, and surrender.

I embrace this much-needed time, space, and freedom to re-search and re-visit.

I trust that theory, in whatever form it might take, will show itself when ready.

Xenoglossia and Xenagogue (200)

Xenoglossia: an ability to use language and phrases intelligibly that are unknown in our ordinary states of consciousness (Stevenson and Pasricha).

Xenagogue: a fancy word for tour guide—someone tasked with guiding strangers or newcomers along their journeys (WordSense).

I am struck by the parallels of xenoglossia and xenagogue to m/othering. We are (re)birthed into this world. We are instructed, encouraged, and expected to embody a set of clichés, even stereotypes, that are never really brought into the light of our maternal consciousness (Rose). Xenoglossia is assumed, and with little guidance, we escort those we m/other along their journeys, never quite knowing why we do what we do, where we are going, the language(s) needed for the journey, or how/when we are going to arrive. Just as we seemingly get a handle on today's language and guidebook, they change yet again.

Matricentric feminist xenagogues steer us away from repeating and re-enacting a past that has not been unpacked or deconstructed within new contexts and waves of feminism (Jeremiah). Surfing the waves, we let what does not serve us wash away, break free of gendered stereotypes and inequities, elevate m/others' needs for equality, and make matricentric feminism visible in our m/otherworlds.

Wandering and Wilding (200)

I am lusting for "An expansiveness of time. An unhurried pace.... Wandering brings mind and movement into a healing congruity.... Wandering is goalless, aimless, directionless—the motion of our steps guided not by a set path or route, but by the inclination of our spirit. Off grid, offline, off map.... Wandering tilts us out of the everyday measure of chronological time and into the eternal spirit of *kairos*—sacred time.... It takes pausing and remembrance to wander" (Kaupf 63–67).

Seeking to (re)wild mothering (Evans), I (re)draw boundaries (Parr and Martin), stay true to myself, my own needs, and my voice, and resist conformity (Parr, "Breaking"). I wander deeply in matricentric feminism with no clear destination outside of seeking meaning afforded by sacred time—time that is pulled in all directions by my ordinary m/othering practice and my experience of motherhood, time that is not bounded by theory or external expectation, time that is mine to choose.

My dream for m/otherworlds is one where mothers can (re)wild mothering, run with the wolves (Estés, *Women*), embrace the freedom of knowing, being, and creating, all the while imagining, for future children and mothers, the healing congruity offered by sacred, expansive, and unhurried time.

Hope and Home (200)

> Hope lives inside the artist: instrument, brush, voice, pen, sculpture, body. Hope breathes life inside those shadowy crevices where doubt waits to feast on our weakened and dimmed inner light. Hope gives us strength to trudge through the muck and the mire to find solid ground. Hope is the home of curiosity, imagination, intelligence, and compassion. Artists are an empathic link between hope and the outside world. Hope frees, hope relieves; hope moves us. Artists move people from inspiration to action and direct hope toward a new reality that can be shared by everyone.
>
> In the end, hope matters.
>
> —Lee Maracle et al. 11

"Hope gives us a sense that there is a point to working things out, working things through. Hope ... carries us through when the terrain is difficult, when the path we follow makes it harderto proceed" (Ahmed 2). Hope breathes life into m/others' shadowy crevices, carries us when the terrain is difficult, and lends strength to trudge through the muck and mud of subjugation, marginalization, and disempowerment. Matricentric feminism opens new possibilities for m/others and calls us to our homeplace (hooks), bringing with it curiosity, imagination, intelligence, and compassion.

Matricentric feminism, like hope, matters.

Empowerment and Expectation (100)

For Erika Horwitz, mothering exists within unique sociohistorical contexts that influence and constrain resistance. As a site of resistance, empowered m/othering moves away from maternal sacrifice by insisting that m/others meet their own needs, many of which are not fulfilled by motherhood; accepts that it takes a village to raise a child; refuses dominant and mainstream parenting and m/othering discourse; dismisses the notion that m/others are solely responsible for their children; and challenges that mothers always feel love towards their children.

I love her absolute rejection of patriarchal motherhood and active interrogation of externally and internally imposed expectations on mothers.

Micro and Macro (200)

Motherhood is a large-scale, worldwide institution, governed by dominant assumptions, cultural ideals, family expectations, political ideologies, and more. Yet the experience of mothering is so isolating. When we share and voice our experiences, reach out, and (re)story our encounters with mothering, we expose and problematize the larger scale of the institution of motherhood. This is the breathwork of matricentric feminism: We need this push and pull, stretch and contract, inhale and exhale. This is where we (re)birth and grow into our own. I am cautious of the macro, the observation of patterns, and trends that risk erasing the lived realities of mothers who hit the ground running. I attempt to balance these micro realities with the larger forces at work in the world. I consider those around me, those who have come before me, and those yet to come. I walk in both worlds yet again, in that liminal space of theorizing and knowing, practising and doing, being and becoming, settling into what is and reaching for a more inclusive and empowered m/otherworld.

Inhale: Our individual mothering experiences are valid.
Exhale: Release the bonds imposed by the institution of motherhood.

Collectively, we've got this.

Liberating and Loving (100)

I return to Horwitz's work and the need for mothers to make conscious choices to love and liberate themselves and to embody inclusive and empowered mothering. Although our children make us mothers, we experience motherhood through agency and imagination. Voicing our stories and articulating our being and becoming as m/others, we "correct the child-centredness that defines much of the scholarship and activism on motherhood" (O'Reilly 46). We show our children how to lay claims to their own lives, how to be fully alive, and how to be writers, makers, creators, and architects of their own stories (Martin and Parr).

Umbilical and (Un)Tethered (100)

umbilical...
    the original tether

inwards
    the me-in-there
    innate knowing of self
    insights of authenticity and nakedness
nurturing, feeding, connecting

(un)tethered...
    the first cut is the deepest

outwards
    the me-out-there
    discerning self and m/other
    shadows of strength and surrender

testing, stretching, (un)knotting

umbilical and (un)tethered...
    assumption of separation, reality of connection

umbilical/(un)tethered inward/outward
    the me-in-there-out-there/me-out-there-in-there
    mirrored reflections of self and other
    echoes of acceptance and forgiveness

mysteriously (un)tethered
miraculously umbilical
magically threaded

umbilical-(un)tethered
m/other bond

I learn to live in harmony with these seeming contradictions (Lorde), seeking ways to raise my voice in unison with a vision for a harmonious future.

Intuition and Insight (100)

Much of mothering is intuitive: an experienced and continuous process where things naturally unfold. We sense the solution with or without an explicit rationale or explanation. Insight is more fragmented and discontinuous (Zander et al.). In m/othering, insights often come long after the children have left home, and we have time to feel, (re)live, process, and deconstruct, ultimately arriving at a defining aha moment: "We made the best choices we could with the tools and resources we had available to us" at the time (Martin and Parr 209).

Inhale: I make space.
Exhale: I forgive myself and my m/others.

Queering and Quirky (200)

I disrupt and distort the binary thinking about sacrifice and mothering, knowing and doing, motherhood as experience and institution (Rich). I reach instead for m/othering as being and becoming. Accepting the efficacy and agency as m/other that is only mine to claim, carry, and hold sacred, I turn inwards instead of outwards.

I accept tender moments of care, time spent deep in writing still in yesterday's pajamas, and the gentle exhaustion that allows a certain creativity to emerge: unedited, unsanctioned, and uncensored. I fear the completion of this project with full awareness that the theorizing and practising, doing and knowing, have just begun. I keep a firm rein on sharing and steering my journey of wonder and discovery, allowing theory and knowing to emerge naturally in this moment of m/othering and doing. I fear that this is far less than what the editors want to see in a chapter about the theory and praxis of matricentric feminism. Yet knowing that I cannot dismantle the master's house with the master's tools (Lorde), I continue. I settle into my quirkiness as m/other, as a theorist, as a scholar, and I allow this tendency to queer to be active, restorative, and hopeful (Butler).

Vision and Voice (200)

M/othering is ongoing creation, destruction, and (re)imagination and commitment, openness, and willingness to see the world of m/othering for what it is and what it is not:

> The world of doing is busy and loud and the people who live there like it that way. In the world of doing, noise and agitation mean things are getting done. In the world of knowing, things tend to get done with silence and stillness.... In the world of knowing, we are happy to live without many of the things that are needed in the world of doing.... The world of doing cares only for what can be seen; the world of knowing flows from the unseen world of being. The people who live in the world of knowing love what can be seen because they know where it comes from and where it is going. In the world of knowing, nobody ever does anything—yet everything gets done. (Gates 306)

I dream of a matricentric feminist collective that rejects the status quo of mothers trapped in a doing world filled with systemic violence, oppression, marginalization, subjugation, and silencing, those for whom raising children is the obligation and main responsibility of women alone (Green).

Footsteps and Fragments (200)

Retracing my scholarly footsteps, I search for evidence of the reciprocity between my m/othering theory and praxis: that to know something we must first do. Looking for continuity, I call forward fragments of my scholarly past, allowing the seed to go where I feel most empty today. I find a legacy to draw from:

> I acknowledge that my processes of understanding and knowing stem from my personal experience and my actual doing. I also recognize that knowing is a relative term ... we can never know everything about everything because the world is continually changing, but we can know something about something which will help us to know something more than we knew yesterday. We can know our reality, where we are situated right here, right now, and we can choose to explore the many dimensions of our reality in an effort to truly understand ourselves and the world around us. Our understanding of the world is not only shaped by our current perception of reality and our experiences, but as well, it is shaped by our perspectives and understandings of how we actually come about knowing "something." (Parr, "Knowing")
>
> Now I see: Doing is knowing. I am grounded in gratitude.

Gaps and Gratitude (400)

I stay in the space of my past and search for gaps in my awareness as one who m/others and engages in scholarly work. For years, I claimed that I could seamlessly walk in both worlds:

> One step at a time.
>   Baby step by baby step.
>   There was no other way to do it.
>   No shortcuts, no secret passages, no escape hatches.
> Simply loving the slow process of learning, of growing, of becoming—
>   Loving the work as it unfolded.
>   Loving each achievement and each goal as they were reached.
>   Taking time–doing the right thing.
> Baby steps—that was the way to do it.
>   Walking, running, balancing—
>   Adjusting each step along the way.
>   No misstep, no wasted moments, no regrets.
> Always moving in the direction of my dreams—
>   The believe of childhood,
>   The do of academia,
>   A balance of the personal and the professional. (Parr, "Baby" 257)

Perhaps, I was (re)claiming my right to be/become m/other on my terms.

Perhaps, I had no other choice. Perhaps, no one has any other choice.

Perhaps, this was an early attempt to resist and/or reconcile the duality of creation and consciousness, the false separation of maternal and professional selves, the rigid polarization of masculine and feminine, the illusion of public and private, the difference between dream and reality, and the division of m/other and scholarly work.

Perhaps, I was trapped by "acceptable standards of collegial interaction" and "the very process of knowledge creation" where I was expected "to center Eurocentric, hierarchical, and individualist ways of thinking, speaking, and being ... orientations [that] privilege the intellectual work of white academics, especially those unencumbered by the rigors of home labor, as they produce knowledge in a society created to support their livelihood" (Yu et al.).

I am grateful for the privileges afforded by academia and wonder about mothers who continually "negotiate and perform their identities from their individualized subject positions, which are uniquely constituted through diverse intersections of identities" (Yu et al.) that exist within complex institutional, political, cultural, and economic contexts that influence what it means to m/other.

I fear the widening gap in how m/othering is enacted around the world. I conjure hope for those who have no other choice but to fragment their bodies and work in ways more palatable to white society (Yu et al.).

I recognize that even our collective identity is fragmented and individually negotiated (Spradley et al.).

Defiance and Demands (200)

Years ago, I fell in love with *Wicked* (Schwartz), a story told through the opposing perspectives of Glinda and Elphaba, the witches of the land of Oz. I felt my life was being performed on a New York stage (See Parr, "Letting Go"). Those who were with me can attest to my intense reaction to "Defying Gravity," sung by Kristin Chenoweth and Idina Menzel; I heard a plea to embrace change and break free of patriarchal motherhood:

Something has changed within me
Something is not the same
I'm through with playing by the rules
Of someone else's game

Too late for second guessing
Too late to go back to sleep
It's time to trust my instincts
Close my eyes and leap

It's time to try defying gravity
I think I'll try defying gravity
Kiss me goodbye, I'm defying gravity
And you won't pull me down

I'm through accepting limits
'Cause someone says they're so
Some things I cannot change
But till I try, I'll never know...

While it's impossible to defy gravity, I can defy the conflation of m/othering and motherhood and demand that matricentric feminism have a room of its own in the larger house of academic feminism (O'Reilly).

Justice and Journey (100)

This journey seeks justice for all m/others but especially for those pulled down by political, cultural, familial, and quite-often self-imposed shackles. Matricentric feminist theory "commits to social change and social justice," "regards mothering as a socially engaged enterprise and a site of power," "understands mothering and motherhood to be culturally determined and variable," and "is committed to exploring the diversity of maternal experience across race, class, culture, ethnicity, sexuality, ability, age, and geographic location" (O'Reilly 47).

Inhale: This journey begins within me. I am powerful.

Exhale: I "can and do create social change through child-rearing and activism" (O'Reilly 47).

Nature and Nurture (100)

"Central to matricentric feminist theory is a critique of the maternal stance that positions maternity as basis to and the basis of female identity; as well, matricentric feminism challenges the assumption that maternity is natural to women (i.e., all women naturally know how to mother) and that the work of mothering is driven by instinct rather than intelligence and developed by habit rather than skill" (O'Reilly 43–44). We learn(ed) to mother by observing, being mothered, and practising mothering.

We did not learn to nurture our inner child and m/other ourselves.

With this mother wave, the tides are shifting.

Yearning and Yielding (100)

I am learning to yield: to give way under pressure, sometimes gently and quietly. Like my children once did, I am learning to take baby steps, to risk, and to (re)balance. I yearn for time to speed up and time to slow down. I yield to the inevitability of time, liberatory structures, and loving myself as I love others. I spend long days and nights theorizing, but the real magic happens when I breathe life into my theory and reach out with consciousness, artistry, and activism, where resistance becomes hopeful yielding, and gratitude for my privileges (re)imagines empowered m/otherworlds.

Oracles and Originaries (400)

No stone is left unturned in my search. Trusting intuition and looking for insight, I turn to "Wild & Sacred Feminine," an oracle deck that authors Niki Dewart and Elizabeth Marglin and illustrator Jenny Kostecki-Shaw refer to as a "broader reincarnation of The Mother's Wisdom Deck" (5). Honouring my originaries, I choose a four-card spread to "access the wisdom of Grandmother Moon" who "rules the tides and can offer perspective on the ebb and flow of life" (14).

Card 1 represents Waning Moon: a symbol that energy is fading, discernment is afoot, and new becoming is on the horizon. I pull Rainbow: "an ancient symbol of promise who offers herself as a vision of integration" (88), pointing "to the overall truth that diversity of perspective is the keystone to forgiveness" (87). I tiptoe around her shadow of resentment as I consider past perspectives of mothers, re-searchers, theorists, and feminists. I wonder how we've come so far, when we have so much yet to cover.

Card 2 represents New Moon: renewal, unmanifested potential, and being in the mystery. The mother goddess Kali Ma shows up: "Simultaneously devouring and life-giving, [she] summons fierce love that frightens and transforms" (169); she challenges us to "dance upon the corpse of that which no longer serves" promising that "something greater will emerge" (170). I work to avoid her shadow illusion as I balance the private and public, personal and collective, theory and praxis.

Card 3 represents Waxing Moon: a call out of the dark, towards awakening, self-realization, and light. Divine matriarch Oshun is present: "The Yoruba orisha of love, negotiation, and diplomacy indicates that harmony is at hand.... Oshun's wisdom teaches that harmony is dynamic, encompassing a range of voices through finely tuned scales and adjusting to variations in pitch, frequency, and tone" (177–78). Oshun's shadow is discord: I avoid waging war instead seeking harmony of perspective and insisting on my authority as m/other (O'Reilly).

Card 4 represents Full Moon: the highest expression of our potential in the radiant face of being. I fall under Raven's spell, acknowledging this work "as a force for good," aiming to embody her assertion, with humility, that "every word [I] utter casts a spell, every thought [I] nurture shapes reality" (46). Like Mother Night who walks in two worlds, the blue-black, magical Raven flies between worlds, courting the unknown and staying out of the shadows of manipulation.

Carrying and Comforting (200)

I carry a spell in my heart as a reminder to meet myself in a space of gratitude, where I am in this moment. I cast this spell for all m/others of the world reaching for recognition, justice, and liberation. I am indebted to adrienne maree brown for her witchy ways and willingness to share her spells with the world. It takes a village to make a m/other.

radical gratitude spell by adrienne maree brown

you are a miracle in motion
i greet you with wonder
in a world which seeks to own
your joy and your imagination
you have chosen to be free
every day, as a practice
i can never know
the struggles you went through to get here
but i know you have swum upstream
and at times it has been lonely.

i want you to know
i honor the choices
you made in solitude
and i honor the work
you have done to belong
i honor your commitment
to that which is larger
than yourself
and your journey
to love the particular vessel of life
that is you.
you are enough
your work is enough
you are needed
your work is sacred
you are here
and i am grateful.

Kaandossiwin and Kinship (200)

Looking back and in at how I came to know (Kaandossiwin) and m/other, I hear Kathy Absolon's words that self-location matters: Who you are matters and informs how you search. I didn't come to this work of m/othering on my own. Guiding my journey was a long lineage of mothers, each existing in a particular time and place. From my m/others, I learned how to be and become, what (not) to do, who I wanted to be and become.

And most importantly, who I didn't want to be and become.

I pause.
I breathe.
I know.

I re-search and (re)story my learnings (Absolon) throughout the matricentric feminist life I've lived. I tease out the threads passed from generation to generation. I become aware of the complexities of living in a different time and place that may not have placed value on the work of mothering or that may have imposed arbitrary and unreasonable expectations on mothers.

Today, my originaries continue to walk with me: each butterfly I see, each hug I give, each game I play, and each cup of tea I share. I wish for them to know:

your work was enough
you were needed
your work was sacred
you were here
and I am grateful.

Zephyr and Zealous (200)

soft, gentle zephyr
untethered in the world
bringer of light and early spring breezes
an end to winter
a breath of fresh air
a time of (re)birth

impassioned, energetic zealous
devoted to person, cause, or idea
symbol of strength and conviction
seeds to be scattered
a strident, gusty wind
a time of growth

I resolve the contradictions and binaries that have accompanied me throughout this process, the ones whose path has been less than smooth, requiring continual (re)negotiation of going where the wind blows, walking gently, barreling on through, surfing the wave, and pausing amid the still, silent doing. There is no one path but all roads lead to my homeplace: a space of resistance, peace, and congruity that allows me to reach outwards because I am resolving inwards.

As I push back against contradiction, assumption, expectation, judgement, hierarchy, and patriarchy, I wonder about "other ways of imagining the world, ways that do not depend so much on oppositions as they do on co-operations" (King 110). I reimagine the tethers that have held me captive, accept the nuances and privileges of being a white, cisgender, able-bodied, Canadian M/otherScholar, and position myself as activist for myself, my children, and other m/others.

The At-One-Ment: Theory Meets Praxis (200)

Writing this chapter, amid the intensity of my m/othering practice, enabled me to stand in the possibility afforded by life, dig around in my understanding of matricentric feminism, and set aside practices that no longer serve. This is not always easy or possible when there are children to be fed, loved ones to be cared for, societal expectations to be met, and survival to be ensured. A reciprocal balance between knowing and doing serves me well and calls me to question: What matters most to me, m/others, and future generations? What is worth keeping? What needs weeding out? And who is to decide?

I arrive at this place of at-one-ment (Singer). I settle into a deep awareness that theorizing and knowing does not and cannot sit outside praxis and doing. We must change from within to understand the resources needed and the paths forward in our quest to raise a more global matricentric feminist consciousness that considers m/othering simultaneously personal, political, and pedagogical (O'Reilly).

In essence, who we are matters; how and who we m/other matter.

In m/otherworlds, it is only the m/other's tools that will dismantle and (re)build the m/other's homeplace.

All this and time. Sacred time.

Works Cited (790)

Absolon, Kathy. *Kaandossiwin: How We Come to Know, Indigenous Re-Search Methodologies*. Fernwood Publishing, 2022.

Berlant, Lauren, and Kathleen Stewart. *The Hundreds*. Duke University Press, 2019.

brown, adrienne maree. *Fables and Spells: Collected and New Short Fiction and Poetry*. AK Press, 2022. Ebook.

Butler, Judith. *Bodies That Matter: On the Discursive Limits of "Sex."* Routledge, 1993.

Carlin, David, and Nicole Walker. *The After-Normal: Brief, Alphabetical Essays on a Changing Planet*. Rose Metal Presss, Inc., 2019.

Chenowith, Kristin, and Menzel, Idina. "Defying Gravity."*Wicked*, Universal Music Corp., 2003, Transcript of lyrics.

Dewart, Niki, and Elizabeth Marglin. Illustrator Jenny Kostecki-Shaw. *Wild & Sacred Feminine, A 52-Card Oracle and Guidebook*, Shambhala, 2022.

Elias, Camellia. *The Fragment: Towards a History and Poetics of a Performative Genre*. 2004. Eyecorner Press, 2021.

Elias, Camelia. "Clowns of Potentiality, Repetition, and Resolution." *Cercles*, no. 14, 2005, pp. 41–57.

Estés, Clarissa Pinkola. *Mother Night: Myths, Stories and Teachings for Learning to See in the Dark*. Sounds True, 2010. Audiobook.

Estés, Clarissa Pinkola. *Women Who Run with the Wolves*. Ballantine Books, 1992.

Evans, Shannon K. *Rewilding Motherhood: Your Path to an Empowered Feminine Spirituality*. Brazos Press, 2021.

Fivush, Robyn. "Speaking Silence: The Social Construction of Silence in Autobiographical and Cultural Narratives." *Memory*, vol. 18, no. 2, 2010, pp. 88–98.

Gates, Rolf, and Katrina Kenison. *Meditations from the Mat: Daily Reflections on the Path of Yoga*. Anchor, 2002.

Green, Fiona Joy. "Re-Conceptualising Motherhood: Reaching Back to Move Forward." *Journal of Family Studies*, vol. 21, no. 3, Sept. 2015, pp. 196–207.

Haupt, Lyanda Lynn. *Rooted: Life at the Crossroads of Science, Nature, and Spirit*. Little, Brown Spark, 2021.

hooks, bell. *Yearning: Race, Gender, and Cultural Politics*. South End Press, 1990.

Horwitz, Erika. "Resistance as a Site of Empowerment: The Journey Away From Maternal Sacrifice." *Mother Outlaws: Theories and Practices of Empowered Mothering*. Edited by Andrea O'Reilly. Women's Press, 2004, pp. 43–58.

Jeremiah, Emily. "Motherhood to Mothering and Beyond." *Journal of the Motherhood Initiative for Research and Community Involvement*, vol. 8, no. 1-2, 2006, pp. 21–33.

King, Thomas. *The Truth About Stories: A Native Narrative*. Anansi Press, 2003.

Lathrap, Mary T. *Judge Softly. AAA Native Arts*, 1895, https://www.aaanativearts.com/walk-mile-in-his-moccasins. Accessed 4 July 2024.

Lorde, Audre. *Sister Outsider: Essays and Speeches*. Crossing Press, 1984.

Maracle, Lee, et al. *Hope Matters*. Book*hug Press, 2019.

Martin, BettyAnn, and Michelann Parr. "From Mourning to Greeting: The Predicament and Possibilities of Maternal Regret." *Maternal Regret: Resistances, Renunciations, and Reflections*. Edited by Andrea O'Reilly. Demeter Press, 2022, pp. 201–19.

McDermott, Mairi. "Stories (of) Carrying Forth M/otherworlds From Our Matricentric Carrier Bags." *Mothering Outside the Lines: Tales of Boundary-Busting Mamas*. Edited by Michelann Parr and BettyAnn Martin. Demeter Press, 2023, pp. 7–13.

O'Reilly, Andrea. *Matricentric Feminism: Theory, Activism, Practice*. 2nd ed. Demeter Press, 2021.

Parr, Michelann. "Letting go: Writing Through the Pain." *The Pain Mothers Must Never Expose: Confronting the Silences of Maternal Life*. Edited by Michelann Parr. Demeter Press, 2024, pp. 207–28.

Parr, Michelann. "Breaking The Silences of Motherhood: Rabbit Holes, False Starts, (Un)Finished Fragments, and Hopeful Connections." *Mothering Outside the Lines: Tales of Boundary-Busting Mamas*. Edited by Michelann Parr and BettyAnn Martin. Demeter Press, 2023, pp. 39–67.

Parr, Michelann. "'Knowing by Doing': We Must Do! Teacher Development through Engagement in Learning Opportunities." *International Journal of Learning*, vol. 12, 2005/2006, pp. 1447–9540.

Parr, Michelann. "Baby Step by Baby Step: That Was the Way to Do It." *The Parent-Track: Timing, Balance, and Choice within Academia*. Edited by Christina DeRoche and Ellie Berger. Wilfrid Laurier University Press, 2016, pp. 257–66.

Parr, Michelann, and Martin, BettyAnn, eds. *Mothering Outside the Lines: Tales of Boundary-Busting Mamas*. Demeter Press, 2023.

Rose, Jacqueline. *Mothers: An Essay on Cruelty and Love*. Farrar, Straus and Giroux, 2019.

Schwartz, Stephen. *Wicked: A New Musical*. Directed by Joe Mantello, Original Broadway Cast. April 2004, Gershwin Theatre, New York, NY.

Singer, Michael. *Living Untethered: Beyond the Human Predicament*. Sounds True, 2022.

Spradley, Elizabeth, et al. "Proving Our Maternal and Scholarly Worth: A Collaborative Autoethnographic Textual and Visual Storying of MotherScholar Identity Work during the COVID-19 Pandemic." *Journal of the Motherhood Initiative*, vol. 11, no. 2, 2020, pp. 189–209.

Stevenson, Ian, and Satwant Pasricha. "A Preliminary Report on an Unusual Case of the Reincarnation Type with Xenoglossy." *The Journal of the American Society for Psychical Research*, no. 74, 1980, pp. 331–48, https://med.virginia.edu/perceptual-studies/wp-content/uploads/sites/360/2018/03/STE7A-Preliminary-Report-on-an-Unusual-Case-of-the-Reincarnation-Type-with-Xenoglossy-.pdf. Accessed 4 July 2024.

Waheed, Nayyirah. *salt*. CreateSpace Independent Publishing Platform, Kindle Edition, 2013.

"Xenagogue." *WordSense Online Dictionary*, 7 Aug. 2023, https://www.wordsense.eu/xenagogue/. Accessed 4 July 2024.

Yu, Min, et al. "Remember. (Re)member. Re-member: Theorizing the Process of Healing, Sustaining, and Transforming as MotherScholars," *Peabody Journal of Education*, 2022. DOI: 10.1080/0161956X.2022.2055892.

Zander, Thea, et al. "Intuition and Insight: Two Processes That Build on Each Other or Fundamentally Different?" *Frontiers in Psychology*, vol. 7, 2016, https://www.frontiersin.org/journals/psychology/articles/10.3389/fpsyg.2016.01395/full.

6.

Mother's Speaking: Towards An Ethics of Maternal Monstrosity

Abigail L. Palko

Every summer since 2012, The Mamalogues, a staged reading of personal monologues about motherhood created and nurtured by Nicole and Kate, has offered a microphone to South Bend women: "Everyone has a story. We give you the platform to share it" ("The Mamalogues"). While ultimately, the timing never worked for me to submit a monologue, I thought about it often. Each time I considered it, the same opening line ran through my mind: "When my child was five, I abandoned her."

I don't really think I abandoned her (not really...). But my husband was having a health crisis, and I had to choose: Take the medical flight from New Jersey to Illinois with him and leave her with my parents, or stay with her and send him halfway across the country alone, newly paralyzed from the neck down. Who could choose? And yet I had to.

Was I a bad mother for choosing to meet my husband's needs over my child's? The circumstances were extreme. Maybe this choice was unquestioningly justifiable? When I reflect on this moment, a decade later, this is always the point when I remember Ayelet Waldman's scandalous essay, wherein she confesses: "If a good mother is one who loves her child more than anyone else in the world, I am not a good mother. I am in fact a bad mother. I love my husband more than I love my children."

The line, it seems, is drawn somewhere between her reality and mine.

But.

Why am I looking for this line? Why am I not just upending the whole expectation that prompts the line?

In this chapter, I trace the connections that form a matricentric feminist understanding of the maternal voice and the obligations mothers bear when using this voice. I begin with autoethnographic reflections juxtaposed against a critical analysis of the intersections between Sara Ruddick's work on peace politics and Jude Doyle's exploration of maternal monstrosity. I argue that Ruddick and Doyle, philosophers of motherhood, offer avenues into thinking about the role that mothers' storytelling plays in the liberatory possibilities of matricentric feminism. Untangling this knot is essential to realizing the potential of matricentric feminism. This analysis leads to a consideration of the impact that maternal voices can have through a micro case study of mommy blogs and other maternal writings as a matricentric feminist practice. Jude Ellison S. Doyle's incisive analysis of horror films in *Dead Blondes and Bad Mothers: Monstrosity, Patriarchy, and the Fear of Female Power* (published as Sady Doyle) has helped me think this through. As he notes of monster stories, tales of monstrous mothers also "let us directly perceive the script of male dominance and female subjugation, which is usually just a set of nameless anxieties fluttering under and around our day-to-day interactions" (xix).

In a distinction that I hold firmly, I define maternal monstrosity as breaking the commitment of Ruddick's three tenets to ensure the preservation, growth, and social acceptability of children without securing alternate mothering for the child (17). In contrast, neoliberal Western culture often deploys the label "monstrous" against mothers who break under the pressure of institutional motherhood, which, in Adrienne Rich's terms, "aims at ensuring that that potential [of maternal experience]—and all women—shall remain under male control" (13). How do mothers develop and enact a praxis of mothering that they can confidently assess as "good enough" (in D. W. Winnicott's terms, 10) in opposition to sociocultural constructions of maternal monstrosity, which are themselves constructed in dialogue with ideologies of intensive mothering? In other words, maternal monstrosity is a control mechanism that operates under the cover afforded by socially imposed, context-specific norms of good mothering; thus, as culturally constructed in the early twenty-first century, monstrous mothering is marked by the mother's failure to accept and abide by the demands of intensive mothering and neoliberal ideologies. One of the most pernicious ways that this label "monstrous mother" impacts real mothers' mothering practices is via its power to induce judgment—both societal and self-judgment.

I follow Andrea O'Reilly's hope that matricentric feminism—a "mother-centred perspective" that "positions mothers' needs and concerns as the starting point for a theory and politic on and for women's empowerment" (3, 2)—can empower mothers and their maternal practices outside of the controlling mechanisms of the "good mother" ideology. My engagement with matricentric feminism is grounded by two principles O'Reilly articulates. According to her, matricentric feminism "contests, challenges, and counters the patriarchal oppressive institution of motherhood and seeks to imagine and implement a maternal identity and practice that is empowering to mothers"; it also "commits to social change and social justice, and regards mothering as a socially engaged enterprise and a site of power, wherein mothers can and do create social change through childrearing and activism" (7). I must caution us, however. Although I understand the impulse propelling the question, "Why can we not simply demand that motherhood be made better for mothers themselves?" (O'Reilly 182), this impulse is rooted in the individual and perhaps unsuited for undoing the impacts of institutional motherhood. Efforts to "correct the child centredness" without harming the child (my abiding concern) pose challenges, suggesting that the path winding between the two principles has the greatest potential to succeed, guided by an ethics of maternal monstrosity. This ethics recognizes that the label "monstrous" is deployed against mothers, advocates for the needs of the vulnerable, and champions the right of mothers to own their voices in relationship-affirming ways.

Two foundational factors mean that attempts to delineate a healthier maternal model, one shaped by matricentric feminist principles, can perhaps only ever be partially successful: the relational nature of mothering (i.e., whether they are present or not, a child whose autonomous identity must be honoured is involved) and the pernicious nature of this control mechanism (which creates multiple vulnerabilities for the mother who is mothering in a setting that does not support her maternal work). If "motherhood is, in Western discourse, the place in our culture where we lodge, or rather bury, the reality of our own conflicts, of what it means to be fully human" (Rose 1) and "becoming and being a mother shape a woman's sense of self and how she sees the world" (O'Reilly 1), then we must ask, how does a mother grapple with the sociocultural, political, and historical messages that tell her how she should view mothers—that is, how she should view herself? These foundational factors create a paradox we must contend with: How do we make sense of O'Reilly's claims (both of which I affirm) that "for women who are mothers, mothering is a significant, if not defining dimension of their lives" (2) and "matricentric feminism ... positions mothering more as a practice than an identity" (4)? The practice, I argue, can account for, but cannot rest solely, on the identity; the child, the object of the practice, must also be accounted for.

As the children of the mommy blogs, the personal essays, and the social media posts grow up and find their lives online, a reckoning is coming: "The shock of realizing that details about your life—or, in some cases, an entire narrative of it—have been shared online without your consent or knowledge has become a pivotal experience in the lives of many young teens and tweens" (Lorenz). What does matricentric feminism have to say to the children who inherited a "digital persona that's already been created, and that they have no power to erase" (Lindsay) through their mothers' efforts to gain self-actualization? How can matricentric feminism guide these mothers in processing this cost and impact?

As I have deepened my research on mothering practices, I find my analytical eye returning again and again to the figure of the monstrous mother. I don't care, though, what makes her bad (that seems simplistically obvious to the point of being boring: we ask mothers to do the impossible and/or mothers are human). I want to know why the rest of us are so fascinated by her. How do we dare to claim the right to judge her while refusing the obligation to support her? Our current fascination with maternal monstrosity is at least partly linked with evolving norms guiding maternal expression. The careful reader will note that I insistently refuse to define "maternal monstrosity" as monstrous mothering practices or maternal actions. Although I recognize that some mothers do behave in horrific ways, and I do not want to minimize the impact of those actions, especially on their children, my matricentric feminism demands that the structural ways that the label is deployed against women be centred when defining "maternal monstrosity"; if individual maternal actions are centred, a form of double jeopardy is imposed whereby mothers are denied the resources needed to mother well and then are also persecuted for their resulting failure.

Or maybe it's fear rather than fascination. Doyle argues that there is a self-reinforcing loop between patriarchy and maternal monstrosity:

> We can use monster stories to trace the shape of patriarchy; the key junctures in a woman's life when male control and violence are deployed to domesticate her sexuality or her reproductive agency into something less fearsome, and the monstrosities that invariably show up at these junctures, justifying male violence by demonstrating what the patriarchy fears women may become. (xx)

Doyle's reading of myths across geography and time demonstrates how "mother" is meant to be understood as the monster (which is itself a stand-in for power, autonomy, and bodily self-determination) latent in all women (123). One result, so beneficial to patriarchy, is the silencing of maternal voices; when voices are silenced, false narratives stand unchallenged.

In the early blogging years, mommy blogs were lauded by readers, bloggers, and researchers as a powerful vehicle for maternal self-expression and self-realization; the perception was that mommy blogs offered mothers a way to avoid losing their identity in motherhood (see Freidman and others). For that moment, it seemed mommy blogs had achieved the aspirations of matricentric feminism by offering mothers a mode of expression organically originating from their identity as mothers, intimately connected to their motherwork. As technology companies and their algorithms have monetized and reshaped the virtual world, the position and power of blogging about children have evolved in ways that inflict harm on them rather than (or even as they) empower the bloggers. (Social psychologist Jonathan Haidt calls the past decade a "uniquely stupid" time in which Americans are "disoriented, unable to speak the same language or recognize the same truth.") When mothers develop and deploy their maternal voices, consciously or not, they contribute to a collective mother-centred exploration of what role these maternal voices should play in a matricentric feminist praxis.

Although mothers now share their stories, the challenge inherent in mothers' storytelling, however, is the bedrock of motherhood. To be a mother is to be in relationship with another human being, the child, whose story is not the mother's story—but whose story is inextricably linked to the mother's story. Exploring the complicated linkage between Ruddick's posited role for mothers vis-à-vis peacemaking and the social impulse to label mothers monstrous that Doyle analyzes can help us understand this paradox. I use a mix of autoethnographic explorations of the label "bad" mother and critical readings of cultural messages about maternal voices; juxtaposing the autoethnographic with the theoretical sustains a focus on the impact of the label "monstrous" on mothers and their children and informs my articulation of an ethics of maternal monstrosity. This linkage is indelibly shaped (deformed?) by the fear driving patriarchy: "Women are meant to completely efface themselves in motherhood; to live for, and in, and through their children. But this means that a bad child infects the mother with his [sic] own sins, and vice versa. In these stories, a woman who raises a monster is that monster. He [sic] would not exist, on any level, if not for her" (Doyle 190).

If I could set up my own "Table for Three" dinner conversation, I'd sit down with Ruddick and Doyle to explore the edge between their thoughts, Ruddick's on peacemaking and Doyle on monster labelling. I would ask them to help me connect the three points of the triangle: maternal peacemaking, patriarchy, and monstrous mothering. Therein lies the ethics of maternal monstrosity I seek. Both note the "fusion of self and other" (Ruddick 191) that marks motherhood with significant implications. As Ruddick argues, "Birth, more than any other experience, except perhaps sexuality, undermines the individuation of bodies" (191). Doyle extends this observation and connects it to patriarchy:

> After a life of being violently warped and scarred by patriarchy, women are given the responsibility of recreating patriarchy, by raising their sons to hold dominion over the world and women. We are also given the blame for everything that may go wrong. Stalin and Stalin's mom, Ed and Augusta, Norma and Norman: we blame mothers, not men, for the violence that male domination has unleashed on the world. (191)

Blamed and responsible does not equal empowered, though.

> *Driving into work, half of my mind is thinking through my argument in this essay, and half is worried that my kiddo doesn't understand the decision they've just helped us make—to move from Virginia to New York. Then Patty Loveless's song "How Can I Help You Say Goodbye?" comes on the radio. I am sitting at the traffic light, waiting to turn left. I sob. The ugly kind of tears that will leave my face splotchy, my eyes a marine-blue shade, my soul soothed. How to make sense of this?*

In a move that repudiates stereotypes of monstrous mothers, Ruddick carefully delineates between the power that mothers exercise over their children and the powerlessness that mothers experience under patriarchy (26, 34). With that distinction articulated, her evocation of maternal peace politics can only make sense when viewed through a matricentric feminist lens. Otherwise, it is just another way that patriarchy perverts motherhood, just another way that patriarchal impositions distort mothering practices. Our current fascination with maternal monstrosity is linked, at least in part, with evolving norms of maternal expression. The twenty-first century calls for a matricentric feminist understanding of the maternal voice and the obligations mothers bear with using this voice, lest it be co-opted in service of patriarchal neoliberalism. As Doyle argues: "The bad mother is patriarchy's saving throw, its ultimate loophole: by moving the blame for male violence back one generation, it makes guilty parties out of the women who are its victims." (191).

There is an irresolvable paradox driving Ruddick's thinking about a maternal politics of peace: "The weak have powers to resist and seduce that belie any absolute division between strong and weak" (180). She advocates for "an opposed and superior conception of conflict resolution rooted in a maternal view of relationships" in recognition that equality is not achievable in a family structure (180). This view of conflict empowers both mother and child:

> In the maternal view of conflict it is not necessary to be equal to resist violence. Most mothers try to teach their children when self-respect demands a fight. Their own peace-making—their attempt to create conditions of peace—includes training for active, engaged nonviolent fighting. Rather than depending on an illusory state of equality, they aim to fight as they live, within communities that attend to and survive shifting differences in power. (180)

How does a mother live out this peace-making orientation (which should not be confused with conflict avoidance)? I follow Ruddick in turning to the practice of maternal thinking through self-reflection. This brings us back to the trap I identified earlier: the possibility that ungrounded reflection can lead to the unwarranted acceptance of the label "monstrous."

For years, I've tried to write an essay about the ethics of mommy blogging while watching the rise of the momfluencer. I still remember the visceral jolt I felt more than a decade ago when I opened a favourite mommy blog to read the paragraph: "[He] transformed into a teenager somehow in one snowy week in February. It wasn't a gradual change in personality. It was an abrupt change. One day he was a kid, and the next day he was an asshole." Did she just call her son an asshole? On the internet? Questions about how to balance what mothers owe their children with respect to privacy with their own right (and need) to express themselves swirled through my mind. I have grappled with varying comfort levels in my impulse to judge how and how much mothers share in public forums (mommyblogs, Facebook, Instagram) while trying to calculate my personal ethical approach.

Although the mommy blogger evolved to momfluencer as social media platforms evolved, perhaps the ethical calculation is best worked out in reverse. The momfluencer who uses their child as a prop fails Ruddick's precepts by accepting the false assurances that shape social media's logic—a logic I would argue, that is designed to suggest liberation from the patriarchal fear Doyle has identified while actually working to replicate and reinforce it. As Elisabeth Van den Abeele, Ini Vanwesenbeeck, and Liselot Hudders note of Flemish momfluencers: "A privacy openness paradox arises: momfluencers want to protect their children's privacy, yet want to enjoy the benefits of openness." (305). The momfluencer chases false promises of power and monetizes their posts, but their children pay the cost. Other mothers write in search of self-awareness, communal connections, or both. There is a difference between speaking about your experience and understanding your own identity and speaking about your child's experience and shaping their identity. One prompts introspection; one practices exploitation. [*When my child was five, I abandoned her.*] Whereas the former empowers mothers and supports them in crucial ways in their motherwork, the latter risks harming their children and perpetuating a patriarchal cycle of disempowerment.

On March 13, 2021, I reposted a photo on Facebook of a pair of purple flip-flops, adding this reflection:

> *March 12, 2020 was the last day my team and I all worked together in-person in our center, and March 13, 2020 was the last day N went to school in-person. I've been watching friends reflecting this week on where they were this time last year, posting their last photos from before the scope of the pandemic hit us. But in our family, we're marking a different, more personal milestone. Today is the tipping point when John and I have been married longer post-accident than we were pre-accident. I lost my husband that day, and he lost his wife that day. We have the new versions of each other now, but there is a peculiar form of grief in the question of who would we be if it weren't for that wave. It's a disorienting experience to mourn something so personal in the midst of a different collective grief that also impacts you, and I've waffled about posting this. But it feels important to honor this moment.*
>
> *This is my last photo, taken around noon on July 30, 2012.*

The photo, a still-life of our child's flip-flops kicked off at the at the entrance of the beach, suggests the easy abandonment of daily routine on vacation. The photo also keeps the secret of its composition and taking: After my child kicked off their flip-flops, I carefully arranged them at the edge of the dunes for the photo I knew I wanted to capture—yes for the memories but really for Facebook. I posted that photo mere hours before my husband's life-altering accident. In the process of trying to curate the public presentation of our family vacation, I unknowingly preserved a visual of the before-and-after moment for our family. So much of our post-accident journey has been an isolated experience for our family. When I saw the flood of photos on Facebook in March 2021, the captions a record of the "before COVID" world and a reflection on all the ways life had changed in a year, I was struck by the poignancy of marking a personal post-traumatic growth milestone at the same time that the whole world was marking a complementary moment. And even as I posted my own "last photo," I grappled with the ethical question, what of this is my story to tell?

A friend who read this chapter for me posed the provocative question: "Is this a monstrous act as a mother? We are shamed for not performing motherhood correctly, but shamed for cultivating the performance, too." If we accept that this double standard sets the terms of the debate, we commit ourselves to a zero-sum perspective wherein either mothers can speak publicly about their experiences or children's right to privacy is protected. The performance in itself is not monstrous. The public use of the child as a stage prop, however, is monstrous to the extent that it causes (irreparable) harm. An ethics of maternal monstrosity offers us the tantalizing possibility that we do not have to choose between the mother's voice and the child's safety.

Last fall, I decided it was time to start excavating the self that had been buried over the past fifteen years by caregiving responsibilities, personal and professional. I took an online writing course, and the final submission included this reflection[1]:

My kiddo demands hugs with a ferocious frequency. Somewhere in the middle of the height of the pandemic, we looked at each other and realized that even when I adopt my very best posture and their teenager slouch is unmistakable, I am not the taller person. Awkward and unwieldy as they are, though, these hugs that destabilize my stance and threaten to knock me to the floor remain constant.

How do we know our children?

I have lived in Virginia for 2,723 days. Apparently, I needed 2,718 days to learn to ask questions when someone invites me to an event at a "farm."[2]

When I go online to do my belated, overdue diligence, I peruse two websites. The official site for the farm—branded as "an 1814 plantation where weddings, tours, and events are hosted"—shares the ownership lineage: originally a wedding gift to William and his widow, "Maria (pronounced Mariah)," who kept it financially stable through "her dedication to continuing her husband's legacy" and her "diligence" until her death.

The SAH (Society of Architectural Historians) Archipedia site shares that William ran an "efficiency-driven plantation." The entry also catalogues with careful dignity the 154 enslaved people he controlled at the time of his death: "The names of the people he owned and who farmed his lands and cared for him and his family were: ..."

Neither website recounts the story shared with us as we twisted together clippings from the grounds, sprigs of boxwood and magnolia branches growing from a wire frame.

The original owners had a cook named Elvira, we are told, whose culinary skills were so renowned that a neighbouring plantation owner purchased her. At her new home, Elvira had a daughter, whom she named Mathilda after her mother, who was still held at the first plantation. Elvira's skills and reputation continued to grow, and her original owners decided to repurchase her. She was allowed to bring her daughter with her. But no two enslaved people ("workers" was the euphemism used) are allowed to have the same name, we're casually told, and since her mother Mathilda was still there, Elvira had to rename her child.

My child recently changed their name. This is their story to tell, not mine. But when I hear the new name come out of my mouth in my voice, I wonder how Elvira felt, using a new name for her child.

When my child was five, I abandoned her. Others are quick to contradict me. But I left my only child with my parents, got on an airplane with my husband and without our child, and flew to Chicago to help him settle into the Rehabilitation Institute of Chicago before I took the South Shore line back to South Bend and a night alone. Irish mythology fascinates my child, especially tales of the selkies. But I can't banish thoughts of changelings from my ruminations. The child that my parents drove west to me was not the one I had kissed goodbye just days earlier in my childhood bedroom.

Is it in our power as mothers to protect our children? Ruddick ascribes to mothers the task of committing to the child's preservation. She also reminds us with devastating clarity:

> Maternal peace politics begins in a myth: Mothers are peace-makers without power. War is men's business; mothers are outsiders or victims; their business is life. The myth is shattered by history. Everywhere that men fight, mothers support them. When powerful men have not discouraged them, women, and sometimes mothers, have fought as fiercely as their brothers. As feminists insist that women and men share fairly the burdens and pleasures of battle, many young women expect their lives to include, without contradiction, both fighting and mothering. (219)

It seems that there is all too often a connection between Ruddick's posited role for mothers vis-à-vis peace and those deemed monstrous—not a direct correlation but a complicated linkage.

As we conceptualize a maternal politics of peace, Doyle forces us to grapple with the fear undergirding patriarchy: "It's hard to believe that our terror of femininity could possibly run that deep; that we see women who give life as more frightening than men who take it" (206). The challenge then for matricentric feminism is to embrace the "needs of care," what Ruddick terms "the dependencies in which connection begins" (132) and develop an "attentiveness to ethics" (225). The alternative is "an attach[ment] to detachment, developing ideals of objectivity that turn on separation and distance" (132). But detachment begets violence, and violence threatens maternal work.

I've grappled for more than a decade with analyzing monstrous mothering, and I still cannot resolve my great difficulties labelling a mother "monstrous," despite evidence of monstrous actions. Perhaps this is because of the complicated history of power. Anyone paying attention to how mothers are judged knows that the label "monstrous" is a weapon deployed unevenly: The mother with power, with access to resources, shielded by the patriarchy and white supremacy, will find her behaviour easily explained away. The mother who lacks those protections, who eschews patriarchal comforts (privileges which may or may not be available and accessible to her), will find the label weaponized against her, sabotaging her efforts to mother successfully. Similarly, but not completely overlapping, is a near-ubiquitous inability to directly confront monstrous maternal behaviour without deflecting the possibility that any mother could behave that way. The mother who deliberately harms her child and who commits unspeakable atrocities must be explained away as unnatural; the very notion that a mother could behave that way is too threatening to the worldview that depends upon maternal benevolence.

In this environment, mothers try to speak (up) for themselves, but institutionalized motherhood can only accommodate mothers speaking in a problematic way. Even Ruddick outlines a women's politics of peace that leans into gendered norms about social roles:

> What I am calling a women's politics of resistance affirms obligations traditionally assigned to women and calls on the community to respect them.... A women's politics of *resistance* is composed of women who take responsibility for the tasks of caring labor and then find themselves confronted with politics or actions that interfere with their right or capacity to do their work. In the name of womanly duties that they have assumed and that their communities expect of them, they resist.... While some people fear that "feminine" resistance is inevitably limited—and their fears seem to me not groundless—I place my hope in its unique potential effectiveness, namely, women's social position makes them inherently "disloyal to the civilization" that depends on them. (223–24, 225)

Ruddick, thus, indirectly activates fears about feminine identities, maternal roles, and the intersection of the two. Scholars (see, for example, Jaqueline McLeod Rogers and Fiona Joy Green) and popular writers (Sara Petersen) have begun to consider the implications of the platforms promoted as the ideal(ized) microphone for maternal voices. Although I struggle with the label "monstrous," it seems most fitting for a particular way of mothers speaking—but that judgment feels unfeminist.

Was the timing never right? Is that why I never submitted a monologue? Did I doubt I had the right to tell this story? Make this decision? Consider my own needs? Or did the inherent disconnect between a monologic mamalogue block my words? (This seems the appropriate place to note that although I wrote this chapter alone, my husband and child read it, and I incorporated all of their requested revisions.)

One of the greatest challenges in creating realistic representations of motherhood and mothering practices, I argue, is embedded in the question, "whose story is it?" How do you separate the mother's story and an attempt to articulate her reality from the child's story and an impulse to protect their privacy? Just at a moment when it seemed that technology might offer an open path for mothers to speak their truth in mommy blogs, the corresponding danger of overexposing their child on the internet and the capitalistic opportunity to monetize formerly uncompensated labour complicate any such attempt. Matricentric feminism must take up this question: How can the mother ethically tell her story? How can she speak without behaving monstrously? Kelly McMasters describes the focus of a recent panel she spoke on as exploring "issues of exposure and protection, particularly of our children, in our pages." She poses the question I grapple with: "How do we, as mothers and writers, pull the plastic sheet so that it covers enough? And who, more importantly, determines when it is, in fact, enough? The children? The reader? The writer herself?"

Unsurprisingly to me, her answers map onto the triangle I described earlier: Why don't we pose these questions of fathers, only of mothers? Creation requires breaking: "At our best, memoirists hope it is silence we are breaking, and not another person. At our worst, we create anyway, knowing it will." But this story is not the only story: "Even though it feels to me like they don't remember much of their childhood, I understand that the difference is that they don't remember my version of their childhood" (McMasters).

Trying to disentangle institutionalized motherhood from mothering practices can feel like tracing your finger along a Möbius strip. On one side, systemic inequalities are perpetuated and reinforced through idealized norms of the good mother. Think about the ways that images of good mothers are deployed to political ends, of ways that labels like "welfare mother" police the mothering practices of women who do not fit the stereotypical ideal: poor mothers, mothers of colour, too-young mothers, and all the mothers whose maternal identity we feel compelled to diminish through an adjective. On the other side, which is also the same side, systemic inequalities perpetuate and reinforce idealized norms of the good mother. Think about the ways that cultural messages reinforce expectations and boundaries of acceptable mothering practices.

Consider a recent United States (US) political advertisement as an example of how motherhood is deployed politically and how norms are reinforced. The advertisement features a woman talking about her son's experience reading a book assigned to his high school English class. The script focuses on her (white) motherhood the entire time, never naming the book, Toni Morrison's *Beloved*—nor acknowledging either Morrison's (Black) motherhood or the ways that motherhood and the questions of what a mother owes her children or how she is to mother in circumstances of extreme duress form the very heart of the novel. The script suggests the good mother protects her child from an assignment she fears will harm him. The enslaved Black mother who acts to save her child from slavery and the Black mother who wrote the story she herself needed to read are both erased. ("Laura Murphy") If we want to deploy the label "monstrous," which of the three mothers has embraced monstrosity?

But those erased stories continue to reverberate today. Historians Deidre Cooper Owens and Sharla M. Fett trace the ways that obstetrics and gynecology as a field advanced at the expense of enslaved Black women and connect this history to the significantly higher rates of maternal and infant mortality that harm Black mothers and children today. Yet making another loop around that Möbius strip, mothers (going back to Ruddick's definition) also hold responsibility for ensuring the social acceptability of their children. For too long, this has meant that mothers of colour have had to raise their children to fit into dominant norms to preserve their lives, and for far too long, white mothers have not put comparable energy into raising their children to resist racism.

How do we teach the mother in the advertisement that her fears for her child are not more important than Elvira's fears for her child? How do we teach the current owner of Elvira's plantation to recognize Elvira's maternity? If the matricentric feminist approach is to be truly liberatory, its goals must be understood through an intersectional lens; in the vision I aspire to, mothers will speak for themselves while recognizing as equally significant the maternal stories of mothers who live in very different circumstances. Matricentric feminism must hear the wisdom of intersectional feminism. In this ethics, mothers will not weaponize their own maternal identity against others' mothering practices.

We simultaneously idealize mothers (or at least, the right mothers), weigh them down with unachievable expectations, and deny them the social supports that might enable them to meet those expectations. We live, after all, in a political moment marked by escalating restrictions on access to abortion services and a partisan refusal to take up the legislature to strengthen the social safety net in a way that would support mothers in their childrearing work. The US is one of only eight countries that does not guarantee paid maternity leave and the only industrialized country without a national paid family leave policy. The mother who breaks under these pressures is the mother typically labelled "monstrous."

Fragments of a class discussion:

One warm April afternoon, we discuss the experiences of disabled mothers: the ways that they have to overperform good mothering to ward off losing custody of their children, as part of the hypersurveillance they are subjected to.

I pose the question: What if their physical condition means they can't safely take care of a child?

The class thoughtfully answers: There are adaptive aids.

What if they choose not to use them?

This is a level of scrutiny and advance planning we don't require of nondisabled mothers, they counter, advocating for the autonomy of the person mothering with/through disability.

Yes, and: the reality of some disabilities is that they preclude mothering (parenting) a child autonomously.

I quietly say, "Our child was five when my husband was disabled. He could not have taken care of the kiddo on his own."

I am a feminist to the marrow in my bones. And I want to question the fetishization of autonomy. Have we misled ourselves into sacrificing collective care for self-actualization?

To return to the question that I posed at the beginning of this chapter: How do we make sense of the impulse to label mothers monstrous? To what extent does it stem from the "unwitting acknowledgement of our [women's] power—a power great enough, in their [men's] own estimation, to end the world" that Doyle identifies (xiv)? Can we stand to view the messiness of motherhood without judgment? For writing session after writing session, working on this chapter, I struggled with my conclusion, until the morning I realized: "I can't record what hasn't been achieved yet." Ultimately, I see resolving the intertwined tensions swirling around the fascination with monstrous mothers and efforts to articulate a maternal voice as one of the great, yet-to-be-realized elements of matricentric feminism: "The empowerment of mother must be the primary aim of feminist mothering if it is to be a truly transformative theory and practice. To fully and completely liberate children from traditional childrearing, mothers must first seek to liberate themselves from traditional motherhood; they must, to use Rich's terminology, mother against motherhood" (O'Reilly 180).

More concrete goals are being pursued in the mother wave: paid leave, access to childcare, and reproductive justice. Lingering over to the side is the matter of maternal voice, with a generational split in approaches to the same bedrock dilemma (with, broadly speaking, Generation X mothers embracing mommy blogs and Millennials becoming momfluencers on social media platforms). A relationship is never a single person's story.[3] Nor should a relationship subsume an individual's identity: "Real change for mothers cannot be achieved if it is always defined as for and about children" (O'Reilly 183). Can we find in the matricentric feminist approach a way to talk about the pressures we put on motherhood and the expectations we hold of mothers—and the fear at the base of them? Doyle reminds us that monsters invoke fear:

> Fear of women may be the single most important truth of misogyny. A cage, after all, has two purposes. Of course, it serves to keep women confined, hemmed in—to prevent us from going out into male territory and getting what men have, the jobs and money and respect and power that are so much more accessible if you're male. But the second purpose of a cage—the more interesting one—is to protect the world from what is inside it. On some level, the cage exists to keep women from getting *out.* (xv)

At the same time, Ruddick inspires mothers to resist acquiescing to the environment of fear: "Some mothers struggle to create nonviolent ways of living with and among children. They school themselves to renounce violent strategies of control" (xix). If matricentric feminism is to have the impact it aspires to, mothers must resist modes of self-expression that simultaneously inflict violence (whether physical, psychological, or verbal) on their children.

A clear-eyed, full-hearted ethics of maternal monstrosity is, like the Möbius strip, multi-dimensional. Let's trace that strip again: one side must be a society that supports mothers and their motherwork, values children, and not only recognizes their needs, but provides for them willingly. On the other side are mothers who embrace the fact that although they haven't lost their identity, they have chosen, per Ruddick, to assume responsibility for another, vulnerable person and are willingly entering into a relationship of unequals. Ethical maternal monstrosity makes space for the maternal voice while recognizing reasonable constraints to it. As mothers exercise their voices, a matricentric feminist approach demands attention to the wisdom of intersectional feminism: a feminism focused solely on the self, with no regard for the needs of the vulnerable or the community, is no true feminism and reinforces the cage as a strategy of control – and here I find a use for the label "monstrous mother." Alice Randall reminds us, "Mother-love is not inevitable. The good mother is a great artist ever creating beauty out of chaos." For the Mother Wave to be successful, we need to have messy conversations about the maternal Möbius strip of judging mothers and mothers speaking, and then we might find the beauty in the chaos.

Endnotes

1. Actually, it was a version of this draft, the original painfully lost in Google docs. It seems like there's some metaphor for maternal thinking and practice in this...
2. "Farm" being the euphemism often deployed in the US South for former plantations built and run by enslaved laborers.
3. My thanks to Summer Cunningham for this particular formulation; to Katie Garner and Nicole Willey for reading earlier versions of this chapter and generously responding to them; and to the three of them, treasured "mompanions" in this mothering journey, for the conversations that helped me clarify my thoughts.

Works Cited

Doyle, Jude Ellison S. [*published* as Sady Doyle]. *Dead Blondes and Bad Mothers: Monstrosity, Patriarchy, and the Fear of Female Power.* Melville House Publishing, 2019.

Haidt, Jonathan. "Why The Past 10 Years Of American Life Have Been Uniquely Stupid." *The Atlantic*, 11 Apr. 2022, https://www.theatlantic.com/magazine/archive/2022/05/social-media-democracy-trust-babel/629369/. Accessed 5 July 2024.

"Laura Murphy—McAuliffe Shut Us out (:60)."*Facebook*, 25 Oct. 2021, https://www.facebook.com/watch/?v=577186750024310. Accessed 5 July 2024.

Lindsay, Kate. "The First Social-Media Babies Are Growing Up—And They're Horrified." *The Atlantic*, 23 May 2023, https://www.theatlantic.com/technology/archive/2023/05/parents-posting-kids-online-tiktok-social-media/674137/. Accessed 5 July 2024.

Lorenz, Taylor. "When Kids Realize Their Whole Life Is Already Online." *The Atlantic*, https://www.theatlantic.com/technology/archive/2019/02/when-kids-realize-their-whole-life-already-online/582916/. Accessed 5 July 2024.

"The Mamalogues."*The Mamalogues®*, http://www.realmamalogues.com/. Accessed 5 July 2024.

Martinot, Steven. "Motherhood and the Invention of Race." *Hypatia*, vol. 22, no. 2, 2007, pp. 79–97.

McLeod Rogers, Jaqueline, and Fiona Joy Green. "Mommy Blogging and Deliberative Dialogical Ethics: Being in the Ethical Moment." *Journal of the Motherhood Initiative Research and Community Involvement*. Spring/Summer 2015, vol. 6(1):31–49. 11 Aug. 2023.

McMasters, Kelly. "The Ethics of Writing Hard Things in Family Memoir." *Literary Hub*, 31 May 2023, https://lithub.com/the-ethics-of-writing-hard-things-in-family-memoir/. Accessed 5 July 2024.

O'Reilly, Andrea. *Matricentric Feminism: Theory, Activism, Practice*. Demeter Press, 2016.

Owens, Deirdre Cooper, and Sharla M. Fett. "Black Maternal and Infant Health: Historical Legacies of Slavery." *American Journal of Public Health*, vol. 109, no. 10, Oct. 2019, pp. 1342–45.

Petersen, Sara. *Momfluenced: Inside the Maddening, Picture-Perfect World of Mommy Influencer Culture*. Beacon Press, 2023.

Rich, Adrienne. *Of Woman Born: Motherhood as Experience and Practice*. W. W. Norton, 1995.

Rose, Jacqueline. *Mothers: An Essay on Love and Cruelty*. Farrar, Straus and Giroux, 2018.

Ruddick, Sara. *Maternal Thinking: Toward a Politics of Peace*. 1989. Beacon Press, 1995.

Singletary, Michelle. "Yes, Black Americans Are Entitled to Reparations. We've Earned Them." *Washington Post*, 30 Oct. 2020, https://www.washingtonpost.com/business/2020/10/30/black-americans-reparations/. Accessed 5 July 2024.

Van den Abeele, Elisabeth, et al. "Child's Privacy Versus Mother's Fame: Unravelling the Biased Decision-Making Process of Momfluencers to Portray Their Children Online." *Information, Communication & Society*, vol. 27, no. 2, 2024, pp. 297–313.

Waldman, Ayelet. "Truly, Madly, Guiltily." *The New York Times*. 27 Mar. 2005, https://www.nytimes.com/2005/03/27/fashion/truly-madly-guiltily.html. Accessed 5 July 2024.

Winnicott, D. W. "Transitional objects and transitional phenomena; a study of the first not-me possession." in *Playing and Reality*. Routledge, 1989, pp. 1–25.

7.

Choosing Matricentric Feminism in an Era of Choice Feminism: A Way Forward

Katie B. Garner

Individual choice does not override cultural injustice.
—Clare Chambers 40

Introduction

In comedienne Michelle Wolf's 2017 *Nice Lady* tour, she claims: "I don't want to have a baby or a family. I want a career." ("Michelle Wolf"). While this assertion fits into the notions of financial independence that neoliberal feminism[1] espouses, it is provocative in its refusal to adhere to the belief that women should desire familial relationships and motherhood above all other goals. Wolf then iterates the advice bestowed on her: "But, Michelle, you don't have to choose. You can have it all. *Women can have it all*" (my emphasis). "You act like 'all' is good," she admonishes: "'All' does not mean good. You've never left an all-you-can eat buffet and thought, 'I feel really good about myself.'" The welcome comic relief is followed by the crux of her argument: "Even if a woman out there definitely wants it all, we've put up too many obstacles in your way to make it possible." Wolf then draws attention to the pressures mothers face, including pressure to be fit, nurse, be with their kids when needed (but not miss work), and earn more than childcare costs. She concludes this portion of the routine by telling her audience that she would rather be a dad than a mom because "a great dad is still just an okay mom."

Wolf effectively pushes back against the rhetoric central to choice feminism, which many American women absorb via mass media, their parents, partners, employers, and friends: Settling for just a career or a family is to sell one's self short. A capable woman can have (dare I say, is expected to have) both. What Wolf does not mention but implies is that each woman is on her own to craft success within broken systems that do little to support sustainable outcomes. A mother's labour is expected to be on behalf of helping others float (or thrive) even though she drowns—a fate, Wolf notes, that is not assigned to fathers. Indeed, mothers' carework is the backbone of society, businesses, and our government even though these systems implicitly and explicitly frame parenting, and mothering more specifically, as a personal goal that, if done well, yields personal success. This framing of motherhood as a choice is critical, as it places nearly all responsibility for that choice on the shoulders of individual women. Meanwhile, mainstream, contemporary, white feminism is now arguably one and the same as choice as neoliberal feminism.

Choice feminism troublingly aligns with neoliberal tenets in which "ideas of the public good are transformed into economic individual interests" (Toft 225) while persuading women to view their gains and setbacks as personal successes or failures that are dictated by one's commitment to self-improvement. The self, in other words, is a commodity, and capitalism, at its core, aims to deactivate communities' esprit de corps. Motherwork is, thus, positioned outside the economic market, and women enter motherhood as a matter of choice—a choice that is cast as a personal success but simultaneously decreases her earning potential (Crittenden). (The recent overturning of Roe v. Wade has not had much impact on viewing motherhood as a choice.) Becoming a mother should, of course, be an unconstrained choice, but the issue here is that intensive mothering, which remains the gold standard, is nearly impossible in a labour market that is increasingly extractive and rife with under remuneration, particularly for work deemed feminine (i.e., pink collar jobs). Too often, mothers are encouraged to see their inability to achieve balance as personal failures.

We are encouraged to view motherhood as an individual pursuit that should not require community, government support or both when both types of support are critical to the health of both mother and child. Maternal scholar and coeditor of this volume, Andrea O'Reilly, posits, "motherhood regards motherwork as privatized labour undertaken in the domestic sphere," while mothering "is an explicitly and profoundly political-social practice" (*Rocking the Cradle* 13). Choice feminism generally views any choice a woman makes in good faith to be inherently feminist, including motherhood, regardless of how much this choice disadvantages her or may be coerced (Hirshman). This includes "opting into" patriarchal motherhood, which can be detrimental to women's ability to be full humans who are engaged in civil, personal, and financial pursuits that permit a greater sense of freedom. Although many forms of feminism are valuable, choice/neoliberal feminism is problematic. Economist Nancy Fraser claims feminists, particularly those influenced by second-wave feminism, have become "handmaidens" to neoliberal-driven capitalism ("How Feminism"). In light of this, we must make space for matricentric feminism, which successfully creates space for both mothers' agency as individuals and carework more broadly in ways few other feminisms currently address.

Matricentric feminism centres on mothers, women, and carework while it advocates for the disruption of systems that prevent liberation. Choice feminism never was and never will be good for the majority of women, particularly women who belong to historically marginalized communities. Feminisms focussing on women of colour as well as feminisms supporting reproductive justice, prison abolition, and queer rights address issues that affect the majority of women (and people!), particularly those whose liberation is most jeopardized. Loretta Ross and Rickie Solinger accurately posit that access to "material resources is justified on the ground that safe and dignified fertility management, childbirth, and parenting together constitute a fundamental *human right*," which "governments owe to the people they govern" (10). Although SisterSong and other similarly aligned groups are gaining traction in the United States (US), particularly after the 1973 *Roe v Wade* decision was overturned in 2022, relatively little attention has been paid to the social and political merits of matricentric feminism, which value "agency, authority, autonomy, and authenticity" and, by extension, aim to empower women to advocate for stronger supports at work, via their politicians, and at home

(O'Reilly, *Rocking the Cradle* 46).

bell hooks acerbically notes that feminists in the 1960s (including Betty Friedan) saw the home and motherhood as sites of oppression, whereas Black feminists then (and arguably now) would not have named motherhood as a "serious obstacle" to freedom (87). Instead, hooks argues that "racism, availability of jobs, lack of skills or education" present greater challenges (87). Indeed, mothering is a practice influenced by our social placement and the cultural norms we, as mothers, are expected to uphold. O'Reilly writes that motherhood "is specifically and fundamentally a cultural practice that is continuously redesigned in response to changing economic and societal factors" ("Introduction" 4). Matricentric feminism may not centre issues that hooks cites directly, but as a framework, it aims to support all who are engaged in (liberatory-based) carework, mothering, and motherwork, as well as advocating for more equitable systems of education, employment, and division of reproductive labour that permit mothers to engage fully with their community.

In no way should this chapter be construed as advocating that mothers should be expected to remain full-time caregivers and forsake waged work based on cultural norms of femininity and care. Instead, I align with communication scholar Helen Hester and digital humanities scholar Nick Srnicek who posit: "For many, it is an established fact that the emancipation of women comes through the labour market. While waged work has undoubtedly granted women a measure of financial independence and social recognition, the generalised expectation that everybody must earn a wage is hardly something to be celebrated" (10). In other words, I am arguing that carework should be valued as essential labour and that those doing this labour should be entitled to economic, physical, emotional, and temporal support that allows them to continue working in this capacity even when done for kin.

This chapter presents a brief context of the US government's failure to support mothers and the current application of neoliberal feminism in the US before addressing how mothers and women experience separate subjectivities under capitalist-driven, neoliberalist institutions and explains why the rhetoric of choice is so perilous for women and mothers. The chapter closes with three suggestions to help realize the primary goals of matricentric feminism.

Care-Less Nanny State

Although the tangled roots of neoliberalism extend far back, the most notable increase in austerity measures in the US is often associated with President Ronald Reagan's administration (1981–89), with Prime Minister Margaret Thatcher's administration (1979–90) simultaneously carrying forward similar measures in the United Kingdom. However, in 1996, President Bill Clinton, a Democrat, was the one that signed one of the most impactful pieces of neoliberal legislation for mothers: the Personal Responsibility and Work Opportunity Reconciliation Act (PRWORA) (ASPE). The benign-sounding term "responsibility" cloaks its emphasis on a specific form of responsibility—engagement with waged work. "Responsibility" is nearly synonymous with wage-earning regardless of care responsibilities in the home, and the bill all but ensured that labour costs would remain low for employers while providing no increase in social supports needed to engage in work, such as subsidized childcare. Simply put, carework is not seen as labour. Congress and ensuing presidents have doubled down on austerity-driven government policies. One recent example occurred in 2022 via the Build Back Better bill, which was developed in response to COVID-19 and would have provided at least a modicum of childcare support via tax credits and four weeks of paid family leave. The bill was defeated, leaving the US to stand alone as the only global North country to withhold paid leave support from those who have given birth.

Sociologists and other researchers will likely be studying the impacts of COVID-19 on mothers engaged in waged work for decades to come. But one of the most glaring truths is that despite the widespread acceptance of choice feminism, which has generally encouraged women to engage in waged work, women are still the ones charged with the bulk of familial care responsibilities, and mothers remain vulnerable when it comes to retaining equitable employment. According to the US Department of Labor, maternal employment declined more than 15 per cent in April 2020 (compared to 9.5 per cent for fathers), and it took nearly a full year longer for mothers to return to prepandemic levels of work (Landivar).[2] More than 2.3 million women left the workforce between February 2020 and 2021, compared to 1.8 million men, even though men are more likely to be employed (Connley, Ewing-Nelson). Nearly one in three women cited childcare as a major issue, compared to 12 per cent of men (Heggeness). Carework, then, remains marked as women's work even though the current mode of (largely white, upper-middle-class) feminism encourages women to choose to stay committed to their careers after having children, effectively ignoring the bulk of working mothers who have no choice but to engage in waged work.

The US government's use of welfare, tax laws, and other legislation can have a strong impact on individual women's choice to maintain employment, ultimately making mothers' waged labour a faucet of sorts that is easily controlled.[3] According to sociologist Leah Ruppanner, due to conflicting approaches towards governance, conservative-leaning (Red) states often approach the "problem" of maternal employment differently than progressive-leaning (Blue) states. The former tend to have few legal protections for working mothers but strong child-care resources, and the latter tend to have strong institutional support for female employment but weak childcare resources (Ruppanner 25).[4] Blue states show worse maternal employment outcomes (Ruppanner). Particularly within the Republican party, however, there is deep ambivalence when it comes to supporting maternal employment. In 2021, during a debate regarding federal funding for kindergarten, Republican Charlie Shephard, an Idaho state representative, said, "I don't think anyone does a better job than mothers in the home, and any bill that makes it easier or more convenient for mothers to come out of the home and let others raise their child, I don't think that's a good direction for us to be going" (qtd. in Russell). He apologized a couple days later. Other opponents were concerned about young children being indoctrinated with left-leaning school curricula (Krutzig). The bill ultimately failed. More recently, Project 2025, which outlines the Republican platform moving beyond the 2024 election, describes efforts to strip Head Start funding and restrict access to reproductive care. Project 2024 also claims "married men and women are the ideal, natural family structure because all children have a right to be raised by the men and women who conceived them" (Mandate for Leadership, 489) and "Families comprised of a married mother, father, and their children are the foundation of a well-ordered nation and healthy society" (451).

Mothers, particularly mothers of colour, are disproportionately affected by the damaging repercussions of government policies. Even with federal protections, mothers are left vulnerable because despite federal policies designed to restrict employer discrimination against mothers, discrimination remains both rampant and difficult to prove. Mothers, and not fathers, are still presumed less competent in the workplace, which influences the motherhood penalty (Correll et al.). This penalty occurs regardless of race (Correll et al.). Legal scholar Tamar Kricheli-Katz posits that mothers also experience greater discrimination by employers who believe that this status is a choice, claiming that when "homosexuality and motherhood are perceived to be beyond individuals' control, people who hold these traits are actually placed at an advantage" (688).[5]

Without federal laws in place, many US businesses fail to support mothers adequately. Only half of women aged eighteen to thirty-four qualify for Federal Medica Leave Act (FMLA) benefits, and these tend to be the women with access to more social privilege (IMPAQ and IWPR). These dire statistics take shape within a culture that still places the majority of responsibility for childcare and domestic work on women's shoulders, according to the Organisation for Economic Co-operation and Development ("Gender Inequality and Unpaid Work"). Although Congress passed the Pregnancy Protection Act in 1978, discrimination remains an ongoing problem, particularly in hiring practices, with increasing numbers of claims being filed (Chester and Kleiner; US Equal Opportunity Office Commission). Moreover, many companies, including Hobby Lobby, have been emboldened by Republican leaders to push back against covering birth control (Al-Faruque; Liptak). With the *Roe v. Wade* ruling being overturned in 2022, companies based in states controlled by Republicans may find themselves in murky legal waters when it comes to supporting women's reproductive needs.

Choice feminism seldom relies on policy as a solution. Instead, self-improvement is the name of the game. We see this reified through legal and cultural measures that mandate responsibility but offer little to no support. This is untenable and disproportionately affects mothers. Matricentric feminism encourages mothers to advocate for empowered mothering not only for their children but also for themselves. It also sees the state as an agent of cultural change. O'Reilly aptly highlights that the "Three models of motherhood activism—maternalism, equal rights, and an ethic of care—must be understood as complementary" (*21st Century*, 25). In essence, this queering of traditional capitalist norms—focussing on reproductive labour rather than productive labour—is what permits this model to work for the majority. Matricentric feminism emphasizes "maternal power" and positions the work of mothering specifically as a "socially engaged enterprise that seeks to effect cultural change in the home through feminist child rearing and the world at-large through political/social activism" (O'Reilly, "Introduction" 10). The social and political engagement aspect is critical to effecting progressive change for the majority.

Modern Neoliberal Feminism and Waged Work

How we frame waged work and motherhood in the US, and many other neoliberal countries in the global North, is cause for concern, particularly as it relates to the illusion of choice. Unremarkable to most people is the fact that many choices we make are actually constrained choices. All humans experience constrained choices regarding who we associate with, where we live, the type of car we (cannot) buy, our health outcomes as they connect to genetic predilections towards certain illnesses, and so on. What is more remarkable is how many women still feel that the choice to become a mother is a constrained one, with 50 per cent of US women who vote Democrat reporting that they feel pressured to have children (Orth). Pressure can be due to parents, friends, partners, societal expectations, religious dogma, and more, as well as combinations of any of the above. People who choose not to have children, particularly women, are still viewed as selfish, since they have not experienced the quasi-spiritual joy of forsaking material, psychological, and physical comforts to benefit another person (Morison et al).

This pressure to have children is certainly not new. What has changed, particularly for white women, is the pressure to engage in waged work simultaneously. Women of colour and immigrant women have seldom had the opportunity to be full-time, stay-at-home mothers, but the "angel in the house" figure was permitted to be removed from waged work and less savory household tasks that could sully her. Employment has been seen as optional for middle-class, white women in ways that motherhood was not for most of the twentieth century; however, employment has become arguably less optional than motherhood today. There has also been increased pressure to mother intensively (Hays).

Although an increasing number of US families all but require two incomes to thrive (Kochhar and Sechopoulos), the cultural pressure to be employed is also placed on economically wealthy mothers whose family may not require their income. Some of the most notable feminist writers addressing this within the past twenty years include Linda

Hirshman (2006), Sheryl Sandberg (2013), and Anne-Marie Slaughter (2015), all of whom have extolled the virtues of remaining in waged work. Neoliberal feminism is at the core of the belief that more women in the board room and c-suite will be a win for all women when it reeks of trickle-down feminism and has been just as unsuccessful as trickle-down economics. Journalist Koa Beck proposes a reason for this:

> Whether it's for themselves, their companies, their business enterprises, or their families, white feminism's willingness to adopt a "conqueror" understanding of their rights and power, specifically unconsciously, underscores the vast ideological space between white feminist ideology and what Native women and two-spirit people have been organizing against for centuries. (37–38)

A pseudo-caste system evolves from capitalist-driven work structures, and, with a lack of meaningful social supports in place, mothers are forced to find individual solutions to the common problem of balancing waged work and motherhood. Some hire childcare providers, who are often Black, brown, or immigrant women, whereas others attempt to carve out increased flexibility by being self-employed or reducing their hours at work, both of which often disqualify women from employee-based health insurance and may stall career growth.

Although not all women can rise to the apex of what choice feminism envisions for women either at work or in their personal lives, part of its allure is its ability to assure women that any outcome is a fair one. Everything between being a child-free business executive and a #tradwife is a legitimate choice if it fulfills a woman's goals for herself—regardless of the impact these choices have on her community. Due to biological aspects of procreation and norms regarding carework and parenting, however, natal-born/AFAB (assigned female at birth) women who become mothers have few options other than to deviate from ideal worker norms even though opting out is often not an option due to economic need, government welfare regulations, and social pressure to be financially independent. At its core, however, the inherent problem is one that feminist philosopher Catherine Rottenberg discusses in *The Rise of Neoliberal Feminism*—Neoliberal capitalism provides no framework for carework. Although cis-hetero men and nonbinary folks also provide care, the majority of care globally and in the Western world is done by natal-born/AFAB women. Mothering, then, becomes an impossible puzzle in which there is no right choice. Mothers can either be good, neoliberal subjects, or they can become needy via their demands for childcare, maternity leave, equitable coparent/spousal engagement, and structural support in the forms of healthcare, education, and so on.

We need to be more articulate and strident about the ways that mothers are pushed out of employment. Opting out, which connotes choice, is seldom the full picture. Many women rightly want to engage in waged work, but without systems promoting genuine financial, career, and parenting equity, it is asinine to claim women are making true choices. Moreover, many other women would prefer to be full-time mothers but cannot without adequate financial support. We need to think more holistically about women's bodies, subjectivities, lives, waged work, carework, and motherhood with a firm stance that privileges equity in an unequal system so all of us have the opportunity for economic stability and meaningful community relationships.

Matricentric feminism, which values agency and authentic authority, pushes back against constrained choice while empowering women and mothers to recognize the value of the carework they do in and out of mothering. Drawing from philosopher Patricia DiQuinzio, O'Reilly notes that matricentric feminism, which is based on a feminist ethic of care framework, "serves to reinvent normative motherhood both in terms of individualism and essentialism" (*21st Century* 9). This is important in terms of choice because, as political philosopher Clare Chambers notes, "In order to distinguish between influence that does and influence that does not threaten justice, we must consider whether individuals are encouraged to make choices that threaten their equality" (172). She also aptly notes that "if there are identifiable pressures on the choosing group to make that choice," in this case motherhood, then those choices are not freely made, "especially if those pressures come from the group who choose differently and thus benefit" (120). In this case, only seven per cent of US men choose to become full-time fathers. (Fry). It is hard not to read the economic and mental health data on mothers, which is nearly always more dire than it is for fathers, and come to the conclusion that women, as a whole, are not thriving even though we continue to do our best within broken systems.

Mother versus Woman under Neoliberalism

Choice feminism also fails as a mode of feminism that benefits the majority of women because it fails to acknowledge the ways women function in society differently than mothers. In *Rhetorics of Motherhood*, English scholar Linda Buchanan argues that in the dyad of good and evil, mother is good, and woman is evil (8–11). Buchanan lists the traits of women that tend to be culturally maligned, such as "childlessness, self-centeredness, work, materialism, hysteria, irrationality, the sensual/sexual body, and the public sphere" (8), whereas a mother holds its meaning culturally via praised traits in females, such as "children, love, protection, home, nourishment, altruism, morality, religion, self-sacrifice, strength, and the reproductive body, the private sphere and the nation" (8). The term "mother," according to Buchanan, is a "god term" and is thus an "ultimate expression to which all others are subordinate" (8). Women can and do become mothers, but if we accept Buchanan's thesis, then their status as a woman, which Buchanan deems a "devil term," is deeply inferior to their status as a mother. Arguably, Buchanan's work may overlay more completely on white, (upper-) middle-class mothers since, as many scholars have noted, Black and brown motherhood and mothers are labelled "monstrous" and/or "deviant" (Chang; Collins; Solinger).[6] Rottenberg similarly acknowledges how "neoliberalism feminism increasingly produces a splitting of female subjecthood" dividing the "worthy capital-enhancing feminist subject" from the "'unworthy' disposable female 'other' who performs most of the reproductive and care work" (20). This is a point I will return to later.

The qualities Buchanan describes as feminine (in that they are associated with cis-hetero women) are often the same ones that we compare negatively against masculine ones, such as illogical (bad/not valued) versus logical (good/valued) or private (bad/not valued) versus public (good/valued), or are ones that are valued in men but are maligned in women, such as strong commitment to work and assertiveness. In Western societies, this method of privileging masculine traits as they appear in cis-hetero men (and the social power simultaneously conferred) remains fairly consistent. Within economic paradigms, however, people are not always gendered in the same ways they are as social beings, with neoliberalism (and some have argued communism) allowing people to function as ungendered beings as long as they can perform as ideal, unencumbered workers. Thus, a childfree woman can be redeemed of her motherless status via her success in the marketplace, even though she will simultaneously be disparaged socially for not choosing motherhood.[7]

This is relevant to the work in this chapter because as neoliberalism becomes increasingly entrenched culturally, politically, and economically, it is only women (i.e., not mothers) whose work has meaning and can be valued. Motherwork has historically been made invisible via capitalism's effort to maintain free labour, but the values we associate with mothers (and are socially lauded according to Buchanan) cannot be extolled within the framework of neoliberalism, which sanctifies self-sufficiency, independence, and personal success. Although there are many problems with this, we face this splitting of the female subject in a time when antiessentialism is de rigueur in most US gender and women's studies programs. Exploring this debate in detail is beyond the scope of this chapter, but, as psychoanalyst Julie Stephens insinuates, because we are so "cautious" and even "queasy" about the "essentialist connection between women and care," the "debate about care and justice in the social and political sphere" can be silenced (13). It is thus important to critique the ways that one's sex affects (and limits) one's access to power and privilege in our society. We cannot achieve the progress we need by willfully ignoring the lived reality of (racialized) women. This becomes of the utmost importance as we consider the ways society enforces feminine norms of carework while neoliberalism refuses to acknowledge and even erase these same socially enforced sex-based norms.

Ultimately, mothers are in an impossible bind. Mothers are inferior neoliberal subjects because by becoming mothers, they are no longer unencumbered workers, even though they are inferior women if they do not become mothers, a choice that ultimately provides the human material and labour that capitalism requires. Matricentric feminism provides a different framework by refusing the neoliberal terms of the debate. Its ability to honour complex notions of the caregiving self and encourage a form of mothering provides space for personal fulfillment and stands in contrast to the either/or binary previously described.

Rhetoric of Choice for Mothers: Flexibility, Responsibility, and Blame

Today, the term "choice," particularly for women, is intrinsically linked with access to abortion. This is not by accident. Rather than talk about abortion or pregnancy by name in the 1960s and 70s, Planned Parenthood, the National Abortion Rights Action League, and NOW centred their work around the idea of "children by choice" in part because it was an attractive framing to independent and conservative voters (Swinth). The rhetoric of choice is problematic, and many feminist scholars (e.g., Rickie Solinger, Lynn O'Brien Hallstein, and Amrita Nandy) have addressed how the fault lines of this concept can be deeply detrimental for mothers. Certainly, the rhetoric of choice has become even more challenging since the overturning of *Roe v. Wade* in 2022 by the US Supreme Court in *Dobbs v Jackson. Dobbs* effectively put legislative control of abortion into the hands of states—a move that was forewarned by many activists working towards reproductive justice and full access to abortion.

Women, particularly (upper-) middle-class white women, are still presumed to choose motherhood and to choose work. This is not entirely true. I am not arguing that women do not have agency, but this choice is shaped by government policies, cost and access to childcare, income level, men's engagement with domestic labour and childcare, access to support from extended kin, and many other factors. *Some* women do have *some* degree of choice (for now) regarding whether they become pregnant or continue a pregnancy. Moreover, their (unwaged) carework is theoretically valued enough that it gives some mothers (particularly white, middle-class ones) permission to opt-out without stigma. However, whereas the ideal mother a generation or two ago was encouraged to stay at home full-time, mothers today are increasingly pressured to engage in waged work even though they remain the primary parent with extreme temporal demands and little to no care infrastructure to rely on. Waged work is not the primary problem, even though we need more robust laws around exploitative and extractive labour conditions. Neoliberalism, at its core, espouses self-sufficiency and free will.

Women have been creative in their attempts to manage private and public identities, including self-employment, multi-level marketing endeavours, and flexible gig jobs (Anderson and Moore). Journalist Sara Petersen notes that even in the very modern field of influencing, companies "have no problem saying 'no' to a momfluencer demanding to be paid fairly for her time and skill" (23), with mothers of color experiencing even more egregious underremuneration. Jobs that permit a mother to be both a full-time caregiver as well as a productive labourer and earner too often count flexibility as part of remuneration. Women's atypical employment still provides an economic benefit to the government and businesses as women attempt to find solutions to time shortfalls.

Although the notion of responsibility is highly regarded in the US, the ugly underbelly of this virtue is blame. Mothers, as many maternal scholars have highlighted, are castigated for all of society's sins.[8] Fathers, who are better able to remain unencumbered workers due to feminized norms of care, remain outside the fray almost entirely. Ultimately, women remain in a "damned if you do, damned if you don't" framework that casts blame for not fulfilling impossible norms of intensive mothering and retaining their status as productive workers. The reason for this, according to Rottenberg, is that neoliberalism as an economic order "relies on reproduction and care work in order to reproduce and maintain human capital ... [yet] as a political rationality ... has no lexicon that can recognize let alone value reproduction and care work" (16). People, even full-time caregivers, who do not engage in waged work are barely tolerated within neoliberal and capitalist regimes, despite the fact that Keynesian and neoclassical economists are leery of full employment's impact on inflation (Barcena and Wessel).[9] Legal scholar Joan C. Williams argues: "Women may choose not to perform as ideal workers, but they do not choose the marginalization that currently accompanies that decision" (*Unbending Gender* 6). One of the core fissures in our society rests on social inequities, but in the case of motherhood, the root of inequity is framed as a choice but one that is a social good. Matricentric feminism works to correct these fissures by viewing children, mothers, and carework as social goods. These values ultimately help all people feel supported, loved, and connected in ways that do not put a greater toll on material resources and our climate.

Where to Go from Here?

One of the inherent tensions in the fight for liberatory mothering is, to borrow from Audre Lorde, whether to work within the (capitalist) "house" that has been built and remodel it via subsidized childcare, better family leave options, and fairer hiring practices or to dismantle the house altogether and start anew with economic systems that are not nearly as destructive to individuals, families, and the flora and fauna of our planet (112). Pragmatically, most people recognize that we all must navigate broken systems as ethically as possible until the systems we aim to fix are repaired. Importantly, a person's privilege may permit them to perform their ethics in ways that align well with their goals, for instance, being able to pay a childcare provider well. Yet even in these cases, it is important to consider what we are gaining and losing more broadly when we remain complicit with exploitative systems that perpetually extract time and labour from certain groups to benefit others. Political scientist Joan Tronto presents this complicity in "The Nanny Question in Feminism," as a central question and, I argue, it is one that matricentric feminism is particularly suited to address in its adherence to rebuilding broken structures that often do not align with our values and needs as humans.

The first major argument my spouse and I had concerned whether to hire a housecleaner. We were far from wealthy; he repaired industrial machines, and I was completing my master's in English education. His work required extensive travel, and I was adamant that we split domestic chores fairly on weekends. He agreed I should not be solely responsible, but he did not want to spend his scarce free time cleaning on weekends. Armed with the economic fact that he outearned a housecleaner, his logic was hard to refute. Capitalism endorses this method of labour output and extraction. Still, I did not feel that it was fair to outsource underpaid work, and we could not afford to pay more than the market rate. I struggled to articulate my discomfort and ultimately lost the argument, and we had someone clean our home every other week. Meanwhile, my professional life was taking the scenic route. I left a fairly lucrative position at a tech firm, got certified to teach high school, and obtained my first teaching position in my late twenties. As a new teacher, I was incredibly stretched for time and was still untenured when I became pregnant at twenty-nine. My spouse was still travelling extensively for work and leisure, and my school district would only renew my contract on a full-time basis. Knowing something had to give, I resigned.

To retain my sanity, sense of self, and good social standing, I continued to earn credits towards my PhD part-time and ultimately got hooded at the age of thirty-nine. While I was pursuing my studies, we (really, I) hired women to care for our kids for about ten hours a week. We paid market value or better (because we could by then), and I remain in touch with most of the women. My cis-male, self-employed spouse was happy to support my goals financially, but he could not see the logic of scaling back his work when he easily outearned those we hired. (I would not be surprised if patriarchal norms also influenced his choices since stay-at-home fathers, even part-time ones, were and remain rare.) He continued to grow his business, provided well for our family, and fulfilled the norms of heteropatriarchal capitalism, whereas my professional ambitions treaded water. When I was ready to go onto the national market, we decided it would be too disruptive to move our children two or three times for a salary that paled in comparison to his and would ultimately disrupt his ability to run his business.

Despite being well-steeped in feminist theory, which seldom if ever addresses motherhood, I saw this confluence of events as a perfect storm. I took responsibility for my choices and viewed my failure to launch as a result of personal shortcomings, not part of a systemic problem. I realized much later, particularly after interviewing nearly one hundred US mothers regarding their role as mothers, the rhetoric of choice, and childcare, how unexceptional my story is. Indeed, I now compare this perfect storm to a George Rhoads's ball machine sculpture.[10] Choice, or the illusion of it, which is at the core of neoliberal feminism, has encouraged mothers to believe our inability to thrive is a personal failure when this is not the case. Mothers must demand that those who benefit from our labour (e.g., our governments, corporations, and cis-hetero men) help carry the responsibility, blame, and labour of mothering.

I now run the International Association of Maternal Action + Scholarship, née MIRCI, which was started by Andrea O'Reilly, the coeditor of this collection. I am passionate about this work, but it is entirely pro bono. I am the woman Linda Hirshman warned women not to become. Looking back, I wonder if I should have sacrificed as much as I did professionally. I still question if hiring women so I could read, write, and think about the exploitation of domestic workers made (or makes) any sense at all. I know that the work I do, even in this chapter, is the result of their labour in my home and with my children, and I feel a sense of obligation to do what I can to make the world we live in more equitable. I share this story only to assert that I am not outside the fray or talking from a pedestal. I continue to struggle with how to effect change and somehow craft a way forward that is better for all. There are no simple answers, but below are four shifts that need to take place to achieve the policy changes mothers need and align with the framework of matricentric feminism. Although access to universal healthcare, paid family leave, and subsidized childcare are the most critical, significant ink has been spilled on these topics already, so I have chosen to focus on less common places for change.

The first and shortest, in part because it is so indisputable, has been addressed throughout this chapter. We all must carefully consider the ways we participate in and resist the pressure to engage in neoliberal-informed feminism and motherhood. As noted, I have outsourced domestic labour; I have also fretted over my children's ability to function in a capitalist world, and I feel guilty when I am not engaged in productive tasks. It is nearly impossible to be an outlaw mother all the time. There are good reasons to share the load of carework with people outside our inner circle. While outsourced care is currently problematic, it does not need to be as problematic as it is. Carework and domestic labour are not inherently exploitative and extractive; it is often this way now due to toothless government policies, a culture that devalues women's labour and carework, and because we have no infrastructure within capitalism to value carework appropriately. In line with the goals of matricentric feminism, we must work collectively to craft a society that respects carework and domestic labour (alongside mothering), and remunerates those doing this work equitably.

Second, we must work to centre the idea that children are a social good and act accordingly. This means all children. Whereas current norms of intensive mothering exist, partly, because of poorly designed policies that address globalization, employment, and welfare, it is not healthy for mothers, parents, or children (Edlynn). We must return to an approach to carework that values all people regardless of their ability to engage in a capitalist society. According to The Care Collective, "If care is to challenge capitalism as a source of ethics and a site of resistance, not only must the capitalist value of profit at all costs be contested, but so too must the deeply gendered and racialized hierarchical social order that underpins it" (56). Matricentric feminism provides the footing for this, even though it recognizes that not all women want to be mothers. The Care Collective also posits, "Promiscuous care recognises that not all women want to be mothers, whether they can be or not; and that caring for children who are not your own, caring for the community and caring for the environment are equally valuable tasks that must be adequately resourced and appreciated" (43). Children today are too often viewed as a personal hobby of sorts, which are taken on by individual parents whose success or failure (both parents and children) determines their overall worth in society. Matricentric feminism values a community approach towards the carework taking place in mothering children and others.

Part of valuing children means holding those who benefit from their rearing responsible for contributing fairly. One of the dubious advantages of neoliberalism is that while it glorifies the individual worker, no individual business owner is responsible for systemic abuse. Ironically, businesses, according to the 2010 *Citizens United* ruling by the US Supreme Court, are political entities, whereas the people running the companies often remain immune to prosecution.[11] Lobbying groups supporting US businesses, including the US Chamber of Commerce, influence elected officials via campaign donations (that go largely to Republicans) and the policies they enact (Barney). Since the 1950s, unions have lost much of their bargaining power (Vachon and Wallace), and in turn, worker protections have stalled, been rolled back, or never voted on. Unions can have a powerful role moving forward when it comes to securing equitable pay, reasonable work demands, and subsidized childcare. Mass boycotts are also effective ways to encourage companies to behave responsibly.

Third, we must normalize work that values the family while being careful about what we ask for. Feminists have long fought for women's right to engage in waged labour for good reason. Women benefit from financial independence and the diversity of experiences that come from engaging in work outside the home. Some neoliberal (self-professed) feminists have suggested women are to blame for their shortcomings in waged work (including Lisa Belkin, Hirshman, and Sandberg). Others rightly identify current systems that need to be reformed and posit that increased flexibility is the answer (Slaughter). Over the past decade at least, there have been countless articles highlighting the advantages of flexibility for both employers and employees, and there are certainly benefits to some types of flexibility for some people. During COVID-19, many workers decided that they enjoyed having the option to work from home at least some of the time, but as shown earlier, this did not necessarily benefit everyone equally. Similarly, the ability to tailor one's work hours can be an alluring perk in a job, including in academia. Flexible work, however, can also mean erratic hours, unstable hourly wages, schedules that may not provide enough hours, and restricted access to federal programs like FMLA and company-based health insurance.

Last but not least, I would like to address the importance of making part-time work more accessible and realistic. Most employed mothers (and many others) prefer but may not engage in part-time work due to how it is undervalued in the US.[12] Christine Williams and Gretchen Webber also point out that higher-status, part-time female workers tend to take on part-time work as a short-term strategy even though they still identify with and support ideal work norms. Conversely, women working in lower-status jobs see their work as a means to "enhance their families' well-being" (756). Interestingly, both groups of women claim "responsibility for any job penalties they experienced" (756) even though, as cited earlier, this is often not the case. Economist Claudia Goldin rightly warns against the perils of "greedy work," which occurs as a result of (often gendered) specialization both in waged work and in the home due to the intensification of work demands, presenteeism, and lack of policies limiting employers from extractive labour practices.

Many feminists have disparaged part-time work due to negative outcomes women experience, namely being "mommy tracked," which can decrease financial earnings and potential for career advancement (Hirshman).[13] Women, particularly mothers, are overrepresented in part-time work, which, importantly, is not always preferred. The benefits of part-time employment are only advantageous if they are useful to the employee and offer equitable compensation (Chung). It is important to note that part-time work may be a way to address many contemporary problems, and there is little reason not to make this a more standard option, particularly with the growth of artificial intelligence. Feminist scholar Kathi Weeks accurately asserts that work is a "social convention and disciplinary apparatus rather than an economic necessity" (7–8). Calling into question employment perks such as flex-time, working from home, and other nonstandard options, Weeks posits that the goal for feminists should be a "reduction rather than the mere rearrangement of paid work time" (172). Importantly, this argument overlays with (intensive) mothering as well, and it would behoove groups advocating for stronger worker protections to partner with matricentric feminists.

The US needs to implement a two-pronged approach to addressing the dearth of sustainable, family-friendly, and economically viable work. This two-pronged approach consists of reshaping cultural beliefs while providing policies that support progressive change. While not a complete success, the European Union (EU) has policies that cap weekly work times, support employees seeking part-time work, and mandate equitable remuneration for part-time work. It will take considerable effort to curtail engrained beliefs that link morality and work in the US, and some of it involves recognizing carework as valuable labour. Despite the work done by brilliant feminists, ideas regarding who is responsible for childcare and domestic labour remain painfully rigid (McConnon et al.) even though mothers are still expected to contribute financially to their families. We cannot simply wait out the storm; instead, we must implement change however we can. Matricentric feminism provides the tools needed to stay dry even as the storm rages on.

Endnotes

1. Although there are likely shades of differences between choice feminism and neoliberal feminism (e.g., neoliberal may focus more on government and economic aspects, and choice feminism may focus more on social aspects), for this chapter, I will largely use the two terms interchangeably while defaulting to the parsed differences above when it makes sense to do so. In many ways, these two branches of antiliberatory feminism complement one another and give oxygen to similar forms of exploitation.
2. In the US, March 2020 is considered the beginning of strict lockdowns due to COVID-19.
3. The most glaring example of this occurred following WWII when women protested en masse to retain government-supported childcare centers, which were closed when women's labour was considered less desirable than the labour of men who had returned from the war effort. Other, less overt, examples are plentiful.
4. In Ruppanner's analysis, socially progressive states with strong employment protection and weak child-care infrastructure yield lower maternal employment. However, these Democrat-leaning districts also tend to have higher per capita income, making a second income less essential.

5. There was a concerted effort by gay rights groups to position homosexuality as biologically determined, drawing attention to studies that identified a "gay gene." See Robert Alan Brookey's *Reinventing the Male Homosexual: The Rhetoric and Power of the Gay Gene* for more information.
6. One only has to look at Meghan Markle to see how little motherhood can assuage the fears of Black and brown women.
7. It is also important to note that while childfree US women are earning 97 per cent of US men's salary, US mothers are averaging 50 per cent of that with mothers of colour well below that (Rose and Hartman).
8. Psychologist Jacqueline Rose writes: "Motherhood is, in Western discourse, the place in our culture where we lodge, or rather bury, the reality of our own conflicts" (1). Molly Taylor-Ladd and Lauri Umansky accurately highlight the "extraordinary elasticity of the 'bad' mother label" (2). Feminist scholar Jennifer L. Turner highlights the resiliency of the controlling image of the Black "welfare queen" (56). Feminist scholar Gretel H. Vera-Rosas similarly pushes back against "deficit-oriented" rhetoric that "blames parents rather than structural conditions" (66). US mothers, particularly single mothers, experience disproportionate rates of poverty, insecure housing, and food scarcity (Nolan et al). Feminist sociologist Kathleen Lynch aptly writes, "*Security* is a prize also available to those who behave *responsibly*, and who are active in managing themselves and availing themselves of opportunities within neoliberal capitalism" (29).
9. Full employment is often considered 4 per cent and below, but achieving this number can be challenging and often does not account for those who are considered mentally or physically unable to contribute to waged work.
10. Many readers have likely seen one of these sculptures in which a ball that is released sets off bells, lift levers, and may be lowered via baskets as it traverses a predetermined path.
11. The collapse of AIG and ensuing financial chaos led to a single prosecution of a middle-management person. In fact, many massive financial institutions were deemed "too big to fail" and were "bailed out" by US taxpayers.
12. Unlike the EU, the US does not offer much to protect part-time workers, who are often underpaid in comparison to equally positioned

peers, may not have access to company-sponsored health insurance and can be tacitly "mommy tracked" (i.e., perceived as less committed to their company, colleagues, and waged work more broadly).

13. Webber and Williams describe two tiers of part-time work consisting of a lower track that is colloquially deemed "gig" work and "unskilled" (customer service, etc.) and a higher track of elite formally educated folks working on a contract basis, are self-employed, or freelance.

Works Cited

Agonito, Rosemary. *The Last Taboo: Saying No to Motherhood*. Algora, 2014.

Al-Faruque, Ferdous. "Republicans Hail Hobby Lobby Decision as Religious Victory." *The Hill*, 30 June 2014, https://thehill.com/policy/healthcare/210963-gop-hails-hobby-lobby-decision-as-religious-victory. Accessed 6 July 2024.

Anderson, Gillian, and Joseph G. Moore. "'Doing It All ... and Making It Look Easy!': Yummy Mummies, Mompreneurs and the North American Neoliberal Crises of the Home." *Mothering in the Age of Neoliberalism*. Edited by Melinda Vandenbeld. Demeter Press, 2014, pp. 95–115.

ASPE, Office of the Assistant Secretary for Planning and Evaluation. "The Personal Responsibility and Work Opportunity Reconciliation Act of 1996," 31 Aug. 1996, https://aspe.hhs.gov/reports/personal-responsibility-work-opportunity-reconciliation-act-1996. Accessed 6 July 2024.

Barcena, Lorena Hernandez, and David Wessel. "How does the Fed Define 'Maximum Employment?'" *Brookings Institution*, 23 Feb. 2022, https://www.brookings.edu/articles/how-does-the-fed-define-maximum-employment/. Accessed 6 July 2024.

Jopson, Barney. "Business Lobby Puts its Cash Behind the Republicans: Chamber of Commerce Spends $30m to Influence US Congressional Elections."*Financial Times*, 2014 Oct 03, 2014/10/03/, pp. 4. *ProQuest*, https://proxy.cc.uic.edu/login?url=https://www.proquest.com/newspapers/business-lobby-puts-cash-behind-republicans/docview/1619247275/se-2. Accessed: 18 July 2024.

Beck, Koa. *White Feminism: From the Suffragettes to Influencers and Who They Leave Behind.* Atria Books, 2021.

Brookey, Robert Alan. *Reinventing the Male Homosexual: The Rhetoric and Power of the Gay Gene.* Indiana University Press, 2002.

Care Collective. *The Care Manifesto: The Politics of Independence.* Verso, 2020.

Chambers, Clare. *Sex, Culture, and Justice: The Limits of Choice.* Pennsylvania State University Press, 2008.

Chang, Grace. *Disposable Domestics: Immigrant Women Workers in the Global Economy.* South End Press, 2000.

Chung, Heejung. "Part-Time Working Conditions and Part-Time Work Flexible Working-Time Arrangements Across Europe." *Dualisation of Part-Time Work: The Development of Labour Market Insiders and Outsiders.* Edited by Heidi Nicolaisen et al. Policy, 2019. pp. 109–32.

Chester, Nefertiti, and Brian H Kleiner. "Pregnancy in the Workplace." *International Journal of Sociology and Social Policy,* vol. 21, no. 8/9/10, 2001, pp. 137–47, https://doi.org/10.1108/01443330110789899.

Collins, Patricia Hill. "Shifting the Center: Race, Class, and Feminist Theorizing About Motherhood." *Maternal Theory: Essential Readings.* Edited by Andrea O'Reilly. Demeter Press, 2021, pp. 167–86.

Connley, Courtney. "In 1 Year, Women Globally Lost $800 Billion in Income due to Covid-19, New Report Finds." *NBC,* 30 April 2021, https://www.cnbc.com/2021/04/30/women-globally-lost-800-billion-dollars-in-income-due-to-covid-19.html. Accessed 6 July 2024.

Correll, Shelly, Stephen Benard, and In Paik. "Getting a Job: Is There a Motherhood Penalty?" *American Journal of Sociology,* vol. 112, no. 5, 2007, pp. 1297–1338, https://wwwjstororg.proxy.cc.uic.edu/stable/pdf/10.1086/511799.pdf?refreqid=excelsior%3Afcf809c2b0543af82b-36b48886378043&ab_segments=&origin=&initiator=&acceptT C=1. Accessed 6 July 2024.

Crittenden, Ann. *The Price of Motherhood: Why the Most Important Job in the World is Still the Least Valued.* Holt, 2001.

Edlynn, Emily. *Autonomy-Supportive Parenting: Reduce Parental Burnout & Raise Competent, Confident Children.* Familius, 2023.

Ewing-Nelson, Claire. "All the Jobs Lost in December Were Women's Jobs." *National Women's Law Center,* Jan. 2021, https://nwlc.org/

wp-content/uploads/2021/01/December-Jobs-Day.pdf. Accessed 6 July 2023.

Fraser, Nancy. "How Feminism Became Capitalism's Handmaiden—And How to Reclaim It." *The Guardian*, 14 Oct. 2013, https://www.theguardian.com/commentisfree/2013/oct/14/ feminism-capitalist-handmaiden-neoliberal. Accessed 6 July 2024.

Fry, Richard. "Almost 1 in 5 Stay-at-Home Parents in the U.S. are Dads." *Pew Research Center*, 3 Aug. 2023, https://www.pewresearch.org/short-reads/2023/08/03/almost-1-in-5-stay-at-home-parents-in-the-us-are-dads/. Accessed 6 July 2024.

Goldin, Claudia. *Career and Family: Women's Century-long Journey Toward Equity.* Princeton University Press, 2021.

Heggeness, Misty L., and Jason M. Fields. "Working Moms Bear Brunt of Home Schooling During COVID-19." *U.S. Census Bureau*, 18 Aug. 2020, https://www.census.gov/library/stories/2020/08/parents-juggle-work-and-child-care-during-pandemic.html. Accessed 6 July 2024.

IMPAQ International and IWPR. "Qualifying for Unpaid Leave: FMLA Eligibility Among Working Mothers." *Department of Labor*, Jan. 2017, https://www.dol.gov/sites/dolgov/files/OASP/legacy/files/IMPAQ-Working-Mothers.pdf. Accessed 6 July 2024.

Kricheli-Katz, Tamar. "Choice-Based Discrimination: Labor-Force-Type Discrimination against Gay Men, the Obese, and Mothers." *Journal of Empirical Legal Studies*, vol. 10, no. 4, 2013, pp. 670–95.*HeinOnline*, https://heinonline-org.proxy.cc.uic.edu/HOL/P?h=hein.journals/emplest10&i=688.

Krutzig, Sally. "Idaho House Rejects Federal Grant Aimed at Improving Childcare." *The Spokesman-Review*, 3 Mar. 2021, https://www.spokesman.com/stories/2021/mar/03/idaho-house-rejects-federal-grant-aimed-at-improvi/. Accessed 6 July 2024.

Kochhar, Rakesh, and Stella Sechopoulos. "How the American Middle Class has Changed the past Five Decades." Pew Research. 20 April 2022, https://www.pewresearch.org/short-reads/2022/04/20/how-the-american-middle-class-has-changed-in-the-past-five-decades. Accessed July 16, 2024.

Landivar, Liana Christin. "Mothers' Employment Three Years Later: An Assessment of Employment Loss and Recovery During the COVID-19 Pandemic." *Department of Labor*, May 2023, https://www.

dol.gov/sites/dolgov/files/WB/media/Mothers-employment-3-years-later-Final.pdf?_ga=2.92036058.1552035200.1694726433-714315898.1694726433. Accessed 6 July 2024.

Liptak, Adam. "Supreme Court Rejects Contraceptives Mandate for Some Corporations." *New York Times*, 30 June 2014, https://www.nytimes.com/2014/07/01/us/hobby-lobby-case-supreme-court-contraception.html. Accessed 6 July 2024.

Mandate for Leadership: A Conservative Promise. Presidential Transition Project. Heritage Foundation. 2023, https://static.project2025.org/2025_MandateForLeadership_FULL.pdf

McConnon, Annie, et al. "Mother Like Mothers and Work Like Fathers: U.S. Heterosexual, College Students' Assumptions About Who Should Meet Childcare and Housework Demands." *Sex Roles*, vol. 86, Jan. 2022, pp. 49–66, https://doi.org/10.1007/s11199-021-01252-3.

"Michelle Wolf: Nice Lady (2017)—Full Transcript." *Scraps*, 12 Jan. 2018, https://scrapsfromtheloft.com/comedy/michelle-wolf-nice-lady-2017-full-transcript/. Accessed 6 July 2024.

Morison, T., et al. "Stigma Resistance in Online Childfree Communities: The Limitations of Choice Rhetoric." *Psychology of Women Quarterly*, vol. 40, no. 2, 2016, pp. 184–198, https://doi.org/10.1177/0361684315603657.

Nandy, Amrita. *Motherhood and Choice: Uncommon Mothers, Childless Women*. Zubaan, 2017.

O'Brien Hallstein, Lynn. *Contemplating Maternity in an Era of Choice: Explorations into Discourses of Reproduction*. Eds. Sara Hayden and D. Lynn O'Brien Hallstein. Lexington Books, 2010.

O'Reilly, Andrea. "Introduction." *From Motherhood to Mothering: The Legacy of Adrienne Rich's Of Woman Born*. Edited by Andrea O'Reilly. SUNY Press, 2004, pp. 1–23.

O'Reilly, Andrea. *The 21st Century Motherhood Movement: Mothers Speak Out on Why We Need to Change the World and How to Do It*. Demeter Press, 2011.

O'Reilly, Andrea. *Rocking the Cradle: Thoughts on Motherhood, Feminism, and the Possibility of Empowered Mothering*. Demeter Press, 2006.

Organisation for Economic Co-operation and Development. "Gender Inequality in Unpaid Work." *The Pursuit of Gender Equality: An Uphill*

Battle. OECD Publishing: Paris, 2017, https://read.oecd-ilibrary.org/social-issues-migration-health/the-pursuit-of-gender-equality/gender-inequality-in-unpaid-work_9789264281318-18-en#page2. https://doi.org/10.1787/9789264281318-18-en. Accessed 16 July 2024.

Orth, Taylor. "Does Society Pressure Men and Women to Have Children?" *YouGov.*, 8 Feb 2022, https://today.yougov.com/topics/politics/articles-reports/2022/02/08/does-society-pressure-men-and-women-have-children. Accessed 6 July 2024.

Petersen, Sara. *Momfluenced: Inside the Maddening, Picture-Perfect World of Mommy Influencer Culture*. Beacon, 2023.

Rose S. J., and H. I. Hartman. "Still a Man's Labor Market." *IWPR*, 2018, https://iwpr.org/wp-content/uploads/2020/08/C474_IWPR-Still-a-Mans-Labor-Market-update-2018-2.pdf. Accessed 6 July 2024.

Rose, Jaqueline. *Mothers: An Essay on Love and Cruelty*. Farrar, Straus and Giroux, 2018.

Rottenberg, Catherine. *The Rise of Neoliberal Feminism*. Oxford University Press, 2018.

Ruppanner, Leah. *Motherlands: How States Push Mothers Out of Employment*. Temple University Press, 2020.

Russell, Betsy Z. "Governor: 'We'll Try Again' on Early Childhood Learning." *Idaho Press*, 3 Mar. 2021, https://www.idahopress.com/news/local/governor-well-try-again-on-early-childhood-learning/article_fc643fd6-48bf-5041-bc92-58ee2ce49ab2.html. Accessed 6 July 2024.

Stephens, Julie. *Confronting Postmaternal Thinking: Feminism Memory, and Care*. Columbia, 2011.

Solinger, Rickie. *Beggars and Choosers: How the Politics of Choice Shapes Adoption, Abortion, and Welfare in the United States*. Hill and Wang, 2001.

Swinth, Kirsten. *Feminism's Forgotten Fight: The Unfinished Struggle for Work and Family*. Harvard University Press, 2018.

Taylor-Ladd, Molly, and Lauri Umansky. *Bad Mothers: The Politics of Blame in Twentieth Century America*. New York University Press, 1997.

Turner, Jennifer L. "Beyond 'Welfare Queens' and 'Baby Mamas': Low-Income Black Single Mothers' Resistance to Controlling Images." *Black Matrilineage, Photography, and Representation: Another Way of*

Knowing. Edited by Lesly Deschler Canossi and Zoraida Lopez-Diago, Leuven University Press, 2022, pp. 53–72. *JSTOR*, http://www.jstor.org/stable/j.ctv2dd 4714.7.

US Dept. of Labor. "Employment Characteristics of Families—2022." *Bureau of Labor Statistics*, 19 Apr. 2023, https://www.bls.gov/news.release/pdf/famee.pdf. Accessed 6 July 2024.

US Equal Employment Opportunity Commission. "Pregnancy Discrimination Charges—EEOC and FEPAs Combined: FY 1997–2011." *EEOC*, https://www.eeoc.gov/data/pregnancy-discrimination-chargeseeoc-fepas-combined-fy-1997-fy-2011. Accessed 6 July 2024.

Weeks, Kathi. *The Problem with Work: Feminism, Marxism, Antiwork Politics, and Postwork Imaginaries*. Duke University Press, 2011.

Williams, Joan C. *Unbending Gender*. Oxford University Press, 2001.

Williams, Christine, and Gretchen Webber. *Gender and Society*, vol. 22, no. 6, 2008, pp. 752–77.

Vachon, Todd E., and Michael Wallace. "Globalization, Labor Market Transformation, and Union Decline in U.S. Metropolitan Areas." *Labor Studies Journal*, vol. 38, no. 3, Sept. 2013, pp. 229–55. *EBSCOhost*, https://doi-org.proxy.cc.uic.edu/10.1177/0160449X13511539. Accessed 18 July 2024.

Vera-Rosas, Gretel H. "Coordinates: A Testimonio on Urban Migration, Mothering, and Teacher." *The Chicana M(other)work Anthology*. Edited by Cecilia Caballero et al. University of Arizona Press, 2019, pp. 58–76.

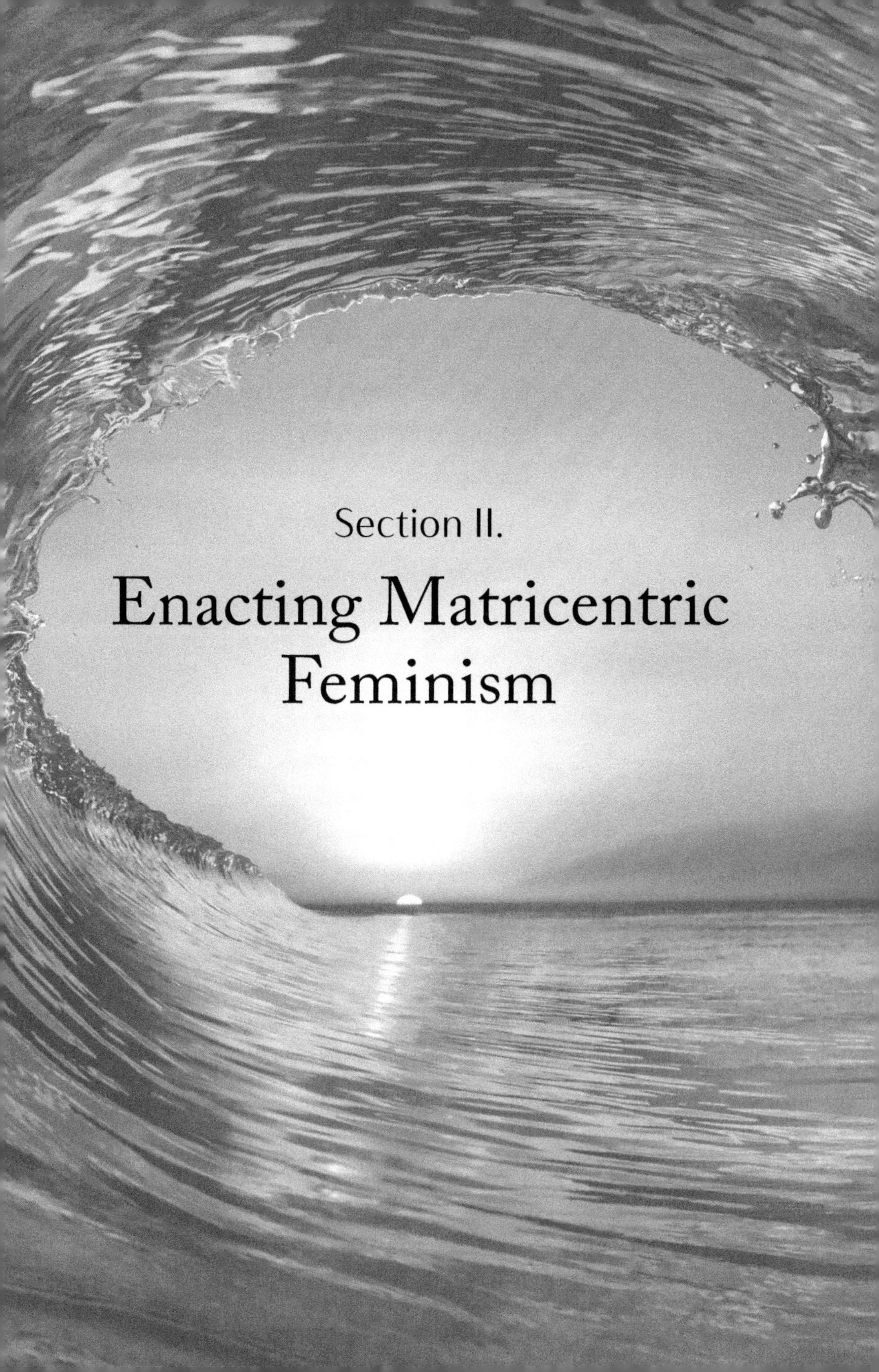

Section II.

Enacting Matricentric Feminism

8.

The Theory and Praxis of Matricentric Feminism in the Lives of Motherhood Studies Certification Course Participants

Sophie Brock

This chapter tells part of my own story of how I developed a praxis of matricentric feminism through my mothering and career, involving the creation of an online motherhood studies professional development course. In this chapter, I share the foundational core of the course—a sociological understanding of motherhood as hegemony described through the analogy of a fish tank. I detail three key findings from the qualitative research I conducted with fourteen graduates from the online course. The research investigated the ways that matricentric feminism has been enacted, created, and explored in participants' own mothering experiences as well as their professional work in supporting other mothers. The first finding explored in this chapter details how matricentric feminism has helped participants contextualize their lived experience as mothers and make visible the social structures they live within, key in breaking down their experiences of shame. The second finding is that education about the perfect mother myth and support in exploring socialization into patriarchal motherhood led to participants' (perceived) diminished guilt, (perceived) enhanced confidence, and facilitated compassion towards themselves and others. The third finding explored is that by initiating and developing matricentric praxis through their lives and work, participants claimed new relationships with feminism and positioned their mothering as a site of activism and power. Through sharing these findings, drawing on the words of mothers interviewed, and sharing parts of my own lived experience, the following chapter demonstrates how waves of matricentric feminism are being realized, enacted, and expanded in theory, activism, and practice across the world.

I became a mother a week after I received the email awarding me my PhD in sociology, specializing in motherhood studies. I focussed my research on the lived experiences, identities, and relationships of mothers of children with disabilities. From the research, I developed a theory on how the social structure of motherhood operated as a form of hegemony in shaping individual mothers' lives, relationships, identities, and experiences. Part of what I learned was how our socialization as mothers into patriarchal motherhood is fluid, and we straddle many paradoxes as we make our way through motherhood and construct our way into our mother identity.

My path to becoming a mother was lined with scholarly feminist literature, such as Adrienne Rich, Sara Ruddick, Andrea O'Reilly, and Patricia Hill Collins. I knew about the perfect mother myth, the concept of the "good mother," and how the new momism has infiltrated its way into our culture and psyches. I knew about Sharon Hays's work on intensive mothering and how it manifests in the day-to-day lives of mothers. I knew about the ways guilt operated as a tool of patriarchal self-surveillance. I knew about the undoing and remaking of identity and was fascinated by maternal subjectivity and the work of Nancy Chodorow, Petra Bueskens, Lisa Baraitser, and Suzanne Juhaz.

Part of the work I needed to do in writing my dissertation was to blend theory and data from lived experience, make connections, and create anew. Part of the work I needed to do in becoming a mother was to blend theory and the realities of my emerging lived experience, make connections, and create anew.

Shortly after I gave birth, my marriage ended unexpectedly, and I felt like the ground I knew had been pulled out from underneath me. The disorientation of early mothering that I thought I had known about intellectually and had prepared for as best I could became a new type of disorientation in processing the loss of my relationship, what I thought life had been, and what I had imagined as possible for our future. That was six years ago, and I've been asked how my knowledge of motherhood studies and matricentric feminism affected or helped me through that period of upheaval, disorientation, and transition. It can be difficult and messy work, looking back at the past and trying to piece together a story that most closely resembles the truth based on my memory and perspective alone.

At the time, I wasn't consciously connecting with maternal theory. I wasn't having conversations about matricentric feminism. I wasn't engaged in how I could make meaning from what I was living through or how I could help others. I was in it and focussed on putting one foot in front of the other or getting through one feed to the next, one wake-up to the next.

I turned to matriarchs, mentors, and my mother. I listened to the wisdom of others' lived experiences to help me connect with my inner knowing. I centred myself to centre my daughter, I fought for our mother-baby dyad to be protected and to help facilitate the relationship between my daughter and her dad.

I didn't want to be robbed of the preciousness of the presence of my much-longed-for baby. I tried as much as I could to be present with her. I learned how to mother and care for my baby while I was being listened to and cared for by my mother and sister. I pulled things apart to try to piece together something new. I was grieving, connecting, gathering information, and using my voice through writing. I had set up a private blog where I posted poetry and journaling to try and untangle my thoughts. All my entries were typed on my phone while breastfeeding late at night.

What I can see now as I reflect on my emerging mother self is how I was constructing my matrifocal narrative to help make sense of what I was experiencing and who I was becoming. O'Reilly coined the term "matrifocal narrative" (*Matricentric Feminism* 45), borrowing from Miriam Johnson's discussion of matrifocality, and suggests that a matrifocal perspective can be used as a tool for unmasking, exploring, and redefining.

My orientation to myself, my daughter, close relationships, the broader social world, the process of my divorce and building of a new relationship with my daughter's father, my work, my creativity, and my voice were grounded in an embodiment of matricentric feminism, which O'Reilly defines as a feminism that positions "mothers' needs and concerns as the starting point for a theory and politics on and for women's empowerment" ("Matricentric Feminism" 13). I am grateful that I had already fought against and spoken back to my own internalized policer of patriarchal motherhood before becoming a mother. I knew my mothering was valuable. I knew I existed beyond my role and identity as a mother. I knew my mothering should not be my sole responsibility, but I also knew the value and power of my knowledge and knowing as my daughter's mother. I knew and could see how structures and systems were impeding me and all the ways that I was privileged. Not only did I know that motherhood was a site of oppression, but I also realized that my journey of becoming a mother could also be my site of power.

When my daughter turned two, I started my own business. I needed to generate income, and I also wanted to make something of my PhD research and pursue my dreams of becoming an academic. Various factors meant I felt it would be too difficult to pursue a university position; as an alternative, I decided to start my own online business sharing my reflections, journey, and what I'd learned through my PhD. I also started a podcast and created an Instagram page to share some of my writing, started building an online community, and eventually created online courses and programs for mothers. I ran an online community called The Liberated Motherhood Membership and each week recorded a live video training on a mother-related topic. One week, I wanted to share my theoretical findings from my dissertation. In trying to find a way to talk about how the hegemony of motherhood is formed and operates, I came up with an analogy of a fish tank.

I asked those watching to visualize a round glass tank and imagine that the tank represents society. The fish inside represents mothers. The fish swimming are mothers doing their mothering—motherwork (Collins 373). And the water represents the culture. Particular rules of idealized motherhood are written on the tank and come to flavour the water (culture) we're swimming (living) within. The fish (mothers) have their identity and self-perception shaped by what they see reflected at them from the tank (society) and how their swimming (mothering) is shaped by the tank (society, structures, and institutions).

The Tank = Our Society

The Fish = Mothers

The Water = Our Socialisation

The Swimming = Practice of Mothering

During the live teaching, community members could type comments as I spoke. One member was Dr. Haya Zedan, an academic in public health specializing in maternal mental health and wellness, based in Saudi Arabia. In talking about the importance of creating change in the "tank" (society), Dr. Zedan commented on the movement of the "fish" (mothers), and the need to reconceptualize our understanding of the collective power of mothers and how they might consciously shift the ways we mother, work, manage relationships, and seek education.

My aim through the membership, podcast, and courses was to break down the theory into smaller teachings or analogies and share them with mothers in a way that could create a difference in their lived experiences and sense of fulfilment and empowerment as mothers. But if I wanted to make a bigger impact, I would have to teach mothers about the social construction of motherhood and the professionals and practitioners who support mothers. I thought: What if I could create a course that taught this fish tank model and key pieces of maternal scholarship and information to mother-supporting professionals all over the world? I hoped they could apply this work on the ground with the mothers they support.

This led to the creation of The Motherhood Studies Practitioner Certification, an online education program teaching the sociological foundations of the social construction of motherhood and an overview of key motherhood studies teachings across eight content modules: sociological foundations (the fish tank model); power and performance (assessing cultural messaging); the socioeconomics of motherhood (institutionalized marginalization); identity and self-creation as mothers (maternal subjectivity); motherhood as relational (the sociology of the family and sex-based inequality); mental labour and emotions (maternal thinking, the mental load, and the anger guilt trap); revolutionizing motherhood (matricentric feminism and liberated motherhood); and motherhood visionaries (a business and practice-based module for integrating content). While matricentric feminism is taught explicitly in the seventh module, the pedagogical underpinning of the entire course is built upon the foundations of matricentric feminism and a matrifocal approach.

I first ran the program in September 2020, and at the time of writing this chapter, I am running the fifth round of the now six-month-long course. The program has been taught to over one hundred participants from twenty countries, including mothers, psychologists, social workers, psychotherapists, parent educators, human resources professionals, physiotherapists, coaches, nongovernment and government organizations, corporations, and small business owners. The course offers scholarships and subsidized positions to support diversity and equity of access. Examples of scholarship recipients include single mothers, mothers from developing nations, Black mothers, mothers building their businesses after escaping domestic violence, those experiencing housing instability, mothers of children with disabilities, and disabled mothers.

At the end of 2022, I sent an invitation and initial survey to all course participants from rounds one, two, three, and four, inviting them to be part of a study I was conducting on course participants' experiences and practices of matricentric feminism. The criteria for inclusion in the study were that a participant was a mother, had previously or was currently working in the motherhood-support space, and had finished their coursework. There were initially twenty-five people who expressed interest in participating in the study, and fourteen of these were interviewed.

I followed a semistructured interview guide exploring their motherhood expectations, their matrescence journey, their introduction to motherhood studies, their experience of paid work, their understanding of matricentric feminism, and the impact of matricentric feminism on their life and careers. Participants were from Australia, the United Kingdom (UK), New Zealand, the United States (US), and Saudi Arabia. Each had children, with the youngest being four months old and the oldest twenty-two years old. Two participants were also pregnant with subsequent children at the time of our interview. They worked in a range of positions, including birth educators, social workers, academics, doulas, speech-language pathologists, parent educators, and small business owners.

All participants signed consent forms and were given participant information sheets; the interviews were audio and video recorded. I transcribed the interviews and then relistened to all of them. I recorded initial notes, manually coded data through the transcripts, and completed thematic analysis to identify predominant and consistent emerging themes. Three predominant themes emerged, demonstrating the matricentric feminism waves being realized, enacted, created, and explored in micro and macro ways.

Below, I provide a brief overview of findings for the first two themes and then turn to a more detailed coverage of the third theme that is most pertinent to the focus of this chapter.

1. Language and the power of words: Matricentric feminism helped to contextualize individual experience and make social structures visible. This contextualizing was key in breaking down experiences of shame.

Matricentric feminism enabled participants to contextualize and locate the challenges they and their clients face as mothers, which provided validation, affirmation, a relieved sense of personal failure, and a perceived individual inadequacy. Being able to name a concept, theory, field of study (i.e., motherhood studies) and form and mode of resistance (i.e., matricentric feminism) was instrumental for participants in several ways.

Emily is a clinical associate professor, speech-language pathologist, and mother of two daughters, five and eight, and speaks beautifully about the power of naming: "Having the name for things, made it real, or more real or three dimensional ... I felt things in the dark—of guilt and shame—but I didn't realize it was because I was internalizing surveillance." Part of what was so powerful for participants in having the language of matricentric feminism meant they were not alone in their experiences of these challenges.

But even more than this, the power of naming concepts and social phenomena when it comes to the marginalization and othering that mothers experience meant that participants could place themselves as individuals within their broader social context. This enabled them to identify the reason for their struggles and challenges. It was not that they were inadequate, failing, or not good enough, but that the systems they lived within had been failing them. Their lived experience was part of a broader collective social pattern.

Keturah, a mother of two sons, one a teenager and the other a young adult, is a postpartum doula who supports mothers with their infants, provides baby massage classes, and runs a meal delivery service. She said that the expectation that good mothers provide self-sacrificial care for their children has been dominant in her mothering experience, but that learning about the perfect mother myth and matricentric feminism "has really put a language and meaning behind things that maybe you've internalized and thought you were the only one doing."

Like Keturah, Brielle is also a mother and is self-employed working in motherhood support. She is a social worker who offers one-to-one and group counselling online and in person. She shared the ways that knowing matricentric feminism provides an underpinning for how she navigates discussions with her clients. Brielle shared examples of using a model from the certification called "growth through guilt," which helps mothers to situate their experiences of guilt and explore whether it reflects their values or is a symptom of patriarchal motherhood. When Brielle shared with her clients a diagram of this model, they recognized it: "They can just see it on a model like that ... it makes it clearer for them to see how things are connected. And that it's not just them ... I've had tears from some moms. I can see it and feel it in their body; there's a bit of a [sighs, drops shoulders], almost a sigh of releasing something but also a sadness a bit as well, I think."

When I prompted Brielle to reflect more on that sense of sadness she perceives, she said: "I see a little bit of relief that it's not just me, some sadness, and then an anger comes out ... you know, well, why don't we know these things? Why are we set up to—I guess "fail" is not quite the word—but experience this? And feel like we're failing and feel like it's just us."

Having the capacity to name and frame mothers' lived experiences provides validation and reassurance, but it can also be a key step in collectivization and mobilization. We need to name and speak about the realities of our daily lives and the specifics of our challenges to connect with others who share similar experiences, and to educate nonmothers.

O'Reilly argues that "The patriarchal institution of motherhood, as a normative discourse, restrains women's power to challenge and change the oppressiveness of their motherhood experience" (*Matricentric Feminism* 58). But by naming and conceptualizing matricentric feminism, she has provided a key tool of resistance that mothers can pick up and use to understand themselves and their experiences and to resist the normative discourse of patriarchal motherhood through shared use and understanding of the language.

2. Education about the perfect mother myth and support in exploring participants' socialization into patriarchal motherhood led to (perceived) diminished guilt and (perceived) enhanced confidence, facilitating participants' compassion towards others and themselves.

The first module of the course asks participants to imagine what the rules of patriarchal motherhood are by reflecting on what they believe their society and culture celebrate as ideal motherhood. We write, discuss, compare, and reflect on all the "shoulds" existing in society that are internalized by mothers. Unpacking the rules of the perfect mother myth was a key area of discussion within the interviews. Decades of research have shown the existence of a socially constructed ideal of the good mother that can shift and change according to culture, location, and historical period. The myth promotes rules about who a mother should be, how she should behave, what she should look like, and how she should feel and think.

Participants reflected on how they had internalized the pressures of the perfect mother myth rules—particularly as new mothers—and on their experience in "shedding the should" and coming to reclaim motherhood more closely defined and aligned with their values. For example, Nada is a thirty-three-year-old Palestinian woman living in Saudi Arabia, who was pregnant at the time of our interview and mother to a five-year-old. She said learning about "the perfect mother myth [in the course] was a wake-up call." Learning about the perfect mother myth and how mothers internalize it shifted her experience "drastically," making her "go lighter" on herself.

Mandy, a mother to three children, one of whom has cerebral palsy, said the following: "I had a real sense that people were judging my mothering right from the beginning. When things didn't go to plan, I felt that was a reflection of my efforts ... as if I wasn't doing it 'right.' I wouldn't think—why is my baby feeling like this or not feeding? Instead, it was: What did I put in my food, or what's in my milk ... I really personalized that I wasn't doing enough and put more on my list." Mandy said she now experiences reduced guilt and greater agency as a mother, but it can be difficult when the environment around her hasn't shifted: "Having found my voice and having stepped into my power, sometimes I just feel like I'm standing calmly with the storm around me—and watching now instead of being swept up in it. And that's a very liberating shift."

Both Nada's and Mandy's comments reflect cultural narratives of who the good mother is, especially when it comes to how children behave, eat, and sleep. These narratives shape how mothers are perceived and how they perceive themselves and the world around them. This was a theme present across all interviews, and participants spoke in various ways about how they moved through a process of unpacking internalized beliefs to move into a greater sense of alignment and power; they then experienced less guilt and self-judgment and greater empathy for others. However, they recognized their continued challenge while living within the institution of motherhood (Rich).

During the process of (un)learning within the certification, Emily said she felt her previous sense of identity "could no longer stand" and she felt a "crumbling of the self," where there were many elements of her former beliefs that she "ditched" because she realized how "bogus" they were in light of understanding the perfect mother myth. Emily said that when she was able to work through and process her internalized "guilt guard" of patriarchal motherhood, she had succeeded in "kind of liberating" herself. Connecting with their inner voice and understanding of the structural and social function of maternal guilt allowed participants to identify and, at times, resist the guilt working on behalf of patriarchal motherhood.

Several participants invoked the idea of zooming in and zooming out to refer to their learning journey with motherhood studies and understanding matricentric feminism. Lucy, a career coach for mothers, said: "[Learning about matricentric feminism] gives me that understanding of the big zooming out. And that understanding helps me to zoom back into myself and ground myself. This technique is used in mindful meditation, And I hope to be able to offer that to other people, too ... the course made me even more empathetic." And Keturah said: "Although the expectations that are placed on mothers are unjust, the awareness of this is liberating. Education is power. This has been so powerful, and I don't believe I could have navigated and still navigate the very challenging issues that have arisen in my current season of motherhood with grace and self-compassion without this education."

The self-compassion experienced by participants was also reflected in the stories they told about their mother-supporting work, where they emphasized the importance of empathy in their teaching and facilitation. Emily reflected on the important role that her students will play as future speech pathology clinicians in being potential enforcers of institutionalized patriarchal motherhood: "[I] have my students be aware of the role and the power that [they] wield by being a part of the hegemony and being a part of the surveillance." They must cultivate genuine relationships with parents to minimize the potential of mothers feeling they need to hold up the mask of perfect motherhood.

The waves of matricentric feminism continue to ripple out far beyond what can be fully realized as participants use education of the institution of motherhood, fuelled by matricentric feminism, to cultivate awareness and empathy in their students and clients.

3. By initiating and developing matricentric praxis through their lives and work, participants claimed new relationships with feminism and positioned mothering as a site of activism and power.

Many participants described a renewed relationship with feminism since becoming mothers and shared the ways this relationship evolved as they became mothers and eventually discovered matricentric feminism. Grace G works in the US creating arts movement programs to support new mothers with their mental health, but she first discovered matricentric feminism six months after having her baby. She became a mother during the height of the pandemic in Los Angeles and said all of her pregnancy was "in near isolation," as she lived in a small high-rise apartment. She only had contact with OBGYN and her partner. In the early stages of mothering, Grace G experienced what she now recognizes as postpartum anxiety and rage:

> I started after about six months going, okay, I can't keep feeling like this, something has to be wrong with me. So I started doing my own research that led me to matricentric feminism and Andrea O'Reilly, and I just got deeper and deeper into that. The more I read, the more I felt like I could let myself off the hook a little bit for what I was feeling. I didn't have to feel so alone and all of those feelings. So all of that led me to this deep, deep interest and the entire realm of motherhood studies that was happening. And why is every other mother not aware of this because it would make it so much easier on them as an individual person.

A sense of validation and being able to see themselves within feminism was echoed through Bridget's experience. Bridget is a mother of three and works as a motherhood coach, mentor, and guide in the conscious parenting space. She said that while she defined herself as a "staunch feminist" throughout university in her twenties, when she became a mother she felt "like feminism devalued motherhood and saw it as a place where women waste away." These feelings made her "resent feminism a little bit for leaving it [motherhood] out of the equation" because she believed it could be a huge journey of empowerment, awakening, and growth for women.

Bridget said that matricentric feminism "is critical to make feminism relevant to women who become mothers and who want to value mothering" and talked about the juxtaposition between what is defined as valuable by economic systems rooted in capitalist patriarchal systems with what is defined as valuable for "this child, this woman, for the emotional health of human beings?"

Ashley is a mother and a social worker who similarly reflected on her changing relationship to feminism from her university studies through to her experience of mothering. She asked: "How do I mother as a feminist when I'm role modelling to boys?" She discussed the ways feminism for her was "about the coming back to values, self-defined." She went on: "I guess that grounding of what liberated motherhood aligns with and acknowledging what choice looks like in a false choice economy... I was no longer independent in the way that I viewed independence ... and so that kind of was the beginning of reassessing [of] what does feminism look like for me."

Sarah is also a social worker, is a mother of two girls, and was pregnant during our interview. Like Bridget and Ashley, she reflected on how her connection with feminism shifted throughout her life. She felt "more closed off to feminism" in her twenties than now: "I feel much more aligned with feminist theory now. I feel like it's more directly applicable to me as an individual. I can see that there's a real role for matricentric feminism moving forward to empower women globally and be fairly inclusive and intersectional as well."

Sarah's comments are illustrative of Ann Crittenden's observation: "Once a woman has a baby, the egalitarian office party is over" (88). Becoming a mother, and therefore becoming subject to the institution of motherhood in a new way, is oppressive and marginalizing in ways that some women have had enough privilege to seemingly avoid. Sarah reflected on this: "I'm a white heterosexual female from a relatively privileged background. It wasn't until I hit motherhood that I realized that there are disadvantages that I can face in my life as a female, as a woman, that I hadn't felt that very much prior ... it wasn't until I had a sense of losing myself, losing a financial income, and a sense of professional identity, that I was much more aware of how those things can affect me."

Emily also demonstrated reflexive practice in thinking about her cultural positioning. As a half-Mexican woman with "white presenting features," she felt disempowered as a mother and validated in learning about matricentric feminism: "I felt so seen as someone who had thought of herself as a feminist and yet felt so disempowered as a mother. I had done the exact thing that I had been told to do ... And to realize you are a second-class citizen." It was through Emily's reflections on the positioning of herself within the "tank"—our social structure—that she came to understand more deeply the intersectionality of oppression: "That is like a vision, a prescription upgrade that I can't, I cannot unsee and nor do I want to. But motherhood studies is just like that, like a new prescription lens after prescription lens of how you see the world and that architecture ... it was like turning on a black light, and all of a sudden you can see all these things you couldn't previously see before, all these connections that have always been there."

How matricentric feminism was integrated into participants' own lives and work with mothers was experienced in varying ways depending on a participants' cultural context. In Dr. Zedan's social and cultural context of the Middle East, which is undergoing significant changes, integrating a matricentric perspective or lens is in "its very early days, as feminism has been misunderstood and considered a taboo in many respects," as Dr. Zedan said.

Dr. Zedan discussed the intricacies of the Middle Eastern cultural context and the educational and technology-literacy barriers for women to engage in learning about matricentric feminist theory, unlike the way it is more readily accessible in the West. Dr. Zedan integrated aspects of matricentric feminism into her public health work and research with mothers by focussing on mothers:

> From a public health perspective, when women are well in themselves, and they understand themselves, and they understand their physiology and understand their rights and their responsibilities

> and understand what it means to be a mother and how to handle motherhood in a better way, it has an impact on her mental and emotional health and wellbeing, and therefore she will be able to better take care of her children, which impacts everything else entirely.

In this way, the waves of matricentric feminism are creating ripples in culturally relevant and adaptive ways, and mothers and mother-supporting professionals are actively crafting ways to embed matricentric feminism within their work. Nada, for example, used her role as a birth educator—and through her social media platform—to push back against the normative cultural story of how mothers should be. Nada talked about some of the feedback and private messages she received from women in her community who thanked her for sharing this information: "This is what I want them to feel; that it's okay to say no. It's okay to raise your son differently to how your husband or your brother or your father was raised."

A matricentric feminist perspective was drawn on and recognized in both subtle and explicit ways by participants. Alison, a mother of two, a former speech and language pathologist, and now a doula and women's circle facilitator, said matricentric feminism drives her mother-supporting work: "Putting mothers first, that's what ignites passion in me." This ignited passion is something that participants integrated into the mothering of their children, and many expressed their desire to contribute to cultural change for other mothers. Andrea, a career coach for mothers from the US said: "For me, having the lens around motherhood studies has just meant that I can actually share that knowledge with other women to say, we are not broken, it is not our responsibility to fix it all. Mothering and doing it in a different way, is a form of resistance, and that is exciting."

Such resistance was enacted through participants' mothering and their paid work. As Keturah said: "As a mother of boys, I realize that I have a unique opportunity to show them that being a mother is also being a human. That in the context of a family, the domestic workload is shared by all members. I role model self-care and having dreams, interests, and passions that are unrelated to being a mother." About her role as a postpartum doula, she said: "It brings me a lot of joy and satisfaction to know that I am facilitating a woman's wellbeing and to bring a little respite to what is otherwise a relentless, often thankless role."

However, the vocalizing of participants' needs as mothers, and how this filtered through their work, was sometimes met with resistance. Lucy shared an experience of delivering a workshop on guilt within a corporate environment where the existence of intensive mothering ideology was refuted. Such resistance may reflect a reaction to matricentric feminism in how it contests normative narratives of motherhood. Some mothers may not have the capacity, space, or support to acknowledge or resist the constraints placed on them.

Participants came to develop and hone modes of resistance to patriarchal motherhood and reconceptualized their own past experiences of mothering through the lens of rebellious or courageous mothering (O'Reilly *Matricentric Feminism*). Brielle became a single mother when she was eighteen years old and said that in hindsight, she could see how because of her age, she was already positioned as a bad mother and that she actively resisted the label: "I had a bit of like, no, just watch me—I'm gonna like, I'm gonna be okay."

Participants could reframe, reimagine, and rethink their past experiences of mothering and frame their mothering as a catalyst for both personal and professional growth. Grace T, a pregnancy and postpartum doula and mother of two, said: "The person that I am now, because of the work of mothering them—it's fulfilling." Grace T also spoke about her positioning of her mothering as a site of activism, particularly through the ways she supports her children in healthily processing their emotions and the potential intergenerational impacts of this "is a kid that can name his feelings, can be angry, can ask me for a cuddle ... again, it's just another way that we can sort of turn the dial."

Through motherhood studies and drawing on matricentric feminism, participants could situate their role as mothers and professionals as a site of power, resistance, and a catalyst for growth and change making. They absorbed the key teachings of matricentric feminism and formed a praxis for both their mothering and careers.

Conclusion

These course graduates have enacted the teachings of matricentric feminism into their lives in diverse ways. Participants have generated a matricentric praxis that contests the structures of patriarchal motherhood and contributes to creating new modes and forms of empowered mothering.

The power of language was the research's first theme, as participants described how matricentric feminism and motherhood studies helped to contextualize their individual experiences. Having a shared language enables participants to recognize the potential of shared experience and provides evidence that their individual experiences are part of a cultural pattern. This contextualizing was a catalyst for breaking down internalized shame when mothers feel as though their struggles are due to their failings or not being good enough. Instead, they could situate their experience in the context of broader structural failures of patriarchal motherhood.

After experiencing the validation that having shared language can provide, participants spoke about the experience of unpacking their internalization of the perfect mother myth. This involved them actively reflecting on their mothering values, their sense of diminished guilt, and their greater confidence. They could reflexively look back on their mothering history with greater self-compassion. Understanding how the perfect mother myth is operationalized through guilt and understanding this guilt as the "guard" of patriarchal motherhood helped participants dismantle and speak back to some of their inner voices of self-regulation and self-policing. This bolstered their sense of strength and agency as mothers and their passion for sharing these teachings and processes with the mothers they support and others in their communities. Participants communicated a deep empathy and compassion for other mothers; they felt connected to a broader social movement of revolutionizing current cultural conceptions of motherhood.

Finally, participants demonstrated how they have initiated, developed, and created matricentric praxis through both their mothering practices and their careers and businesses. In reflecting on their relationships to feminism, participants expressed the pressing need for matricentric feminism in their lives, work, and the world more broadly. The work done by these graduates is testimony to O'Reilly's view: "There is no doubt that a twenty-first century motherhood movement exists. But because it has developed and has expressed itself in ways that do not conform to accepted, traditional, and, more specifically, masculine norms and practices of activism, it remains for many difficult to define and classify" (140).

Some of the other participants in the course who are also making waves of impact include a mother-supporting coach in Slovenia running group programs; a women's circle guide and activist in Kenya sharing resources of support within her community and providing practical support and postpartum care; neuroscientists in Canada and the US combining their motherhood studies training to understand changes in the maternal brain and infant mental health; as well as mother-supporting career coaches across Australia and the UK, psychologists in Uruguay, parent educators in Brazil and Denmark, doulas in New Zealand, academics in the US and Middle East, and women's circle facilitators in France, Portugal, and Egypt.

The waves of matricentric feminism are crashing with power and passion across the world, championing the voices and needs of mothers. Mothers are moving towards liberation through their maternal practices as mothers themselves and through their careers, businesses, and professions. Mothering itself can act as both a catalyst for deeper inquiry and as a "dynamic place for creativity" where mothers "can successfully confront the rules and ideology of motherhood and rework the mould of this patriarchal institution" (Green, 95).

Matricentric feminism helped guide me in my own experience as a mother, prompted me to create The Motherhood Studies Practitioner Certification, and helps me facilitate the courses. This is an example of an evolving and emerging praxis, which moves into new iterations as more course participants take this work and weave it throughout their lives and work. Emily powerfully encapsulated this potential while reflecting on the changes she witnessed in her teaching her university students about motherhood and matricentric feminism:

> It's a real honour to be a part of the wave ... [and] a wave is always building and changing where it has its kinetic energy. And so... seeing myself as one of those atoms of kinetic energy, and then being able to see them and witness and cherish the moments of transmission to my students is such a gift ... to whatever extent they may not remember where they heard it from or how they heard it, but it has at least literally washed over them with this wave, and with that baptism, they're different.

With matricentric feminism, we are changed, and we are initiated into becoming change makers. Within the words, work, and stories of mothers and mother-supporting activists, business owners, creatives, entrepreneurs, professionals, and artists, we find hope for the future of matricentric feminism and the ripples that will continue to be felt across the world, with a purpose of creating a more just, free, safe, and supportive world for mothers and their families.

Works Cited

Baraitser, Lisa. *Maternal Encounters: The Ethics of Interruption.* Routledge, 2009.

Bueskens, Petra. *Mothering and Psychoanalysis: Clinical, Sociological & Feminist Perspectives.* Demeter Press, 2014.

Chodorow, Nancy. *The Reproduction of Mothering: Psychoanalysis and the Sociology of Gender.* The Regents of the University of California, 1978.

Collins, Patricia Hill. *Black Feminist Thought: Knowledge, Consciousness, and the Politics of Empowerment.* 2nd edition. Routledge, 2002.

Collins, Patricia Hill. "Shifting the Center: Race, Class, and Feminist Theorizing about Motherhood." *Representations of Motherhood.* Edited by Donna Bassin. Yale University Press, 1994, pp. 371–88.

Crittenden, Ann. *The Price of Motherhood: Why the Most Important Job in the World Is Still the Least Valued.* Metropolitan Books/Henry Holt and Company, 2001.

Green, Fiona Joy. "Practicing Matricentric Feminist Mothering". *Journal of the Motherhood Initiative*, vol. 10, nos. 1&2, 2019, pp. 83–99.

Hays, Sharon. *The Cultural Contradictions of Motherhood.* Yale University Press, 1996.

O'Reilly, Andrea. *Matricentric Feminism: Theory, Activism, Practice.* 2nd edition. Demeter Press, 2021.

Rich, Adrienne. *Of Woman Born: Motherhood as Experience and Institution.* Norton, 1976.

Ruddick, Sara. *Maternal thinking: Toward a Politics of Peace.* Beacon Press, 1989.

9.

I Am Becoming My Mother: Conjuring Black Motherhood on Our Own Terms

Sheree Mack

Figure 1. *i go to the sea to heal*, 2022, mixed media artist book (acyclic paint, collage papers, ink, stickers, stencils, watercolour paper).

I am becoming my mother.

Dehumanizing the Black woman. Mammy, Jezebel, Sapphire, Bitch.
The Black woman
is seen always as resilient and strong. The mule of the world, mothering all others
except her own. Her children are lost, lost to the auction block, the ocean,
the noose. A Black mother is a source of wisdom and love.
Conjuring, passing on power as well as pain. Her body carries stories,
carries histories, carries an archive.

as a Black woman
resting deep within the meadow
held in softness grass tickling shins
dress billowing about *like blossom is a*
political act.

Figure 2. Four generations of mothers. I'm in my mum's belly, circa 1970. (Family archive).

Dehumanizing the Black woman

In the Spring/Fall 2019 issue of *Journal of the Motherhood Initiative*, in her article titled "Matricentric Feminism: A Feminism for Mothers," Andrea O'Reilly states that "mothers are oppressed under patriarchy as women and as mothers" (15) and mother-centred feminism is necessary because mothers remain disempowered in comparison to women in general. When O'Reilly starts from the point that maternity matters as a given—proclaiming that "Mothers, in other words, do not live simply as women but as mother women, just as Black women do not live simply as women but as racialized women" (20)—this is where I have to step in.

"We search for our mothers in search of self" (Michael 29). Unearthing my matrilineage as a Black woman of African descent is a difficult task due to slavery, the lack of reports and documentation for the enslaved individuals, and the basic disregard of my ancestors as human beings. Looking at Black motherhood through a matrilineage lens widens the current writings,[1] imagery, beliefs, and practices around motherhood and mothering that continue to centre white middle-class women's experiences. With this chapter, I acknowledge the oppression of mothers and motherhood but start from the given that Black mothers are oppressed not just under patriarchy but are oppressed as women, as Black women, and as mothers under imperialist, white supremacist, capitalist heteropatriarchy as bell hooks argues: "This phrase, imperialist, white supremacist, capitalist heteropatriarchy, is precisely useful because it doesn't prioritize one system over another but rather offers us a way to think about the interlocking systems that work together to uphold and maintain cultures of domination" (hooks, *Writing* 4). Black matrilineage acknowledges that Black motherhood deserves to be looked at differently.

I provide a space to explore the historical and political construction of "the Black woman" and interrupt standard academic writing style by including creative personal reflections to tell my story on my terms. I insert myself and my matrilineage back into the archives where gaps have occurred and festered. I welcome matricentric feminism, committed to social change and social justice, as a means of providing space within feminism and the academy and society to explore the diversity of maternal experience across race, class, culture, ethnicity, sexuality, ability, age, geographical location, and history (O'Reilly 18).

Because I was born white, my mum rejected me. Because my hair was jet black and straight and my nose was straight, too, my mum told the nurse to take me away. She thought I wasn't her baby. I was born in 1971 in Great Britain to a mixed-race Geordie mother—someone born and brought up in the northeast region of England, with Ghanian and Bajan heritage—and a Trinidadian father just before the Immigration Act of 1971. Under the Heath Conservative government, this act restricted immigration further by introducing the concept of "partiality," meaning that a person has the right to abode, stay, reside, or make a home in the United Kingdom (UK). But in reality, it meant to gain entry into Britain, migrants had to have been born in Britain, to have a parent or grandparent who was born in Britain, or to have lived in Britain for over five years. "Partiality" was brought into the immigration equation as a means of favouring those from the old (white) Commonwealth, such as Australia and New Zealand, rather than the new (Black and brown) Commonwealth. The right to {BE} has never been a given for Black people. I learned long ago that my mum was rejected by her mother. Growing up into adulthood, my mum was forced to live with her nana and was forced out of the family home as her mother mothered other people's babies instead of her own. We've all seen the iconic images of Black women wet nursing white babies within the dominant overview of womanhood and motherhood since slavery.

When I thought I was grown, I moved to London to go to university, rejecting my mum.

Indoctrinated by education, I believed I didn't need to listen to my mum and her superstitious ways. I knew more. I knew everything. Now, with my mum twenty-four years dead, I'm finding my way back. I need to find my way back to survive. Living in an imperialist, white supremacist, capitalist, and heteropatriarchal world, I'm tasked with living in a hostile environment where I'm judged by how I look, not who I am{BE}, receiving daily messages of being out of place and never good enough (17). I'm always trying to get back, get back home. Create home—. Home to a place where I belong and where I'm loved for {BEING} me. Radical self-love, as explored by Sonya Renee Taylor in her book *The Body Is Not An Apology* (2018), mothering myself, is an ongoing work in process and progress. As matricentric feminism recognizes and acknowledges, returning to the source—that is, mothering as first and foremost—has the potential to change not just me but society as a whole.

All my ancestors come from the sea: the Atlantic, Middle Passage, and transoceanic crossings. While I'll never know the exact origins of my people, I explore fluidity as an archive where nothing is fixed, and the entirety will never be known, but knowledge and selfhood will be developed in the process. As M. Jacqui Alexander writes: "Emotional memory. Bodily memory. Sacred memory" (290). The trauma of slavery has been haunting us, haunted us, our beings, and our aliveness. I know my first home was my mum, her womb, and her waters. Water. "Water flows with memory" (290), as Alexander writes. Conjuring the opening lines from Grace Nichols's poetic homage to her mother, "Praise Song for My Mother": "You were / water to me / deep and bold and fathoming" (24). In the words of Mindy Tsonas, who advocates for collective belonging, "We all already belong."

Mammy, Jezebel, Sapphire, Bitch

In *Black Feminist Thought: Knowledge, Consciousness, and the Politics of Empowerment*, Patricia Hill Collins examines the issue of "controlling images" of Black women:

> As part of a generalized ideology of domination, stereotypical images of Black womanhood take on special meaning. Because the authority to define societal values is a major instrument of power, elite groups, in exercising power, manipulate ideas about Black womanhood.... These controlling images are designed to make racism, sexism, poverty, and other forms of social injustice appear to be natural, normal, and inevitable parts of everyday life. Even when the initial conditions that foster controlling images disappear, such images prove remarkably tenacious. (69)

If matricentric feminism understands motherhood to be socially and historically constructed, the lived reality of Black women has to be seen as the driving force in challenging the assumption that maternity is the natural identity of women. These images were born in slavery but are still used by dominant society to subordinate Black women. These "controlling images" have become narratives played out within the media, literature, photography, and education through which Black women have been perceived negatively by others and ourselves. These images—mammy, jezebel, sapphire, and bitch—have cemented in Western society's imagination that Black women are unfit mothers and Black motherhood is a social ill to be curtailed. A Black mother is invisible and dehumanized while her own experience as a mother is denied.

Within British society, the lowest of the low is the baby mother. She is the mother of one or more of a man's children and who is not his wife or current partner (Brathwaite 2). Having a baby out of wedlock to multiple men and being a single black mother are branded as shameful, demeaning, and something to be avoided. It is a label assigned to black motherhood which left no room for their multifaceted journeys and experiences. The baby mother stereotype lies on top of a series of other stereotypes and beliefs projected onto Black women that I'm trying as a Black woman and mother to escape.

The asexual mammy is a dutiful, happy-go-lucky, and soft-bodied caregiver, grateful to look after other people's babies. The perfect slave. She loves her white family, wet nursing good, yessir. But this position didn't stem from the belief of her maternal skills because she was still directed and controlled in her mothering duties by the white mistress of the house. Sapphire, the matriarch, is aggressive and strikes fear in her children. The jezebel is hypersexual and lascivious, the site of sexual diseases (Gilman).

Let's get one thing straight here about the sheer horror of being an enslaved Black woman.

These popular myths were constructed to justify the sexual abuse of Black women by white men. Black women were raped by white men and enslaved men daily for control, breeding, profit, and fun. Violence was perpetuated against the Black female body to bring forth babies that would be ripped from their arms to be sold. How this must have felt, how to live this way, I cannot imagine because I freeze at rape. It was thought Black women were unrapeable because their bodies are made ready and willing for sex. These stereotypes were deliberately and systematically perpetuated after slavery ended for the state to continue to control and abuse Black women's bodies. As Marly Pierre-Louis observes, "The thread that unites these images in our imagination is the enduring idea that black mothers are inherently 'bad' and incapable of having loving bonds with their children" (84). The Black woman was also placed in opposition to the virtuous, pure, and ideal (white) woman and mother.

Figure 3. There Is Much Disruption after Ingrid Pollard, 2022, digital collage.

A final layer that can be placed over these controlling images of Black women from the contemporary context is that of the Mothers of the Movement, which extends these stereotypes further. Started after the acquittal of George Zimmerman for the unlawful killing of teenager Trayvon Martin in 2013, to raise awareness around police brutality in the US, Mothers of the Movement is the publicly projected image of Black mothers in perpetual mourning who are also judged for their failure to protect their children from harm. Mother-focussed feminism argues that maternity matters more than gender and that in terms of the workforce and pay, for example, mothers hit a "maternal wall" (O'Reilly 15). What I'm attempting to bring into focus is Black mothers do not have the luxury or energy to focus on work issues while their humanity is still brought into question daily due to these prevailing, dehumanizing stereotypes.

The Black woman is always seen as resilient and strong

You go to the sea to heal. When you overcome your fears to enter the North Sea, you do so knowing within your body, you will be held by the waters. You fall in love with the sea after suffering a miscarriage. The sea, just like Mother Nature, does not judge or reject you. She accepts you in all your messed-up glory. She heals you. You have to be present when you enter the cold waters. You must be present in your body, feeling all the feels, as you are wrapped in a cold caress, which soothes and awakens you. Here with the sea—"a watery body whose history continually splashes into the present" (Alexander 290)—I realize a Black woman is never seen in her entirety.

I didn't see you, mum. I stripped you of all identity and personage before I came along, an absent presence. When it came to you, I had blind spots. Still do. To imagine you before I was born is inconceivable. To think you had a life before me, that you too were once a little Black girl with dreams of love, motherhood, and careers, never crossed my mind. To imagine you enjoying a relationship with nature, especially as I've just begun my own (re)connection with nature in the past few years, is difficult to grasp. But you can't see what you're not looking for, can you? And I didn't see what was in plain sight, your relationship with Mother Earth. You were brought up in a semi-rural village running along the River Tyne. Knowing fragments of you didn't always mean I saw you. But also, I have to wonder, how much were you guarding from me?

Turning to Toni Morrison, I sense "another way of knowing" is needed (342). To journey back to the womb, back to the waters. And to the blood of our mothers. Back to your archived body, mum, to practise this continuous act of conjuring as Marcia Michael argues. To conjure is to imagine, to call to mind, and to remember. Invoking other ways of knowing, like magic, means journeying between what's known and unknown. Where the familiar mum becomes the unfamiliar, coming back again and again in different forms, with wisdom to help me to exist, survive, and thrive.

The mule of the world, mothering all others except her own

At the Northumbria Riviera, I began to explore the liminal shoreline and take refuge in this connection. It is here that the words of artist Ellen Gallagher leave their wake as she "considers the ways in which the Atlantic Ocean wasn't simply a conveyance of the slave trade, it was a geography rife with meaning: a place of transformation from human to cargo, a graveyard for people whose place on land had been called into ruthless question" (qtd. in Miranda).

When my ancestors were kidnapped and stolen from West Africa, enduring the Middle Passage, a liminal space, between countries, cultures and lives, bodies under the force of violence, no Black person arrived at the New World. This horrendous journey was meant to strip enslaved Africans of all identities and humanity. No man, woman, child, mother, father, sister or brother, son, or daughter disembarked the slave ship in the Caribbean and Americas; only property did. There was no distinction between man and woman, all were "ungendered" slaves, to be sold, used, and abused as argued by Hortense Spillers.

Outside of being commodities, there were no Black family, no Black children to be mothered. Through slavery, colonialism, and capitalism, the Black woman was never given a chance to mother, to keep her children close, holding bonds together to make a family whole, therefore, denying their "claims to dominant conceptions of motherhood" (Williams 20). As I allow this to sink in, words from Theresa Hice-Fromille return to reclaim my senses, "Just as slavery reduced the African woman's body to flesh ungendered, it rendered her unmothered" (548).

Her own children are lost

The law partus sequitur ventrem, passed in colonial Virginia in 1662 and then throughout the other English crown colonies in the Americas, translated to "that which is brought forth follows the womb."[4] In practice, this was a mandated doctrine to get around white men having to claim paternity during enslavement. The status of children born to enslaved women would legally be slaves, too. Following Roman civil laws regarding cattle and personal property, a Black child was not kin but the property of the biological (white) father. This ensured the enslaver's right to profit from the sale and labour of Black children. Nowhere within this system were the rights, feelings, or humanity of Black children considered, never mind those of Black mothers. However, children born from the womb of white women were free. White mothers were given the status of mother, while Black mothers were negated. Black mothers were never recognized as having the right to such a status as motherhood. A Black woman would never be a mother to her children. They were breeders, chattel, and dispensable and were solely responsible for labouring for others. This haunts Black mothers to this day; Avery Gordon describes this haunting as a "seething presence" that shapes and meddles with our realities (qtd. in McLemore 48).

I'll not lie. This angers me as wherever I turn, until quite recently, all I see is white middle-class parenting and motherhood. I never see myself reflected as a Black mother of two beautiful human beings who came into this world whole. White middle-class motherhood is the ideal, the standard, with no room for anything else. I'm speaking from a Black female perspective, but what about disabled, Asian, or lesbian mums? Hence, finding the Make Motherhood Diverse account on Instagram provided the space I was craving to breathe and lean into recognition and acceptance.[2] Thank you.

Lost to the auction block, ocean, and noose

"I'm struggling right now, with the stress and everything," said Erica Garner. "The system beats you down to where you can't win" (qtd. in Cauley). Mobilizing for justice after the unlawful killing of her father Eric Garner in 2014 by New York City Police in Staten Island. Erica also died at the hands of the system in December 2017. I have to agree with Jennifer C. Nash when she asserts that "black mothers are in crisis" (29).

Erica, a twenty-seven-year-old mother of two children, died due to heart complications after the birth of her second child. Stroke, heart condition, heart attack, coma, and death. The Reverend Al Sharpton declared Erica died of a broken heart after she couldn't obtain justice for her father, as the police officer who killed him, Daniel Pantaleo, was not indicted (Mays). Erica was let down by the system. But her death is also an indication of how Black women's bodies are treated by racist systems, particularly the medical one, where Black women's concerns about their bodies are not listened to but ignored.

What is alarming and infuriating is that Erica's death after childbirth is not an isolated incident of Black women dying during pregnancy, labour, and after childbirth. In the UK and the United States, Black women are five times more likely to die in childbirth compared to white women.[3] This is a "life or death crisis" facing Black mothers and infants as described by Linda Villarosa in her 2018 *New York Times* article: "Black babies have a 121% increased risk of being stillborn and 50% increased risk of neonatal death (i.e. dying within 28 days after birth) compared to white babies" (qtd. in Brathwaite 105). Thus, Black mothers need feminism in both theory and practice that takes into account their identities and experiences as mothers, which are different and more life-threatening than some other mothers'.[3]

Black women shouldn't be dying in childbirth in the twenty-first century with the advances in medicine. For decades, the reasons for this rise in death rates were placed on the backs of Black women, the victims themselves. Poor health choices, poverty, and lack of self-care, intelligence, and education were given as the causes of this mortality rate. *They're dying, but it's their fault.* I think not.

To fully understand the limitations of Black motherhood, we must first have a reckoning with death. The Black maternal body, a Black woman's body has always been abused because of anti-Blackness and misogynoir. Racism and patriarchy work hand in hand to make sure a Black woman is always operating within a "state of injury" as stated by philosopher Achille Mbembe (McLemore), which is a liminal space between life and death. Two years after the murder of Bibaa Henry and Nicole Smallman in June 2020, the British Metropolitan Police finally apologized to their mother, family, and friends for their murdered bodies being photographed by police officers and shared with the tag "dead birds" (qtd. in Dodd).

Venerable Mina Smallman, the mother of Bibaa and Nicole Smallman, had to instigate legal action against the police for them to admit their failing to act when the two sisters were reported missing. It was a matter of neglect, as the murder of two Black women once again did not receive the rightful attention, care, and diligence that the murder of white women would receive. The family had to search for the missing Black sisters themselves. Nicole's boyfriend, Adam Stone, found their bodies in undergrowth on June 7, 2020. This is just another example of how black women are devalued, dehumanized and disposable.

Smallman said the following about the two policemen charged with taking and disseminating the photographs of her daughters: "The offending stripped Ms Henry and Ms Smallman of dignity in death. That factor is weightier given that the offenders were charged with protecting their bodies" (qtd. in Dodd). The volume and frequency of the dissemination of images and video recordings depicting the brutality and death of black people reinforce this dehumanization. State-sanctioned violence and institutional racism within the medical and health system result in modern-day lynchings.

The sharing of these images does not just add to the spectacle; it also acts as a warning of how to behave towards Black people. The activist and writer Ashlee Marie Preston states: "The purpose of publicly torturing Black bodies, then and now, is to deter Black Americans from challenging white supremacy. And by re-sharing, liking, or posting videos of Black people being murdered, you're inadvertently helping to spread that message" (Preston). We see photos of dead Black women, particularly Black mothers, as images of grief. Mothers of the Movement imagery becomes the public face of different causes, such as Black Lives Matter. Black mothers are held in the vice-like grip of grief and mourning, frozen, which can obscure the systematic violence metered out to another Black son or daughter by the police.[4] I remember watching *Two Daughters*, a BBC film about the murders of Bib Henry and Nicola Smallman, and the centring of the grief of their mother, Venerable Mina Smallman, as if this is the only role she has to play in this tragedy played out on our screens. That a Black woman is not allowed to grieve in her own safe space with other ways of feeling and being human. *Remember, she doesn't feel pain; her feelings are immaterial.* As a result, Black mothers will only exist in the white imagination as always grieving and are therefore easily dismissed. As Kellie Carter Jackson argues: "We never get to see them parent, or be with their child in a very regular way. And so, it takes away this ability to see Black motherhood outside of a space that's not grief, loss or even to see motherhood outside of a movement" (79).

A Black mother is a source of wisdom and love

My mum, Anita Rose Mack, née Melgram, lost the love of her life, my dad, too young to claim a full widow's pension from the government. She had to bring up two, then three daughters as she fostered children for a living and then adopted one alone. It was a struggle. She "robbed Peter to pay Paul," as the saying goes. There was never enough money to pay for the rent, the bills, and the food. She got into life-crippling debt to keep her family afloat.

My mum never disclosed her finances. I didn't know about her struggles until she died prematurely from a stroke after a lifetime of high blood pressure, and I had to settle her estate after her death. The psychic and emotional impact of running her household as a single mum for so long must have added to her stresses and taken a toll on her body. There wasn't any money or property to pass on to her two remaining daughters or financial literacy. Instead, I wrote fifty-plus letters to credit card companies, banks, and money lenders telling them that they wouldn't be getting their money back and to leave my mum to rest in peace. To rest, finally. But to meet my mum, you wouldn't believe she was carrying such a heavy burden. She was the epitome of joy. She was love. I think she passed this on to her children and her children's children. My mum embodied "the radical concept of mothering—creating, nurturing, affirming, and supporting life" (Gumbs 9).

In *Mama's Baby, Papa's Maybe: A New American Grammar Book,* literary critic and Black feminist scholar Hortense Spillers reminds us that motherhood is not a given for Black women. Patriarchy grants white middle-class mothers certain rights not afforded to Black mothers. However, Spillers recognizes that mothering is different because it's an action and a work undertaken. It's vital nurturing for the survival of children.

Mothering can come from other women who are not the birth mother. Rooted in our ancestral tradition brought with us to the New World from Africa is the practice of other women stepping up to take care of children in the absence of their biological mother. Sisters, aunts, and grandmothers become the othermothers. Othermothering stems from a community's desire to survive through mutual care. Once my dad died, my mum returned to the supportive unit of her family, back in the northeast of England, renting the flat above her mum and dad. Nana Amber, my mum's mum, mothered me and my sisters. Her othermothering broke my wings time and time again, as I attempted to stretch beyond the accepted boundaries imposed on Black girls, internally and externally to the family. I feel this overprotection from my nana might have come from a place of love, maybe even an attempt to ready me for the world outside the family home. But I also think that the criticisms and harsh treatments came from a place of trauma. Brought up as a mixed-race woman in a predominately white society by a white mother who probably knew nothing about what being Black was about must have been soul-crushing for my nanny, too.

Conjuring, passing on power and pain

As a Black British woman of Afro-Caribbean descent, I understand conjuring to be a practice we pass on within our matrilineage, tracing our heritage through the maternal line. It's another way of knowing that supports our bodies as we move through this world in which we were never meant to survive. I feel this knowledge within our bodies support our survival, using found text from Krista Franklin's book *Too Much Midnight*:

black girls are mothers who are forced to birth
themselves into a world offered weary scar-scripts
within a death machine /wounded/
& their bodies never their own belonging to whomever
wants to violate them. (1)

Reproductive justice is "the human right to maintain personal bodily autonomy, have children, not have children, and parent the children we have in safe and sustainable communities" (Cole 197). It became necessary after the devaluation of Black motherhood and the belief Black women are not fit to mother, evidenced, for example, by the forced sterilization of Black women. Through coercion, trickery, or blatant disregard for a Black woman's right to choose, the medical profession, adhering to government policies, sterilized Black women for decades for the good of society (Roberts 14). These practices were built upon the field of gynaecology, which originated from a series of operations performed, without anaesthesia, by Dr. J. Marion Sims (1813–83) on enslaved women. I agree with Heidi Downes, who suggests that the contributions to medicine made by Dr. J. Marion Sims's patients should be more widely recognized.

Through these operations, Black women became specimens, not human beings. The body has a way of responding and holding on to distressing and disturbing experiences (Sharpe). Generational traumas, along with the day-to-day demands of living within a Black woman's body, are heavy and exhausting responsibilities to carry.

Her body carries stories

As I've mentioned before, excavating my matrilineage as a Black woman is a difficult and frustrating endeavour. Matricentric feminism, as it positions the needs and concerns of mothers at the forefront of the women's liberation movement, holds the promise of bringing about societal change. I want to make sure that the foundations of motherhood are true and solid, so when I highlight that science can be used to identify our lineage through the mitochondrial DNA we inherit from our mothers, I do so to (re)insert erased links. By tracing maternal genes through mitochondrial DNA, scientists have identified the Mitochondrial Eve as the most recent common ancestor of all living human beings. One woman who lived 150,000 to 200,000 years ago is probably the source of all mothers, grandmothers, great-grandmothers, and so on. This one woman probably came from the modern-day Kalahari Desert in Botswana (Arney). This scientifically proves the mother of all of humanity was an African woman, a Black mother. Without this Black mother, no one else would exist. However, with anti-Blackness being the dominant system, Black mothers and women do not receive their rightful respect, recognition, and appreciation. If you're paying attention to mainstream media in the UK, we're still deemed as "not mothers at all" (Roberts 24).

Figure 4. *My Body's My Home. My Body's at Home in Nature*, 2022, mixed media artist book (acyclic paint, collage papers, ink, stickers, stencils, and watercolour paper).

Carries histories, carries an archive

The Country Journal of a Blackwoman (Northumberland) is a composite, multidisciplinary palimpsest exploring the matrilineal line within the Northumberland landscape to remember and reclaim evidence of Black women's presence. Then and now. Fictionalizing maternal histories, this creative archive lays bare the identity and life of a composite Black woman through her visual country journal.

This installation plays with the multiple manifestations of the palimpsest concept. There are palimpsest manuscripts in which past writings bleed through the words superimposed on top—a haunting. There are palimpsest landscapes where different layers of bedrock, soil, and vegetation cover connect and support each other, with outcrops erupting through the surface at moments of weakness. Finally, I argue we human beings are living, breathing palimpsests. We experience our day-to-day events, happenings, and traumas, storing data and memories in our bodies which come into this world with our ancestors' stories. Over time, memories are processed and changed and become narrated stories. While traumas are never processed and remain stuck,[5] stored in our bodies and psyches, the transgenerational hauntings are metaphorical palimpsests; the body remembers. Through the visual spreads within her country journal, with her hands and heart conjuring, this Black woman peels back the ancestral layers to examine her sense of belonging within language, landscape, and her body. She manages to conjure self-love, with the help of Mother Nature, against the odds.

As a Black woman

The weathering hypothesis was first proposed by Arline Geronimus in 1992 (Geronimus et al.). It holds that African American women's health deteriorates in early adulthood as a result of their cumulative exposure to socioeconomic disadvantages. What this means is that the accumulative effects of living day in and day out as a Black woman, the stress of experiencing the world through a Black woman's body, and living with the effects of a racist, sexist and misogynistic society take its toll on Black women's bodies more than others.

Weathering is the physical consequence of social inequality and inequity. High mother mortality and infant birth deaths used to be linked to teen pregnancy, particularly among white women. However, new research has shown that there are more deaths among older Black women during childbirth than Black teenagers (Geronimus). This has been explained by the fact that these Black women have lived longer under unfair and unjust systems. Nevertheless, the stereotypes and images perpetuated within mainstream society around Black mothers are that they are undeserving of motherhood because they are deviant and criminal. Dorothy E. Roberts examines the interaction between racism and patriarchy in the social construction of motherhood and insists, "Patriarchy denied to Black mothers the authority and joy of mothering which it allowed white mothers" (6).

In the words of Alexandra Elle, "I am the matriarch of my lineage for healing" (qtd. in Whitney). I'm the first in my matrilineage to intentionally lean into my healing practice, a journey of becoming free. As Elle says, "To heal is to remember, to return to and to reclaim" (qtd. in Whitney). I'm taking responsibility for my own mental, emotional, physical, and psychological health and wellbeing because I want to break the cycle of trauma within my ancestral and present lineage.

I heed the wisdom bell hooks shares: "When we love the Earth, we are able to love ourselves more fully. I believe this. The ancestors taught me it was so" (hooks, *Belonging* 34). I fell in love with nature, just {BEING} with her. Closer to her. As a consequence, in return, I fell in love with myself. We are one. Nature and me. Me and Nature. Nature made me feel safe inside my body probably for the first time in my life. Who wouldn't you want to return to this feeling again and again as often as possible?

Resting deep within the meadow

I can see the picture so clearly in my mind. Sepia-toned, greys, and distressed creams. She is young, my mum. Lying back on both hands, in the grass with bushes behind. A white blouse and a dark full skirt. Smiling comfortably in her natural element. Mum in the meadow. I keep coming back to this image, the beginning of it all. Maybe it's because this is one of the few photographs of her outside. Peeling back the layers each time I see it. The image is an example of how we can use the few artifacts we have to construct narratives about ourselves and our kin. Narratives where we centre ourselves rather than relying on the official stories we've been force fed around Black motherhood.

Held in softness

I am drawn to the waters. It may be that I am searching for something. Looking for home? Searching for myself? Or maybe it's just I'm susceptible to change as the sea is never the same sea twice. "Seas" is a more correct term, as the tides and the weather change the physical shape of the sea, bringing different treasures to marvel at. The sea is never the same sea twice. I know now that to heal is to remember to return to and to reclaim.

I go to the sea to heal. I go to the sea to heal. I go to the sea to heal.

I'm not sure what healing looks like or what being sound of body feels like. I just know how I move through this world before I get into the sea, then how I feel afterwards. I feel lighter.

My first home was my mom. Her womb. Her water. I return to the water. Water carries memories. As drea brown, a poet and scholar, maintains, "For so many disposed of and dispossessed, perhaps water is the closest thing to kin and country. Because Blackness has been fed by so much loss, lost at sea, vanished in the veil, we return almost obsessively, for closure, opening, or suture" (487).

Grass-tickling shins

My mum, Anita, and Amber, my nana, kept house for white middle-class women, mothering their white children as a means to feed and clothe their own. I remember one white woman my mum used to clean the house for who gave me a doll. This doll was outside in the garden, sticking out of the dustbin. I turned up and was gifted the doll with the long blond hair. Its forehead was crinkled and puckered, burnt plastic. The doll had no eyes in her head, either. Gaping holes in her head where her blue eyes should be. An absent presence. Even though this scared me, it didn't stop this doll from becoming my prized possession. I mothered and loved her. Feeding, changing, and brushing her hair. Kissing and cuddling on her. Always looking for eyes to fit the holes. I tried marbles. Too small and falling into her head. I'd have to take her head off and shake them out.

I rejected all other dolls for this doll. Crinkled and puckered forehead, no-eyed doll. I kept her close even sleeping with her, as I gained great joy in loving her. Mothering made me feel needed. I played with dolls long after the age that seemed normal or was socially accepted. This was my way of feeling loved by giving love to others. This doll didn't reject me. I feel this is where my need for being needed began. But that's not true, as when I looked around me, all I remember seeing were Black women in service of others, be that inside or outside the home.

Dress billowing about

Figure 5. *Mom, Sharon, and Me*, circa 1976 (family photograph archive).

As a Black child, I'm chasing the water. During the summer holidays, mum organises coach trips from our small village to the coast. The whole village gets involved. Mum hires a coach and collects the money, so everyone contributes. It's a commitment. We descend on mass onto Whitley Bay sands. Mum labours for her community, and her children because she knows how good being by the sea is for our health and well-being. She says the seas have healing properties. She takes to the seas for her. She can't swim, but she paddles. Dress billowing about her knees she paddles. Bunions, callouses, varicose veins, arthritis. So many ailments made easier to bear after time spent at the seaside. I think to myself that the sea must have reminded us of where and to what we belonged.

An invocation to Yemoja from "the pagan book of hours," Ocean Mother, "whose blood runs with the tides / whose pulse is the turning of the moon." Yemoja—whose name within Yoruba tradition means, "Mother whose children are like fish"—is the giver of life and mother of all living things. Yemoja, Black feminine energy, and full spirits we conjure, giving birth to all the waters, "mama watta," Mother Water. I have learned to mother myself.

Like blossom

Even as our spirits are being crushed like blossoms underfoot, Black women continue to show up for themselves and others. Michele Wallace says this: "We exist as women who are Black who are feminists, each stranded for the moment, working independently because there is not yet an environment in this society remotely congenial to our struggle—because, being on the bottom, we would have to do what no one else has done: we would have to fight the world" (227).

Cat Brooks, an organizer from Oakland, California, reminds her twelve-year-old daughter: "I tell my daughter all the time—and it's harsh—but we don't live for the I. We live for the we" (qtd. in McClain 3). To conjure is to take back our power. Our dreamscapes. But not for selfish reasons. Yes, self-care is community care. We take back out power for us, for them and for you.

Black women have fought for their rights to be mothers and to keep their children safe and alive through organizing within communities. Black collective action has brought about, for example, reproduction justice, movements like Black Lives Matter, and community cohesion, where multiple groups with divergent interests have come together to fight against racism and sexism. One such multicultural group was the Organisation for Women of Asian and African Descent (OWAAD).[5] Not waiting to be granted our freedoms, we conjure to liberate ourselves even though we live in fear—fear for our children's survival as we try to protect them while preparing them for a world that does not see their worth.

Is a political act

Black mothering is a political act. To exist, survive and thrive. Death, fear, sacrifice, state-sanctioned violence, enslavement, infant mortality, and a self-perpetuating cycle, we endure along with deep joy and love. The trauma of black mothering wraps around our bodies (Davis 9). If mothering is central to (white) feminism, the image associated with motherhood is always going to be white women and white children. When you say "mother," you actually mean white mother. Motherhood = whiteness. White motherhood is sacred. This is anti-blackness. I would love to get to a point where the term "mother" is conjured and a multicultural, diverse image comes to mind for all of us. I would love to get to the point where all qualifiers and descriptors before "woman," never mind "mother," were no longer necessary because I would feel and know that when these nouns are being used I am included. But we're not at this point yet. "Yet," I say, because I have hope.

Within this imperialist, white supremacist, and capitalist heteropatriarchy, Black mothers never receive the recognition and true appreciation we deserve and labour hard for, from ourselves and others. The centuries of misrepresentation of Black women's bodies have been damaging. In the words of Fannie Lou Hamer, "A black woman's body was never hers alone" (qtd. in McGuire 23). And to a certain degree, this still holds today.

It's time to see ourselves reflected on our terms. Black matrilineage acknowledges that Black motherhood deserves to be looked at differently. Looking at Black motherhood through a matrilineage lens widens the current writings, imagery, beliefs, and practices around motherhood and mothering, which continue to centre white, middle-class women's experiences. Representation is resistance, and matricentric feminism supports this mission. As the author Kevin Quashie reflects on Blackness, "We are not the idea of us, not even the idea that we hold of us. We are us, multiple and varied, becoming" (154). I am, and I am becoming as I choose to heal. I choose to love myself, "regardless," as Alice Walker would proclaim (xi–xii). I choose me.

I go to the sea to heal.
I go to the sea to heal.
I go to the seal to heal.

Figure 6. *I Am the Matriarch of Healing for My Lineage*, 2020.

Self-love is only possible when we reclaim our gaze. Repeatedly. I can't do this, {BEING}-for-myself, if the gaze comes from elsewhere.

The sun dances across the waves. The sea is full to bursting. It moves like a steel-coloured blanket pleating against the shore. Walking in, cold sharp water, rises up my body. Once water reaches my waist, it's time to release my whole body into its liquid embrace. It's a shock to the system. Short, quick, shallow breaths as I attempt to acclimatize. I swim farther out, bob upon the waves, feel the pain in my bones. I keep moving, trying to warm up but never do. My flesh just numbs and comes alive at the same time. I flip onto my back, direct my glaze towards the charcoal sky, and remember why I do this. All my ancestors come from the sea. I read somewhere that when we're born, our bodies are made up of about seventy to seventy-eight per cent water. Our bodies are almost the same density as water. This is how we can float. The mineral composition of the water in our bodies is the same as water's mineral composition. We are the same. We are one. I remember, return, and reclaim.

Endnotes

1. Current academic writings around motherhood have focussed on motherhood, COVID-19, and working from home, for example. There is *The Journal of Mother Studies:A Peer-Reviewed, International, Interdisciplinary Open-Access, Digital Humanities Hybrid Project*, founded by M. Joy Rose, which adds to the diversity of voices around motherhood.
2. This page was created in 2017 by three women from London including Candice Brathwaite, to ensure that the diversity of motherhood is represented in social media.
3. For more information see the report *Black People, Racism, and Human Rights,* which highlights the tragedy of baby loss and in particular the disproportionately high levels of Black baby loss and neonatal deaths in the UK.
4. For evidence of deaths in police custody in the UK, see, https://blacklivesmatter.uk/deaths-in-custody/. For the US, see the recent report published by Statista Research Department, Jun 5, 2023, https://www.statista.com/statistics/585152/people-shot-to-death-by-us-police-by-race/
5. From 1978 to 1981, OWAAD campaigned on issues including immigration and deportation; domestic violence; exclusion of children from school; industrial action by black women; policing and defense policies; and health and reproductive rights. Their campaigns on reproductive rights included protesting against the testing of the contraceptive drug Depo-Provera on women from marginalized communities (History@Manchester).

Works Cited

Alexander, M. Jacqui. *Pedagogies of Crossing: Meditations on Feminism, Sexual Politics, Memory, and the Sacred.* Duke University Press, 2005.

Arney, Kat. 'Would You Adam and Eve It? In Search of Our Earliest

Genetic Ancestors." *Genetics Unzipped,* The Genetics Society Podcast, January 2023, https://geneticsunzipped.com/transcripts/2023/01/26/eve-mitochondrial-dna. Accessed 7 July 2024.

Black Lives Matter UK. "Institutional Racism." *Black Lives Matter,* https://blacklivesmatter.uk/deaths-in-custody/. Accessed 7 July 2024.

Brathwaite, Candice. *I Am Not Your Baby Mother: What It's Like to Be a Black British Mother.* Quercus, 2021.

brown, drea. "Conjuring the Ghost: A Call and Response to Haints." *Hypatia,* vol. 36, no. 3, 2021, pp. 485–502.

Collins, Patricia Hill. *Black Feminist Thought: Knowledge, Consciousness, and the Politics of Empowerment.* Routledge, 2002.

Cauley, Kashana. 'Erica Garner and How America Destroys Black Families.' *New York Times,* 2 Jan. 2018, https://www.nytimes.com/2018/01/02/opinion/erica-garner-black-families.html. Accessed 7 July 2024.

Cole, Haile Eshe. 'Worth a Thousand Words: Visualizing Black Motherhood and Health." *Black Matrilineage, Photography, and Representation: Another Way of Knowing.* Edited by Lesly Deschler Canossi and Zoraida Lopez-Diago. Leuven University Press, 2023, pp. 194–215.

Davis, Dána-Ain. "The Bone Collectors' Comments for Sorrow as Artifact: Black Radical Mothering in Times of Terror." *Transforming Anthropology,* 24, 1, 2016, pp. 8–16, https://anthrosource.onlinelibrary.wiley.com/doi/abs/10.1111/traa.12056.

Dodd, Vikram. "Two Met police officers jailed over photos of murdered sisters." *The Guardian,* 6 Dec. 2021, https://www.theguardian.com/uk-news/2021/dec/06/two-met-police-officers-jailed-photos-murdered-sisters-deniz-jaffer-jamie-lewis-nicole-smallman-bibaa-henry. Accessed 7 July 2024.

Downes, Heidi. "The Forgotten Women of Gynaecology." *British Journal of Midwifery,* vol. 27, no. 10, 2019, pp. 614–15, https://doi.org/10.12968/bjom.2019.27.10.614.

Elle, Alexandra. *How We Heal: Uncover Your Power and Set Yourself Free.* Chronicle Books, 2022.

Franklin, Krista. *Too Much Midnight.* Haymarket Books, 2020.

Geronimus, Arline. "On Teenage Childbearing and Neonatal Mortality in the United States." *Population and Development Review*, vol. 13, 1987, pp. 245–79.

Geronimus, Arline, et al. "'Weathering' and Age Patterns of Allostatic Load Scores among Blacks and Whites in the United States." *American Journal of Public Health*, vol. 96, no. 5, 2006, pp. 826–33.

Gilman, Sander L. "Black Bodies, White Bodies: Toward an Iconography of Female Sexuality in Late Nineteenth-Century Art, Medicine, and Literature." *Race, Writing and Difference*. Edited by Henry Louis Gates, Jr. University of Chicago Press, 1985, pp. 223–61.

Gumbs, Alexis Pauline, et al. *Revolutionary Mothering: Love on the Front Lines*. PM Press, 2016.

Hartman, Saidiya. *Lose Your Mother: A Journey along the Atlantic Slave Route*. Serpent's Tail, 2021.

History@Manchester. "Black Women Organising. What We Can Learn from the Rise and Fall of OWAAD." *University of Manchester*, 1 Oct. 2020, https://uomhistory.com/2020/10/01/black-women-organising-what-we-can-learn-from-the-rise-and-fall-of-owaad/. Accessed 7 July 2024.

hooks, bell. *Belonging: A Culture of Place*. Routledge, 2019.

hooks, bell. *Writing Beyond Race: Living Theory and Practice*. Routledge, 2013.

House of Commons and House of Lords. *Black People, Racism, and Human Rights*. Joint Committee on Human Rights, 2020, https://committees.parliament.uk/publications/3440/documents/32850/default/. Accessed 7 July 2024.

Hice-Fromille, Theresa. "The Queerness of Black Matriarchal Praxis." *Hypatia*, vol. 36, no. 3, 2021, pp. 547–54, doi:10.1017/hyp.2021.37.

Jackson, Kellie Carter. "Black Motherhood Online: A Reimagined Representation, A Conversation with Tomi Akitunde." *Black Matrilineage, Photography, and Representation: Another Way of Knowing*. Edited by Lesly Deschler Canossi and Zoraida Lopez-Diago. Leuven University Press, 2023, pp. 72–81.

Lorde, Audre. *The Collected Poems of Audre Lorde*. W. W. Norton & Company, 1997.

Mays, Jeffery C. "Mourning Erica Garner: 'When Her Father Died, an Activist Was Born.'" *The New York Times,* 9 Jan. 2018, www.nytimes.com/2018/01/08/nyregion/erica-garner-funeral-black-lives-matter.html. Accessed 7 July 2024.

McClain, Dani. *We Live for the WE: The Political Power of Black Motherhood.* Bold Type Books, 2019.

McGuire, Danielle L. *At the Dark End of the Street: Black Women, Rape, and Resistance–a New History of the Civil Rights Movement from Rosa Parks to the Rise of Black Power.* Alfred A. Knopf, 2011.

McLemore, Brie. "Regarding the Pain of Our Own: Jazmine Headley, Portraiture, and the Sorrow of Black Motherhood." *Black Matrilineage, Photography, and Representation: Another Way of Knowing.* Edited by Lesly Deschler Canossi and Zoraida Lopez-Diago. Leuven University Press, 2023, pp. 36–81.

Michael, Marcia. "The Impossibility of Breathing When the Sun Covers Your Face". *Black Matrilineage, Photography, and Representation: Another Way of Knowing.* Edited by Lesly Deschler Canossi and Zoraida Lopez-Diago. Leuven University Press, 2023, pp. 262–71.

Miranda, Carolina. "Painter Ellen Gallagher's tragic sea tales: How African slaves went from human to cargo on the Atlantic." *Los Angeles Times,* by 7 Nov. 2017, https://www.latimes.com/entertainment/arts/miranda/la-et-cam-ellen-gallagher-hauser-wirth-20171117-htmlstory.html. Accessed 7 July 2024.

Morrison, Toni. "Rootedness: The Ancestor as Foundation." *Black Women Writers (1950–1980): A Critical Evaluation.* Edited by M. Evans. Anchor Press / Doubleday, 1984, pp. 339–45.

Nash, Jennifer C. "Birthing Black Mothers: Birth Work and the Making of Black Maternal Political Subjects." *WSQ: Women's Studies Quarterly,* vol. 47, no. 3, 2019, pp. 29–50. *Project MUSE,* doi:10.1353/wsq.2019.0054.

Nichols, Grace. *I is a long memoried woman.* Karnak House Publishers, 1983.

O'Reilly, Andrea. "Matricentric Feminism: A Feminism for Mothers." *Journal of the Motherhood Initiative,* vol. 10, no.1 & 2, 2019, pp. 13–26, http://journalofmotherhoodinitiative.org/product/matricentric-feminism/. Accessed 7 July 2024.

Pierre-Louis, Marly. "Thotty Mummies: The Erotic Potential of Black Mothers Online." *Black Matrilineage, Photography, and Representation: Another Way of Knowing*. Edited by Lesly Deschler Canossi and Zoraida Lopez-Diago. Leuven University Press, 2023, pp. 83–91.

Preston, Ashlee Marie. "Sorry, Consuming Trauma Porn Is Not Allyship." *Marie Claire Magazine*, 10 June 2020, www.marieclaire.com/politics/a32802688/stop-sharing-trauma-porn-black-deaths/. Accessed 7 July 2024.

Quashie, Kevin Everod. *Black Aliveness, or a Poetics of Being*. Duke University Press, 2021.

Roberts, Dorothy E. "Racism and Patriarchy in the Meaning of Motherhood." *Faculty Scholarship at Penn Law*, vol. 595, 1993, https://scholarship.law.upenn.edu/faculty_scholarship/595. Accessed 7 July 2024.

Sharpe, Christina. *In The Wake: On Blackness and Being*. Duke University Press, 2016.

Spillers, Hortense J. *Black, White, and in Color Essays on American Literature and Culture*. University of Chicago Press, 2003.

Statista. "Number of People Shot to Death by the Police in the United States from 2017 to 2024*, by Race." *Statista*, 5 July 2024, https://www.statista.com/statistics/585152/people-shot-to-death-by-us-police-by-race/. Accessed 7 July 2024.

Tsonas, Mindy. "We Belong". *Collective Belonging*, https://collectivebelonging.org/. Assessed 7 July 2024.

Villarosa, Linda. "Why America's Black Mothers and Babies Are in a Life-or-Death Crisis." *The New York Times Magazine*, 11 Apr. 2018, https://www.nytimes.com/2018/04/11/ magazine/black-mothers-babies-death-maternal-mortality.html. Accessed 7 July 2024.

Walker, Alice. *In Search of Our Mothers' Gardens: Womanist Prose*. Houghton Mifflin Harcourt, 1983.

Wallace, Michelle. "Anger in Isolation: A Black Feminist's Search for Sisterhood." *Words of Fire: An Anthology of African American Feminist Thought*. Edited by Beverly Guy-Sheftal. *The New Press*, 1995, pp. 220–27.

Whitney, Ev'yan. *Sensual Self Podcast*, Episode 74, 21, Dec. 2022, https://shows.acast.com/5b0e0cdb0372226f4661c637/63a237a9981c02001

048707a. Accessed 7 July 2024.

Williams, Rhaisa Kameela. "Toward a Theorization of Black Maternal Grief as Analytic." *Transforming Anthropology*, vol. 24, no. 1, 2016, pp. 17–30, https://doi.org/10.1111/traa.12057.

10.

Black Mothers' Responses to Systems of Oppression: Navigating Work, Family, and Self-Actualization

Nicole Dezrea Jenkins

Introduction

Motherhood is central to challenges faced by mothers (O'Reilly). In this chapter, through an intersectional analysis of race and gender and transnational feminist framework, I explore how Black women conceptualize motherhood and navigate work-family balance. Drawing on two years of participant observation, ethnography, and unstructured interviews conducted in a Black, immigrant, and women-owned and operated hair salon in the Western United States (US), which was part of my dissertation research, I highlight the experiences and problems faced by Black women navigating institutions in the US.

This chapter explores the experiences of Black mothers from West African countries and Black American women in a hair braiding salon setting; it argues that they experience paradoxes in their understanding and enactment of motherhood. First, using the concept of matricentric feminism as a foundation, I examine how mothers conceptualize their roles and enactment of mothering through a lens that prioritizes patriarchal understandings of motherhood roles, yet, in practice, they are queering motherhood by mothering in the community. Next, I discuss how the challenges of motherhood compounded with narratives about strong Black women complicate motherhood for Black mothers. Lastly, I explain how mothers value their children's education but must prepare their children to respond to the racial violence often experienced in educational institutions. I demonstrate how the racialized motherwork of Black mothers in this salon shows up as mothers anticipate and share encounters of racism involving their children. This chapter centres on the experiences of Black mothers by demonstrating how they must navigate the paradox of motherhood as they aspire to perform both paid work and motherwork while managing their own and their children's racial identities.

Matricentric Feminism

Matricentric feminism, coined by Andrea O'Reilly, is a feminist framework focussing on motherhood and the experiences of mothers. This theoretical framework seeks to specifically highlight the political significance and motivations for a feminist framework that centres on motherhood and challenges patriarchal structures that devalue and marginalize mothers. How motherhood is conceptualized often accounts for the many problems that mothers face, meaning that societal expectations and norms surrounding motherhood can create significant challenges and burdens for Black women. The pressures to be strong, adequate, and perfect as mothers can be overwhelming and lead to feelings of inadequacy and stress.

In this chapter, the concept of "empowered mothering" is pivotal. Empowered mothering, in this context, refers to the agency and resilience Black mothers exhibit in challenging and redefining traditional patriarchal roles of motherhood. These mothers demonstrate empowered mothering by actively balancing work and family responsibilities, navigating systemic racial challenges, and advocating for their children's wellbeing and educational success. The term "queering empowered mothering" extends this concept to include how these mothers subvert traditional motherhood norms. This is evident in their adoption of communal and nonconventional parenting practices that reject heteronormative, nuclear family structures, embracing a more inclusive and flexible approach to motherhood that is responsive to their unique social and cultural environments.

The relationship between empowered mothering and matricentric feminism is deeply interwoven. In this framework, empowered mothering is seen as a form of resistance against patriarchal norms and an assertion of autonomy and strength in the face of societal challenges specific to Black mothers. By embracing matricentric feminism and queering empowered mothering, Black mothers in this study display a transformative approach to motherhood. This approach not only confronts the traditional patriarchal constraints but also addresses the complexities of race, identity, and systemic oppression. The chapter thus explores how these mothers, through their lived experiences and practices, contribute to a deeper, more nuanced understanding of motherhood, advocating for the recognition and empowerment of Black mothers within the broader discourse of feminism.

Within the framework of matricentric feminism, this chapter explores how Black mothers navigate work-family balance using patriarchal frames. While demonstrating real and prevalent oppression of motherwork, these mothers adopt strategies, such as the queering of empowered mothering, to negotiate patriarchal expectations, and confront the challenges of racism within educational institutions through racialized women's motherwork. By centring the voices and challenges Black mothers face, this research sheds light on the complexities of motherhood and emphasizes the need for inclusive policies that support diverse families. Through the lens of matricentric feminism, this study contributes to a deeper understanding of motherhood as a central aspect of women's experiences and advocates for the recognition and empowerment of Black mothers within feminist discourse.

Mommy Ethnographer: Methodology and Insider-Outsider Status

I am a mother and have been one for over a decade now. This aspect of my identity provided me with the most salient opportunities for building rapport while in the field. I am an Afro/Latina and have identified as a Black woman my whole life. In graduate school, I knew I wanted to do ethnography and was interested in the natural hair experiences of other Black women who donned natural hairstyles and textures like me.

In my two-year ethnographic research in a hair-braiding salon located in a Western US city, I observed Black mothers navigating work-family balance in a child-friendly space. The braiders were West African immigrants, and the primary customer base was Black or African American women. I learned the salon's daily operations and assisted with various tasks, which enabled me to engage with the braiders and customers regularly. My insider-outsider identity was unique. My status as a mother helped me to develop intimate relationships with the women in the salon. My identity as a Black woman and an American, however, left me in limbo, sometimes being an insider as a Black woman and other times being an outsider as an American.

For two years, I visited the salon a few times a week, for several hours each visit. I made myself useful by running food errands, sweeping and taking out trash, answering the phone, and greeting customers. I eventually became the salon's receptionist, scheduling, confirming, and cancelling appointments. As a graduate student and mother, I, too, had to balance my professional life with my motherhood identity. This fact made for an intimate experience as the theme of motherhood began to emerge in my data. I used unstructured interviews with both customers and employees of the salon. I coded my data by hand and used grounded theory to analyze my data. The findings I share in this chapter are just one aspect of a larger story on Black womanhood in the US.

Mothers in this study participate in collective mothering in their workspace: an African-owned hair salon. In the salon, women share the responsibility of caring for children. The decision or need to work outside of the home in combination with the belief that mothers are the primary parents responsible for most childrearing results in a need for collective mothering and queer-parenting strategies. In addition to collective mothering within the workplace, Black mothers also adopt queer parenting strategies and cocare for children that rely on communal networks beyond their partners for support in child-friendly work environments. Strategies employed include bringing children to work and allowing other women present to assist with childcare. These strategies challenge traditional notions of parenting and highlight the resilience and resourcefulness of Black mothers in achieving work-family balance. The strategies employed demonstrate the queering of empowered mothering based on the mothers' conceptualization of the role of motherhood, demonstrating the real and prevalent oppression of motherwork.

Exploring Work-Family Balance through the Real and Prevalent Opression of Motherwork

Implementing work-family balance strategies involves the collective sharing of childcare responsibilities within the workplace. This integration of childcare and work allows Black women to achieve personal fulfillment while fulfilling their perceived parenting duties. Their strategies for managing parenting and work are influenced by the women's conceptualization of motherhood that frames mothers as the primarily responsible parents in the variety of care necessary for childrearing. Matricentric feminism highlights how conceptualizations of motherhood can intensify the difficulty of the role. The conceptualizations by mothers in my study, which are shaped by patriarchal ideas of parenting responsibilities, are problematic and further aggravate the already challenging role of Black motherhood. However, their unique response demonstrates the queering of empowered mothering.

Gina,[1] a braider at the salon, had an interesting encounter with a new customer one day. The customer was a young mother from Los Angeles, California, who had recently returned to work at the United States Postal Service after giving birth and exhausting all her maternity leave options. During their conversation, the new mother expressed how difficult it was for her to leave her infant daughter and return to work. To Gina's surprise, other mothers in the salon echoed the sentiment, yet they collectively agreed that it is a mother's responsibility to ensure that her job allows her to take care of her children:

> "Child, it ain't never enough time. These jobs want you back to make them money. They don't care about your baby, so you have to." said Pam, a forty-six-year-old Black American woman.
>
> "Ya, my job already knows that if something comes up with my kids, then I am going to take care of that without a doubt. They understand that, so that's why I like working there," said Quianna, a Black American and a twenty-five-year-old paralegal.
>
> "She is right," said Adina, a thirty-eight-year-old Senegalese braider. "A good mother has a job that lets her take care of her children."

As the author of this study, I couldn't help but ponder whether this burden of responsibility should solely rest on the mothers' shoulders. What role should partners and employers play to alleviate this burden? I reflected on my own experiences as a mother returning to work after childbirth. I was an active-duty police officer in the United States Air Force when I gave birth to my son. I had to return to service when my son was six weeks old. To say I was not ready would be a severe understatement. Leaving my infant in the care of strangers was one of the hardest moments of my life. Yes, weeks after my delivery, I toured several nearby daycare facilities in preparation. Working mothers, such as Gina and her customer, value their work for self-actualization. However, they also prioritize their childcare responsibilities and work obligations for their families' sake.

The comments here demonstrate the real and prevalent oppression of mothers discussed in matricentric feminism. This oppression occurs as mothers try to balance paid work with mother work. Women navigate parenting and career differently from men and fathers, as mothers. They must navigate a capitalist society that does not value their commitment to their families and careers in the same way they do. Mothers are held to expectations that pressure them to negotiate their work and careers in ways that men and fathers do not. While the mothers in my study expressed aspirations to work, their reliance on capitalism and patriarchal understandings of motherhood and responsibility highlights their oppressive circumstances.

Some working mothers seek child-friendly work environments to achieve a work-family balance aligning with their values. The concept of "child friendly" varies drastically depending on the line of work and environment. Perhaps children can visit work, maybe an office has a "bring your kid to work day," or maybe children are regularly welcome for extended amounts of time. In child-friendly work settings, such as the salon, parents feel more comfortable bringing their children along while they work. These environments foster an atmosphere where caring for children is normalized, allowing employees to fulfill their professional duties while still tending to their children's needs. The salon is a child-friendly environment to the greatest extent. Children are welcome in the salon for as long as they need to be present. Braiders brought their children to the salon for the day while they worked. Customers brought their children to the salon as they received their styles. Visits could range from one to twelve hours. Highlighting metacentric feminism, I describe this salon setting as a radical queering of empowered mothering.

This example of Gina and her customer illustrates the central dilemma faced by many working mothers. They grapple with the responsibility of providing for their families while also ensuring their children receive the care and attention they deserve. The prevailing question is whether it should solely be the mother's duty or if partners, employers, and society at large should share the burden of supporting working mothers. Mothers parenting in patriarchy must radically queer mothering to successfully combine labour work with motherwork in ways that meet their expectations of good mothering. These strategies implemented within the salon function as a result of parenting in patriarchy as well as a response to oppression. While women in the salon are paradoxically recycling pejorative narratives about good mothering, they are also responding in ways that empower mothering using queer strategies.

Strategies for Parenting in Patriarchy

The challenges and strategies faced by Black mothers in this study in balancing work and family are reflected in their experiences and practices within the salon. The salon environment serves as a child-friendly space that supports the integration of work and childcare, allowing women to meet their expectations of motherhood while pursuing their careers. This section explores the unique dynamics and practices arising in this setting, highlighting the significance of radical queering of empowered mothering and the supportive community fostered among salon workers.

Child-Friendly Salon Environment

Within the braiding salon, a child-friendly working environment exists. In this chapter, I use the term "child-friendly working environment" to describe spaces that combine labour and childcare in ways that support business operations and allow for communal type childcare. In the salon, Black women employ strategies for work-family balance based on their conceptualizations of good mothering practices by leveraging the established community in salons and collectively sharing childcare responsibilities. I demonstrate how their strategies highlight the real and prevalent oppression of motherwork as well as the racial queering of empowered mothering. Mothers conceptualize themselves as the primary parent of their children and the ones most responsible for the variety of care required.

Mimi, the salon owner, demonstrates her approach to work-family balance by bringing her children to the salon and incorporating them into daily operations. This is not done every day but is common, especially during summer months and holidays when school is out. This practice is not limited to Mimi alone, as other mothers also utilize the salon as a place where their children can accompany them during work hours. The salon provides ample space, assistance, and a supportive atmosphere accommodating children of various ages. The children are engaged and helpful, demonstrating the normalized inclusion of parenting tasks within the salon. While mothers braid hair or have their hair braided, kids watch television, play on iPads, read, do homework, and even help with small tasks in the salon. The space works to accommodate families. I argue that this space queers motherhood by allowing mothers to fulfill their professional roles while also actively participating in childcare. This queering of motherhood aligns with the principles of matricentric feminism, which seeks to challenge and deconstruct patriarchal norms limiting women's roles to caregivers.

Othermothering and Supportive Community

Within the salon, the concept of othermothering is embraced, reflecting African American and queer parenting practices that challenge the traditional nuclear family structure. Mothers in the salon support and assist one another in childcare responsibilities, creating a strong sense of community and mutual aid. This collective approach to parenting acknowledges and values the diverse experiences and aspirations of women beyond their roles as parents. It provides a supportive space where mothers can bring their children to work, receive assistance from fellow salon workers, and build meaningful connections. The concept of othermothering in the salon challenges the traditional nuclear family structure and contributes to the empowerment of mothers. Through othermothering, the roles and responsibilities of motherhood are shared by other women. The supportive community within the salon is an example of women collectively sharing childcare responsibilities, a key aspect of queering motherhood. This practice aligns with matricentric feminism, which highlights the importance of foregrounding mothers and mothering in feminist discourse. How does this relate to matricentric feminism?

Normalizing Dual Roles of Motherwork

The salon environment actively normalizes and integrates the dual roles of work and caregiving. For example, one day, when a new mother arrives at the salon with her family, she is warmly welcomed, and her family members, including the father and teenage daughter, actively participate in caring for the infant. The salon owners and workers embrace parental tasks and provide support to the family. The teenage daughter asks for a microwave to heat the baby's bottle. While one of the braiders heats the bottle for the baby, the father holds the baby close enough to see its mother. While the father feeds the baby, the braider positions herself around the mother and child to ensure the baby can see mommy while eating and until he falls asleep. The collective attentiveness and care create a sense of inclusivity and understanding. By creating a family-friendly atmosphere, the salon enables mothers to fulfill their perceived responsibilities as caregivers, fostering their success in both domains. Within the salon, the normalization and practice of dual roles of work and caregiving challenge patriarchal ideals of motherhood that often place undue strain on women. By accommodating both work and childcare, the salon creates an inclusive atmosphere that allows mothers to succeed in both domains. This queering of motherhood aligns with matricentric feminism's goal of challenging and dismantling societal expectations surrounding motherhood.

The communal childcare practices observed in the salon reflect the unique ways that Black mothers navigate the challenges of balancing work and family. By providing a child-friendly environment, embracing othermothering, and normalizing dual roles, the salon provides a supportive and inclusive space where Black women can thrive together. These practices align with the principles of matricentric feminism by challenging traditional family structures, promoting collective care, and recognizing the mothers' diverse experiences and aspirations.

Mimi, the salon's owner, is a married mother of two, who is considering having another baby. During our conversation, she shared some of the challenges women face when contemplating having a child, such as the physical changes during pregnancy and postpartum body image concerns. Childcare was also discussed, but Mimi had a plan. She explained that she would have to arrange for childcare when she returned to the salon, since her husband was not interested in caring for small babies. However, she had a solution: bring her new baby to work and have the baby on her back or chest, just like she did when I first met her. When I arrived at the salon on my first day, I saw a busy woman moving about the salon—sweeping, taking out the trash, answering the phone, talking to customers, and pencilling down appointments—before coming over to greet me. I only then noticed the baby wrapped closely around her body. "Wow! You are doing all of this with your baby strapped to you? I ask. Mimi smiled. "Oh, this is not my baby; this is her baby," she said, pointing to another woman. "How can I help you?" Her warmness was inviting, and the salon was captivating. I knew this would be my research site. So, Mimi's plan to bring her child to work is not without experience. Her confidence in her childcare plan reflects a strategy used by working mothers to combine work and childcare in unique ways that enable them to work outside of the home and meet their expectations for motherhood. These expectations often aid patriarchal and limiting ideals of motherhood that place strains on women. However, the salon's child-friendly environment makes a blend possible for the braiders and customers.

It's election day in 2018, and Mimi arrives at the salon with five children—her two children, Joleen's children (who is a nurse), and Adeana's children (a veteran braider in the salon). Mimi jokes about having to babysit, since there is no school that day. The children enter the salon and make themselves comfortable. They go around and hug each braider before sitting in the waiting area or empty chairs. Before the first customer arrives, Mimi directs the children to the break room, which has a couch, a small TV, a table, and packs of synthetic hair covering the walls. Adeana's children share their new Duolingo app for learning French with me, and they talk about their school, friends, and favourite apps. Throughout the day, the children behave and help in the salon when needed. Mimi gives each of Joleen's children five dollars for their help at the end of the day.

The above scenario demonstrates how the women and children at that salon can share the accommodating space in ways that support working mothers and mothers tending to their beauty needs. A paradox exists in which women carve out professional and personal identities for themselves but must also feed the narrative that childcare is their responsibility to navigate as mothers. Customers and employees regularly brought their children to the salon, allowing braiders working in the salon to work while also being able to care for their children and any other children present. This allows customers tending to their beauty regimens to bring children along. These spaces are important as Black mothers are often concerned about the potential mistreatment of their children in US institutions, such as schools.

The salon's practices enable mothers to navigate the challenges imposed by patriarchal norms. Mothers in the salon employ strategies to balance work and motherhood, and this reflects the real and prevalent oppression of motherwork, a concept central to matricentric feminism. The practices are a unique response to patriarchal challenges and demonstrate the queering of empowered mothering, where mothers find innovative ways to fulfill their responsibilities.

Motherhood: Racialized Women's Motherwork

The societal expectation for Black women to continuously strive for excellence has profound implications for their life experiences (Hooks; Collins; Cooper; Crenshaw) and, of course, their motherhood. Internalizing the pervasive Strong Black Women narrative, Black women often find the boundaries between productivity and overextension blurred (Scott). While based on truths about resilience and strength, this narrative is harmful. The socialization of Black women to embody the ideals of strong Black womanhood begins early and is reinforced by family members and other Black women.

These points emphasize how the expectations placed on Black women to be strong and resilient directly tie into the overarching argument of the salon as a space that challenges traditional notions of motherhood and aligns with the principles of matricentric feminism, which seeks to empower and support mothers in their diverse experiences. For example, within the family, young Black girls may be socialized to exhibit strength and resilience from an early age (Beauboeuf-Lafontant; Collins; Cooper; Harris-Perry). They may be encouraged to be strong and "keep it together" in the face of adversity, such as family challenges, financial difficulties, or racial discrimination. This socialization often comes from older female relatives, such as mothers, grandmothers, aunts, or sisters, who believe that displaying strength is necessary for survival and success in a world that may be hostile towards Black women (Harden-Bradford).

These examples underscore how the family dynamic contributes to the perpetuation of strong Black womanhood, which is a key element to consider in the context of matricentric feminism and the queering of motherhood. Furthermore, Black women may also receive reinforcement of the strong Black womanhood ideal from other Black women in their community (Beauboeuf-Lafontant; Collins; Cooper; Harris-Perry). This reinforcement can occur through various forms of support, such as mentoring, role modelling, and cultural practices. For instance, community organizations or women's groups may emphasize the importance of resilience, perseverance, and self-sufficiency as essential qualities for Black women to navigate systemic barriers.

These community-based interactions and shared experiences are essential components of the broader argument that Black motherhood is shaped by societal expectations, reinforced by family and community dynamics, contributes to the socialization process, and reinforces the expectation of strength among Black women. This directly ties into the central argument of my work, which explores how the salon serves as a space to challenge these expectations. These experiences are not universal for all Black women, as we are not a monolith. However, they illustrate common patterns in the socialization process and the role that family and community play in reinforcing the ideals of strong Black womanhood.

This pressure to constantly achieve and excel leads many Black women to neglect self-care in their pursuit of doing as much as they can. These expectations have deep roots in the dehumanization of Black people during slavery, perpetuating the myth that Black individuals are superhuman and can endure any amount of work and hardship. While Black women may be perceived as strong when taking on an excessive workload, the need for self-care becomes evident (Scott).

Karla D. Scott proposes a self-care manifesto as a new mandate for strength, emphasizing the importance of self-care in challenging the harmful effects of the Strong Black Women narrative. This discussion on the neglect of self-care and its historical roots is crucial to my argument as it illustrates how societal expectations placed on Black women intersect with the principles of Matricentric Feminism. It emphasizes the need to challenge the harmful effects of the Strong Black Women narrative and make space for more vulnerability and self-care through queering motherhood.

The pressures of strength and adequacy extend to the role of motherhood for Black women as observed in studies (Barnes; O'Reilly). The idealized image of a perfect mother, wife, and daughter places a significant burden on Black women and falling short of these expectations can result in intense scrutiny (O'Reilly). Riché J. Daniel Barnes's study *Raising the Race: Black Career Women Redefine Marriage, Motherhood, and Community* on Black middle-class women reveals their efforts to uphold an image of respectability and challenge stereotypes about Black women and families to protect themselves and their loved ones. However, these pressures can become unattainable for Black mothers who are simultaneously juggling career and family responsibilities.

The weight of these expectations adds an additional layer of complexity to their experiences of motherhood. The pressures of motherhood and the challenges faced by Black mothers who balance career and family responsibilities directly relate to my central argument. They highlight the need to challenge traditional ideals of motherhood within the context of matricentric feminism and the salon as a space for redefining these expectations. Black mothers often face negative stereotypes perpetuating harmful narratives, such as the "welfare queen" or the "angry Black woman" (Collins). These stereotypes can lead to heightened scrutiny and assumptions about their parenting abilities or choices. Additionally, Black mothers may experience heightened surveillance from various sources, including healthcare providers, child welfare agencies, and educational institutions.

Racial biases can drive this surveillance, leading to increased scrutiny of their parenting practices, decisions, and their children's wellbeing (Roberts; Roberts and Sanders-Phillips). Black mothers may also face specific expectations and pressures related to raising their children in a society marked by racial inequalities. They may be judged for how they navigate discussions about race and racism with their children, how they protect their children from discrimination, and how they instill a positive racial identity (Collins; Lewis). When Black mothers face challenges or difficulties, they may be subjected to victim-blaming and shaming instead of receiving support and understanding. This can further contribute to feelings of guilt, isolation, and stress (Collins; Dowd).

Lastly, Black mothers may face compounded discrimination due to the intersection of their race, gender, and other social identities. This can include experiences of racism, sexism, and classism, which can all shape the unique ways in which they are scrutinized and judged as mothers (Crenshaw; Dowd). Stereotypes, surveillance, and expectations faced by Black mothers are vital to my argument, as they illustrate how Black motherhood is subject to external pressures and judgments, reinforcing the need for a salon space that challenges and redefines these narratives within the framework of matricentric feminism.

In the context of matricentric feminism, these struggles highlight the ways in which patriarchal systems shape and constrain Black women's experiences of motherhood. The Strong Black Women narrative, rooted in patriarchal ideals of strength and resilience, imposes unrealistic expectations on Black mothers, denying them the space for vulnerability and self-care. By recognizing and critically examining these dynamics, matricentric feminism seeks to challenge and dismantle oppressive systems hindering Black women's ability to navigate the complexities of motherhood on their own terms. In the context of matricentric feminism, this argument aligns with the aim of challenging the patriarchal systems placing unrealistic expectations on mothers. I now turn to how matricentric feminism allows Black women to challenge these patriarchal systems and redefine motherhood on their own terms.

Matricentric Feminism and Strong Black Motherhood

Black mothers who deviate from societal expectations of motherhood, which prescribe qualities such as unwavering nurturing, self-sacrifice, and availability for their children, are often met with intense judgment and scrutiny (Collins; O'Reilly). These challenges in the context of matricentric feminism highlight the significance of feminist framework and provide an alternative perspective that actively challenges these societal pressures. Matricentric feminism centres on motherhood and aims to dismantle patriarchal norms that undermine the wellbeing and autonomy of mothers, including Black mothers (O'Reilly).

First, matricentric feminism emphasizes self-care as an act of resistance against oppressive patterns in society that devalue it as a priority for mothers. It acknowledges that self-care for Black mothers is often viewed as a luxury they cannot afford due to the demands placed upon them. By highlighting self-care as a necessary and integral part of motherhood, matricentric feminism advocates for mothers' wellbeing and self-actualization, recognizing them as priorities in being an effective caregiver (Dowd).

Second, matricentric feminism highlights the significance of community support and collective action in redefining motherhood. In the face of societal judgment and scrutiny, Black mothers can find solidarity and strength in the community via other mothering and child-friendly workspaces. These collective efforts can reimagine isolation that stems from societal expectations into empowerment for mothers to define their roles in ways that prioritize well-being and autonomy in motherhood (Roberts). Furthermore, matricentric feminism aims to create inclusive spaces where the diverse experiences and voices of Black mothers are valued and recognized. In doing so, it actively counters the mainstream discussions of motherhood that silence and devalue these experiences (Smith).

Through the lens of matricentric feminism, we can examine the experiences faced by Black mothers and more effectively dismantle the patriarchal norms contributing to their challenges and burdens. Advocacy, empowerment, and liberation for mothers regardless of their race or ethnicity harmonize with the overarching objective of feminist frameworks in support of motherhood (Crenshaw). This section demonstrates how matricentric feminism identifies the challenges Black mothers face and provides a framework for comprehension, action, and advocacy towards these challenges within broader feminist discourse. Within this framework, we can truly value championing the health and sovereignty of Black mothers as crucial for the advancement of gender equality.

Protecting and Empowering: Black Mothers' Education Advocacy

Matricentric feminism recognizes the central role of mothers in shaping society and seeks to challenge and transform oppressive systems devaluing and marginalizing motherhood. By amplifying the voices of scholars like bell hooks and Patricia Hill Collins, matricentric feminism highlights the racialized motherwork that is necessary for Black motherhood. Collins emphasizes how Black mothers find empowerment in their identities as mothers despite experiences of oppression (57), while hooks speaks about the importance of safe spaces where mothers can discuss racialized oppression (42). In the context of education, Black mothers navigate the challenges of a patriarchal and racist institution while prioritizing their children's success and wellbeing, demonstrating the racialized women's motherwork highlighted in matricentric feminism theory.

Mothers in my study actively engage in academic preparedness, engage in open and honest conversations about race and racism with their children, and advocate for their children's rights within the educational system. Their motherhood responsibilities are primarily focused on the care and development of their children, with a central emphasis on their Black children's success within mainstream US institutions, particularly schools. Furthermore, these mothers prioritize their children's education by assigning them academic tasks to keep them engaged while they accompany them at work. At the same time, they navigate and strategize on how to address anticipated instances of racism within their children's schools.

Clearly, racialized women's motherwork, a concept described in the theoretical framework of matricentric feminism, demonstrates how intersections of race and gender complicate motherhood (O'Reilly). While prioritizing their children's education, these Black mothers also recognize that these institutions can be hostile towards children of colour (Ray). Consequently, they aim to shield their children from the experiences of racism, sexism, and nationalism they will likely encounter in school while equipping them with the necessary tools to face these challenges.

Their efforts to protect and empower their children align with the principles of matricentric feminism, which calls for the recognition and empowerment of mothers as agents of change in society. By highlighting the experiences and strategies of Black mothers in navigating the hostile institution of education, this section contributes to a deeper understanding of matricentric feminism and how motherhood intersects with systems of power and oppression.

The preparation undertaken by Black mothers in anticipation of the hostile institution of education reflects their dedication to their children's success and wellbeing. This section explores how these mothers prioritize academic preparedness and engage in discussions with their children about race and racism. It emphasizes the importance of Black mothers' involvement in their children's education and the protective role they assume in navigating the challenges of a racially biased educational system. Matricentric feminism highlights the role mothers play in society at large.

Mothers within the salon recognize the significance of academic preparation for their children due to the racial hostility often encountered in educational institutions. They incorporate academic tasks and additional support outside of school to ensure their children's success. This dedication showcases their role in society at large by emphasizing the importance they place on their children's education and their commitment to equipping them with the necessary tools to overcome systemic barriers.

Matricentric feminism discusses how children learn their culture and community at home, highlighting Collins who emphasizes how children of colour must learn how to survive in systems that oppress them. Black mothers in this study teach their children how to navigate racism at school.

Black mothers also teach one another how to navigate instances of racism involving their children through sharing stories. Mothers in the salon often exchanged stories with one another about the experiences that their children had had with racist encounters at school. In anticipation of these incidents, mothers engage in open and honest conversations with their children about race and racism, including discussions on police interactions. These conversations aim to make children aware of instances of racism and empower them to protect themselves while addressing the injustice of such experiences.

Avery, a Senegalese woman in her mid-fifties who has been a braider at Mimi's for about five years, has three children who have all left home. She started having children at a young age and stressed the importance of communication in parenting. Avery told a story about her son's encounter with racism in middle school. When a teacher asked the children what they aspired to be when they grew up, and her son said that he wanted to be an engineer, the teacher scoffed in front of the entire class and told him that he would be on the street instead. Avery was angry and heartbroken when her son arrived home and shared what had happened in his classroom. She immediately contacted the school and asked for the teacher to be reprimanded for his comments and apologize to her son.

When the school refused to do either, Avery acted and moved her son to another school. Unfortunately, he also experienced racism while playing football in high school, and he experienced frequent harassment, including being spat on and told to "go back to his country with his people." As she shared the story, her eyes filled with tears at the thought of someone speaking to her son that way and spitting on him. "My son is so sweet and so calm; he will not fight. He is not mean at all. He knows only to defend himself, not just react. So, to hear this from him make me so angry and sad all at once. But I taught him how to handle tings like dis." He handled the situation by speaking to the student and making him aware of the consequences of his actions. They eventually became close friends.

Avery's experience highlights the importance of communication between parents and children, especially when discussing instances of racism, and serves as an example of racialized women's motherwork. Avery believes that there is no problem too big that they cannot solve and encourages her children to talk to her about anything. She also emphasizes that there are no bad kids, only kids who are told they are bad and feel the need to please others. However, parents must also be mindful of the racism that exists within institutions, which can be particularly hostile to youth of colour. The story of Avery exemplifies the necessary communication in parenting and the proactive measures taken to address racism encountered in school.

Matricentric feminism recognizes the central role of mothers in shaping society and challenges oppressive systems that marginalize motherhood. Scholars like hooks and Collins have highlighted the racialized motherwork essential in Black motherhood. For example, Collins emphasizes how Black mothers derive empowerment from their motherhood identities despite facing oppression. This empowerment demonstrates the recognition and empowerment of mothers advocated by matricentric feminism (Collins 57). Furthermore, hooks emphasizes the importance of safe spaces for mothers to discuss racialized oppression. The experiences I documented at the salon, such as Black mothers engaging in open and honest conversations with their children about race and racism, align with hooks' perspective (hooks 42).

Avery's story exemplifies the core principles of matricentric feminism. Her proactive response to her son's encounter with racism in school, where she immediately contacted the school and later moved her son to another institution, demonstrates her commitment to protecting and empowering her child. This aligns with matricentric feminism's call for recognizing mothers as agents of change in society (O'Reilly). Moreover, Avery's emphasis on communication with her children about racism and her belief that there are no bad kids, only kids influenced by external judgments, aligns with matricentric feminism's recognition of the role mothers play in nurturing and guiding their children's understanding of the world, especially in systems that oppress them.

In summary, the experiences and strategies of Black mothers in this study offer valuable insights into how matricentric feminism operates in the context of racialized motherhood and education. These mothers actively engage in protecting and empowering their children, which aligns with the principles of matricentric feminism, since it seeks to advocate for mothers to influence policy. The Black mothers from this study take on the role of advocacy for their children in unique ways. The connection between matricentric feminism and how the Black mothers prepare their children for racist encounters at school highlights the intersectionality of motherhood, as it includes race and gender through racialized women's motherwork. In a white supremacist and patriarchal society, parents and mothers, especially mothers of colour, must equip their children with the knowledge for how to best navigate situations that are likely to occur. Marginalized mothers protect their children from emotional and psychological harm by preparing them for racist encounters and additionally empower their children in doing so.

Addressing the racial challenges that children face aligns with the broader goals of matricentric feminism by empowering mothers and their families. Mothers play a crucial role in nurturing children's resilience and self-confidence in the face of societal prejudice. Aligning with matricentric feminist theory that highlights the racialized motherwork necessary for Black mothers as well as the importance of identity formation of their children for Black mothers, these strategies used by Black mothers to prepare their children for racist encounters provide a unique insight into the responsibilities of raising children and addressing racial discrimination as a significant aspect of empowering families within marginalized communities.

Conclusion

Researchers have acknowledged the challenges involved in achieving a balance between work and family life, yet little attention has been given to how people of colour manage this delicate balancing act. Despite Black women's long history in the workforce and their significant contributions as earners, their experiences with work-family balance are seldom the centre of research. To address this, I conducted research to explore how

Black mothers conceptualize motherhood and the associated responsibilities and how they achieve work-family balance. Using the concept of matricentric feminism as a foundation, I examined how mothers conceptualize their roles and enactment of mothering within the space and context of patriarchal schemas, demonstrating the real and prevalent oppression of motherwork. Through radical queering of empowered mothering within child-friendly working environments, Black women employ strategies for work-family balance by leveraging the established community in salons and collectively sharing responsibilities for childcare. Their motherhood responsibilities are primarily focussed on the care and development of their children, with a central emphasis on their Black children's success within mainstream US institutions, particularly schools. Furthermore, these mothers prioritize their children's education within the workplace by assigning them academic tasks to keep them engaged.

My findings suggest that Black mothers define good motherhood based on patriarchal understandings that position motherhood as a singular identity and as the primary caretaker responsible for childcare and childrearing. Mothers recycle harmful narratives about what it means to be a good mother and also carry out the duties of motherhood with these restrictions in mind. Women prioritize their duties as mothers while also valuing the ability to work outside of the home, which is critical for their self-actualization. A paradox exists as women enact unique ways of mothering in the community while also relying on patriarchal understandings of what it means to be a good mother. For example, finding a job that allows for the blend of responsibilities between work and mothering. Mothers in this study prioritize their children's educational preparedness, including academic and racial concerns, and employ racialized women's motherwork as a strategy.

Child-friendly work environments supporting working parents are highly valued but not always feasible. These findings highlight the importance of centring on Black mothers' experiences in discussions about work-family balance and family policy. By recognizing their values and practices, we can develop more inclusive policies that benefit all families, including headed by single-parent families, international families, and queer families. Furthermore, the collective efforts of Black mothers in childrearing, as well as the concept of othermothers, demonstrate the potential for community-based support systems to assist in achieving work-family balance.

Overall, this research underscores the need for greater attention to the complex realities of diverse families' experiences with work-family balance and the potential for inclusive policies and support systems to promote greater equity and wellbeing for all families.

Endnotes

1. Pseudonyms have been used for the participants' names.

Works Cited

Barnes, Riché J. Daniel. *Raising the Race: Black Career Women Redefine Marriage, Motherhood, and Community*. Rutgers University Press, 2015.

Beauboeuf-Lafontant, Tamara. "You Have to Show Strength: An Exploration of Gender, Race, and Depression." *Gender & Society*, vol. 23, no. 1, 2009, pp. 28–51.

Collins, Patricia Hill. *Black Feminist Thought: Knowledge, Consciousness, and the Politics of Empowerment*. Routledge, 2000.

Cooper, Brittney. *Beyond Respectability: The Intellectual Thought of Race Women*. University of Illinois Press, 2019.

Cooper, Brittney. *Eloquent Rage: A Black Feminist Discovers Her Superpower*. St. Martin's Press, 2018.

Crenshaw, Kimberlé. "Mapping the Margins: Intersectionality, Identity Politics, and Violence against Women of Color." *Stanford Law Review*, vol. 43, no. 6, 1991, pp. 1241–99.

Harris-Perry, Melissa. *Sister Citizen: Shame, Stereotypes, and Black Women in America*. Yale University Press, 2011.

Dowd, Nancy E. Reimagining Equality: A New Deal for Children of Color. New York University Press, 2018.

hooks, bell. *Ain't I a Woman: Black Women and Feminism*. South End Press, 1981.

Jenkins, N. D. "Contested Identities: African Diaspora and Identity Making in a Hair Braiding Salon." *Journal of Contemporary Ethnography*, vol. 48, no. 6, 2019, pp. 806–35, https://doi.org/10.1177/089124161 9829210.

Lewis, A. E. *Race in the Schoolyard: Negotiating the Color Line in Classrooms and Communities*. Rutgers University Press, 2006.

McClain, D. *We Live for the We: The Political Power of Black Motherhood*. Hachette UK, 2019.

O'Reilly, Andrea. *Matricentric Feminism: Theory, Activism, Practice*. 2nd ed. Demeter Press, 2021.

Roberts, Dorothy E. *Killing the Black Body: Race, Reproduction, and the Meaning of Liberty*. Vintage, 1998.

Roberts, Dorothy E., and K. Sanders-Phillips. "Racial, Ethnic, and Gender Differences in the Societal Consequences of Maternal Incarceration." *Journal of the American Academy of Child & Adolescent Psychiatry*, vol. 37, no. 4, 1998, pp. 448–55.

Scott, Karla D. *The Language of Strong Black Womanhood: Myths, Models, Messages, and a New Mandate for Self-Care*. St. Louis University, 2017.

Smith, Candis Watts. *Black Mosaic: The Politics of Black Pan-Ethnic Diversity*. New York University Press, 2014.

11.

Using Matricentric Feminist Research to Create Space for Mothers on Campus

Alexis Carrion and Andrea DeKeseredy

Introduction

Despite women outpacing men in university enrollment and graduation (Lopez and Gonzalez-Barrera), mothers continue to face systemic barriers in higher education, being less likely to complete their degrees or move up the academic pipeline (AAUP; Cruse et al., "Parents"). Although the growing presence of women in university has led many to believe that gender equity in higher education has been achieved, the high attrition rates for mothers show us they are still disadvantaged. Just like in the professional world, mothers in higher education are experiencing a "maternal wall" (Williams) where women without children are succeeding on par with men, whereas mothers are still being left behind due to the duelling roles of being a graduate student and an intensive mother. We refer to the disadvantage mothers in higher education face as the "academic maternal wall." Universities continuing to ignore the impact motherhood has on the lives of their students has increased the invisibility of mothers on campus, leaving them without adequate support and little recourse in an increasingly corporatized, neoliberal academic environment.

This chapter shares our experiences as young scholars studying the academic maternal wall through a matricentric feminist lens. Andrea is a cisgender, heterosexual, 31-year-old white woman in graduate school in the sociology department at the University of Alberta. She is married to a man who works in healthcare with long, unpredictable hours. She has one child, a five-year-old son. Alexis is a cisgender, heterosexual, twenty-eight-year-old black woman in graduate school in the Department of Sociology at Temple University who is unmarried and childless.

We begin by defining and discussing the concepts that maintain the academic maternal wall and how the ongoing neoliberalization of universities is exacerbating it. This includes the duelling roles of intensive mother and graduate student leading to work-life balance conflict. When practising intensive mothering, women are expected to shape their lives entirely around their children, preparing them for a competitive society with little social safety net. At the same time, the role of graduate students is now like that of faculty in that it requires students to meet the demands of the ideal worker to be successful and competitive in the job market. An increasingly neoliberalized academy is transforming universities away from places of learning into corporatized job training facilities, leaving students with even fewer support resources. Both roles are nearly impossible to complete simultaneously and are further shaped by race and class.

Next, we address the intersectionality of the oppression of mothers in academia by highlighting the racialized implications of motherhood. We share our experiences as researchers applying matricentric feminism and maternal theory to our work in a field that often does not recognize these theories. We argue for the inclusion of Black matricentric feminism when studying mothering and higher education to gain a more thorough understanding of how race shapes the experience of student mothers.

We conclude by outlining the reasons for including matricentric feminism in our work and discuss the use of public feminist sociology to reach nonacademic audiences while engaging in matricentric activism. By sharing our experiences, challenges, and success in using matricentric feminism in our work, we hope to bring more awareness to motherhood scholarship and inspire other researchers to do the same.

The Academic Maternal Wall

While conversations around the wage gap as a continued threat to women's equality have entered public discourse, white women without kids have been quite adept in closing it, now making nearly the same amount of money as men do (Crittenden). A more accurate way of describing the discrepancy between the wages of men and women is by recognizing it as a maternal wall (Williams), where women with caregiving responsibilities have fewer professional opportunities than men and their childless peers. As theorized by Joan Williams, the unequal bearing of childcare responsibilities contributes to mothers being less likely to be able to adhere to the standards of the "unencumbered man"—someone who can fully commit to their work with few external distractions and is entirely committed to their job and employer (Williams).Being unable to mirror the image of the unencumbered man (or ideal worker) results in women with children receiving lower pay and being concentrated in less prestigious work, part-time work. The COVID-19 pandemic served as a stark reminder of the ongoing presence of the maternal wall, with women being disproportionately removed from the workforce to stay at home and care for their children during school and daycare closures (Calarco et al.; Fuller and Qian)

The academic wall is often ignored. Women with children and caregiving responsibilities encounter systemic barriers to success in higher education, keeping them from achieving their degrees and moving up the academic pipeline. Despite their ongoing erasure, mothers comprise a large portion of the student population. In 2019, in the United States (US), 15.6 per cent of college students were mothers, and most were single (Cruse et al., "Parents"). Recent statistics show that in Canada, the numbers are similar, with an estimate of 6 to 11 per cent of all undergraduate students being mothers (Van Rhijn et al.) and about 20 per cent of graduate students being parents as of 2019 (CGSPA). Student parents are a significant minority of the student body population and experience disproportionately high attrition rates. About half of student parents drop out within six years of enrolling, with mothers being more likely to leave school than men. This has often been referred to as the leaky pipeline, in which the longer a woman is in the academic pipeline, the more likely they are to exit before finishing and securing permanent employment (Goulden et al).

Mothers in university with caregiving responsibilities often cannot adhere to the mould of a traditional student, as they experience several unique barriers explaining their high attrition rates and the other challenges they face. One of the biggest obstacles student parents must first overcome is accessible childcare. Waitlists for campus childcare facilities are highly competitive and require years-long waitlists (Cruse et al., "Evaluating"). Student parents also often compete with faculty for childcare near campus, and they tend to have more knowledge, time, and resources to secure their child a spot (Austin and McDermott; Boyd and Shea).Should a spot become available, being able to afford the services can be insurmountable for student mothers with little financial resources and no additional student aid allotted for care. At the University of Alberta, Andrea's university, the cost of childcare is between six hundred and fifteen hundred dollars a month and has a waitlist of two years. Her graduate monthly stipend is 2, 209.97 dollars, leaving her to use more than half of her salary to pay for childcare (University of Alberta Graduate Student Association). To lessen the cost of care, student mothers will strategically decrease the number of classes they take to reduce the number of hours they need to access and pay for childcare services. Those students in more precarious financial situations often struggle between paying for tuition and childcare. Student mothers often have to discontinue their studies at some point due to the loss of childcare (Augustine et al.; Mahaffey et al.).Another frustration for student parents is that campus housing is virtually nonexistent, and much information on the available options is spread through word of mouth and not through formal communication from the university (Austin and McDermott). Few student housing options are available for families, and the few available spots are too expensive and lack the utilities necessary to care for small children.

Resources and support for student mothers often impose confusing and contradictory policies that discourage mothers from accessing services and in some cases do harm (Goldrick-Rab and Sorensen). For example, single mothers are less likely to complete their Free Application for Federal Student Aid (FAFSA) than students without dependents (Radey and Cheatham). The Free Application for Government Student Aid (FAFSA) form is that which students fill out to get government student aid. It gives them access to government student aid, which is the biggest source of aid, which can help them pay for college or career/trade school.

A lot of states and colleges also use the information from the FAFSA to figure out if students can get state and school help (USA.gov). Those with the time and resources to manoeuvre their way through the process will often use loans as their primary source of income and take out the highest possible amount available to them (Austin and McDermott; Katz; Marx and Turner). Relying on large student loans to access the entirety of their education leaves student mothers in a state of perpetual worry about how they will repay them (Goldrick-Rab and Houle). Of course, paying off these student loans is more difficult for mothers who spend the entirety of their wage-earning years under the motherhood penalty making less money than their male and childfree colleagues (Crittenden).

The Neoliberalization of Academia

Anglo-American universities continue to undergo mass neoliberal restructuring by adhering more to the rules of the market as opposed to ones of learning, thus increasing the barriers mothers face as they pursue higher education. The process of neoliberalization within universities has been spurred by conservative government policies and public distrust in higher education; universities are under pressure to prove their utility and justify access to their increasingly precarious funding (Coté and Pickard). In this environment, universities want to maximize output while minimizing the amount of money it costs to do so, which means increasing the number of graduating students who enter the workforce and doing so as cheaply as possible. Graduating students become the product, and universities want to deliver "the cheapest product to the largest number of customers" (Coté and Pickard 2).

Andrea's university serves as a prime Canadian example of the neoliberalization of academia. Prompted by the election of a hard-right provincial government in 2019, the University of Alberta had their funding slashed by millions of dollars. In response to the cuts, the university engaged in an aggressive restructuring process to recoup its losses, resulting in hundreds of people losing their jobs and an increase in enrolment (Teeling and Williams). The provincial government also released the MacKinnon Report (MacKinnon and Percy), which argues that too many students were not finishing their degrees and that public funding should be tied to graduation rates and the number of students entering the workforce. Of course, this negatively affected mothers, who often cannot neatly fit into the confines of program timelines. In her thesis research on graduate student mothers' experiences during the COVID-19 pandemic, Andrea found that the restructuring of the university had massive consequences for the lives of participants in her research, leaving them with fewer resources and inflexible program deadlines that they were not able to meet due to interruptions from the pandemic. Extensions became harder to claim under a performance-based funding model. There was fear of more funding cuts from the government if the university didn't show they were quickly graduating students into the workforce.

Meanwhile, the corporatization of North American universities was rearing its head in the US at Alexis's university through the refusal to pay graduate students a living wage and provide adequate maternity leave. Union contract negotiations with the university administration proceeded for a full year, and ultimately the administration's lack of seriousness regarding graduate students' attempt to fight for livable wages, dependent care, and adequate working conditions led to a strike in 2023. In the previous collective bargaining agreement (CBA), graduate students with dependents and families had to pay almost a third of their annual salary to add one dependent to their healthcare plan and almost 58 per cent and 86 per cent of the annual salary for two or three dependents, respectively. The situation was even more dire for graduate students who wanted to have or already had children. The previous contract stipulated that graduate students may only take five days of parental leave per academic year. The graduate student union went on strike for the first time in its history, which lasted for almost two months. During this period, strikers had their wages withheld and their health insurance terminated. The new CBA was ratified two months after the strike began, and it now stipulates that the university will cover 25 per cent of dependents' healthcare premiums, regardless of how many dependents are on the plan. Parental leave of twenty-one days is now allotted for childbirth or adoption, which was a considerable win for the graduate student union.

Intensive Mothering

As challenging as it is to be a student in an environment with dwindling resources, mothers in university also struggle with meeting the demands of mothering in an individualized environment outside of the academic world. While adhering to the demands of the ideal student norm, mothers are also encouraged to participate in the practice of intensive mothering, which dictates that to be a good mother one's life must entirely revolve around your children; good mothers spend an exhaustive amount of time, energy, and resources on them (Hays). Intensive mothering emerged as a response to the aggressive government adoption of neoliberal ideology in the 1990s. Resources once provided by the government and community were eliminated through privatization and deregulation and were now subsidized by mothers' labour and resources (O'Reilly). Without a social safety net, mothers now face the stress of preparing their children for a hyper-competitive capitalist society. The new mothering requirements make it nearly impossible for students to adhere to the dual role of student and mother, creating work-life balance conflict as both are too time consuming and expensive.

Based on Hays's conceptualization, intensive mothering has three main elements. First, the mother is the central caregiver to the child as other family members or external help cannot be relied upon to give the same level of care, especially the father. Second, the mother must engage in what is understood to be appropriate childrearing, which is child centred, expert guided, emotionally absorbing, labour intensive and expensive. Finally, the ideology of intensive parenting dictates that a comparison of paid work and childrearing is absurd, since raising a child must always take precedence in a mother's life (Hays).

In practice, intensive mothering is a strenuous process that is often incompatible with the daily requirements of university work. Mothers must always be aware of the latest research about how to best raise a child. They must also have their children enrolled in time-consuming and expensive multiple activities. Today, this often includes competitive sports on top of a strenuous academic schedule. Mothers must always be prepared to leave work to pick up their child if they are sick or have forgotten something they need for school. Successful intensive mothering requires that mothers always put their children before their own goals, which means sacrificing their academic goals. The two roles are impossible to hold at the same time.

Racialized Motherhood in Higher Education

Matricentric feminism recognizes that principles of mothering and motherhood are largely driven by culture, and thus the maternal experience will vary across race, class, culture, ethnicity, sexuality, ability, age, and geographical location (O'Reilly). We argue that to utilize a matricentric feminist lens within sociological research on student mothers, we must include theoretical perspectives on racialized motherhood. We must address the intersectionality of the oppression of mothers in academia, which addresses issues that differently affect nonwhite mothers. Incorporating theoretical perspectives on racialized motherhood is especially important when conducting research aiming to address the barriers faced by Black and brown mothers in academia. More Black women care for children while in American college than any other group of women (Cruse, "Parents"). For Black women, the confines of motherhood are more likely to create a conflict in their attempts to succeed academically and economically. Whether they are a student or a faculty member, the lack of structural support for mothers in academia imposes particularly dangerous implications for Black women who already encounter structural racism and implicit bias.

Matricentric Scholarship in Research on Higher Education

Matricentric feminism recognizes that the oppression of mothers is experienced in different ways than being a woman, and much of the oppression mothers face is specific to their role as caregivers (O'Reilly). As Andrea O'Reilly states in her ground-breaking book, *Matricentric Feminism: Theory, Activism and Practice,* "Mothers need a feminism that puts motherhood at its centre" (2). In many instances, maternity holds more significance in the lives of women than gender. Research on higher education has shown for decades that students who engage in mothering experience barriers to academic success and completion of their degree (Augustine et al.; Goldrick-Rab and Sorensen). Despite this, matricentric feminism is often omitted from broader conversations around inequality in academia, like how it is excluded from mainstream academic feminism (O'Reilly).

For student mothers, it is not a matter of gender holding them back from academic success, but the confines of motherhood. Women are vastly outpacing men in academic achievement on many levels, including enrolment and graduation (Lopez and Gonzalez-Barrera). At the same time, we question why women with children are less likely to graduate than their childless peers. Feminist research on inequality in higher education must adopt a matricentric feminist lens to answer this question because mainstream academic feminism has not centred on conversations about how and why women face unintended consequences, such as higher attrition rates in comparison to their childless peers. Only with maternal theory can we advance sociological research on higher education. In discussing our experiences in applying matricentric feminism to our research, we hope to inspire and move towards a broad inclusion of a matricentric feminist lens to the study of inequality in higher education.

Andrea's Research

Born from her own experiences as a student mother, Andrea's project used a reflexive process in line with her epistemological approach of transactional knowledge creation to conduct research on the experiences of graduate student mothers during the outbreak of COVID-19. Using a qualitative descriptive approach and critical thematic analysis, the project aimed to understand better how graduate student mothers' duelling roles were experienced within an organization that reproduces inequality during a crisis. Based on a theoretical framework informed by maternal theory—specifically that of Williams and Hays—Andrea's project tried not only to gain a better understanding of what impact the pandemic had on graduate student mothers but also to inform future policy recommendations. Maternal theory guided interview questions as well as prompts. Saturation occurred at nineteen interviews. Andrea chose the methodology to collaboratively engage with the research participants and present the findings in everyday language, accessible to the broader public. This is in keeping to create a matrifocal narrative in which scholars "endeavour to unmask motherhood by documenting the lived reality of mothering" (O'Reilly 5).

Andrea's project found that the COVID-19 pandemic exacerbated the family gap in graduate education by making it impossible for student mothers to balance their duelling role of intensive mother and graduate student. To meet all their responsibilities, student mothers had to organize the most important resource they had: time. The pandemic and subsequent closures of childcare facilities led to a loss of control in the mothers' lives, leaving them unable to organize their time in a way that would allow them to complete their duelling roles. In the end, most of the participants were forced to add years onto their degree timelines as they could not complete their academic work. Changes to university structures brought on by austerity measures and budget cuts also exacerbated their work-life balance conflict, with graduate student mothers being less likely to access resources and support within their university.

One of the most important aspects of Andrea's research design from a matricentric point of view was creating an accessible space for conducting data collection. During an ongoing pandemic, the start of "the tripledemic" (the unprecedented circulation of sickness among children throughout the fall and winter of 2022), Andrea decided to give her participants the option of conducting their interviews online or in person. In-person interviews were conducted in the designated feeding and care space to inform mothers of the space on campus, allowing them to bring their children to the interview if they wished. An overwhelming majority of participants used the online Zoom option, often interviewing while sick or caring for their child. We argue online options should always be considered when conducting research with mothers, as the confines of motherhood greatly impact their ability to meet in person.

In keeping with the initial goals of the study, a large part of the interview protocol focussed on what the participants felt would assist them in achieving their academic goals. These suggestions included more online classes and increased flexibility and timeline extensions. Andrea's research findings would later be disseminated among the stakeholders within the broader university community to implement some of the participants' requests, including the campus paper and student-parent working groups. The interviews also served as a source of care between the researcher and participants through their reflexive interview approach. Similar to what other researchers have experienced (Averett), the interviews created a much-needed space for the participants to talk about what they had been through.

Alexis's Research

By the time Alexis finished her first year in graduate school, her mother had just received a diploma in nursing. Alexis conducted research during the fall of 2020; her research explored why some student parents, such as her mother, take longer to earn their degrees and why some do not reach this goal. Alexis used qualitative inquiry to explore the barriers to college persistence for mothers and the strategies they use to overcome them. She conducted semistructured interviews via Zoom with ten mothers who were students at a public state-related university, some of whom were married, while the remainder were either in a domestic partnership or single. Two of the participants were married; the remaining ones were in a domestic partnership or single. Two of the mothers had children under five, and the rest had children old enough to attend primary school or who were adults. Three-fifths of the sample self-identified as white, while the other participants identified as African American and one, Asian American. Alexis asked the participants questions about their daily routine, perceptions of their schools and their experiences, their children's view of their mothers' schooling, and the participants' future aspirations. She used open-ended questions, which allowed the participants to reflect on their experiences.

Five themes emerged from these interviews. The first was the lack of access to financial aid. The mothers insisted their institutions did not provide adequate information about how to access financial aid and the terms of their loans. They also stated that the application process was often tedious and selective, making it less practical for them due to their already limited free time and lack of confidence their efforts would pay off. Next, the mothers experienced an exacerbated time strain, which hurt their ability to complete assignments and their relationships with their children. Mother guilt resulted from time strain, as the mothers expressed negative feelings about their parenting due to the lack of time spent with their children. Teacher, peer, and school support was another common theme. Some of the mothers expressed that they had experiences with teachers who understood that their parenting may affect their ability to turn in assignments on time, or if they had to bring their child to class one day. Yet a few mothers shared discontent with their teachers' and fellow students' lack of understanding and support of their role as parents. Lastly, motivation for attending college was mentioned in every interview, and improving one's financial situation was most often reported.

Regardless of their marital or racial status, these mothers typically encountered the same obstacles while balancing parenting and being a good student. Alexis learned firsthand some of the challenges of being a mother while attending school by watching her mother's almost twenty-year journey to obtain her nursing credentials. The concerns expressed by the mothers Alexis interviewed concern areas not adequately addressed in the existing literature about the issues student mothers face.

Developing a Black Matricentric Feminist Theory

Alexis actively engages in a Black matricentric feminist theory. She argues that the connection between existing Black feminist theory and matricentric feminism will create space for Black mothers to advocate for themselves through the lens of Black womanhood. In her current research, Alexis is developing this theory of Black matricentric feminism by examining the most influential scholarship about how Black feminism and matricentric feminism address issues related to Black mothers. This theory-building exercise begins with a focus on the obstacles faced by Black mothers who seek higher education opportunities. A Black matricentric feminist framework addresses women racialized as Black. This is a key distinction because a racialized society implies specific consequences for women racialized as Black than in a non-racialized society.

Alexis argues that the struggles that Black mothers face living in a racialized society such as the US explicitly stem from racism; thus, any research aiming to help this population must be studied with their experiences centred. A Black matricentric feminist framework has the potential to highlight the unique strategies that Black mothers employ to combat racist beliefs and practices affecting their communities. Alexis's research on Black mothers in higher education uses a black matricentric feminist framework to explicate the value of education in present-day African American communities.

Motherhood Activism and Public Sociology in Higher Education

A tenet of matricentric feminism is a commitment to social justice, where mothers can engage in social change through activism and their own experiences of childrearing (O'Reilly). A goal of each of our research projects was to explore the experiences of mothers in higher education. Andrea's research explored the impact of COVID-19 on graduate student mothers to understand better how an exogenous crisis affected the academic maternal wall. We knew our research would not reveal a perfect utopia in which mothers balanced their duelling roles as students and mothers perfectly. Armed with more knowledge regarding what keeps mothers from achieving their academic goals, we wanted to disseminate our findings to our community and policymakers to advocate for more equitable policies on campus.

We have done this in several ways. Andrea's research became a part of her activism on campus in resisting neoliberal policies affecting students on campus. The intersection of motherhood and the destruction of the academy at the hands of conservative policies became inextricably, intertwined as one issue. Andrea engaged in what Michael Burawoy (64) calls "organic public sociology" (64). This occurs when one pursues immediate engagement with the public as opposed to being filtered through media or other larger institutions. Researchers engage in a face-to-face relationship with the community. Organic public sociology is smaller than traditional public sociology but more determined (Burawoy). Partaking in student governance at the department level, Andrea slowly made connections with other like-minded graduate student associations within varying departments.

Andrea collaborated in a series of open letters and statements by student leaders that were sent to the university administration after graduate students were left to work as teaching and research assistants without contracts for weeks due to staffing cuts and the streamlining of university services. The letters were informed by her research in which she found that budget cuts and restructuring measures at the university were harming student mothers by leaving them without resources, support, and increased pressure to finish their degrees on time despite interruptions in childcare due to the pandemic. Like the mothers in her study, all graduate students were left to toil in uncertainty while the university failed to communicate what was happening with workers' contracts. The statements were disseminated within departments and were eventually covered by the student newspaper, resulting in contracts being issued to the students on time. Had graduate students missed a payment period, it would have been disastrous for student mothers needing to pay for childcare. After the success of the open letter, Andrea formed connections with other student activists and unions on campus who voiced their support for the cause. This included the Association of Academic Staff at the University of Alberta, the Non-Academic Staff Association, and the Campus Food Bank. The connections made throughout the school year amounted to a mass organization of hundreds of people in protest of the 2023 tuition hike at the University of Alberta titled Halt the Hike. Throughout the organizing, Andrea maintained a sense of matrifocality, discussing the importance of keeping tuition affordable for student parents, and was ultimately able to join the university's Student Parents on Campus Working Group based on prior connections. The group works towards advocating and implementing changes to the university that will help student parents.

As the purpose of the research is to create change in the academic community, Andrea also disseminated the research to an academic audience. Andrea organized a session at the 2023 Canadian Sociological Association titled "Impacts of Neoliberalization on Higher Education in Canada." Although the session served as a forum to present research to an academic audience, it also explicitly served as a space to learn about others' experiences and trade strategies of resistance. Faculty and students had designated sessions, ensuring the voices of all were equally heard.

For her dissertation research, Alexis explores how Black mothers navigate higher education under a neoliberal system. Applying matricentric feminism as a framework for research on inequality in higher education presents a unique opportunity to further theorize on Black motherhood and womanhood and to understand better how the inequities in higher education particularly affect Black women who participate in it. Her research aims to explore the hypothesis that Black mothers conceptualize higher education as a space where they can go to be successful in American society, despite the country's racist history and present. She seeks to explore how the mothers' racial, gender, class, and motherhood identities affect them within and outside of academic environments. What are their goals and how do they work towards achieving them? What are the racialized implications of navigating the higher education system?

This research will contribute to the sociology of education literature, particularly the inequality and organizational studies of colleges and universities. Importantly, this study will also explore how Black mothers conceptualize participating in higher education as a tool for survival and how it influences their wellbeing. At the institutional level, the study aims to examine the barriers and opportunities at colleges and universities that allow them to offer support to Black mothers. For example, are Black student mothers better supported at predominately white institutions or historically Black colleges and universities? This method of analysis and narrative-making contextualizes Black mothers' situational knowledge by focussing on their experiences while actively investigating the forces beyond their control.

Conclusion

There are several challenges in conducting sociological research and activism using matricentric feminism. Motherhood has often been excluded from academic feminism in the twenty-first century (O'Reilly 197). One predominant reason for this is the ongoing exclusion of mothers in the academy, specifically in areas of leadership and power (O'Reilly 207). Coupled with the ongoing dismantling of universities from places of learning to job training facilities, matricentric feminism has become even more challenging to use and disseminate in a university setting. Despite women continuing to make advances in both the professional and academic world, mothers continue to be left behind, forgotten, and erased by powerful institutions that have shaped policies around traditional students. Although mothers make up a large portion of the student population, the existence of the academic maternal wall continues to go unnoticed.

Challenges surrounding childcare, finances, and a lack of support continue to plague mothers at university, resulting in their leaving school and falling prey to the leaky pipeline. Exacerbating these issues is the neoliberalization of universities, in which individualism and cost-cutting measures have become the focus of the administration and policy change. Student parents achieve higher grade point averages (GPA) than other students, despite the various hurdles that prevent them from graduating on time. The Institute for Women's Policy Research found that a third of student parents have a GPA of 3.5 or higher, whereas independent nonstudent parents attained this minimum GPA at a rate of 31 per cent and 26 per cent for dependent students (Cruse, "Parents"). Student parents are a largely untapped student population that have immense potential to graduate at higher rates with proper support from their institutions.

To resist the policies that make universities so hostile to mothers, we have adopted a matricentric lens in our sociological research on mothering and higher education. Forming a research framework around a feminism recognizing the unique oppression of mothers under patriarchy has allowed us to inform our methodology in a way that leads to a greater understanding of mothering in university. This includes the addition of Black matricentric feminism to understand how race intersects with mothering experiences in higher education. We also use matricentric feminism to inform our activism, directly applying our findings to advocacy work to assist mothers on campus. We propose using matricentric feminism as a research framework to assist stakeholders in conducting research within their communities while contextualizing the macro-societal influences on the lived experiences of mothers.

Works Cited

American Association of University Professors. "Data Snapshot: IPEDS Data on Full-Time Women Faculty and Faculty of Color." *American Association of University Professors*, 2020, https://www.aaup.org/news/data-snapshot-full-time-women-faculty-and-faculty-color#.YnRkOilh3uQ. Accessed 8 July 2024.

Augustine, Jennifer M., et al. "Doing It All? Mothers' College Enrollment, Time Use, and Affective Well-Being." *Journal of Marriage and Family*, vol. 80, no. 4, 2018, pp. 963–74.

Austin, Sandra A., and Kathryn A. McDermott. "College Persistence among Single Mothers after Welfare Reform: An Exploratory Study." *Journal of College Student Retention: Research, Theory & Practice*, vol. 5, no. 2, 2003, pp. 93–113.

Averett, Kate Henley. "A Feminist Public Sociology of the Pandemic: Interviewing about a Crisis, during a Crisis."*Gender, Work & Organization*, vol. 28, 2021, pp. 321–29.

Boyd, Diana, and Rob Shea. "Socioeconomic Need for Student Parent Success within a University Environment." *Journal of Student Affairs*, vol. 24, no. 176, 2015, pp. 79–92.

Burawoy, Michael. *Public Sociology*, Polity, 2021.

Coté, James E., and Sarah Pickard. "The History and Scope of the Sociology of Higher Education." *Routledge Handbook of the Sociology of Higher Education*. Edited by James E. Coté and Sarah Pickard. Routledge, 2022, pp. 1–7.

Crittenden, Ann. *The Price of Motherhood: Why the Most Important Job in the World Is Still the Least Valued*. Picador, 2010.

Cruse, Lindsey Reichlin, et al. "Parents in College: By the Numbers." *Institute for Women's Policy Research*, 2019.

Cruse, Lindsey Reichlin, et al. "Evaluating the Role of Campus Child Care in Student Parent Success: Challenges and Opportunities for Rigorous Study. IWPR# C506." *Institute for Women's Policy Research*, 2021.

Federal Student Aid. https://studentaid.gov/help/fafsa. Accessed 14 July 2024.

Goldrick-Rab, Sara, and Kia Sorensen. "Unmarried Parents in College." *The Future of Children*, vol. 20, no. 2, 2010, pp. 179–203.

Goldrick-Rab, Sara, and Jason N. Houle. "Student Debt Accountability and Its Unintended Racial Consequences." *In Accountability and Opportunity in Higher Education: The Civil Rights Dimension*. Edited by Orfield G., Hillman N. Cambridge. MA: Harvard Education Press, 2018.

Goulden, Marc., et al. "Keeping Women in the Science Pipeline." The ANNALS of the American Academy of Political and Social Science, vol. 638, no. 1, 2011, pp. 141–62, https://doi.org/10.1177/00027162 114 16925.

Graduate Student Association and University of Alberta Board of Governors. *Graduate Student Assistantship Collective Agreement*, 2022, https://www.ualberta.ca/graduate-students-association/media-library/collectiveagreement/final-ca-2022-2024.pdf. Accessed 8 July 2024.

Hays, Sharon. *The Cultural Contradictions of Motherhood*. Yale University Press, 1996.

Hugo Lopez, Mark and Ana Gonzalez-Barrera. "Women's College Enrollment Gains Leave Men Behind." Pew Research Center, 6, Mar. 2014, https://www.pewresearch.org/fact-tank/2014/03/06/womens-college-enrollment-gains-leave-men-behind/. Accessed 8 July 2024.

Katz, Sheila. "'Give Us a Chance to Get an Education': Single Mothers' Survival Narratives and Strategies for Pursuing Higher Education on

Welfare." *Journal of Poverty*, vol. 17, no. 3, 2013, pp. 273–304.

Koppisch, D., Dahl, S., Magnelia, S., Goldrick-Rab, S., Coca, V., & Gill, J. "Securing the Basic Needs of Philadelphia-Area College Students During a Pandemic: A #RealCollegePHL Report." *The Hope Center for College, Community, and Justice*, 2021. Available at: https://hope4college.com/rc2021-phl/.

Mahaffey, Barbara A., et al. "College Student Mother Needs at Regional Campuses: An Exploratory Study." *Association for University Regional Campuses of Ohio (AURCO) Journal*, vol. 21, 2015, pp. 105–15.

Marx, Benjamin M., and Lesley J. Turner. "Student Loan Nudges: Experimental Evidence on Borrowing and Educational Attainment." *American Economic Journal: Economic Policy*, vol. 11, no. 2, 2019, pp. 108–41.

Radey, Melissa, and Leah P. Cheatham. "Do Single Mothers Take Their Share?" FAFSA Completion among Aid-Eligible Female Students." *Journal of Diversity in Higher Education*, vol. 6, no. 4, 2013, p. 261.

MacKinnon, Janice, and Mike Percy. *MacKinnon Report on Alberta's Finances*, 2019, https://www.alberta.ca/mackinnon-report-on-finances.aspx#jumplinks-3. Accessed 8 July 2024.

O'Reilly, Andrea. *Matricentric Feminism: Theory, Activism and Practice.* Demeter Press, 2016.

Teeling, Katie, and Emily Williams. "Two Years in Review: Academic Restructuring at the U of A." *The Gateway*, https://thegatewayonline.ca/2023/01/two-years-in-review-academic-restructuring-at-the-u-of-a/. Accessed 8 July 2024.

Van Rhijin, Tricia M., et al. "A Profile of Undergraduate Student Parents in Canada." *Canadian Journal of Higher Education*, vol. 41, no. 3, 2011, pp. 59–80, http://dx.doi.org/10.47678/cjhe.v41i3.2490.

Williams, Joan. *Unbending Gender: Why Family and Work Conflict and What to Do About It.* Oxford University Press, 2000.

12.

Without a Village: Motherhood, Childcare, and COVID-19: A Research Journey

Bailey Higgins

Introduction

In May 2023, I graduated with my doctorate of social work (DSW) after completing a dissertation about the impact of the COVID-19 pandemic on mothers of children who had not yet reached school age and used childcare outside of the home. This research took place in the United States. When I started the research project in early 2022, lockdown orders had lifted and life was transitioning to the "new normal" or "post-COVID-19." At this time, COVID-19 was still prevalent in the community. Mitigation efforts—such as masking, social distancing, and quarantines for exposure—were in effect, and people were mostly still advised to stay home or at least away from each other when possible. Some who had worked from home during the height of the pandemic were transitioning back to the office. I was expected to show up at the office to complete my employment duties daily, despite working from home during the lockdown.

During the spring of 2022, quarantines and isolation were still the norm for COVID-19 exposures for those not vaccinated and after positive test results. My two young children were attending preschool (which I also will refer to as childcare), and the policy was if there was exposure in the classroom, everyone needed to stay home to monitor symptoms for eleven days. This happened often and without notice. Many times, I would pull up to preschool and see the director meeting parents at the door, telling them that their children had been exposed to the virus and they could not come back to the facility until they finished their quarantine and were symptom free if they had developed the illness. It was stressful managing both roles: navigating keeping the children safe and well (and at home) and being employed (which, in the eyes of my employer, could only be done from the office). Vaccines were starting to become available for adults, but in early 2022, it seemed impossible that there would ever be a vaccine developed for children under five years old that would be safe and effective.

I observed through my own experience that the tasks (and expectations) of motherhood (at least my brand of it) were impossible. Accessing childcare is complex, expensive, and problematic in many ways. COVID-19 somehow made mothering young children even more impossible for me. Reading mommy blogs and consuming other social media led me to believe that it was not only me struggling: Other mothers were doing a similar complicated dance trying to manage it all. But was this the truth or just the picture being painted by the algorithms set by my internet habits? Did researchers already know about the experience of motherhood?

The same year, I discovered matricentric feminism while exploring the available motherhood studies literature regarding the effects of the pandemic on mothers. This serendipitous discovery helped to validate and normalize not only what I was experiencing as a mother living through the muck of motherhood but also as a budding motherhood researcher who had yet to make any social connections with others in the field of motherhood studies. The matricentric feminism perspective served as an analytical tool I could use in my dissertation.

In this chapter, I will share parts of my dissertation to demonstrate the utility of matricentric feminism. The framework provided me with vocabulary and perspectives to understand my own experiences on a personal level and opened new analytical avenues at the research level.

Exploring What Matricentric Feminism Provided

Matricentric feminism is a mother-focussed feminism that advocates for the enfranchisement of mothers and understands motherhood "not as a 'natural' or biologically given process, but as one which is historically and socially constructed" (O'Reilly, 43). Researchers of motherhood studies agree motherhood is a social and ideological construct without universal meaning or experience (O'Reilly). The practice of motherhood is then defined and restricted by the societal and cultural context in which it happens (O'Reilly). The framework challenges commonly held beliefs about a person's innate ability to be empathetic and have natural skill or knowing (without learning) how to do motherwork (O'Reilly). Matricentric feminism understands the word "mother" as "a practice" (O'Reilly 11) completed by those who place motherwork at the centre of their lives. Engaging in the practice of mothering is done not only by cisgender women but by anyone who voluntarily assumes the role (O'Reilly).

Matricentric feminism acknowledges that gender inequality exists. Patriarchy is foundational in many feminist theories (Napikoski), matricentric feminism included. A patriarchal society "consists of a male-dominated power structure throughout organized society and in individual relationships" (Napikoski). Women are systematically discriminated against as a result of this power structure (Napikoski; O'Reilly).

Provided Perspective

A mother becomes more than "the woman who cares for her biological children" under normative motherhood. Matricentric feminism defines normative motherhood through ten dictates: "essentialization, privatization, individualization, naturalization, normalization, idealization, biologicalization, expertization, intensification, and depoliticization" (O'Reilly 10). Simply put, maternity is essential to a woman's identity, takes place within the private sphere, is the mother's sole responsibility, is natural to women and driven by instinct, is limited to the nuclear family, ascribes to intensive mothering practices, maintains and perpetuates unattainable expectations of and by mothers, and is private and nonpolitical (O'Reilly). From a normative motherhood perspective, a good mother is determined by whether she meets these ten dictates, and if she cannot, or does not, then she is considered a "bad mother" (O'Reilly

11). Therefore, people who take on motherwork and mothering roles who are not from the hegemonic group (i.e., white, cisgender, and heterosexual) will never be able to meet the "good mother" standard (O'Reilly).

In addition to those who identify as mothers and participate in motherwork, other people have parental responsibilities and roles. The organization of family structure and roles is complex and unique for each family (Sanner and Jensen). Much like the concept of motherhood, family is a social construct without a universal meaning (Sanner and Jensen). Patrifocal family structures are based on the romantic relationships between the adults, whereas pedifocal family systems are oriented towards the children (Sanner and Jensen). Patrifocal and pedifocal familial systems have a different emphasis on blood ties, support, purpose and goal of the family, and patterns of how children are cared for and by whom (Sanner and Jensen).

Provided Vocabulary

After considering existing white patriarchal (or as bell hooks calls "white-supremacist capitalist patriarchy") power dynamics and the language used in previously published research, I decided that I would need to use gendered language throughout the research project. It is necessary to use gendered language when talking about mothers and motherwork to acknowledge the gender oppression and assumptions that accompany the current constructed state of motherhood (O'Reilly). We know that the majority of the time mothers are women and that motherwork is carried out by them. The use of nongendered language, such as caregiver or parent, within the field of motherhood studies perpetuates bias against mothers by erasing them as a unique population and equivocating their roles and responsibilities with fathers within the family (O'Reilly).

In making this choice, challenges caused by using gendered language needed to be addressed, especially to honour and acknowledge those who do not identify as cisgender, identify as nonbinary, or have come to be in the care of children without giving birth. Matricentric feminism informs us that mothers are not only cisgender women who give birth to biological children; those who identify as mother and engage in motherwork have various diverse identities. To be a participant in the study one only needed to identify as mother; there was no demographic data collected regarding gender identity or how one came about having children in their care.

It is important to note that matricentric feminism uses the word "motherwork" with intention. While operationalizing the terms of the study, I honoured the visible and invisible duties that mothers carry out in the public and private sphere. The word "motherwork" emphasizes the work aspect of the motherhood role, includes the cultural and political significance and consequences of motherwork, and highlights the complexity of motherhood within a broad spectrum of mothers (Collins; O'Reilly). Patricia Hill Collins and Andrea O'Reilly agree that motherwork is not just the stereotypical duties of birthing children, doing dishes, preparing meals, etc. but also includes navigating racism, violence, and other systemic oppression. The specific goals and actions of motherwork differ among people of cultural and social groups.

Connection to Those Who Came Before

Andrea O'Reilly's writings about matricentric feminism includes the work of others who have made contributions to the field of motherhood studies. Although I was introduced to many motherhood scholars through doing this work, Collins and Sharon Hays were instrumental in framing my research and understanding social, economic, and political dynamics that influence motherhood and mothering practice. As I examined my own power, privilege, and understanding of motherhood, I kept the participants in my mind and heart so as to minimize any potential harm that could come from research. By building from their work, I hoped to avoid perpetuating assumptions of motherwork set by intensive mothering standards (Hays).

Collins

Collins's work addresses the dichotomous perception and organization of normative, nuclear family life as a division between the public (paid labour economy, male) and private (unpaid caregiving labour, female) spheres. Motherwork is the nurturing and loving labour that mothers do. Rather than restricting itself exclusively to reproductive labour, such as bearing children and doing other unpaid tasks to maintain daily life (Duffy), motherwork seeks to balance a myriad of economic, political, and social factors threatening family life in the public and private spheres (Collins). According to Collins, the effort of motherwork is to maintain family and group survival.

When analyzing feminist theorizing of motherhood with a critical lens, Collins argues that white, middle-class mothers' experiences have been foundational to motherhood studies, thus encouraging a myopic understanding of motherhood that renders the experiences of those from different racial or social backgrounds nonexistent. In addition to erasing those women from motherhood theory, the erasure reinforces social inequality and maintains existing power dynamics, further exacerbating the intersectional oppression of women (Collins et al.).

Hays

Mothering practices that are both intensive and demanding are called "intensive mothering" (Hays). Motherwork of this type asks mothers to sacrifice their own needs and autonomy for their children's needs and interests (Hays). One factor contributing to increased stress during motherhood is the societal pressure to do motherwork in a specific and demanding way. In intensive mothering, mothers must sacrifice their own needs and autonomy over their children's needs and interests, with particular mindfulness of what child development experts say is best practice (Hays). The mothers' wellbeing is diminished due to these unrealistic and unattainable standards (Forbes et al.). It has been found, however, that this ideology causes harm to fathers as well by placing them in a secondary role to mothers and leaving mothers to shoulder the burden of parenting (Forbes et al.NICHD).

Matricentric feminism guided how I chose how to describe and operationalize concepts in my research, helped me to make intentional choices about the use of language describing mothers, families, and the power dynamics identified through the perspective, and provided me with a broad foundation to build the work I was engaged in. Finding matricentric feminism led me to find a community of people living this work and honouring mothers and motherwork in both the joys and struggles. I was finding that maybe it was possible that I am not completely alone in being a mom and in being interested in studying the experience of motherhood. I took what I learned about matricentric feminism and applied it during the research process.

Application at the Research Level

COVID-19 mitigation efforts decreased access to formal and informal supports, leaving families without the extra help needed to provide care to their children. In times of natural disaster or increased stress, families tend to fall back on gender norms for organization of family activities and responsibilities (Power), and during the COVID-19 pandemic, women took on increased hours of childcare, housework, and other domestic duties (Lamar et al.; Martucci; Petts et al.; Power; Shockley et al.; Zamarro and Prados). For those who use formal childcare, the COVID-19 pandemic exposed and exacerbated inadequacies in the system. These shortcomings included high costs for childcare, low availability, and reduced quality of care (Rawjani).

The COVID-19 pandemic did not create the problems associated with childcare. Before the pandemic, mothers and families used a range of care types to cover childcare. A 2008 report detailed how between 33 and 53 per cent of employed parents utilized informal care networks, such as friends, family members, or neighbours to cover childcare demands (Susman-Stillman and Banghart). Amy Susman-Stillman and Patti Banghart (2008) found grandmothers were the most utilized informal childcare providers for children between newborn and preschool. By 2015, it was estimated that 35 per cent of children under age five were enrolled in a formal childcare centre and 52 per cent of childcare was provided by grandparents, friends, or other informal care providers (Fraga et al.). During the COVID-19 pandemic, families with children were forced to incorporate school, work, and daycare into the home due to the closures of these institutions. Mitigation efforts stopped parents from utilizing formal childcare institutions and halted commonly used informal childcare networks, such as assistance from grandparents, family, or friends.

The initial mitigation efforts, including lockdowns, made the struggles of balancing paid labour and motherwork more pronounced (Pettigrew; Petts et al.; Shockley et al.), but employment was not the only area where the pandemic's repercussions were experienced for mothers trying to provide childcare. Research from the lockdown period examines gendered nuances of pandemic life, including differences in norms around the division of domestic labour between mothers and fathers (Shockley et al.; Zamarro and Prados), the increased mental load mothers took on (Dean et al.; Pettigrew), and mental health, stress, and coping (Dugan and Barnes-Farrell; Ruppanner et al.). In contrast, some evidence suggests that mothers had positive experiences during the lockdown period, such as spending more time with their families (O'Reilly) and feeling closer to their children (Kerr et al.).

The Study

My study explored the implications of the COVID-19 pandemic response on motherhood and motherwork for mothers of children not yet in kindergarten who utilized childcare. After the pandemic began in early 2020, the global public health emergency caused a significant impact on many social institutions, including employment and family life. This research project aimed to explore the answers to the following questions: What are the reported experiences of motherhood for women who utilize childcare outside the home? How has COVID-19 influenced the reported experience of motherhood? What changes in motherwork have been made to accommodate the pandemic concerning childcare?

To answer these questions, I used a feminist hermeneutic phenomenological study. This approach allowed mothers of young children to share their experiences with motherhood, childcare, and COVID-19. Feminist hermeneutic phenomenology was developed from Heidegger's phenomenology philosophy to understand human existence better. Phenomenological approaches are applied in motherhood studies to understand mothers' experiences. There is no attempt to "quantify or find" (Vagle 35) through these approaches, but they do provide a scientific system to explore subjective lived experiences.

To operationalize "mother," I considered the term's geopolitical and historical-societal implications. "Mother" is a social construction and therefore exists differently outside the environment in which it is defined. Through matricentric feminism, "mother" can be defined as anyone who participates in motherwork and who identifies as a mother (O'Reilly). Childcare is defined as care provided by individuals other than the child's primary parents or caregivers, such as a daycare centre, a babysitter, or a family member. To participate in this study, participants had to be at least eighteen years old, identify as a mother with at least one child in their care who had not yet started kindergarten, and have experiences with childcare during COVID-19.

Through reading matricentric feminist literature, I learned that mothers are not a completely invisible or erased group in society (despite the efforts of those trying to keep mothering invisible). They can be seen and recognized for their efforts. Mothers are a group worth talking about and to, which was important, as I was framing my research and justifying my study population. I did not need to expand the research population to "caregivers" or "people who take care of children."

I do not intend to diminish or reduce the experiences, functions, or duties of others who care for children. Making mothers the population of the study, as a subgroup of all those who help to raise and provide care to children, illuminates the complexities of Westernized motherhood, the impacts of assuming that role, and the placement of women in society (Ross).

The data collection plan included completing semi-structured interviews with mothers over Zoom. Interview questions prompted participants to share their experiences with motherhood, childcare, and how the COVID-19 pandemic influenced their experience. Participants were recruited from mom affinity groups on Facebook, which was selected as the recruitment tool for this study because it made it possible to recruit mothers from varying backgrounds and locations. Using internet-based recruitment tools and virtual meeting spaces excludes participants who do not have access to Facebook or the internet. After completing a cost-benefit analysis regarding both the researcher's and participants' access to resources, the potential to reach a diverse pool of mothers, and increasing ease of access for mothers, I decided that Facebook, Google Forms, and Zoom would be best suited for this study.

Calls for participants to participate were posted on the Facebook affinity groups inviting interested mothers to sign up via Google Forms. The Google Form included information about the study, consent to participate, and demographic questions. These questions included age; geographical location; the number of adults and children in the household; the children's age; the number of children not yet in kindergarten; how the participant identifies in relation to the children (such as mother, father, grandparent, step-parent, etc.); employment status; if their childcare responsibilities affected their employment; if their employment changed because of childcare responsibilities; how often they used childcare and for what purpose; the range of annual household income; work location (work from home or not); and types of childcare used. Gender identity was not asked because there was no gender qualifier for the inclusion criteria, only that you identify as a mother. This research did not collect racial or ethnic identity data from participants to avoid drawing false conclusions or correlations (Zuberi and Bonilla-Silva). Discussion about these identities was welcomed as part of the interview to understand better the mothers' experiences, but such questions were not explicitly asked as part of the demographic or interview questions.

In total, eight mothers participated in the interview process. Interviews were conducted from November 13, 2022, to November 18, 2022. I did not conduct interviews after American Thanksgiving (November 24, 2022) because if there were an increase in COVID-19 cases or other illnesses after the holiday it would create two distinct sets of data. It was anticipated that increases in illnesses after holiday gatherings—such as respiratory syncytial virus (RSV), influenza (flu), and COVID-19—would disrupt childcare arrangements and routines, potentially causing families to quarantine or childcare classrooms to close to mitigate the spread of illnesses.

Interviews were conducted and recorded via encrypted Zoom and then transcribed by Otter.ai software. Otter.ai provides verbatim transcriptions that need scrubbing for accuracy, clarity, and depersonalization, which I completed manually. This process was completed by listening to the interviews, correcting any mistakes that the Otter.ai software produced, removing vocal disfluencies, such as "like," "yeah," "so," and "um," as well as any personal information, such as names or other identifiable information. During this scrubbing process, the researcher also connected sentence fragments and removed instances where the participants corrected or repeated themselves.

I used NVivo 12 Qualitative Analysis Software to complete the analysis of the transcriptions because of its ability to organize data into themes and create visual representations of the data, such as word clouds. I completed the coding by using emergent codes (meaning units) based on the content of the interviews. Unitization of the data was not rigidly defined but consisted of the complete response to a question or a response fragment. I coded the data multiple times to identify the appropriate meaning units, categories, and final themes. The three identified themes that emerged from the data analysis were "motherhood," "impacts of COVID-19," and "childcare."

Motherhood

At the start of each interview, the participants were asked to share what it meant to them to be a mother. There was a consensus that "being a mother" meant "being everything," even if that meant sacrificing their self-care, career, or relationships. The participants described motherhood as being all-consuming, challenging, frustrating, and rewarding. The negative and positive aspects of the experience of motherhood were not expressed in a mutually exclusive way. It was all those things and more, all at the same time. As one participant said: "It is all in, it is just all-consuming. It is all-consuming in every single way. I guess it is just pure love. Just empathy and just every emotion that goes into what I would consider amazing things. That is motherhood."

Being Everything

"Being everything" took on different meanings in different contexts. During the lockdown period, mothers reported they had to be "everything"—from a speech therapist to teacher, entertainer to protector, employee to supervisor, and more. The focus on "being everything" from that time is discussed mainly through the additional roles that mothers did to fill the gaps created by lockdown measures. Nevertheless, "being everything" during lockdown encompassed the same essence as it does in the post-COVID-19 "new normal."

Mothers reported a continued sense of "being everything" to their children and within their families after the lockdown period, suggesting that how "everythingness" is framed was impacted by the COVID-19 pandemic but not a result of it. "Everythingness" appears to be a quintessential characteristic of the motherhood experience. An all-encompassing state of "everythingness" transcends what may be considered formal professional titles (teacher, chef, chauffeur, etc.) and includes and exceeds abstract roles (provider, protector, supporter, etc.).

Self-Care

During the interviews, participants shared feelings of increased stress, obligation, and hardship because of their mother role and its many intersections with their other identities. I asked them what self-care strategies, if any, they implemented for wellness. At first glance, this may seem outside of the topic of the study and unrelated to childcare and the COVID-19 pandemic, but self-care is part of the role of motherhood.

As one mother put it, "I have to take care of myself to take care of them."

Mothers joked about "just going to the bathroom alone" or "painting their nails during a Zoom call" as small acts of self-care. Others listed other small but intentional acts, such as drinking water during the day or taking breaks during long stretches of work. At the same time, the tone shifted from jocular to serious when mothers shared their experiences of not being able to prioritize their needs. As one mother said, "That's probably the hardest thing for your own emotional well-being is just... losing yourself into motherhood." Another mother expressed similar feelings: "What are you gonna do for self-care? Take a bath? Like that's going to help anything. Honestly, it's just about surviving."

The Village

One mother said: "There is no village. My husband and I are each other's people. It's frustrating at times because you never feel like you're getting a break." The mothers reported limited access to others outside their homes to support them with childcare during the post-COVID-19 period. Within the household, mothers and fathers shared in the completion of childcare tasks, such as bathing, packing lunches, bedtime routines, and picking up and dropping off children from childcare. Mothers did report a sense of doing more of the unpaid labour tasks associated with childcare and homemaking, stating that their schedules and employment responsibilities allowed them to engage more readily in those activities.

Participants shared that the social groups available to assist and support with childcare ("villages") were limited to only a few people or were nonexistent. Mothers identified that without a village they were without a babysitter, mom friends to share in the experience of mothering, and others to assist with childcare tasks outside what was offered through formal childcare settings. Some of the mothers interviewed reported having one best friend or close relatives (typically others in a mother role such as grandmother, mother-in-law, or sister) who they could ask for help with childcare if necessary. "If she [best friend] is unable to help me with them, my sister and mother are close by."

Isolation

Isolation was another theme: "Because that isolation, that lack of community, that lack of being a part of something—not having that, I think is a lot of the part that had me thinking 'I can't do this.'" While going through memos as part of the analytic process, I found this note etched in the margin: "If I had to put one word from each interview that I've done so far: isolation. I think it is the one thing that people are saying. It has affected people the most."

During the lockdown period, people were restricted to their homes and advised not to be in physical proximity to others, resulting in bouts of isolation. The isolation of the lockdown and afterwards, when mothers continued to limit social gatherings to reduce potential exposure to the virus, had negative consequences on their mental health and spousal relationships: "I think part of being a mom, which shouldn't be a part of being a mom, is that you are isolated. And that was true, honestly, before COVID-19. It's the problem of our modern society. And I would say, post-COVID-19 that it became even more extreme, the isolation." The sense of isolation these mothers experience did not only materialize because of policies limiting physical proximity to others. The experience of being a mother itself is isolating because of the time needed to care for children and balance multiple tasks, limiting that time spent with others.

Impacts of COVID-19

Changes to Employment

The COVID-19 pandemic changed the national conversation about working and where it can be done. For some mothers, remote working allowed them to care for their children at home while working. Some of the mothers interviewed did not entirely benefit from remote working, disclosing that working from home while trying to mother made them feel bad and guilty because they were not showing up one hundred per cent for either role. They reported feelings of "letting down" their coworkers and supervisors, even though they completed all their assigned work. They felt like they were not doing enough at work because their attention was divided between employment and childcare.

Families took different approaches to accommodate mothers working from home. One mother reported that she felt positive about working from home with her child home with her: "I actually get more done when he is here!" Because of her hybrid schedule, she could reduce the number of days her child attended childcare outside the home, saving the family money and limiting the child's exposure to illness. In contrast, another mother shared that to accommodate her work-from-home schedule and the children's schedules, her husband had to take a demotion at work to ensure the children were cared for when needed: "My husband, he actually stepped down from his position. Because I needed more when I switched jobs, I couldn't do it myself anymore." According to another mother, her office did not allow parents to have their children at home while working from home. However, she kept her children at home during the day as needed, risking disciplinary action and termination from her position.

Privilege

The COVID-19 pandemic has exposed the challenges and hardships that mothers face with navigating and providing childcare. A common thread that tied all the interviews together was outlining how COVID-19 was impactful but not necessarily the cause of the hardships: "A lot of the stuff that I'm experiencing are things I would have experienced in 2018 if I had a kid when there was no pandemic, or COVID, or whatever. I think that is the part that bothers me the most is that I knew I was gonna have the issues of childcare. So for me my frustration lies in the fact that I did not have the basic needs."

While mothers were working from home, people who might not have had prior experience seeing motherwork in action had real-time exposure. Mothers' Zoom meetings and phone calls were interrupted by children, and home life was visible on screen, which speaks to the invisibility of motherhood as identified by the matricentric feminist framework and to the privilege of being unaware that others were facing these challenges.

Another privilege this research exposed was doctor appointments and childcare centres' requirements for negative COVID-19 tests and return to school/work notes from doctors. One mother described her experience trying to make an appointment: "There are no sick visits available at the doctor's office. They are full, and there are no urgent care centre appointments either. And if you do walk in, they'll ... send you away and have you come back, [or] they'll call you or text you if there's an availability, or they'll just tell you they have no room, and they'll direct you to go to the ER." Another mother shared the additional burden of the cost of seeing the doctor: "You are paying for that out of pocket. That's another bill." Mothers also noted that when children did not attend formal childcare, they were still billed for those days. Avoiding illness became not only about not getting sick but also preventing the strain of having to access medical care and pay for it and taking time off work to care for the sick children.

Childcare Closures

One mother said: "Everything's COVID. There [are] no more ear infections or sinus infections. It's [assumed to be] COVID." In the period after the COVID-19 lockdown, the winter of 2021, childcare centres reopened and people started to engage in their daily routines outside the home once more. Mitigation efforts were still in place, and vaccinations were not available yet to children under five years old, resulting in childcare closures when there was a COVID-19 case in a classroom. During this time, mothers recalled struggling with the disruptions to childcare:"I think it was six times being quarantined. It came down to, what, once a month at least. And then at one point, one [child] was going out on quarantine, and then another one was just getting off of quarantine. It was a mess."

Of the mothers who used formal childcare services, all reported that the classrooms no longer closed for a COVID-19 case, but policies were put in place to extend absence periods and other requirements to return to childcare when a child was experiencing any type of illness. The mothers expressed frustration, yet understanding, of the new procedures.

Many of the mothers reported that if the child could not attend childcare, they had to take time off work because it was easier or more affordable than if their spouses did. The extended time that children needed to be away from childcare centres in the event of a fever had mothers missing multiple days of work. These stretches away from work become prolonged when there were multiple people at home who become sick at different times or when community resources were not available, such as medical care or COVID-19 testing.

Other Illnesses

One mother said: "You hear all the stuff on the news about Respiratory Syncytial Virus (RSV) and about them ending up in the hospital and getting really sick, and it's stuff that normally you wouldn't think a two-year-old would get this sick. But then I have friends that are people in his daycare, his friends, that are ending up in the hospital with it."

The COVID-19 pandemic brought illness to the forefront of the concerns the mothers mentioned. COVID-19 had become less central to the conversation of illness and safety because of the increase of other illnesses affecting young children, such as RSV and influenza. Eighty-seven and a half per cent of mothers interviewed mentioned that RSV had affected their household in the last year: "I'm not feeling as concerned about

COVID itself; however, I'm concerned about some of the flu and RSV that's going around."

Childcare

Regarding the necessity of having childcare, one mother said, "Just the juggling; it's a constant juggle. I can't possibly do everything at once, right?" All of the mothers interviewed reported that they used childcare services during work hours. The other reasons listed were to socialize children, to educate them, to complete tasks unrelated to unemployment, and to access early intervention services.

During the interviews, mothers shared strategies that they used to accommodate changes in childcare since the pandemic. These strategies ranged from changing employment to "just reacting to survive." One of the mothers was not able to get her children back into childcare after having lost their spot during COVID-19 lockdown. The strategies to accommodate childcare were to get assistance from their spouse, ask friends or family members (although this appeared to be a limited option or a last resort), or take time off work themselves.

Conclusion

This research sought to answer three questions. The main question, in accordance with phenomenological research approaches, was "What are the reported experiences of motherhood for women who utilize childcare outside the home?" Two subquestions were also asked and helped to guide the study: "How has COVID-19 influenced the reported experience of motherhood?" and "What changes in motherwork have been made to accommodate the pandemic in relation to childcare?" The findings from this study reveal that mothers are experiencing a sense of having to be "everything" for their children and families. Being a mother means there is little available time for self-care activities and it is isolating. Despite these negatives, the experience is also positive, full of love and empathy.

The COVID-19 pandemic continues to have consequences for motherwork in that it has changed childcare policies, brought illness to the forefront of thought and worry, and changed employment. COVID-19 changed the conversation about how people engage in employment.

Mothers will continue to have to navigate the childcare system and illnesses even after the COVID-19 pandemic is declared endemic.

The research would not have been possible without matricentric feminism, as it centres mothers and their experiences. Matricentric feminism guided all the steps of this research process through the operationalization of terms, identifying the research population, guiding the development of the questions, and structuring how the study would take place. The findings are supported by matricentric feminism in that cultural, societal, and political factors influence the experience of motherhood. Matricentric feminism has proven to be useful in guiding and informing my research.

Works Cited

Collins, Patricia Hill. "Shifting the Center: Race, Class, and Feminist Theorizing about Motherhood" *Mothering: Ideology, Experience, and Agency*. Edited by Evelyn Nakano Glenn et al. Routledge, 1994, pp. 45–65, https://doi.org10.4324/9781315538891-3.

Collins, Patricia Hill, et al. "Intersectionality as Critical Social Theory." *Contemporary Political Theory*, vol. 20, no. 3, Sept. 2021, pp. 690–725, https://doi.org10.1057/s41296-021-00490-0.

Dean, Liz, et al. "The Mental Load: Building a Deeper Theoretical Understanding of How Cognitive and Emotional Labor Overload Women and Mothers." *Community, Work and Family*, vol. 25, no. 1, Jan. 2022, pp. 13–29, https://doi.org10.1080/13668803.2021.2002813.

Duffy, Mignon. "Reproductive Labor." *Sociology of Work: An Encyclopedia*. Edited by Vicki Smith. SAGE Publications, Inc., 2013, pp. 729–30, https://doi.org10.4135/9781452276199.n260.

Dugan, Alicia G., and Janet L. Barnes-Farrell. "Working Mothers' Second Shift, Personal Resources, and Self-Care." *Community, Work and Family*, vol. 23, no. 1, Jan. 2020, pp. 62–79, https://doi.org10.1080/13668803.2018.1449732.

Elias, Nicole M., and Maria J. D'Agostino. "Care in Crisis: COVID-19 as a Catalyst for Universal Child Care in the United States." *Administrative Theory and Praxis*, vol. 43, no. 2, Apr. 2021, pp. 217–229, https://doi.org10.1080/10841806.2020.1813456.

Fraga, Lynette, et al. https://www.childcareaware.org/wp-content/uploads/2016/05/Parents-and-the-High-Cost-of-Child-Care-2015-FINAL.pdf. Accessed 9 July 2024.

Kerr, Margaret L., et al. "Exploring the Complexity of Mothers' Real-Time Emotions While Caregiving." *Emotion (Washington, D.C.)*, vol. 21, no. 3, Apr. 2021, pp. 545–56, https://doi.org10.1037/emo0000719.

Lamar, Margaret R., et al. "The Mental Health of U.S. Parents during the COVID-19 Pandemic." *Journal of Mental Health Counseling*, vol. 43, no. 4, American Mental Health Counselors Association, Oct. 2021, pp. 319–335, https://doi.org10.17744/mehc.43.4.03.

Larossa, Ralph, and Sharon Hays. "The Cultural Contradictions of Motherhood." *Social Forces: A Scientific Medium of Social Study and Interpretation*, vol. 76, no. 3, 1998, p. 1159–61, https://doi.org10.2307/3005721.

Martucci, Sara. "He's Working from Home and I'm at Home Trying to Work: Experiences of Childcare and the Work-Family Balance among Mothers during COVID-19." *Journal of Family Issues*, vol. 44, no. 2, 2023, pp. 291–314, https://doi.org10.1177/0192513X211048476.

Napikoski, Linda. "What Is a Patriarchal Society and How Does It Relate to Feminism?" *ThoughtCo*, 9 June 2010, https://www.thoughtco.com/patriarchal-society-feminism-definition-3528978.

O'Reilly, Andrea. *Matricentric Feminism: Theory, Activism, Practice*. 2nd ed. Demeter Press, 2021.

Pettigrew, Rachael N. "An Untenable Workload: COVID- 19 and the Disproportionate Impact on Women's Work-Family Demands." *Journal of Family and Consumer Sciences*, vol. 113, no. 4, 2021, pp. 8–15, https://doi.org10.14307/jfcs113.4.8.

Petts, Richard J., Daniel L. Carlson, and Joanna R. Pepin. "A gendered pandemic: Childcare, homeschooling, and parents' employment during COVID-19." *Gender, Work & Organization*, 28 (2021), pp. 515–534.

Power, Kate. "The COVID-19 Pandemic Has Increased the Care Burden of Women and Families." *Sustainability: Science Practice and Policy*, vol. 16, no. 1, 2020, pp. 67–73, https://doi.org10.1080/15487733.2020.1776561.

Rawjani, S. "The Child Care Crisis Is a Threat to Our Nation." *Columbia Public Health*, 2021, https://www.publichealth.columbia.edu/public-health-now/news/child care-crisis-threat-our-nation. Accessed 9 July 2024.

Rose, Evan K. "The Rise and Fall of Female Labor Force Participation during World War II in the United States." *The Journal of Economic History*, vol. 78, no. 3, Cambridge University Press (CUP), Sept. 2018, pp. 673–711, https://doi.org10.1017/s0022050718000323.

Ross, L. R. *Interrogating Motherhood*. Athabasca University Press, 2016.

Sanner, Caroline, and Todd M. Jensen. "Toward More Accurate Measures of Family Structure: Accounting for Sibling Complexity." *Journal of Family Theory and Review*, vol. 13, no. 1, 2021, pp. 110–127, https://doi.org10.1111/jftr.12406.

Shockley, Kristen M., et al. "Work-Family Strategies during COVID-19: Examining Gender Dynamics among Dual-Earner Couples with Young Children." *The Journal of Applied Psychology*, vol. 106, no. 1, pp. 15–28, https://doi.org10.1037/apl0000857.

Susman-Stillman, Amy, and Patti L. Banghart. "Demographics of family, friend, and neighbor child care in the United States." 2008.

Vagle, M. D. *Crafting Phenomenological Research*. 2nd ed. Routledge, 2018.

Zamarro, Gema, and María J. Prados. "Gender Differences in Couples' Division of Childcare, Work and Mental Health during COVID-19". *Review of Economics of the Household*, vol. 19, no. 1, 2021, pp. 11–40, https://doi.org10.1007/s11150-020-09534-7.

Zuberi, T., and E. Bonilla-Silva. *White Logic, White Methods: Racism and Methodology*. Rowman & Littlefield, 2008.

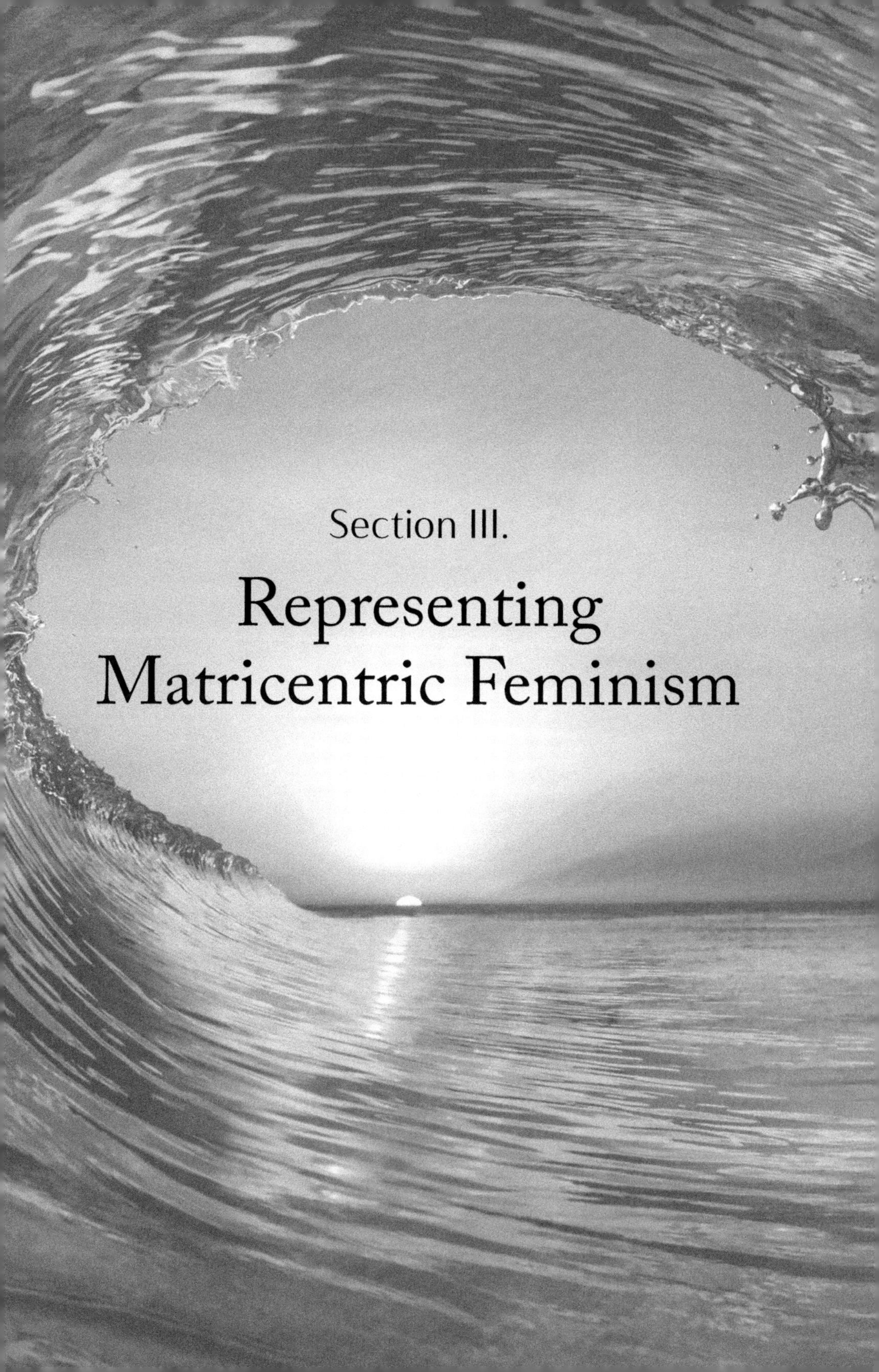

Section III.

Representing Matricentric Feminism

13.

Towards a Literary Theory and Criticism of Matricritics: "Begin with the Mother in Her Own Right" to Deliver "New Meanings of Motherhood" and "Transform Maternal Thinking Itself"

Andrea O'Reilly

Adrienne Rich opened the Foreword to her book *Of Woman Born: Motherhood as Experience and Institution* with the observation: "We know more about the air we breathe, the seas we travel, than about the nature and meaning of motherhood" (lix). Over the last thirty years, I have published over thirty-five books on motherhood that seek to explore its nature and meaning across many topics, including maternal theory, feminist mothering, young mothers, monstrous mothers, maternal regret, normative motherhood, mothers and sons, mothers and daughters, and maternal texts. In 2006, I founded the discipline of motherhood studies and its subfield maternal theory in 2007. In 2016, I developed matricentric feminism, a feminism for and about mothers and in 2021, matricritics, a literary theory and practice for reading mother-focused texts. Although close to half a century has passed since the publication of *Of Woman Born* in 1976 and despite hundreds of books and articles written on motherhood, including my own, it would seem that we still do not yet fully understand the nature and meaning of motherhood. In her 2018 book *Mothers: An Essay on Love and Cruelty*, Jacqueline Rose writes: "It is still the case that today, in public, the bodily necessities of mothering are brushed under the carpet and/or consigned to another hidden, intimate world" (46). Lucy Jones opens her 2023 book *Matrescence: On the Metamorphosis of Pregnancy, Childbirth and Motherhood* by noting that when she became pregnant she felt that she had been "hoodwinked"; that her experiences of pregnancy, birth, and motherhood "did not match up with the cultural, social and philosophical narratives [she] had grown up with… that [she] had been fundamentally misinformed about the maternal experience" (3, 4). In May 2024, I published my collection *In (M)other Words: Writings on Mothering and Motherhood, 2009 to 2024* to continue this conversation on the meaning and nature of motherhood initiated by Rich to present, in Rose's words, "other ideas" (47) on motherhood so to, in Jones's words, find the "language to articulate the reality of motherhood" (9). In this chapter, I consider how my theory and practice of matricritics contributes to matricentric feminism to enrich and expand our conversations on mothering and motherhood.

In her 2018 *Paris Review* article "Why All the Books about Mother?," Lauren Elkin writes: "These books are putting motherhood on the map, literarily speaking, arguing forcefully, through their very existence, that it is a state worth reading about, parent or not." Indeed, as Lily Gurton-Wachter notes, "These writers are making a space in the literary world where there didn't seem to be room before; a space in which pregnancy, childbirth, and the postpartum experience are neither ignored nor pathologized, but simply—at long last—described." Earlier, in the introduction to our 2010 edited collection *Textual Mothers/Maternal Texts: Motherhood in Contemporary Women's Literatures*, Liz Podnieks and I noted that all but one of the thirty-plus maternal narratives examined in the collection were published after 1970. Over the last fifty years, novelists, poets, and memoirists have been writing about maternal themes, identities, and experiences to an unprecedented degree. Critics and theorists are not only documenting and anthologizing the expanding tradition of maternal literature but also recovering and retracing the origins and development of this tradition. I argue that this unprecedented proliferation of maternal narratives in women's writing, particularly over the last decade, calls for a new mother-centred mode of literary theory and criticism, what I have termed "matricritics." The late Sara Ruddick once wrote: "It is hard to speak precisely about mothering. Overwhelmed with greeting card sentiment, we have no realistic language in which to capture the ordinary/extraordinary pleasures and pains of maternal work" (29).

Matricritics, as both literary theory and criticism, is the language we need to capture and convey the maternal in women's writing. Developed from two of the central principles of my theory of matricentric feminism—challenging child centredness and countering normative motherhood—while using Olivia Heal's theory of maternal poetics and Elaine Showalter's concept of gynocritics and a female literary tradition, this chapter will propose a literary theory of matricritics for reading maternal narratives and establishing a matrilineal tradition in women's contemporary fiction. Overall, the chapter considers what matricritics looks like and what it reveals about normative motherhood. Following Heal, it will ask: "How can we as critics, as theorists, and/or mothers read this literature? What might a matricentric feminist methodology look like?" (118). More specifically, the chapter will show how matricritics in countering child centredness to foreground a maternal standpoint and the unmasking of motherhood allows for and enables a critique of normative motherhood to challenge and change this institution. Moreover, in discovering and delineating the maternal in matrifocal narratives, matricritics creates and delivers a matrilineal tradition of maternal texts.

Maternal Poetics: "Tune in as Matricentric Feminists"

In her article "Towards a Matricentric Feminist Poetic," Heal explains that the title of her article is taken from Showalter's "Towards a Feminist Poetics," in which she calls for a "gynocritics"—a mode of "feminist criticism ... concerned with the woman as writer—with woman as the producer of textual meaning, with the history, themes, genres and structures of literature by women" (5). Her article's aim, as Heal explains, is the following: "[To] delineate a poetics of maternal literature ... and consider what a matricritics may look like. How can we as critics, as theorists, and/or mothers read this literature? What might a matricentric feminist methodology look like? (118)." Heal argues that maternal writing is fundamentally a political act and is characterized by four strategies: misreproduction, queering, formal engagement, and new materialist and phenomenological approaches (120). Misreproduction refers to "a practice that purposefully reproduces maternity defectively and which, through audacity and authenticity, reveals the contradictions and complexities of lived mothering to disrupt idealized normative motherhood" (120). To queer motherhood is to destabilize patriarchal motherhood—particularly its ideological mandates of essentialization, normalization, naturalization, and biologicalization—whereas formal engagement refers to aesthetic practices of "interruption, splintering, fragmentation, polyphony, multiple figures, and shifting of pronouns" (121) to create texts that "frustrate any attempt to produce a coherent subject and resist the possibility of a singular interpretation" (121). And, finally, the fourth strategy "champions phenomenology over ontology to," as Heal explains, to situate "the maternal in the everyday, multiple, disparate, and episodic experiences of mothering" (122). These four strategies enact, as Heal concludes, "a politics that works to demythologize and de-essentialize the mother" (121).

Drawing upon Marianne Hirsch's argument that "the psychoanalytical frame ... has made us unable to hear maternal stories," Heal astutely observes that normative theoretical paradigms—whether they are historical, social, or even feminist—do not allow for the comprehension and elucidation of maternal texts. Such texts demand new theories and methods that "reangle our ways of reading and tune out the hefty discourses that may be preventing us from hearing what is actually being said" (Heal 122). In other words, maternal texts require critics to "tune in as matricentric feminists" (122). In the second part of her article, Heal delineates a mode of inquiry that "is informed directly by the experiences, ethics, and aesthetics of maternal texts," and she offers specific reading strategies for its implementation: "read reparatively," "describe not interrupt," "listen to the lesser beats," and "refrain from essentialization and biologicalization" (124). Building upon the four strategies of maternal texts demarcated by Heal and in response to her call that readers "tune in as matricentric feminists," I now move to Showalter's framework of gynocritics and a female literary tradition and then to two of the central principles of matricentric feminism.

Gynocritics and Female Literary Tradition: Templates for Matricritics and a Matrilineal Literary Tradition

In her classic 1979 article "Towards a Feminist Poetics," Showalter develops a theory of gynocritics for reading woman-authored texts. Gynocritics, as Showalter explains, is concerned with the following:

> woman as producer of textual meaning, with the history, themes, genres, and structures of literature by women. Its subjects include the psychodynamics of female creativity; linguistics and the problems of female language; the trajectory of the individual or collective female literary career; literary history; and ... studies of particular writers and their works. (5)

The aim of gynocritics, as Showalter explains, "is to construct a female framework for the analysis of women's literature, to develop new models based on the study of female experience, rather than to adapt male models and theories" (8). She argues that "gynocritics begins at the point when we free ourselves from the linear absolutes of male history, stop trying to fit women between the lines of male tradition and focus instead on the newly visible world of female culture" (8). Gynocritics, thus, signifies a new literary project intended to construct a female framework for the analysis of women's literature.

Significantly, gynocritics is also attentive to what Showalter defines as a female literary tradition and studies the "patterns and phrases" of the evolution of this tradition. In her 1977 book *A Literature of Their Own: British Novelists: From Bronte to Lessing*, Showalter classifies and organizes the writings of British women writers into three stages: feminine, female, and feminist. Similarly, Sandra Gilbert and Susan Gubar, in their monumental *The Madwoman in the Attic*, identify and chart a distinctive female literary tradition in nineteenth-century women's literary imagination, which is one of enclosure and escape to represent and enact "a common, female impulse to struggle free from social and literary confinement" (xii). In *Archetypal Patterns in Women's Fiction*, Annis Pratt detects and chronicles archetypes across three hundred years of women's writing that, in her words, "manifest a considerable degree of continuity, uniformity of concern, and an abundance of analogue in both subject and method" (iii). Although the framework differs with each of these literary studies—whether they are political, stylistic, thematic, or archetypal—

they each locate "coherence" and "continuity" in the particular female tradition studied. I suggest that maternal texts likewise require matricritics that, to paraphrase Showalter, positions the mother as a producer of textual meaning and is attentive to the history, themes, genres, and structures of literature by mothers.

A Taxonomy of Matricritics as Literary Theory and Criticism

My proposed taxonomy builds from Heal's theory of maternal poetics, as well as Showalter's framework of gynocritics and female tradition to describe a matricritics, as literary theory and criticism, for the reading of maternal texts and to delineate a matrilineal tradition of mothers' writing. This taxonomy is thematic in focus and draws upon two of the central principles of matricentric feminism to configure the themes of maternal texts and its matrilineal tradition. These principles are correcting the child centredness defining much of the scholarship and activism on motherhood while developing research and activism from the experience and the perspective of mothers; and countering the patriarchal/normative institution of motherhood to imagine and implement a maternal identity and practice that empower mothers. These two frameworks are not the only way matricritics may be exercised, nor do all maternal texts enact these two principles. Rather, I suggest that matricentric feminism, with its matrifocal perspective and emphasis on critiquing normative motherhood, affords us the required vocabulary and methodology to "begin with the mother in her own right" and "deliver new meanings of motherhood and transform maternal thinking itself."

Matrifocality: Correcting the Child Centredness Defining Much of the Scholarship and Activism on Motherhood While Developing Research and Activism from the Experience and the Perspective of Mothers

Matricentric feminism works from one particular and constitutive assumption: Mothering matters and is central to the lives of women and others who are mothers. In this, matricentric feminism is consciously and deliberately matrifocal in its foregrounding of a maternal perspective and in positioning mothers' needs and concerns as the starting point for a theory and politic on and for women's empowerment. Matricritics foregrounds this matrifocality in its reading of a maternal text, wherein a mother plays a significant cultural and social role and in which motherhood is thematically elaborated and valued and is structurally central to the plot. In her introduction to *The Mother/Daughter Plot*, Marianne Hirsch queries why in Sophocles's *Oedipus Rex*, the voice of Jocasta, Oedipus's mother, is missing, and she connects this narrative silence to a larger literary lacuna: "In asking where the story of Jocasta is in the story of Oedipus, I am asking not only where the stories of women are in men's plots, but where the stories of mothers are in the plots of sons and daughters" (4). She concludes that "Clearly, to know Jocasta's maternal story ... we would have to begin with the mother" (5). Brenda O. Daly and Maureen T. Reddy emphasize that even in the limited number of fictional or theoretical texts that do "begin with the mother in her own right, from her own perspective ... [they] seldom hold fast to a maternal perspective; further when texts do maintain this perspective, readers and critics tend to suppress the centrality of mothering" (*Narrating Mothers*, 2–3). Daly and Reddy have coined the term "daughter-centricity" to describe the perspective wherein "we learn less about what it is like to mother than about what it is like to be mothered, even when the author has had both experiences" (2).

Within the last three decades, as motherhood studies has emerged as a distinct and established academic discipline, this daughter-centricity has been countered and corrected in fiction and theory. Indeed, a central aim of matricentric feminism is to articulate and theorize "the voice of the mother"—that is, to analyze becoming and being a mother from the perspective and subjectivity of mothers themselves. Adrienne Rich concludes *Of Woman Born* with these words: "The words are being spoken now, are being written down, the taboos are being broken, the masks of motherhood are cracking through" (239). Whether such "unmasking" (Maushart) is conveyed by way of a sociological study of mothers or maternal fiction, feminist writers and scholars alike endeavour to unmask motherhood by documenting the lived reality of mothering. In so doing, they counter the daughter-centricity, described by Daly and Reddy above, to create and compose what I have termed a "matrifocal narrative."

Specifically, the matrifocal perspective of matricentric feminism as enacted in matricritics excavates and emphasizes the maternal subject in women's literature. Indeed, as Heal notes, "Maternal writing begins with an 'I'; in a deft step, it pulls the mother out of the third person into the first" (119). By positioning the mother as a subject, Heal continues, maternal writing "begins to unravel those discourses, notably patriarchal and psychoanalytic ones, that have long held 'mother' in the third person as object or 'other'" (119). However, I suggest that the narrative point of view of the text does not necessarily need to be first person—although it frequently is—to enact matricritics. Rather matricritics, to borrow from Daly and Reddy's words, "begins with the mother in her own right, from her own perspective, and holds fast to a maternal perspective" (2–3). Matricritics, in other words, attends to and accentuates the maternal thematic in any given text by excavating the matrifocal perspective denied and distorted by a daughter-centric standpoint, masculinist readings, or both and seeks to articulate mothers' voices—in all their rhythms and ranges—moving them from silence to speech.

Countering the Normative Institution of Motherhood to Imagine and Implement a Maternal Identity and Practice Empowering for Mothers through this Challenge to Child Centredness

In *Of Woman Born*, Rich distinguishes "between two meanings of motherhood, one superimposed on the other: the potential relationship of any woman to her powers of reproduction and to children; and the institution—which aims at ensuring that that potential—and all women—shall remain under male control" (7). The term "motherhood" refers to the patriarchal institution of motherhood, which is male defined and controlled and is deeply oppressive to women, whereas the word "mothering" refers to women's experiences of mothering and is female defined and centred and potentially empowering to women. In *Of Woman Born*, Rich emphasizes, "We do not think of the power stolen from us and the power withheld from us in the name of the institution of motherhood" (275). Empowered mothering aims to reclaim that power for mothers and to imagine and implement a mode of mothering that mitigates the many ways that patriarchal motherhood, both discursively and materially, regulates and restrains mothers and their mothering.

Feminist scholars contend that motherhood, as it is currently perceived and practised in patriarchal societies, is disempowering if not oppressive for a multitude of reasons—such as the societal devaluation of motherwork, the endless tasks of privatized mothering, the current incompatibility of waged work and motherwork, and the impossible standards of idealized motherhood. The overarching aim of empowered mothering is to confer to mothers the agency, authority, authenticity, autonomy, and advocacy-activism denied to them in patriarchal motherhood. A literary theory of matricritics achieves this principle of matricentric feminism—countering normative motherhood to achieve empowered mothering by enacting another central principle of matricentric feminism, correcting the child centredness defining much of the scholarship and activism on motherhood while developing research and activism from the perspective and experiences of mothers. More specifically, enacting one central principle of matricentric feminism—correcting child centredness through a matrifocal perspective—allows for the attainment of a second central principle of matricentric feminism, specifically the critique of normative motherhood. In so doing, matricritics generates explorations on how mother protagonists can and do challenge, defy, and destabilize normative motherhood to make possible empowered mothering and deliver, in Rich's words, "new meanings of motherhood to transform maternal thinking itself" (286).

Enacting Matricritics as Literary Criticism: Reading the Maternal in Post-2010 Women's Narratives

Over the last four-plus years, first on sabbatical, then in COVID-19 lockdown, and then working and teaching remotely due to a health condition, I read dozens upon dozens of maternal narratives to enact and test my proposed theory of matricritics. I chose to look at women's fiction and memoirs published since 2010 across various genres and from multiple maternal perspectives. The genres include gothic fiction, dystopian fiction, speculative fiction, psychological thriller, domestic fiction, commercial fiction, climate change fiction, historical fiction, and autofiction. The authors studied are from Australia, Canada, Ireland, India, Jamaica, Mexico, Spain, South Africa, the United Kingdom, and the United States, and include writers who identify as Basque, African American, Canadian, Caribbean, Chinese American, Indigenous, Irish, Irish Canadian, Japanese American, Nigerian/South African, Palestinian, and queer/lesbian. I have completed fourteen articles on my theory of matricritics, which examine twenty-nine maternal narratives. Another seven papers are in progress or planned on an additional thirteen maternal texts.[1] The papers will be published as a monograph tentatively entitled *Matricritics as Literary Theory and Criticism: Reading the Maternal in Post-2010 Women's Narratives*. When I first began the project in 2018, I did not have a clear hypothesis let alone a coherent argument; I only knew that I wanted to write on maternal texts, which deliver, through a matrifocal standpoint, an authentic and candid account of the maternal experience. With their matrifocal perspective, these narratives all enact a central principle of matricentric feminism—namely, correcting the child centredness defining much of the scholarship and activism on motherhood while developing research and activism from the experience and the perspective of mothers. With each text, I sought to perform what I have defined elsewhere as an archeology of maternity: an excavation of the truths of motherhood that are disguised and distorted beneath what Susan Maushart has called the mask of motherhood (*Textual Mothers*).

With each reading, I asked the following: What do we learn about the mother protagonist's experiences and perspectives on mothering when motherhood is unmasked? What new understandings of motherhood are unearthed through this archeology of maternity? One cold winter afternoon, at the height of yet another COVID-19 lockdown, as I was pondering these questions while writing my fourth paper on this topic, my son, who was copy-editing an earlier article of mine, walked by my desk in the cottage loft and jokingly commented: "These mothers are rightly and certainly pissed off at normative motherhood." At that exact moment, I was trying to understand my current mother protagonist's rage. It was a lightbulb moment, as I then understood what the unmasking of motherhood through a matrifocal narrative allowed and enacted: a critique of normative motherhood to make possible a change to this institution and the attainment of maternal empowerment. More specifically, I realized that enacting one central principle of matricentric feminism—correcting child centredness through a matrifocal perspective—could allow for the attainment of a second central principle of matricentric feminism, specifically the critique of normative motherhood.

Ten assumptions and mandates define normative motherhood: essentialization, privatization, individualization, naturalization, normalization, idealization, biologicalization, expertization, intensification, and depoliticalization of motherhood. Essentialization positions maternity as basic to and the basis of female identity, whereas privatization locates motherwork solely in the reproductive realm of the home. Similarly, individualization causes such mothering to be the work and responsibility of one person, and naturalization assumes that maternity is natural to women—all women naturally know how to mother—and that the work of mothering is driven by instinct rather than intelligence and developed by habit rather than skill. Normalization limits and restricts maternal identity and practice to one specific mode: the nuclear family. The mother is a wife to a husband, and she assumes the role of the nurturer, and the husband assumes that of the provider. The expertization and intensification of motherhood—particularly as they are conveyed in what Sharon Hays has termed "intensive mothering," and what Susan J. Douglas and Meredith W. Michaels call "the new momism"—cause childrearing to be all consuming and expert driven. Idealization sets unattainable expectations of and for mothers, and depoliticalization characterizes childrearing solely as a private and nonpolitical undertaking, with no social or political import. Finally, biologicalization, in its emphasis on blood ties, positions the birthmother as the authentic mother. Normative motherhood is only available to mothers who can enact and fulfill these ten dictates: Mothers who cannot, or will not, do so because they are, for example, young, queer, single, racialized, trans, or nonbinary are defined and positioned as de facto bad mothers.

As I continued to read and write on maternal narratives through matricentric criticism, I developed and implemented a theory and practice of queering motherhood to explore how the maternal narratives sought to challenge and change one or more of these dictates. Queering, as theory and practice, troubles the presumed gender, family, and sexual scripts of the dominant relations and makes "mother" a contested and unstable social category. Indeed, queering, as Margaret Gibson explains in the introduction to her book *Queering Motherhood: Narrative and Theoretical Approaches*, "makes the things we otherwise take for granted suddenly unpredictable, uncooperative, and unexpected" (1). Thus, the concept of queering motherhood extends beyond the experiences of queer and trans parents—although they are central to this endeavour and start, in Gibson's words, "where any of the central gendered, sexual, relational, political and/or symbolic components of 'expected' motherhood are challenged" (6). This act of queering is thus similar to Heal's concept of misreproduction: "a practice that purposefully reproduces maternity defectively and which, through audacity and authenticity, reveals the contradictions and complexities of lived mothering to disrupt idealized normative motherhood" (120). As I read and wrote on each narrative, I analyzed how normative motherhood functioned in each text, explored how each text queered and misreproduced motherhood, and considered which mandates were revealed and challenged through the text's matrifocal unmasking of motherhood. In all the twenty-nine narratives I have written about, the texts reveal normative motherhood to be oppressive; each exposes and challenges one or more of the ten mandates to render possible a practice and identity of empowered mothering.

Earlier, I referenced Showalter's *A Literature of Their Own: British Novelists: From Bronte to Lessing*, Gilbert and Gubar's *The Madwoman in the Attic*, and Pratt's *Archetypal Patterns in Women's Fiction* and discussed how they each locate coherence and continuity in the particular female tradition studied. Based on the forty-two maternal texts I read for my current study on motherhood in post-2010 women's narrative, I suggest that we can similarly identify a matrilineal tradition in women's contemporary fiction that manifests, to use Pratt's words, "a considerable degree of continuity, uniformity of concern, and an abundance of analogue in both subject and method" (iii). Or, to paraphrase Showalter's words, this chapter has sought to define a program of matricritics by constructing a new theoretical model for reading mother-centred literature ("Feminist Poetics" 8). It seeks to deliver, in other words, a matrilineal tradition of maternal texts elucidated and developed through a theory and practice of matricritics.

Conclusion: If Feminist Theory Is Not the Means to a Resolution, Matricritics May Well Be

In her recent book *The Book of Mothers* (2024), author Carrie Mullins considers "how literature can help us reinvent motherhood" and argues that "one of the joys of fiction is that it can teach us about the human experience" (2). However, as Mullins continues, "that doesn't mean the lessons always land" (2) and that, concerning maternal narratives, this is because readers "do not notice" (3) what the texts are saying about motherhood. The problem, however, Mullins emphasizes, is "not the books; it's the way we talk about them" (4). To correct this, Mullins argues, readers must engage in the act of "revision, or seeing a text with fresh eyes and entering it from a new critical direction" (5). I suggest that matricritics enacts this revision and enables us to enter a text from a new critical direction. Feminist theorist Patrice DiQuinzio has argued, "It is impossible for feminist theory to avoid the issue of motherhood, and it is impossible for feminist theory to resolve it" (xx). However, I suggest that matricritics, as literary theory and criticism, developed from two central principles of matricentric feminism—challenging child centredness and critiquing normative motherhood—allows for such encounters and resolutions. Through its maternal standpoint and matrifocal unmasking of normative motherhood, matricritics exposes and counters the oppressive mandates of normative motherhood to provide a formidable critique of it and render possible maternal empowerment. Perhaps, to paraphrase the words of DiQuinzio, if feminist theory is not the means to a resolution, matricritics may well be (xx). Indeed, in beginning and staying with the mother, matricritics delivers new meanings of motherhood to transform maternal thinking itself.

Notes

Chapters Published and Forthcoming:

Published

"A 'Motherhood So White': Normative Motherhood as Enacted and Resisted in the Motherhood Memoir. Through a Reading of Nefertiti Austin's Memoir *Motherhood So White: A Memoir of Race, Gender, and Parenting in America*." *Artemis*, vol. XXXI, no. 1&2, 2021, pp. 35–55.

"Breaking the Rules of Normative Motherhood and Family: Matrifocality, Motherlines, and the Mask of Motherhood in Sally Hepworth's *The Secret of Midwives* and *The Family Next Door*." *Hecate*, vol. 45, no. 1&2, 2019, pp. 43–52.

"Imagining Motherhood in a Post-Apocalyptic World: Reifying and Resisting Normative Motherhood in the Climate-Change Novels *Clean Air* by Sarah Blake and *The New Wilderness* by Diane Cook." *The Pain Mothers Must Never Expose*. Edited by Michelann Parr. Demeter Press, 2024, pp. 181–203.

"Redemptive Mothering; Reclamation, Absolution, and Deliverance in Emma Donoghue's *Room* and *The Wonder*." *Writing Mothers: Narrative Acts of Care, Redemption, and Transformation*. Edited by BettyAnn Martin and Michelann Parr, Demeter Press, 2020, pp. 141–66.

"'The Damage Done and May This Madness Be Over': Exposing and Eradicating Matrophobia through a Reading of the Nanny Trope in the Psychological Thrillers *The Nanny* and *Nanny Dearest*." *Care(ful) Relationships between Mothers and the Caregivers They Hire*. Edited by Katie Garner and Andrea O'Reilly. Demeter Press, 2024, pp. 149–68.

"'The Terror of Mothering': Maternal Ambiguities and Vulnerabilities in Helen Phillips's *The Need* and Melanie Golding's *Little Darlings*." *Monstrous Mothers: Troubling Tropes*. Edited by Abigail Palko and Andrea O'Reilly. Demeter Press, 2021, pp. 243–68.

"The 'Wildness of Motherhood': Transforming Maternal Rage, Transgressing Patriarchal Motherhood to Realize Maternal Empowerment: A Reading of Rachel Yoder's *Nightbitch*." *Coming into Being: Mothers on Finding and Realizing Feminism*. Eds. Andrea O'Reilly, Fiona Joy Green and Victoria Bailey. Demeter Press, 2023, pp. 215–236.

"'There Must Be Something Good about Me': Dystopian Satire, Maternal Resistance, and the Undoing of Normative Motherhood in Jessamine Chan's *The School for Good Mothers*." *Wild with Child: Outlaw Mothers and Feminist Representations of Female Power*. Edited by Rebecca Bromwich and Elena Fineston. Demeter Press, 2024, pp. 149–67.

"'They Both Begin with Blood, Pain, and Terror': Transgressing Normative Motherhood in and through the Contemporary Psychological Thriller: *The Perfect Mother* by Aimee Molloy, *Little Voices* by Vanessa Lillie, and *Little Disasters* by Sarah Vaughan." *Mothering Outside the Lines: Tales of Boundary Busting Mamas*. Edited by Michelann Parr and BettyAnn Martin. Demeter Press, 2023, pp. 197–218.

"'What Finally Dragged Her under the Water and Who Carried the Spark': The Intergenerational Trauma of Normative Motherhood in Celeste Ng's *Everything I Never Told You* and *Little Fires Everywhere*." *Normative Motherhood: Regulations, Representations, and Reclamations*. Edited by Andrea O'Reilly. Demeter Press, 2023, pp. 169–88.

"'What Is Incomprehensible': The Myth of Maternal Omniscience and the Judgment of Maternal Culpability in Sue Klebold's *A Mother's Reckoning* and Monique Lepine's *Aftermath*." *Monstrous Mothers: Troubling Tropes*. Edited by Abigail Palko and Andrea O'Reilly. Demeter Press, 2021, pp. 201–22.

Forthcoming

"Critiquing, Correcting, Defying, and Displacing Normative Motherhood: Reading Five Narratives of Mothers Who Leave as Demon Texts: *Hiroshima in the Morning* by Rahna Reiko Rizzuto, *Patsy* by Nicole Dennis-Benn, *The Shame* by Makenna Goodman, *I Love You But I've Chosen Darkness* by Claire Vaye Watkins, and *When I Ran Away* by Ilona Bannister." *The Missing Mother.* Edited by Andrea O'Reilly and Martina Mullaney. Demeter Press, Fall 2024.

"'How Sometimes They May Get It Wrong': The Survival of Black Mothers, the Safekeeping of Children, and the Loss of Homeplace in *Caul Baby* by Morgan Jenkins." *Home(place): Honouring, (Re)membering, and (Re)storying the process of Matriarchal Worlding as Kinship.* Edited by Jennifer Brant, Whitneé L. Garrett-Walker, and Qui Alexander. Demeter Press, Winter 2025.

"Misrepresentations and Rerepresentations: Queer Mothering as Challenging and Changing Heteronormative Motherhood and Family in Kristen Arnett's *With Teeth* and Francesca T. Royster's *Choosing Family: A Memoir of Queer Motherhood and Black Resistance.*" *Palgrave Handbook on Parenthood in Popular Culture.* Edited by Elizabeth Podnieks and Helena Henriksson. Palgrave Press, 2025.

Chapters Planned on the Following Novels

Agirre, Katixa. *Mothers Don't.* Translated by Kristin Addis. 3TimesRebel, 2022.

Audrain, Ashley. *The Push.* Penguin, 2022.

Bennett, Brit. *The Mothers.* Riverhead Books, 2016.

Elliott, Alicia. *And Then She Fell.* Dutton, 2023.

Kilroy, Claire. *Soldier Sailor.* Scribner, 2024.

Maxwell, Kate. *Hush.* HarperCollins, 2010.

Naqvi, Zehra. *The Reluctant Mother: A Story No One Wants to Tell.* Hay House, 2022.

Nettel, Guadalupe. *Still Born.* Fitzcarraldo Editions, 2022.

Omtosos, Yewande. *An Unusual Grief.* Cassava Republic Press, 2021.

Shree, Geetan Jaili. *Tomb of Sand*. Translated by Daisy Rockwell. Harper Via, 2023.

Stage, Zoje. *Baby Teeth*. St. Martin's Griffin, 2019.

Williams, Mai'a. *This is How We Survive: Revolutionary Mothering, War, and Exile in the 21st Century*. PM Press, 2019.

Woodson, Jaqueline. *Red at the Bone*. Riverhead Books, 2020.

Works Cited

Arnett, Kristin. *With Teeth*. Riverhead Books, 2021.

Austin, Nefertiti. *A Motherhood So White: A Memoir of Race, Gender, and Parenting in America*. Source Books, 2019.

Bannister, Ilona. *When I Ran Away*. Doubleday, 2022.

Blake, Sarah. *Clean Air*. Algonquin Books of Chapel Hill, 2022.

Blakely, Mary Kay. *American Mom: Motherhood, Politics, and Humble Pie*. Algonquin Books of Chapel Hill, 1994.

Chan, Jessamine. *The School for Good Mothers*. Simon & Schuster, 2022.

Cook, Diane. *The New Wilderness*. HarperCollins Publisher, 2020.

Daly, Brenda O., and Maureen T. Reddy. *Narrating Mothers: Theorizing Maternal Subjectivities*. University of Tennessee Press, 1991.

Dennis-Benn, *Patsy*. W. W. Norton & Company, 2019.

DiQuinzio, Patrice. *The Impossibility of Motherhood: Feminism, Individualism and the Problem of Motherhood*. Routledge, 1999.

Douglas, Susan J., and Meredith W. Michaels. *The Mommy Myth: The Idealization of Motherhood and How It Undermines all Women*. Free Press, 2004.

Elkin, Lauren. "Why All the Books about Motherhood." *The Paris Review*, 2018, https://www.theparisreview.org/blog/2018/07/17/why-all-the-books-about-motherhood/>. Accessed 7 July 2024.

Gibson, Margaret. *Queering Motherhood: Narrative and Theoretical Approaches*. Demeter Press, 2014.

Gilbert, Sandra M., and Susan Gubar. *The Madwoman in the Attic: The Woman Writer and The Nineteenth Century Literary Imagination*. Yale University Press, 1979.

Goodman, Makenna. *The Shame*. Milkweed Editions, 2020.

Hays, Sharon. *Intensive Mothering: The Cultural Contradictions of Motherhood*. Yale University Press, 1996.

Heal, Olivia. "Towards a Matricentric Feminist Poetics." *Journal of the Motherhood Initiative*, vol. 10, no. 1&2, 2018, pp. 117–29.

Hirsch, Marianne. *The Mother/Daughter Plot: Narrative, Psychoanalysis, Feminism*. Indiana University Press, 1989.

Jeremiah, Emily, "Troublesome Practices: Mothering, Literature, and Ethics." *Mother Matters: Motherhood as Discourse and Practice*. Edited by Andrea O'Reilly. ARM Press, 2004, pp. 231–41.

Johnson, Miriam. *Strong Mothers, Weak Wives: The Search for Gender Equality*. University of California Press, 1988.

Jones, Lucy. *Matrescence: On the Metamorphosis of Pregnancy, Childbirth and Motherhood*. Penguin Random House, 2024.

Lillie, Vanessa. *Little Voices*. Thomas and Mercer, 2020.

Maushart, Susan. *The Mask of Motherhood*. Penguin Books, 2000.

Mullins, Carrie. *The Book of Mothers*. St. Martin's Press, 2024.

Ng, Celeste. *Everything I Never Told You*. Penguin, 2014.

Ng, Celeste. *Little Fires Everywhere*. Penguin, 2017.

Molloy, Aimee. *The Perfect Mother*. Harper, 2018.

O'Reilly, Andrea. *In (M)other Words: Writings on Mothering and Motherhood, 2000–2024*. Demeter Press, 2024.

O'Reilly, Andrea. *Matricentric Feminism: Theory, Activism, Practice*. 2nd Edition. Demeter Press, 2021.

Podnieks, Elizabeth, and Andrea O'Reilly, eds. *Textual Mothers/Maternal Texts: Motherhood in Contemporary Women's Literatures*. Wilfrid Laurie University Press, 2010.

Pratt, Annis. *Archetypal Patterns in Women's Fiction*. Indiana University Press, 1981.

Rich, Adrienne. *Of Woman Born: Motherhood as Experience and Institution*. Norton, 1986.

Riizzuto, Rahna Reiko. *Hiroshima in the Morning*. Feminist Press, 2010.

Ruddick, Sara. *Maternal Thinking: Toward a Politics of Peace*. Beacon Press, 1989.

Rose, Jacqueline. *Mothers: An Essay on Love and Cruelty.* Farrar, Straus and Giroux, 2018.

Royster, Francesca. *Choosing Family: A Memoir of Queer Motherhood and Black Resistance.* Abrams Press, 2023.

Showalter, Elaine. "Towards a Feminist Poetics." *Historia Cultural,* https://historiacultural.mpbnet.com.br/feminismo/Toward_a_Feminist_Poetics.htm. Accessed 7 July 2024.

Showalter, Elaine. *A Literature of Their Own: British Novelists: From Bronte to Lessing.* Princeton University Press, 1997.

Vaughan, Sarah. *Little Disasters.* Simon and Schuster, 2020.

Watkins, Claire Vaye. *I Love You But I've Chosen Darkness.* Riverhead Books, 2021.

Yoder, Rachel. *Nightbitch.* Doubleday, 2021.

14.

Swimming against Plato: Rachel Cusk's *Outline*

Else Werring

> It is in Plato that the founding rite of matricide achieves its philosophical completion…these ancient mothers … are brought back to life in the sober gestures of a thousand daughters weaving together in their mother's home
>
> —Adriana Cavarero 9

This chapter argues that Rachel Cusk's *Outline* (2014) is a work of matricentric feminism—a feminism for mothers aiming to avoid the pitfalls of maternalism[1] and essentialism (O'Reilly). The reception of the *Outline* trilogy has made much of Cusk's device with "the invisible narrator" and her reinvention of the novel form. Little attention, however, has been granted the trilogy's treatment of motherhood.[2] *Outline* (2014), *Transit* (2016), and *Kudos* (2018) expose what Julia Kristeva and Luce Irigaray have pointed to—namely, that a "matricidal" way of thinking is still alive in European, late capitalist culture and that feminist thought so far has failed to deal adequately with this problem. *Outline's* narrator, Faye, is a feminist mother in a frozen state, speechless under neoliberal conditions that still discriminate against mothers despite having a seemingly feminist façade. Faye's journey points towards motherhood as a privileged site from which to explore gendered subjectivity beyond the body-mind distinction. Rather than ignore motherhood, feminism should consider it a valuable tool to think with. Building on Fanny Söderbäck's theory of revolutionary time, I read Cusk as a proponent of the view that feminism must work through a movement of return "from the present of our here- and- now to a past that by and large has been silenced and repressed, into a future that might be otherwise" (5). Such a nonlinear temporal movement is needed to uncover matricidal repressions before we can spiral into the future with a deessentialized mission that is nevertheless fully embodied. *Outline* urges us to "stay with the trouble" of the maternal body, even as we reject essentialism.

My chapter begins by introducing matricentric feminism and pointing out which aspects of it are relevant to my reading of *Outline.* I then present Söderbäck's theory of revolutionary time as a useful lens through which to read *Outline's* Faye as a contemporary feminist mother who needs to travel back in time to untie herself from certain strands of the Western intellectual tradition. I then show how Faye's journey alludes to the matricidal beginnings of philosophy (Plato) and literature (Homer) and how Cusk's play with the novel form alerts us to historical constructions of gender. Next, I describe Faye's journey through 1950s Beauvoirian existentialism, which, despite its enormous contribution to the feminist cause, seems to have left its daughters with a maternal excess. The final section explores the watery undercurrent running through *Outline*, which I read as an allusion to the unresolved issue of maternity in contemporary feminism and the new materialist attempt to bring the sexually differentiated body back to life in a deessentialized form.

Matricentric Feminism and *Outline*

In her book *Matricentric Feminism: Theory, Activism, Practice,* Andrea O'Reilly argues that motherhood is feminism's "unfinished business" and that mothers need a feminism of their own (41–42). This stance should not be confused with gender essentialism: Matricentric feminism does not argue that mothering is all that matters to women, that only women can mother, or that women are incomplete unless they mother. What it does argue is that "mothering is a significant, if not a defining dimension" of mothers' lives and that "arguably, maternity matters more than gender" to people who identify as mothers (41). The definition of a "mother" is a person who engages in "maternal practice" (Ruddick). Contrary to essentialism, it is because the category of mother is distinct from the category of woman that mothers need a feminism of their own, since mothers are oppressed under patriarchy both as women and as mothers. Matricentric feminism, therefore, is an intersectional approach but one which, unfortunately, has been largely ignored by feminist scholars (O'Reilly 213). Although mothering was briefly explored and even celebrated by cultural-difference feminism from the mid-1970s through the early 1990s, this tendency was eclipsed by the end of the 1990s as cultural-difference feminism fell out of favour in academia (219).[3]

O'Reilly offers three possible reasons for the academic disavowal of motherhood. First, it has been necessary to reject essentialism, as any celebration of the maternal body risks sliding into biological determinism or reified images of femininity. Second, feminists like Betty Friedan and Shulamith Firestone conflated the oppressiveness of the patriarchal motherhood institution with the empowering mothering experience, distinguished by Adrienne Rich in her 1976 book *Of Woman Born*, a distinction of crucial importance to matricentric feminism (O'Reilly 228). Third, O'Reilly contends that there exists today "a cultural anxiety around nurture, human dependency, caregiving and emotion," labelled by Julie Stephens as "postmaternal thinking" (qtd. in O'Reilly 231–32). This anxiety connects contemporary neoliberal tendencies to an "unmothering of society as a whole." (ibid, 32).

Cusk's *Outline* trilogy aligns with O'Reilly's theory in all of these respects, and it does so in its own specific way by linking maternity to temporality. Many of Cusk's books[4] portray contemporary mothers who are jolted out of time and pose difficult questions about how their maternity might be made to fit with their feminism. In *Outline*, this leads Faye to time travel, instigated by the troubling question of what exactly happened to make contemporary mothers speechless and seemingly without feminist sisters. *Outline* argues, between the lines, the matricentric point that motherhood deserves serious and sustained inquiry (O'Reilly 46). The novel shows that motherhood is not, and should not be, the sole responsibility and duty of mothers by alerting readers to how alone and miserable Faye's sons become when she leaves her children to go to work, and no one is there to perform her care duties. Through depicting a diversity of maternal experiences, *Outline* deessentializes motherhood and reveals it as a maternal practice rather than a biological reality. The multifarious parental voices depicted in *Outline* form a Greek chorus challenging patriarchal child centredness (O'Reilly 54) and the ideology of intensive motherhood, revealing that motherhood ought to be a collective rather than an individual concern.

Maternity and its relation to temporal experience is a theme running through the *Outline* trilogy, which one critic refers to as mimicking "the sensation of being underwater" (Julavits).[5] Narrator Faye is a mother of two whose life bears a striking resemblance to Cusk's alter egos in autobiographies *A Life's Work* (2001) and *Aftermath* (2012). Timothy Bewes, therefore, refers to the trilogy as exemplifying our postfictional age, and Ella Ophir highlights how Cusk's shifts between fiction and memoir signal a specific in-betweenness. In *A Life's Work*, Cusk relates her arduous process of finding herself anew after a maternal blow for which culture had left her unprepared. Eventually, this process led to divorce, after having attempted to switch roles with her husband, who for a while took care of the children, so that Cusk could pursue her writing career. Even so, we learn in *Aftermath* that this experience did not alter her identification with Clytemnestra, the murdered mother in Aeschylus's tragedy, the *Oresteia*. Although never explicitly stated, the narrator's identification with the murdered mother continues in *Outline*.

Following the publication of her memoirs, Cusk was accused of being a bad mother by several critics and defended herself in a newspaper article by stating that she "was only being honest" (Cusk: "I was Only Being Honest"). In a later interview, she admitted that the public outrage had left her feeling wiped out (Kellaway). And "wiped out" seems an apt description of narrator Faye, an effaced receptacle whose voice we only discern piecemeal—if at all—behind the voices of all the people she meets on her way.[6] Peter Vermeulen describes Cusk's device with the effaced narrator as "literary austerity." He argues that this device has the effect of gendering unsentimentality as a feminine choice rather than a female character trait and that Faye's unsentimental and hollowed-out form converts the traditional muting of women's voices into a deliberate posture. I want to add Faye's maternity to this picture: When read *as a mother*, Faye's hollowed-out character foregrounds, and criticizes, the muting of matrifocal narratives under patriarchal discourse, from psychoanalysis to medical and philosophical history, through the literary canon and continuing into neoliberalism—all of which overwhelmingly see the mother from the outside, as an object rather than subject. O'Reilly points out that strengthening the matrifocal perspective is a central aim of matricentric feminism, which is still a salient issue today, considering that even contemporary manuals for feminist mothering tend to be presented from a child-centred perspective rather than taking a mother-centred approach (O'Reilly 207–08).

A Life's Work depicts a new mother embodying what O'Reilly and Lynn O'Brien Hallstein call a "post-feminist split subjectivity" (O'Reilly 79). They explain how young women grow up with an expectation of being liberated but then encounter a shock as they become mothers: "The lives of women without children have become more and more similar to the lives of men without children; yet, on the other hand, becoming a mother fundamentally changes that similarity" (ibid, Quiney). In *Outline*, we meet a narrator who is in some ways a continuation of the mother depicted in Cusk's memoirs, but this time, she is in what Luce Irigaray calls "a state of dereliction," or feminine homelessness under patriarchy. To untangle Faye from this frozen state, Cusk sends her on a time-travelling voyage to the origins of patriarchal thought that instigated an ideal of disembodiment as the road to freedom. She travels to Greek antiquity, where she runs into remnants of Plato's philosophy and the Homeric epic (as will be explained below). Having engaged with Plato and Homer, Faye is then propelled to the 1950s, to Simone de Beauvoir's feminism, and its implications for contemporary mothers. In all these encounters, Faye notices a connection between constructions of motherhood and temporality. Like O'Reilly, Cusk's implied author in *Outline* seems to mourn the disappearance of difference feminism, with its exploration and foregrounding of the maternal, from the feminist scene of the 1970s and the 1980s. Cusk also portrays how reintroducing the mother to feminist thought is a precarious balancing act because we need to avoid essentialism. Returning to the past is not a nostalgic longing to remain there but rather a constant push and pull, necessary for instigating future change.

Revolutionary Time

According to Söderbäck, feminist questions tend to be linked to questions of time. The claim "me too," for instance, signals a "relational temporality of sorts," the "too" referring to a claim made by another, while inevitably also telling the story of a past to which the speaker must return in order to speak those words" (4). Anyone wanting to contribute to a change for the future must understand that change depends on "a return to the past and a vitalization of the present" (Söderbäck 9). A future capable of renewal does not depend on a break with the past, but rather on our perpetual return to it, argues Söderbäck. (9). She builds her argument on Kristeva's and Irigaray's philosophies of time, and argues that contemporary feminism can benefit from a return to these two thinkers, who were falsely accused of essentialism in the 1990's.

Kristeva and Irigaray, despite differences as thinkers, share the view that any serious engagement with gender must work through an engagement with time because time in the tradition of Western philosophy has been powerfully tied to constructions of gender. Women have tended to be linked to embodied repetition and cyclical time, whereas men have been constructed as "minds," laying claim to linear time. In *The Second Sex,* Beauvoir argues that it is women's task to leave the cyclical time of immanence and transcend into the linear future, previously reserved for men (73).[7] The linear-cyclical binary, however, may be seen as two sides of the same coin, as Kristeva argues in her 1979 essay "Women's Time," in which she urges women to recreate themselves for the future through new time conceptions, in what she calls a future "heretics." Expanding upon Kristeva, Söderbäck argues that the sex-gender dichotomy has tended to work within the linear-cyclical binary rather than challenge it. If we understand sex as aligned with nature, repetition, and immanence and gender with culture, mind, and transcendence, we seem to reach the conclusion that mothers must leave their bodies behind to liberate themselves. But maternal work, even if deessentialized, cannot be carried out by disembodied minds because maternal thinking is an "ethics of care" rooted in practice (Ruddick). Feminist mothers must straddle the linear-cyclical binary to a greater extent than what is required of feminists without dependents. This underlines O'Reilly's point that mothers need a feminism of their own because many of the problems mothers face are specific to women's roles and identities as mothers rather than their being women in general.

Cusk's characters often feel trapped in either linear or cyclical time. Faye's maternity is rarely mentioned in *Outline*, but this elision creates the uncanny effect of a maternal ghost pulsating between the lines. This eerie shadow may be connected to a historical erasure of the maternal across philosophy, literature, psychoanalysis, and many strands of feminism. Feminist reworkings of psychoanalysis, in contrast, insist that Freud's theory of individuation (staged as an Oedipal battle between fathers and sons, one where the mother's voice is missing) glosses over an earlier matricide—a crime that has been committed, then covered up, creating a wound that we cannot mourn properly because it has been given no symbolic representation (Hirsch; Jabobs; Wieland). We learn about Faye's sons only as they disrupt the narrative now and then, with their phone calls, letting Faye know that they are alone and miserable. Their father, who was supposed to be taking care of them, is absent. Faye's maternal guilt has rendered her an empty vessel, channelling other people's stories, yet unable to tell her own. But the stories she channels spool out a web of care and questions of the flesh—a web that we gradually come to perceive as mirroring Faye's own.

Athens: The Past in the Present

In what follows, I present *Outline* as Faye's return to the matricidal beginnings of literature and philosophy. As Faye undertakes her journey through revolutionary time, she is unweaving herself from certain strands of the Western intellectual tradition and attempting to reweave herself into a new fabric. She must first unweave herself from Plato's philosophy because it is a mode of thought—now thriving under neoliberalism—in which freedom seems incompatible with an ethics of care. But Faye also returns to the Homeric epic, in her play with the novel form. Her listening and recounting of other people's stories may be construed as Penelopian, pointing towards a philosophy of birth (Cavarero; Stone). Faye's time travel epitomizes matricentric feminism's emphasis on reclaiming the motherline (Lowinsky qtd. in O'Reilly 128).

Outline begins in an unidentified present, which we soon recognize as our recent past, where Faye undertakes a journey, significantly, to Athens, the cradle of Western civilization. Once she arrives, Faye settles into the apartment of a woman named Clelia. The flat lies atop of a Platonic ladder[8]:

> Clelia's apartment was on the top floor of the building and was reached by a curving marble staircase that passed the doors to the apartments on the other floors one by one.... At the bottom the hallway was darker and cooler than the street, but ... as it rose it became lighter and warmer. Outside Clelia's door, just beneath the roof, the heat—with the strain of the climb up—was faintly stifling. Yet there was also the feeling of having accessed a place of privacy, because the marble staircase ended here and there was nowhere further to go. (51)

Among Clelia's many books is a collection of finely carved wooden boats with sails attached to tiny cords, which Faye feels sure "Clelia had intended to illustrate the relationship between illusion and reality" (52). Clelia's kitchen is immaculately clean, pointing to the fact that Clelia rarely spends any time there. These observations tie in with Plato's philosophy, which argues for an ascent away from the realm of the senses towards the higher, abstract ideals of truth and beauty. Faye's perception of Clelia's flat echoes feminist observations of the way Plato's theory carries within it a disdain for the body and birth, which are somehow, for him, related to fiction and irrationality (Cavarero; Söderbäck *Liminal*).

In the sitting room, Faye finds a tremendous collection of classical music, bearing witness to Clelia's preference for symphonies: "In fact she possessed the complete symphonic works of all the major composers. There was a marked prejudice against compositions that glorified the solo voice" (54): Faye remarks: "I wasn't sure I would sit through symphony after symphony any more than I would spend the afternoon reading the *Encyclopedia Britannica*" (54). It occurs to Faye that in Clelia's mind "they [the symphonies] perhaps represented the same thing, a sort of objectivity that arose when the focus became the sum of human parts and the individual was blotted out (54).

The allusion to Plato's philosophy continues with Faye's observation of Clelia's symphonies. In *The Symposium*, Plato, through his mouthpiece Socrates,[9] argues that love, if pursued properly, is the result of a long process, whereby one starts by desiring an individual body but then moves step by step up a ladder towards the abstract ideals of truth and beauty. This philosophy ties in with temporality: The abstract forms are fixed for eternity, whereas empirical or existential truths are ever changing and ephemeral. The ideal lover, Socrates, is unperturbed by embodied concerns, such as cold, hunger, or sexual desire. Irigaray (*Ethics*) and Adriana Cavarero argue that Socrates ends up distancing himself from anything resembling love the further up the ladder his tale ascends (Nussbaum; Söderback, *Natality*). Faye's reaction to Clelia's flat seems to echo these critiques. It hints that the Platonic view of love (and freedom) is still alive in contemporary western culture, and that this has detrimental effects for mothers and children: there is a children's room in Clelia's flat where pristinely made bunk beds "stood for the concept of children generally rather than any child specifically" (54).

Faye has travelled to Athens on a quest to refind herself after her recent divorce. Arguably, however, her divorce merely scratches the surface of an underlying issue having to do with care in the history of Western thought. What are the conditions of care, asks *Outline*, in an age of neoliberal individualism?

Another relevant Platonic dialogue is *The Republic*, which may be read as an early feminist classic, in its emphasis on women being just as capable as men of becoming philosopher rulers.[10] But this insight is modified by Plato's insistence that a philosopher ruler must be freed of familial ties and children raised in institutions. Care is associated with the body and is incompatible, therefore (due to a strict body-mind separation), with the true liberation of the mind. Two thousand years later, Beauvoir (*Second Sex*), for all her focus on embodiment, seemed to agree with Plato that to "transcend," women need to free themselves of their embodied "situation" and step into the realm of the mind and linear time (73).[11] Where does this line of thought leave the mother?

Significantly, there is an uncanny female statue at the centre of Clelia's flat. Faye has to pass it frequently, and even though it is "surprisingly easy to forget" (55) its presence, Faye is haunted by it:

> Sometimes she looked as if she were about to say something, sometimes as if she were in despair. Occasionally she appeared to be conferring some kind of benediction. Her white garment glowed at dusk. You had to pass her frequently, going from one room to another, yet it was surprisingly easy to forget that she was there. Her white looming figure with its raised hands and its broad flat face, with its swiftly changing mood, was always slightly startling. (55)

Faye is unsettled by this eerie "woman-mother" of the Western cultural imaginary. There is something goddesslike about the statue, saintly, as if about to confer "some kind of benediction," yet it is also volatile, with its "swiftly changing moods." Faye's impression that the statue changes moods signals a profound existential ambivalence, shaking her to the core: "The terracotta woman made reality seem, for a moment, smaller and deeper, more private and harder to articulate" (55). Faye finds herself looking for "something else, a clue, something rotting or breeding, a layer of mystery or chaos or shame" (57).[12]

Faye's reaction is reminiscent of Kristeva and Irigaray's reactions to Plato, who they think instigated a matricidal way of thinking in the

Western imaginary (Kristeva, *Revolution*, Irigaray, *Speculum*).[13] Faye identifies with the statue as the murdered mother glossed over by patriarchal thought but she also bumps into her, as if for the first time, wondering how it might be "so easy to forget" (55) something so intense and unresolved. Faye's thoughts echo those of Irigaray, who, in *Speculum of the Other Woman*, critiques how masculine thought has split from the maternal body. Irigaray thinks of Plato's cave as a metaphor for the womb and of Plato as usurping the maternal when he uses birth and midwife imagery (the philosopher as a midwife) and instigates a male appropriation of the female body. She emphasizes how Plato's allegory of the cave reverses birth's direction. The prisoners of the cave "ascend" out, while an actual birth is a "descent" (Söderbäck, *Revolutionary* 236–40). When Faye inhabits Clelia's flat, she is a mother climbing into masculine space, like Plato's prisoners ascending out of their cave. But this ascent brings on an uncanny homelessness. If the cave is a metaphor for maternal generativity, seen as a passive space from which an active mind projects itself, Faye becomes a split self: to project her mind out of the cave, she must leave her maternal body behind. The part of herself that ascends from the cave is the child that, according to Freud and Lacan, must separate from the mother to become a self.

No route exists for Faye's maternal self, which is rendered fleshless through the cave metaphor. In matricentric feminist terms, Irigaray's reaction to Plato may also be connected to the historical medicalization of pregnancy and birth (Hill 236). Recent research on obstetric violence shows a troubling tendency in pregnancy and childbirth to efface the mother's agency from the birthing process: "By virtue of the nearly microscopic fetus growing in my belly, I was no longer my named self; to my providers, I was 'mama' ... no longer recognized as my own individual person with her own rights and agency" (Hill 234). We can also understand Faye's ascent up Plato's ladder (or out of the cave) as a projection of herself into a secular feminist future but one that has the paradoxical effect of jolting her back to the past. Faye's experience troubles our naive understanding of space and time because on her journey, past and future intertwine, and Faye seems to be in several places at once.

Faye reacts to the conceptual order of Clelia's space while repeatedly bumping into an uncanny, silenced woman at the centre of the flat, rupturing her experience of herself in gendered space and time. She has longed to go on a writer's retreat to transcend into a room of her own,[14] but once she arrives, she feels not only homeless but also speechless.

Homelessness and the Novel

Faye's journey to Greece also alludes to the Homeric epic. This is hinted at by the quest motif, the Athenian setting, the recurring theme of homelessness, and the lack of interiority to Faye's character. In the final chapter, as Faye has finished her mission in Athens, a new writer, Anne, comes to take over the flat. Anne's story mirrors Faye's and illustrates how all the stories we are presented with in *Outline* "echo and repeat like slant rhymes" (Valihora 21). With Georg Lukács, we might say that Anne, Faye, and other characters are trying to overcome their alienation. In his *Theory of the Novel*, Lukács argues that novels are culture's attempt at healing the dissonance between our empirical selves-in-flux and our dreams of ascending to the eternal ideals of truth and beauty. In the epic, there is no clash between so-called inner and outer life.[15] The novel, by contrast, arose in the context of modernity and its new individual with their unique inner (temporal) life that tended to conflict with their surroundings. Alienation results in protagonists being in a state of homelessness, longing to transcend (185–89). Yet they are tragically bound to fail due to being trapped in temporal immanence.

For Lukács, characters try to transcend in two different ways: a) into a metaphysical realm, like the protagonists of abstract idealist novels or b) into a social realm, like the protagonists of sociohistorical novels (Jameson 181). In the former case, we may think of religious or metaphysical longing, and Faye's climb up Plato's ladder may be read as a remnant of this old wish. In the latter, we can think of the existentialist view of liberation as throwing oneself into projects in a secularized society, which is more aligned with Faye's bid for freedom as a feminist writer. What both these sorts of transcendence have in common is that they are premised on linear time.[16]

According to Söderbäck, this linear logic suppresses the past, cyclical time and embodiment in its effort to thrust itself into the future (*Revolutionary* 24). Both these forms of transcendence, moreover, depend on a binary model of sexual difference, "which is another way of saying that they both depend on a mono-sexual model or a logic of identity" (ibid) : for one gender (female) to liberate itself, it must take on the values and ideals of the dominant (male) gender[17]. Taking on mono-sexual values is likely to leave mothers in a bind because these values idealize disembodied rationality as the road to freedom. Maternal practice, by contrast, underlines how "the mind is not a substance separate from the body"

(Ruddick 91). Instead, argues Sara Ruddick, the mental, in maternal thinking, expresses itself physically, and "the physical is mentally interpreted" (91).

Maternal thinking troubles the idea of the bounded rational agent, traditionally linked to masculinity, because maternal rationality arises in relation. "A 'self,'" states Ruddick, "however fixed and personal it may seem, is always in the process of being socially constituted. Mothers themselves often suffer from a sense of fragmentation"...(92). The specific sort of rationality required of mothers stems from children's need for protection, nurturance, and training. These needs vary in different contexts, requiring mothers to have a perennial capacity to adapt to new circumstances and to renegotiate their principles.

Contrary to Plato's ideal, mothers "have to take the near and banal quite seriously" (Ruddick 78). Mothers are in flux because children are in flux. They have a fundamental duty to "keep safe whatever is vulnerable" (80) and respond to it with care rather than abuse, indifference or flight (19). This requires an embodied presence, flexibility, and attunement that has historically been constructed as feminine even if men, of course, might perfectly well inhabit it and even though many mothers do not display maternal thinking but rather subject their children to neglect, control or abuse.

What Faye needs is neither linear transcendence nor cyclical immanence but both and neither: Faye needs a different route through time. Söderbäck suggests that we think of transcendence in nonlinear ways. Alongside the two above-mentioned linear models of transcendence that we may picture as vertical, there are two horizontal routes to transcendence. One is her own theory of revolutionary time, or a return to the past that is necessary, to produce change in the future. The other is a horizontal movement between sexed subjects, or what we might, inspired by Irigaray, call "immanent transcendence" (*Revolutionary* 53–83).[18] Faye's journey through *Outline* epitomizes both these horizontal movements: She encounters the past in the present as she returns to Plato's philosophy, the Homeric epic, and, as we shall see, Beauvoir's existentialism. She also performs an immanent transcendence between situated subjects inhabiting a common, intersubjective social space.

Faye's return to Homeric time is a return to a time before Platonic dualism had imprinted itself on narrative form. Karen Valihora has highlighted how we might read Faye as a doubling of Odysseus and

Penelope. The fact that Faye is on a journey links her to Odysseus. In what follows, however, I expand on what Valihora calls the *Outline's* "Penelopiad" by relating Faye's narrative strategy to Penelope's activity of weaving and how weaving may be linked to Söderbäck's Irigarayan notion of immanent transcendence.[19]

Penelopian Time

According to Cavarero, Odysseus and Penelope epitomize the linear (masculine) versus cyclical (feminine) binary. Cavarero, however, re-reads the *Odyssey* from a feminist angle and finds that even though Penelope is stuck in the repetitive time of immanence, her activity of weaving and unweaving "cannot be reduced to either of the two tempos that are alien to it: the tempo of the men's actions and the tempo of wifely domestic production" (16). Her tempo, rather, has the cadence of "infinite repetition," which "nullifies any usefulness through its rhythmic undoing" (17). Penelope's time "carves out a feminine space where women belong to themselves" and grounds a philosophy of birth and rootedness, rather than one of "death and adventure" (22); her weaving is an act of "retying the soul to the body" (23). In this vein, we may read Faye's listening and recounting as Penelopian weaving.

One of the students in Faye's writing course is named Penelope, and her story revolves around the theme of sisterhood (*Outline* 217–20). Penelope's narrative describes a glass ceiling breaking under the weight of water. Valihora connects this, and other water imagery in the trilogy, to the breaking down between subject and object. It seems important to add, however, how profoundly wet imaginaries are connected to the mother and birth in the "material imagination" (Bachelard). I shall come back to this watery current below. First, however, I want to connect Faye's journey to the origins of second-wave feminism.

Cyclical and Linear Mothers: Simone de Beauvoir

One evening, Faye meets feminist writer Angeliki, who ventriloquizes Beauvoir's remarks on "parasite mothers"—namely, the housewives who make their husband and child the central task of their lives, making them "so important in your own mind that your ego has enough sustenance to stay alive" (*Outline* 111; Beauvoir 484–85). These remarks come after

Faye has told the story of her own mother, who, while "she used to be desperate" (105) for her children to go to school, had no idea what to do with herself in the empty space after they had left. The two women are discussing their mothers' generation, who were told to find fulfilment in the home and how this rendered them so helpless that they were unable to fill the empty space of their freedom, once given it. Angeliki then reflects upon current times and remembers meeting some affluent mothers juggling an impressive number of children with successful professions: "The women were of a kind I had never known before in my life: nearly all of them worked in a profession—doctors, lawyers, accountants—and most of them had a large number of children, five or six apiece, whose lives they supervised with amazing diligence and energy, running their families like successful corporations on top of the demanding careers" (111).

These mothers were excellently groomed, "...went to the gym every day, ran marathons for charity.... They went to church, baked the cakes for the school fete, chaired the debating society, held dinner parties..." (111-12). Curiously, however, notes Angeliki, she could never remember their names or "recall a single one of their faces" (112). Moreover, there seems to linger some forbidden feelings beneath these mothers' facades: "Sometimes, she said, I almost wonder whether the exhaustion I felt when I returned from Berlin was in fact the collective exhaustion of these women, which they refused to feel themselves and so had passed on to me. One always seemed to see them running ... in their enormous white shoes ... supremely practical and supremely ugly" (113). The shoes, Angeliki feels, might unlock the whole mystery of these mothers: "'I myself,' she continued, extending a silvered foot out from beneath the table 'developed a weakness for delicate shoes when we returned.' Perhaps it was because I had begun to see the virtues of standing still" (113). For the character in Angeliki's novel, delicate shoes represent something forbidden: "She looks out the window at the women running, and she asks herself whether they are running towards something or away from it. If she looks long enough she sees that they are simply running around in circles" (114)

What feminism and affluence have brought to these mothers is more freedom to realize themselves professionally, but this freedom has come at the price of physical and emotional exhaustion, since working life is still not attuned to an ethics of care. Whereas the cyclical mothers of the previous generation were stuck in immanence, the linear mothers under late capitalism are still performing most childcare and domestic work, leaving them no free time. To Angeliki, these mothers seem robotic. Another mother Angeliki met, Olga, shares her maternal obligations in a strict fifty-fifty arrangement with her husband, as they alternate "strictly every six months, one working and the other looking after the children" (108). But there seems to be little pleasure in Olga's life. Olga appears trapped inside her preordained schedule, leading an instrumentalized life, illustrative of how contemporary parents juggle conflicting temporal regimes, as they try to attune to their children's tempos while remaining in the loop of demands they meet elsewhere. One strategy out of the resulting moral dilemmas is to set up schedules for everything, but this has a cost. Faye, like Angeliki, seems to long for drifting along and letting go of clocks and calendars:

> I had come to believe more and more in the virtues of passivity, and of living my life as un-marked by self-will as possible. One could make almost anything happen, if one tried hard enough, but the trying—it seemed to me—was almost always a sign that one was crossing the currents ... and though you might argue that nothing could ever be accomplished without going against nature to some extent, the artificiality of that vision and its consequences had become ... anathema to me. (170–71)

We are back with the oceanic imagery that runs like an undercurrent through the trilogy. Faye is digging up "the liquid ground" (Irigaray, *Marine*) buried by patriarchal history. I return to this watery theme below. First, however, I want to point out how Angeliki's story of German and Polish mothers highlights how the patriarchal motherhood institution has joined hands with neoliberalism and how the feminist disavowal of motherhood has allowed this toxic combination to continue unchecked.

Outline alerts us to a troubling neoliberal tendency whereby motherhood and creativity (which are linked) have become products that affluent people can buy. Faye's first interlocutor, a billionaire with "liberal credentials," (3) has eleven children and poses as a man of success. Yet, Faye observes, there is an unreal quality to what the man says. He is "like a child with too many Christmas presents" (3). She finds it hard to assimilate the billionaire's talk because he seems oblivious to the labour that, in his case, is performed by other people. Unlike the billionaire, the German and Polish mothers described by Angeliki do not buy their way out of maternal practice but instead try to do it all on their own. They are harmed by neoliberal ideology, whereby the ideal worker is the "unencumbered worker" (O'Reilly 243).

This ideology repeats the patriarchal dictum that motherhood is an individual responsibility to be shouldered by mothers alone. The 1990s, moreover, saw the rise of "intensive mothering"—an ideology requiring that mothers expend enormous amounts of time, energy, and material resources on their children, in contrast to the more "laissez-faire upbringing" advocated by stay-at-home mothers of the 1950s. Rather than spending time roaming around the neighbourhood with other children, kids today look to adults for entertainment. Mothers are taught to turn to experts for instruction on almost any matter, to enrol their children in an enormous range of extra-curricular activities, and to have their social lives revolve around their children (84-85).

Contemporary mothering, states O'Reilly, "demands far more from mothers than was asked from them from the 1950s to 1980s," as the ideology of intensive mothering "parallels the increase in mothers' paid labour force participation" (87). Highly educated mothers are often uncomfortable with the every day, devalued, and invisible work of mothering, hence they fill up their days with public activities that can be documented as productive and visible work" (88). Moreover, the patriarchal motherhood institution will almost always blame a mother for the faults of her children. To avoid this threat, middle-class mothers succumb to "helicopter parenting" to secure their children's "competitive advantage" (91). While neoliberalism needs mothers to produce new workers and consumers, it is also committed to cutting state expenditures, such as maternity leave and childcare, leaving mothers without support systems (Vandenbeld Giles qtd. in O'Reilly 92). This means that neoliberalism allows a space for women who are willing or able to be like men but no real space for an authentic liberation of the mother.

Remember Your "Liquid Ground"

In *Marine Lover of Friedrich Nietzsche,* Irigaray urges her masculine interlocutor—Nietzsche—to "remember his liquid ground " (37). She thinks of Nietzsche as a productive philosopher who reaffirmed the value of embodiment after a long history of disembodied thought. Even so, she also thinks that Nietzsche's *Zarathustra* epitomizes a masculine overman who gets stuck in an eternal recurrence of the same due to his devaluation of the feminine and fear of "liquid embodiment," which has so often been associated with femininity (Shildrick; Theweleit). As Astrida Neimanis points out, even though men too are "bodies of water,"—a long tradition has construed man as a disembodied mind, leaving it up to women, queer people, and people of colour to carry the burden of the body for him. Water serves as a reminder of human beings' intrinsic condition of being born, being embodied subjects, and coming from somewhere rather than nowhere.

The Western philosophical tradition has prioritized death (moving forward, into the future) over birth (an awareness of one's past and one's entanglements) at the expense of embodiment and repetition (Stone). One way of reframing our fundamental ontology in terms of birth is through watery thinking. Astrida Neimanis recommends that we ponder our "fishy beginnings" because water "connects bodies across times and spaces" (94) and facilitates a "posthuman gestationality" that is not necessarily tied to the female human (68–69) but leaves room for the important insight that bodies are comprised of water, and water is what "bathes us into being" (3).

A wet imaginary underlies Faye's journey in *Outline*—one alluding to the maternal ghost of history and hinting at the embodied, porous, enmeshed, and interrelated aspects of subjectivity. Included in this watery journey is what Faye pays attention to in the narratives of people she meets on her way. Their stories seem to mirror Faye herself (Valihora). The neighbour from the plane positions himself as coming from a ship-owning family, one that is also significantly "matriarchal" (8). He urges Faye to stay close to the water in Athens, lest it should get too hot (6–7). The neighbour takes Faye out on his boat, where their dialogue continues to revolve around motherhood, care, and divorce. Another character, Ryan, describes how it was necessary for him to "dry up" to liberate himself from remnants of his "damp childhood" (32–33). Ryan's narrative illustrates the historical construction of masculinity as a wilful projection of oneself into the future through a disciplining and hardening of the body. In the United States, Ryan could "decide how to be, and then be it," something he achieves by climbing frantically on a Stairmaster (39). Faye, by contrast, climbs down the "Platonic stairs" from Clelia's apartment and links swimming to her desire for freedom as an "escape from what she had" (73–74). Having descended from Clelia's Platonic space with its uncanny woman-mother centre, Faye undertakes a "swimming through the Freudian death drive" where she confronts her own past and relives her experience of maternity through observing a family on a boat (75–8). This experience brings on a childhood memory, after which Faye feels her "body being borne blindly through space" and everything in her life "having become atomised, all its elements separated as though an explosion had sent them flying away from the centre in different directions" (87).

These pages point to Faye's digging up her "liquid ground" through a circular movement. Faye almost drowns, as she zig-zags, swirls, and spirals through time—both in the trilogy as a whole and in *Outline*'s swimming scene (86–89) because her experience of maternal splitting is something she refuses to, or perhaps feels unable to, gloss over. She is in several places at once, both mother and child, feminist, and artist. Her memory of her maternity propels her back to her childhood and then swiftly swivels back again to her maternal self as she starts thinking of her children and wonders "where they are at this moment" (87). Ryan and Faye seem to be contrasted as binary masculine versus feminine embodiments of time: one linear, the other cyclical. But *Outline* also shows that there is no necessary connection between feminine embodiment and a cyclical experience of motherhood. Paniotis is a father whose divorce story invokes images of a wet and circular death rebirth (118–19). Significantly, however, Paniotis's rebirth begins with a divorce, after which he is left alone with his children, having to take responsibility on his own, his ex-wife refusing his pleas for help.

Along *Outline's* watery undercurrent, we find Angeliki talking of having another child as becoming "submerged" (125), and Penelope's above-mentioned story of sisterhood rivalry ending with a glass ceiling breaking under the weight of water (155). The neighbour later tries to seduce Faye in a story alluding to "Leda and the Swan" (176–77; Valihora 26–27), but Faye rewrites the Leda script by refusing the neighbour and longing, instead, for her children (177). Melete recounts a menstrual dream (196–97), which may also be connected to a wet imaginary, since, according to Gaston Bachelard, all liquids, including blood and milk, are like water to the material imagination.

Faye is a feminist mother whose antiessentialism is unsettled by her embodied experience of motherhood. Throughout the *Outline* trilogy, however, motherhood is tentatively deessentialized. We meet men who have taken on the task as primary caregivers (*Transit*, 10–36), biological mothers who do not deserve the label "mother" at all (*Outline* 25–28), as well as biological mothers like Faye, who try to let the idea of the essential mother go and trust that others pick up where they occasionally leave off. The novel shows, however, that as long as no one picks up where the mother leaves off, both mothers and children suffer. Feminism and motherhood become irreconcilable, and Faye is left a speechless victim of the patriarchal motherhood institution, telling mothers that motherhood is their sole, individual responsibility and that they will be blamed almost no matter how they react to this. If they remain in immanence they are bad feminists, but if they try to transcend, their children (and hence also the mothers) suffer. The political imperative is that we need public support like state-sponsored childcare, maternity leave and a general care consciousness in society.

Simultaneously, *Outline's* watery undercurrent suggests that social and political reform is not enough. We also need to dig deeper into the philosophical underpinnings of subjectivity. Like all feminisms, matricentric feminism must battle the patriarchal distinction between mind and body, and, arguably, the maternal standpoint is in a privileged position to do so because of the embodied presence required in maternal work, as Ruddick has shown. We also, however, need to travel back in time to dig out the origins of our understandings of subjectivity, and we need to uncover how such understandings have consistently failed the mother, rendering her a ghostly presence in our contemporary symbolic and even a stranger to certain strands of the feminist canon. Faye's journey alludes to the symbolic and historical significance of the maternal body, while simultaneously letting go of biological determinism. As Tatjana Takševa points out, "In ... much feminist theory, the concepts of female empowerment, self-direction, and gender equality are still largely based on Western neoliberal views of individualism, self and agency" (27). Motherhood troubles the idea of the bounded and self-sufficient rational agent and opens those willing to think with rather than against the mother to a relational understanding of feminist subjectivity.

Outline expresses Faye's quest towards a horizontal rather than linear transcendence. Her journey gets complicated, however, by the cerebral posture she has come to inhabit. She seems to be stuck, and some serious unweaving—and swimming—has to occur before she can move into a more embodied state, which she arguably does in *Transit*.

Conclusion

Cusk's *Outline* epitomizes a return to the matricidal beginnings of literature and philosophy in ancient Athens as well as to feminisms articulated by Beauvoir, Kristeva, and Irigaray. As such, Cusk supports O'Reilly's claim that motherhood is the unfinished business of feminism.

As Faye undertakes her journey through revolutionary time (Söderbäck), she is unweaving herself from matricidal strands in the Western intellectual tradition and attempting to remember her motherline. Through listening to and retelling other people's narratives, Faye also epitomizes a philosophy of birth, which involves a reorientation towards one's past rather than focussing exclusively on the future (Cavarero; Stone). Natality is connected to a watery reframing of transcendence as horizontal and interrelational rather than the vertical journey of the more bounded character whose gender is either essentialized or entirely a social construct. Faye's time travel performs a Penelopian weaving, aimed at rethinking feminism from the maternal perspective through a return of the body, albeit in a deessentialized form. As Olivia Heal points out, new materialist and phenomenological approaches have recently opened a space where writers can explore and depict the maternal without essentializing it (121).

If feminism throws maternity out with the bathwater, it risks partaking in the patriarchal tradition of treating the feminine as the silent ground—the passive matter—from which active humans construct themselves as disembodied and free-floating bounded agents. This burdensome body refers to the body as an enmeshed, porous, and interrelated slice of conscious matter, indistinguishable from the mind. In Rosi Braidotti's words: "Being embodied means being in and of sexualized matter… intrinsically and multiply connected to social and political relations; it is anything but an individualistic entity" (243).

Endnotes

1. Essentialism is the view that there are essential properties which all women share (Stone 135). Maternalism is a form of essentialism that views women as having special access to motherly knowledge and argues that women, therefore, ought to be the moral conscience of humanity (O'Reilly 229)

2. Although critical attention has been paid to the theme of motherhood in Cusk's other work (Braun; Foster; Hanson; Quiney).
3. For statistics on the alarmingly low percentage of mothering content in academic feminist journals, syllabi and conferences, see O'Reilly (220–24).
4. *A Life's Work* (2001), *Arlington Park* (2006), *The Bradshaw Variations* (2009), and *Aftermath* (2012).
5. Cusk herself has referred to the novel in an interview by stating that she thinks of experience as "lateral and oceanic" (qtd. in Schwarz).
6. Although as we proceed through the narrative, we come to notice that Faye's voice intertwines with all the other voices through the use of irony and free indirect discourse.
7. Simone de Beauvoir connects the maternal body to the time of "immanence" and argues that maternity renders women prey to their biological destiny, whereas men are free to "transcend" their "animal" condition (*Second Sex* 73, 84, 165, 194, 524). It should be noted, however, that Beauvoir grounds consciousness in the body and instigates a philosophy of sexual difference (Moi). Patrice DiQuinzio argues that the tensions inherent in Beauvoir's thought on maternity are caused by her adoption of Sartre's distinction between "immanence" and "transcendence," as well as Hegel's theory of self/other (91–114).
8. In *The Symposium*, Plato—through his mouthpiece Socrates—presents the road to truth, beauty and love as an ascent up a ladder.
9. Even though Socrates is Plato's mouthpiece in *The Symposium*, this dialogue is unique in that Socrates is recounting the wisdom of Diotima, the only woman speaking in Plato's dialogues (even if she needs to speak through a man to be heard). Not surprisingly, therefore, the *Symposium* has been of particular interest to feminists.
10. A third reference to Plato enters with the story of Georgeou, one of Faye's writing students (*Outline* 137, 206–07), whose narrative seems to allude to Plato's dialogue *Gorgias*.
11. My argument is not that Beauvoir's overall philosophy aligns with Plato's, as her theory is largely successful in challenging the androcentrism of the Western philosophical canon. My reading aligns with Söderbäck's view that although most feminists would agree with

Beauvoir's descriptive claims about patriarchy in *The Second Sex*, feminists tend to disagree about the prescriptive implications of her philosophy (*Revolutionary* 34–36).

12. This search for mystery, chaos, or shame, something "rotting or breeding," (*Outline*, 57) may be linked to Kristeva's theory of abjection in *Powers of Horror.*
13. For Kristeva's reaction to Plato, see *Revolution in Poetic Language* and Söderbäck, *Revolutionary* 212–14).
14. Cusk reactualizes Virginia Woolf's *A Room of One's Own* in the essay "Shakespeare's Sisters" (*Coventry*) and Woolf's *Room*; gendered space is arguably the main theme of her 2021 novel, *Second Place.*
15. Ella Ophir links Cusk's effacement of the boundary between inner and outer life to her Woolfian affinities—that is, as following in Woolf's footsteps in aiming to convey a collective rather than individual existence, the return to the epic form may be seen as an attempt to constrict herself to exteriority.
16. Although Plato builds his philosophy on cyclical time, later appropriations of his thought in the Western intellectual tradition have tended to think linearly about Platonism. (Söderbäck, *Revolutionary*).
17. Cusk writes in her essay "Aftermath": "What I lived as feminism were in fact the male values my parents, among others, well-meaningly bequeathed me—the cross-dressing values of my father, and the anti-feminine values of my mother" (123).
18. The term "immanent transcendence" is one way of rethinking feminist liberation without a strict separation between body and mind and may also be linked to the philosophy of Gilles Deleuze, as interpreted by new materialist feminists Rosi Braidotti and Elizabeth Grosz. See also Tamsin Lorraine on Irigaray's "Sensible Transcendental".
19. Valihora's focus is on the story of Penelope, one of Faye's writing students, whereas what I focus on is the more general theme of weaving as a Penelopian theme recurring throughout the trilogy.

Works Cited

Bachelard, Gaston. *Water and Dreams—An Essay on the Imagination of Matter.* The Dallas Institute of Humanities and Culture, 1983.

Beauvoir, Simone de. *The Second Sex*. Translated by Constance Borde and Sheila Malovany-Chevallier. 1949. Vintage, 2011.

Bewes, Timothy. *Free Indirect: The Novel in a Postfictional Age*. Columbia University Press, 2022.

Braidotti, Rosi. "META (L) FLESH." *The Future of Flesh: A Cultural Survey of the Body*. Edited by Zoe Detsi-Diamanti, et al. Palgrave Macmillan, 2019, pp. 241–61.

Braun, Alice. "A Compound Fenced Off from the Rest of the World: Motherhood as the Stripping of One's Self in Rachel Cusk's *A Life's Work: On Becoming a Mother.*" *Études Britanniques Contemporaines*, no. 53, 2017 doi: https://doi.org/10.4000/ebc.3802.

Cavarero, Adriana. *In Spite of Plato—A Feminist Rewriting of Ancient Philosophy*. Polity Press, 1995.

Cusk, Rachel. *A Life's Work—On Becoming a Mother*. Faber & Faber, 2001.

Cusk, Rachel. "I Was Only Being Honest." *The Guardian*, 21 March 2008, https://www.theguardian.com/books/2008/mar/21/biography.women. Accessed 10 July 2024.

Cusk, Rachel. *Aftermath: On Marriage and Separation*. Faber & Faber, 2012.

Cusk, Rachel. *Coventry—Essays*. Faber &Faber, 2019.

Cusk, Rachel. *Kudos*. Faber & Faber, 2018.

Cusk, Rachel. *Outline*. Faber & Faber, 2014.

Cusk, Rachel. *Second Place*. Faber & Faber, 2021.

Cusk, Rachel. *Transit*. Faber & Faber, 2016.

DiQuinzio, Patrice. *The Impossibility of Motherhood. Feminism, Individualism, and the Problem of Mothering*. Routledge, 1999.

Foster, Verna A. "Mother Medea and her Children: Maternal Ambivalence in the Medean Plays of Marina Carr, Cherríe Moraga and Rachel Cusk." *Comparative Drama*, vol. 55, no. 1, Spring 2021, https://scholarworks.wmich.edu/compdr/vol55/iss1/4/. Accessed 10 July 2024.

Grosz, Elizabeth. *Volatile Bodies. Toward a Corporeal Feminism*. Indiana University Press, 1994.

Hanson, Clare. "The Book of Repetition: Rachel Cusk and Maternal Subjectivity." *E-Rea*, vol. 10, no. 2, 2013, https://doi.org/10.4000/erea.3259

Heal, Olivia. "Toward a Matricentric Feminist Poetics." *Journal of the Motherhood Initiative*, vol. 10, no. 1&2, 2019. DOI: https://jarm.journals.yorku.ca/index.php/jarm/issue/view/2314.

Hill, Nicole. "Understanding Obstetric Violence as Violence against Mothers through the Lens of Matricentric Feminism." *Journal of the Motherhood Initiative*, vol. 10, no. 1&2, 2019. DOI: https://jarm.journals.yorku.ca/index.php/jarm/issue/view/2314.

Irigaray, Luce. *Speculum of the Other Woman*. Translated by Gillian C. Gill. 1974. Cornell University Press, 1985.

Irigaray, Luce. *Marine Lover of Friedrich Nietzsche*. New York: Columbia University Press, 1991.

Irigaray, Luce. *An Ethics of Sexual Difference*. Cornell University Press, 1994.

Jameson, Frederic. *Marxism and Form*. Princeton University Press, 1971.

Julavits, Heidi. "Rachel Cusk's 'Outline.'" *New York Times*, 7 Jan. 2015, https://www.nytimes.com/2015/01/11/books/review/rachel-cusks-outline.html. Accessed 10 July 2024.

Kellaway, Kate. "Aftermath Was Creative Death. I Was Heading into Total Silence." *The Guardian*, 24 Aug. 2014, https://www.theguardian.com/books/2014/aug/24/rachel-cusk-interview-aftermath-outline. Accessed 10 July 2024.

Kristeva, Julia. *Revolution in Poetic Language*. Translated by Margaret Walker. Columbia University Press, 1984.

Kristeva, Julia. "Women's Time." Translated by Alice Jardine and Harry Blake. *The Kristeva Reader*. Edited by Toril Moi. Blackwell Publishers, 1984, pp. 187–213.

Lorraine, Tamsin. *Irigaray and Deleuze. Experiments in Visceral Philosophy*. Cornell University Press, 1999.

Lukács, Georg. "The Theory of the Novel: A Historico-Philosophical Essay on the Forms of Great Epic Literature." *Theory of the Novel—A Historical Approach*. Edited by Michael McKeon. The Johns Hopkins University Press, 2000.

Moi, Toril. *What is a Woman?* Oxford University Press, 2001.

Neimanis, Astrida. *Bodies of Water: Posthuman Feminist Phenomenology*. Bloomsbury Academic, 2016.

Nussbaum, Martha. "The Speech of Alcibiades: A Reading of Plato's *Symposium*." *Philosophy and Literature*, vol. 3, no. 2, 1979, pp. 131–72.

Ophir, Ella. "Neomodernism and the Social Novel: Rachel Cusk's *Outline Trilogy*." *Critique: Studies in Contemporary Fiction*, vol 64, 2023, pp. 353–64.

O'Reilly, Andrea. *Matricentric Feminism—Theory, Activism, Practice*. 2nd ed. Demeter Press, 2021.

Plato. "Republic". *Plato. Complete Works*. Edited by John M. Cooper. Hackett, 1997, pp. 971–1224.

Plato. "Gorgias". *Plato. Complete Works*. Edited by John M. Cooper. Hackett, 1997, pp. 791–870.

Plato. "Symposium". *Plato. Complete Works*. Edited by John M. Cooper. Hackett, 1997, pp. 457–506.

Quiney, Ruth. "Confessions of the New Capitalist Mother: Twenty-first Century Writing on Motherhood as Trauma." *Women: A Cultural Review*, vol. 18, no. 1, 2007, pp. 19–40.

Ruddick, Sara. *Maternal Thinking—Toward a Politics of Peace*. 1989. Beacon Press, 1995.

Schwartz, Alexandra. "I Don't Think Character Exists Anymore: A Conversation with Rachel Cusk." *The New Yorker*, 18. Nov. 2018, https://www.newyorker.com/culture/the-new-yorker-interview/i-dont-think-character-exists-anymore-a-conversation-with-rachel-cusk. Accessed 10 July 2024.

Shildrick, Margrit. *Leaky Bodies and Boundaries—Feminism, Postmodernism and (Bio)Ethics*. Routledge, 1997.

Stone, Alison. "Essentialism and Anti-Essentialism in Feminist Philosophy." *Journal of Moral Philosophy*, vol. 1, no. 2, 2004, pp. 135–53.

Söderbäck, Fanny. "Liminal Spaces: Reflections on the In-Between." *Architecture and Culture*, vol. 5, no. 3, pp. 383–93.

Söderbäck, Fanny. "Natality or Birth? Arendt and Cavarero on the Human Condition of Being Born." *Hypatia*, vol. 33, no. 2, 2018, pp. 273–88.

Söderbäck, Fanny. *Revolutionary Time—On Time and Difference in Kristeva and Irigaray*. Suny Press, 2019.

Takševa, Tatjana. "One is Not Born But Rather Becomes a Mother: Claiming the Maternal in Women and Gender Studies." *Journal of the Motherhood Initiative*, vol 10, no. 1&2, 2019. DOI: https://jarm.journals.yorku.ca/index.php/jarm/issue/view/2314.

Theweleit, Klaus. *Male Fantasies, Vol 1: Women, Floods, Bodies, History.* 1987. University of Minnesota Press, 2003.

Valihora, Karen. "She Got Up and Went Away: Rachel Cusk on Making an Exit." *English Studies in Canada*, vol. 45, no. 1–2, 2019, pp. 19–35.

Vermeulen, Pieter. "Against Premature Articulation: Empathy, Gender, and Austerity in Rachel Cusk and Katie Kitamura." *Cultural Critique*, no. 111, Spring 2021, pp 81–103. Project *MUSE*, doi:10.1353/cul.2021.0013.

15.

Matricentric Feminism and Nonnormative Migrant Mothering in Recent Contemporary Fiction from Spain and the United States

Carolina Toscano

> The subjectivity of mothers often disappears from the most sensitive feminist discussions of mothering
>
> —Brenda Daly and Maureen Reddy 3

In "Matricentric Feminism: A Feminism for Mothers," Andrea O'Reilly provides the foundation for a growing and adaptive definition of matricentric feminism. This definition considers the need for mothers to have their own school of feminism that encompasses and builds upon the different schools of feminism that have been developed until now (17). "Practicing Matricentric Feminist Mothering," by Fiona Joy Green, adds to this growing movement by emphasizing what matricentric feminism looks like when it is put into practice through "the process of joining one's feminism together with one's parenting" (83). In this chapter, I add to this conversation by exploring fiction as an example of the praxis of matricentric feminist mothering. By examining three matrifocal contemporary novels written by transnational authors, I observe that fiction and reality influence one another through storytelling and argue that these contemporary novels studied as cultural artifacts reflect the growing wave of matricentric feminism enacted through these examples of nonnormative feminist mothering. I contend that by providing examples of varied matrifocal voices in literature, authors are providing readers with alternate ways of examining the tensions inherent in motherhood and feminism and helping them explore ways in which we can build "a feminism for mothers" (O'Reilly 13).

The three novels chosen for this study share the common threads of migration and maternity: *Mare de llet i mel* (2018), by Najat El Hachmi, takes place in Spain, whereas *Afterlife* (2020) by Julia Álvarez and *Lost Children Archive* (2019) by Valeria Luiselli both take place in the United States (US). By examining fiction from different parts of the world, we can observe that useful examples of nonnormative mothering can be found in a global context. Although all three novels explore marginalized maternal voices, they highlight different aspects of nonnormative mothering: *Mare de llet i mel* emphasizes migrant mothering and the role of the maternal body as a mode of analysis; *Afterlife* explores maternal ambivalence and the choice not to mother; and *Lost Children Archive* examines the tension between family and career that mothers experience and how feminist mothering can be enacted through work and motherwork. By placing these three novels together, readers can reflect on these matricentric feminist issues globally. The wave of matricentric feminism can be seen crossing international borders. This is important because while contributing to our growing definition of matricentric feminism, it also adds to how we can explore matricentric feminism in practice. By looking at fiction as a cultural artifact, we understand how our world adapts as the mother wave of matricentric feminism takes form. Consequently, we can broaden our definitions of matricentric feminism and teach empathy and understanding of what it means to mother under diverse conditions, which is one of the tenets of matricentric feminism.

Theoretical Lenses: Matricentric Feminism Definition and Praxis

To examine these three migration novels in the context of a wave of matricentric feminism, I unpack O'Reilly's and Green's definitions of matricentric feminism and its practice to better understand how this movement can be observed in recent fiction around the world. In

"Matricentric Feminism: A Feminism for Mothers," O'Reilly provides a framework for the growing definition of this concept. To observe how these three novels promote matricentric feminism, I emphasize five tenets listed in her article. O'Reilly writes that matricentric feminism spotlights the need for academic explorations of mothering; finds ways to practise feminist mothering; is mother centred and activist; uses mothering to enact social change; and explores the diversity of mothering geographically and conceptually ("Matricentric" 18). The three chosen novels touch upon these five points by using matrifocal voices, presenting alternative ways to mother, undertaking mothering that considers feminism, and sharing the lived experiences of diverse mothers across the globe.

In "Practicing Matricentric Feminist Mothering," Green explains that feminist parents "define and practice mothering on their own terms.... By placing themselves, and not their children at the centre of their lives, feminist parenting becomes a dynamic place for creativity" (95). The words *on their own terms and creativity* stand out because if feminist parenting can be a space for creativity and if feminist parenting in practice benefits from this freedom from boundaries, what better place to explore what it means to mother than in fiction? Fiction provides the palette where reality and imagination can intermingle. In this chapter, I explore three examples of fiction where authors work with concepts related to matricentric feminism and examine and represent mothering across boundaries and cultures. This is important because it provides several iterations of mothering that can add to the understandings and practices of matricentric feminism, "the diversity of maternal experience" that O'Reilly's definition calls for ("Matricentric" 18).

"The Diversity of Maternal Experience": Migrant Mothering and the Maternal Body

Mare de llet i mel (2018) (*Mother of Milk and Honey*),[1] by Najat El Hachmi, traces the life of a young Tamazigh woman from Morocco who finds herself raising her daughter alone on the outskirts of Barcelona, Spain. El Hachmi uses descriptions of migrant mothering and the maternal body in ways that address some of the points outlined in O'Reilly's definition of matricentric feminism. Specifically, this matrifocal novel challenges patriarchal definitions of motherhood, moves the focus from the child to the mother, describes the maternal and nursing body in careful detail, and gives voice to a group of marginalized women who do not often have the chance to share their stories.

Matrifocal literature, as defined by Elizabeth Podnieks, includes narratives emphasizing mothering points of view (first person or limited third person) and exploring motherhood versus mothering (176). In *Mare de llet i mel*, the narrator alternates between first-person narration by the mother character, Fatima, and a limited third-person narration focussing on Fatima's point of view and experiences and, in some instances, her mother, Zraizmas's point of view. This is significant because the character given the central voice of the novel is a migrant mother from a highly patriarchal culture who has had no access to education.[2] Her intersectional standpoint is that of a woman whose gender, class, race, and culture mean that it is rare to be given a voice. However, in this novel she is given a place to share her thoughts and experiences on migration, mothering, and the difficulties women in her position must withstand. El Hachmi dedicates the novel to her own mother in the inscription: "A mi madre, que sin saber leer, me enseñó a escribir." ("To my mother, who without knowing how to read, taught me to write.") El Hachmi demonstrates that there are different epistemologies, or ways of knowing, that can speak to and inform one another and that they need not be hierarchical. In this epigraph, she connects her lived experience to the story she has imagined and articulated, inspired by what she has learned from her own mother.

In addition to making an immigrant mother character the main speaker of the novel, El Hachmi pays tribute to the oral tradition—a way for marginalized, disadvantaged, and oppressed peoples to pass down knowledge—by having Fatima tell her story to her sisters when returning to her homeland of Morocco for a visit. This sets the stage for a focus on the mothering experience, a tenet of matricentric feminism. The novel begins with a scene of sisterhood and an invitation for the migrant mother character to speak and share her experiences. The short epigraph contains a cozy image of seven sisters with warm cups of tea seated at a wooden table on a rug made of palm or raffia strands. It is a humble yet inviting image that informs the reader that what is to follow will be an intimate story meant for close family and friends. Yet, the reader is also privy to this tale: "Cuéntanos tu historia, hermana nuestra. Cuéntanos todo lo que te ha pasado durante este largo tiempo que has estado lejos de nosotras. Cuéntanos que hiciste para llegar al extranjero, para sobreponerte a todos los obstáculos. Nárranos, dulce hermana, nárranos" (epigraph 6). ("Tell us your story, dear sister. Tell us all that has happened during this long period that you have been far from us. Tell us what you did to emigrate, to overcome all obstacles. Tell us, dear sister, tell us.")

Feminist scholars use women's oral histories to give a voice to marginalized women and emphasize that women's experiences are valid parts of history and should be documented. Sherna Gluck and Daphne Patai's groundbreaking work, *Women's Words: The Feminist Practice of Oral History,* explores the need to record women's oral histories in ways that contribute to the feminist project. While their research does not include fiction, El Hachmi's choice to frame the novel as an oral history emphasizes its importance as a transmission of knowledge between marginalized peoples. In the novel, oral history provides a space for respite from the world and to discuss important issues. Oral history connects to matricentric feminism in that it emphasizes the mother's lived experience and acknowledges that the subject merits attention and a wide audience of readers.

According to Podnieks, matrifocal voices in literature do the job of what Susan Maushart describes as "unmasking" motherhood and allowing for new ways of charting and understanding mothering as not only good or bad tropes but as spaces of complex feelings and identities worthy of academic and social exploration (176). Podnieks writes: "Read as a genre in and of itself as part of a tradition of writings about motherhood, matrifocal literatures are sites of textual liberation where women self-consciously and outspokenly chart, confront, debate, and celebrate maternal feelings practices, bodies and identities" (176). In the case of *Mare de llet i mel,* we see this when El Hachmi explores and elevates descriptions of the maternal body, breastfeeding, and the physical bond between mother and daughter and even grandmother and granddaughter. Like the authors that Podnieks describes, who "broke taboos by writing explicitly and graphically about corporeal experiences, for elevating them within the literary realm" (179), El Hachmi uses the character of Fátima as a matrifocal narrator, as well as a limited third-person narrator, to describe these scenes of maternity and the body in conjunction with the experiences of childhood, adolescence, marriage, and immigration.

One of these important corporeal and maternal experiences is the breastfeeding relationship. The entire second chapter, "Salir de madre" ("Out of Mother"), is devoted to describing the breastfeeding journey of Zraizmas and Fatima, one of the central mother-daughter dyads in the novel. This subject area does not often come up in literature, nor is it common to read such a detailed description of breastfeeding and the bond it can create between mother and child. The narrator describes the first time Zraizmas nursed Fatima:

> Fatima era una niña extraordinaria, y eso su madre lo había visto enseguida por cómo, siendo aún recien nacida, había trepado agarrándose a su piel hasta encaramarse al tembloroso pezón de su pecho derecho y por cómo se había aferrado a él como si aquello lo huberia hecho siempre; y también por cómo abrió los ojos en aquel mismo momento, mientras que el resto de sus hijos—y todos quienes habían nacido en aquella casa—habían tardado varios días en hacerlo. (26)
>
> [Fatima was an extraordinary girl, and her mother had realized this right away by the way that she, while still a newborn, had climbed her way up, grabbing at her mother's skin until perching on her shaky right nipple, and how Fatima clung to it as if she had always done so; and also for how she opened her eyes in that exact moment, while the rest of Zraismas' children—and all of the children born in that household—had taken various days to open them.]

What the narrator describes is called the breast crawl: If a healthy baby is left undisturbed after birth, on top of their mother's chest, they should be able to crawl to the mother's nipple and latch.[3] This practice is uncommon because it requires the doctors, nurses, and other adults present to refrain from intervening after birth. However, when done correctly, it is said to promote breastfeeding in the sense that it allows the newborn to learn how to latch properly from birth onwards. This is an example of how this novel elevates the maternal body. The mother character is learning to read her baby's and her own body's signals without patriarchal culture dictating what she should be feeling or experiencing. This is both feminist and matricentric.

The author takes the time to describe, in detail, a postbirthing process that is important to the act of breastfeeding and sets the stage for the maternal-infant relationship. The bond between Zraizmas and Fatima is based on mutual recognition and communication. This connection is described through the breastfeeding relationship and the act of looking into one another's eyes: "Nadie me ha mirado nunca así, se decía Zraizmas, como si pudiera verme completamente- lo que hay en mi cabeza, en mi corazón, en mi higado—como si también conociera mis recuerdos y mis penas" (26). ("No one has looked at me that way before, Zraizmas said to herself, as if they could see me completely, what is in my head, my heart, my liver—as if they knew my memories and my sufferings.") Eye contact between baby and caretaker is important from birth onwards. It causes both the newborn and adult to release oxytocin, the love hormone that promotes healthy bonding (Verny and Weintraub 74).

Furthermore, this relationship is bidirectional. While still an infant, Fatima communicates with her mother through breastfeeding. When she wants her mother to make eye contact, she stops sucking (30). This action recalls her mother's attention to her and reminds her of their wordless connection. By focusing on the description of breastfeeding and bonding between mother and child, the narrator and the author present these maternal acts as important and worthy of discussion. Moreover, by doing this, mothering, which is usually left to the private realm, becomes part of a larger and more public discussion that includes and is connected to world issues, such as immigration. This correlates with one of matricentric feminism's tenets, which is to recognize topics of motherhood and mothering as "deserving of serious and sustained scholarly inquiry" (O'Reilly, "Matricentric" 18).

The narrator aligns Fatima's weaning process with the experience of immigration. This is another example of matricentric feminism in the text because it uses the mother character's lived experience to interpret critical social issues affecting migrant mothers. And it does so by examining a corporeal experience specific to mothering. The weaning transition is painful to both mother and child (39). As readers, we are accustomed to reading about the yearning between lovers, the sighs, and the longing for romantic love. It is less frequent to read about the intimate physical and emotional attachment between a mother and her child. Yet this bond has a profound effect on identity formation, both for mothers and children. The narrator unabashedly describes all of these feelings and, by doing so, identifies the subject of the maternal body and the mother-child bond as worthwhile pursuits of study.

Moreover, the separation of the mother and daughter through weaning is compared to the experiences of leaving one's home through marriage and later through emigration:

> En cualquier caso, fue durante aquellos días cuando Fatima descubrió el desconsuelo, la extrañeza, la sensación de no estar en ninguna parte: se había quedado sin casa por primera vez. Se le formó en el vientre una desazón que con el tiempo fue atenuándose hasta volverse mortecina, pero que ya no la abandonaría nunca; y, desde entonces, siempre que tiene que separarse de alguien, se le viene encima toda esa tristeza cuyo origen, por descontado, ella desconoce. La tristeza de tomar conciencia de ser ella misma fuera de su madre. (39)

> In any case, it was during those days that Fatima discovered the grief, the unfamiliarity, the sensation of being from nowhere: she had become homeless for the first time. In her womb, there formed a disquiet that diminished until becoming weaker, but that never left, and from then on, any time she has to separate from someone, all of this grief falls upon her, whose origin, untold, she does not know. The sadness of realizing her selfhood as separate from her mother.

Every time that Fátima must separate from loved ones, the feelings of this early separation come flooding back to her. The physical bond between mother and child is drawn upon numerous times throughout the novel to describe the experience of immigration and her changing relationship with her daughter under these new conditions. Again, this tells the reader to value and listen to the voice of the mother as she shares her lived experience, which is matrifocal and feminist.

Fátima explains how she draws strength from the physical closeness and need to protect her daughter in their new surroundings. She also takes pride in having a strong work ethic and the ability to perform tasks successfully (166). She finds empowerment in being a single immigrant mother who has escaped a patriarchal country. However, it is important to remember that empowered mothering does not equal perfect mothering. Although Fatima has found a way to live independently from men, when her daughter begins to pull away from her emotionally and physically, and she has trouble accepting certain aspects of her daughter's assimilation, Fatima falls back on what she knows. Fatima pressures her daughter to marry a cousin from her side of the family so that she will keep her honour, and they can remain living together as a family. Her daughter agrees but is miserable, and after giving birth to a baby boy, she abandons her baby and mother and runs away.

In the epilogue, Fatima realizes her mistake and begs her daughter for forgiveness. At the same time, she observes the tension between perfect and authentic motherhood, the mirror that all mothers hold up to themselves and find lacking: "Las madres no nacemos sabiéndolo todo" (365) ("We mothers are not born knowing everything"). Empowered mothers also make mistakes but can learn from them, and her apology is a testament to this idea. This highlights another important aspect of matricentric feminism, which O'Reilly and Green call "authenticity" ("Practicing" 86). Being able to acknowledge and learn from parenting mistakes contributes to a more authentic experience of mothering and allows mothers to step down from the pedestal of the good mother (Thurer).

"Contests, Challenges, and Counters the Patriarchal Oppressive Institution": Maternal Ambivalence and the Choice Not to Mother

Afterlife, by Julia Alvarez, is also a matrifocal text representing empowered mothering. However, in this case, it does so by exploring the concepts of community othermothering (Collins), maternal ambivalence (Parker), and voluntary child-free women[4] (Lewis). By exploring these matrifocal feminist concepts, Alvarez creates a matricentric feminist text challenging patriarchal definitions of motherhood and presents alternative forms of carework.

Afterlife tells the story of Antonia, a retired university professor from the Dominican Republic who lives in a predominantly white college town in rural Vermont. The narrator tells the story from Antonia's point of view as she navigates through a number of major life changes that happen to take place over the course of the same year. On the eve of her retirement, her husband suffers a ruptured aortic aneurysm on his way to meet her for dinner and dies. As she attempts to assimilate this unexpected outcome of events, one of her sisters goes missing. At the same time, she is approached by Mario, a young undocumented Mexican labourer from a neighbouring farm who seeks out her help to get his girlfriend, Estela, safely to Vermont and out of the hands of the coyotes (traffickers of undocumented people) who have helped her to cross the border from Mexico and now hold her hostage.

In her work on feminist and empowered mothering, Green identifies the need to bring "intersectional experiences of mothering to the centre in order to further understand them, as well as to benefit from the contributions they have to make to feminist mothering, in both practice and theory" ("Feminist" 44). Álvarez enacts this by developing a main character who calls forth the concepts of maternal ambivalence, voluntary childfree, and community othermothering and by presenting alternative ways of being part of a community of caring without being forced into a strict gender role where essentialist theories conflate women with motherhood.

The *Encyclopedia of Motherhood* describes maternal ambivalence as the contradiction of emotions that women can experience in relation to motherhood. This concept "captures the simultaneous experience of positive and negative feelings, beliefs, or thoughts about motherhood and the relationship between mother and child" (Brown 50). Maternal ambivalence is a spectrum that can take place during pregnancy, after childbirth, upon adoption, or in the process of deciding whether or not to become a mother. It can range from the slight chafing between the ideal and the real visions of motherhood to extreme suffering and feelings of anger, sadness, depression, and anxiety.[5]

In *Afterlife,* Antonia is past the childbearing age, yet the novel uses descriptions steeped with maternal imagery, and the subjects of motherhood and maternal ambivalence often surface in Antonia's mind. The reader is invited to reflect on these concepts alongside Antonia. This contributes to the goal of matricentric feminism to be mother-centred rather than child-centred and to explore non-traditional aspects of mothering in order to study "the diversity of maternal experience" (O'Reilly, "Matricentric" 18).

The novel is written from Antonia's perspective by a limited third-person narrator, which makes the text matrifocal if we analyze Antonia's character as a maternal figure maternally inclined towards Estela. Estela arrives in the US visibly pregnant. She is rejected by Mario immediately because he is clearly not the father of her child, having been separated for more than nine months. Estela hides in Antonia's garage, where Antonia eventually finds her. As soon as the reader meets Estela, she is defined by her childlike qualities: "Her face has a sweet, girlish roundishness; her eyes, an astonishment that gives a child's tug to the heart" (100). Although she is seventeen years old and pregnant, all of the descriptions of Estela hinge around her seeming like a small child, even a toddler. These descriptions establish Estela and Antonia "as a mother-daughter dyad." For example, when Antonia helps her back to sleep after covering her at night: "Antonia takes the folded blanket and covers the girl, who startles awake but, on hearing the soothing, *Ya, ya duérmete, duérmete*, instantly falls back asleep" (117). The "startle reflex" is one we associate with babies, and the image of her falling asleep immediately at Antonia's soothing also makes her seem like the ideal child. If we remove the knowledge that she is seventeen years old, the reader can be tricked into thinking that Estela is a toddler by the descriptions of her interactions with Antonia, as a mother-child bond forms between them. The magnetic feeling of caring and wanting to be cared for is reciprocal (179).

These descriptions are just two of the many examples that serve to forge the idea that Estela and Antonia are experiencing a mother-daughter relationship and invite the reader to analyze why this relationship is presented in this way. I contend that establishing this relationship as a mother-daughter dyad allows Alvarez to tease out the nonnormative definitions of mothering that she is exploring in this work: community othermothering, maternal ambivalence, and voluntarily childfree women.

Collins examines the concept of "othermothering" in African American communities. She describes how othermothering originated in slave communities whose biological ties were not respected. In more recent times, African American communities have used othermothering as a way to protect and care for their children in a challenging world where they are born with disadvantages (278). Furthermore, as we have seen, othermothering can also transgress family boundaries. This is known as "community othermothering" (278). When Antonia accepts Estela into her home, she reaches out to Beth Trotter, a doctor acquaintance, to navigate the difficult situation of an undocumented and uninsured pregnant minor on the verge of going into labour. Beth Trotter helps her to arrange prenatal care as well as to consult a lawyer on how to protect Estela and her baby from being deported when she goes to the hospital to give birth. In addition, Beth allows Estela to stay in her home when Antonia must go to Boston for a family emergency. In these ways, Beth and Antonia become a kind of team of community othermothers who are helping Estela. This creates a bond between them as well (233).

While Antonia is experiencing a surge of maternal feelings towards Estela in her unprotected situation, she also feels conflicted about how much responsibility she is willing to take on at such a difficult time in her own life. This point of tension continues the work of matricentric feminism by questioning the patriarchal definition of motherhood and testing out new ways of caring for others. Furthermore, finding the balance between her needs and the needs of others is exactly the recipe for maternal ambivalence.

According to Sara LaChance, "Maternal love, in reality, is part of a much more complex picture that includes contradictory impulses and emotions" (*Mad Mothers* 4). Maternal ambivalence is the "competing desires to nurture and to be independent" (6). Antonia cares deeply about the people around her and the world in general, but she also knows the importance of self-care. Achieving equilibrium is not an easy task: "No matter how worthy or commendable taking on Estela and her new family would be, when Antonia asks herself torturously, *What is the right thing to do*? The certainty is not there" (235). Ultimately, Antonia decides to help Estela and her new family but without taking on the responsibility of assuming guardianship. She helps Estela, Mario, and the baby return to Mexico with their papers in order and with money for Mario to start a business and for Estela to attend nursing school. Mario has accepted his girlfriend's baby little by little, and now they are planning to marry when they get settled in Mexico. So rather than accepting the maternal role, Antonia takes on a more distant kind of godmothering role. This could also be considered a community mothering or othermothering role. She chooses to help, and she also chooses self-care. This is significant because Antonia is practising carework without sacrificing her own needs. This is an example of the kind of matricentric feminist work that empowers women and helps them to explore new definitions of mothering.

Voluntary childless or childfree women make the choice not to have children (Lewis 122). This does not mean that they cannot have meaningful and influential relationships with young people. Antonia often remembers her students and the bond she shared with them:

> She misses them, her access to the young. Another downside to being childless, which she read recently, is no longer the politically correct term. *Nonparent* carries no judgment. *Childless mother*, a former colleague called herself. Maybe others share her intense need to get the words right. But what if their right words sound wrong to her? (34)

Perhaps the right words sound wrong because the reasons for not having children can be varied and complex. They can evolve over time, and they can be a result of circumstances over which sometimes we have no control, and at other times we do. The problem with definitions is that their borders are sometimes too defined and do not leave room for flexibility and mischief, for nuance and for change. Antonia is childfree, but she is very much a mother in some ways, although she chooses not to perform all the expected acts of mothering. Her character provides readers with new definitions of carework and reminds us of the importance of choice.

"Mothers Can and Do Create Social Change Through Childrearing and Activism": Feminist and Empowered Mothering

In the third novel, *Lost Children Archive*, Valeria Luiselli provides us with a matrifocal voice that, like Antonia's, is extremely concerned about the state of the world, immigration, her career, her marriage, her children, and the children of the undocumented. *Lost Children Archive* is a matrifocal text and example of feminist mothering because it places value on describing moments of family intimacy and tension; it tells the story from the point of view of a woman with a deep sense of professional identity, who is also a mother. Moreover, she is more than a mother who cares deeply about her own family; she also cares about the issue of immigration and the situation of undocumented children at the US-Mexico border, and she teaches her children about this issue. Green explores feminist mothering as the intent to combine feminism with parenting and emphasizes that "feminist mothers identify as feminist and bring their feminist theory and practice to their everyday motherwork of parenting" ("Feminist" 43). In this section, I observe how Luiselli explores what it means to be a feminist mother in this work.

The novel is narrated by two characters. The first part is told from the perspective of "Ma," the mother character, and the second part is written from the perspective of "the boy," Ma's nonbiological son. It is a story about a blended family: the husband and his biological son, the wife and her biological daughter. By writing about a blended family, Luiselli is choosing to present a family from a less traditional standpoint. Presenting alternative family formations is an example of feminist mothering (Green, "Feminist" 38).

One of the points of tension in the novel is how easily this team of four becomes a family and how difficult it is to separate them when the marriage dissolves. The lack of biological ties between the brother and sister means that there is no legal bond between them, but an emotional connection has formed. The mother figure, Ma, calls herself a "defacto" mother, meaning that she may not have a biological tie to her son, but she performs all of the acts of mothering, which create the bond between mother and son nonetheless (5). This is a reminder that what it means to be a mother is culturally constructed and that mothering is a series of actions (Knott). The matrifocal voice in the novel elevates moments of family time and captures the essence of these intimate scenes in all their, at times, comical splendour:

> Two or three subway minutes and the children were asleep, heads on each of our laps, tangled humid hair, lovely salty smell like the warm pretzels we'd eaten earlier that day on a street corner. They were angelic, and we were young enough, and together we were a beautiful tribe, an enviable bunch. Then, one started snoring, and the other started farting. (10)

These moments of family community and silliness are frequent throughout the novel and make the family portrayal come alive.

Luiselli also describes the home space and how it reflects the time spent together, including both happy and painful scenes. She describes the acts of caring for children that take place over time in the home, as well as the ups and downs of marriage. These candid observations of childhood make the portrayal of the mother and child bond feel realistic and place value on moments of family interaction. The message is that this family time is a story worth telling. This contributes to the matricentric feminist project by reminding us that these mundane moments are, in fact, a series of essential motherwork tasks being performed that merit attention and study (Endnote 8).

Emily Oster writes about "the plague of secret parenting": After maternity leave ends, there is an unspoken office atmosphere that expects parents to pretend at work that they do not have children. One example she provides is of a mother who thinks it is better to pretend to be ill rather than to take a day off work to care for a sick child. Another example is that of a junior professor who does not place any pictures of her children on her desk. Oster asks parents to end this charade because by making visible what parenting is really like, we will be helping to bring about change in the workplace. This call for action is made for both mothers and fathers. Being candid about childcare obligations and what balancing children and a career entails is imperative if we are to make progress on conditions for parents in the workplace.

The matrifocal voice of Ma contributes to a disruption of patriarchal representations of motherhood because she is a woman who is a mother who also values her professional identity, as well as her sensual needs as a woman. Throughout the novel, Ma looks for moments to do her research and read her books: "The girl is still running around, plucking and distributing flowers, so I open the little red book, *Elegies for Lost Children*, ready to read for a while in silence" (138). These moments are often interrupted, as is the case with many parents who try to juggle working and childcare: "Finally tired, and perhaps bored, the girl comes to join me under the cedar, so I close the book and put it in my handbag. I try to take my mind off what I've been reading and concentrate on her" (139). Trying to steal moments to get work done amid childrearing is a relatable moment. The urge to get work done that competes with the urge to be present with one's children is a familiar bind.

Ma also openly discusses her sensual feelings for her husband, the stranger at the Dicks Whiskey bar, and her friend Natalia López (129, 91). This may seem insignificant, yet the development of the maternal figure in this novel is a far contrast from depictions of the Virgin Mary with the Christ child. This mother is not sculpted and placed on an altar. She has a job that she is passionate about, a rich interior life, and sensual feelings that extend beyond her role as a mother and nurturer.

The matrifocal voice in the novel cares deeply about her children, and she also feels a visceral concern for the situation of the undocumented children at the border between the US and Mexico, as well as the situation of immigrants in general. Ma engages in feminist mothering by teaching her children about the undocumented *lost* children. In her definition of feminist mothering, Green lists one of the tenets as "teaching children to think critically about the world" ("Feminist" 39). She writes: "Simply put, feminist mothers, see their parenting practice as no different from or apart from other parts of their lives; their feminism informs and influences everything that they do" ("Feminist" 42). Ma engages in this motherwork by consciously teaching her children about the research that she is doing on the lost children, and this teaches them empathy and encourages them to use a critical lens on the world they inhabit.

Part of the way Ma (and Pa) parent their children is by sharing their professional and personal interests with them. Pa teaches them about the Apache history, and Ma tells them about the undocumented migrant children. At times, Ma reflects on how much they need to know and if the news on the radio or the *Elegies for Lost Children* may be too much for them. Nevertheless, she consciously teaches her children about the world around them, and this teaches them empathy. The migrant children become part of what Ma calls their "family lexicon," the words that their little group of four uses that make sense to them within their family unit:

> Whenever the boy and girl talk about child refugees, I realize now, they call them "the lost children." I suppose the word "refugee" is more difficult to remember. And even if the term "lost" is not precise, in our intimate family lexicon, the refugees become known to us as "the lost children." And in a way, I guess, they are lost children. They are children who have lost the right to a childhood. (75)

The empathy that Ma's children, "the boy" and "the girl," feel for the lost children reaches a peak when they run away to try to find two of the lost children by themselves. They walk through the desert and ride a train, just as migrant children crossing from Mexico to the US often do. They suffer from thirst, hunger, fear, darkness, loneliness, and terror in the same way as the lost children. They follow in their footsteps and experience what they experience. They put their own lives in danger. It is empathy taken to the limit. From a parent's point of view, this section of the novel feels like a nightmare. Part of it is, in fact, written as a twenty-page-long, run-on sentence (319–38), with no chance to stop and breathe. Yet, for the children, it is a way to empathize with the plight of migrant children by making imaginative play come alive. And perhaps it also functions to get some more attention from a set of parents whose marriage is at the point of no return. This extreme act of empathy demonstrates the matricentric feminist idea that "mothers can and do create social change through childrearing and activism" (O'Reilly, "Matricentric" 18).

Current and Future Impact of Matricentric Feminism on Fiction

Although the examined works cannot solve all the problems connected to maternity and migration, they decentre patriarchal motherhood and broaden the definition of what it means to perform the actions of empowered and feminist mothering in the migration context. This contributes to the growing definition of matricentric feminism and provides new examples of "the diversity of maternal experience" (O'Reilly, "Matricentric"). Whereas *Mare de llet i mel* explores empowered mothering through the lens of a migrant mother who independently raises her daughter far from home and places value on the powerful physical bond between mother and child, *Afterlife* explores both the ideas of community othermothering and voluntarily childfree women, exposing the validity of the choice not to mother. *Lost Children Archive* presents an example of feminist mothering in the main character's choices to prioritize her career and teach her children empathy for the undocumented. These works remind us of the importance of empathy in building a world that can perform actions of care for those who come from beyond our borders.

The novels chosen for this chapter function to create the energy needed to form the wave of matricentric feminism we want to see and need to see to enact change. These texts are cultural artifacts that create space for mothers to focus on their own perspectives and positions within the contexts of mothering and migration. These works elevate the study of mothering as worthy of academic and social pursuit. They shift focus from representations of the good mother and make room for depictions of authentic mothers.

These novels break ground by providing alternative renderings of migrant mothering from a mother's point of view. They provide a sample of the different kinds of work that can be done in matricentric feminist praxis through literature and imagination, through creativity and play. The authors create a space for marginalized voices to address the complicated situation of mothering in a migration context. Furthermore, they invite (and incite) readers to empathize with issues that ultimately affect everyone on the planet. To paraphrase Adrienne Rich again, we are all born of mothers, and the situation of migratory movement from less prosperous to more prosperous countries is not just a political issue; it is a supremely human issue, and it is here to stay.

To further our understanding of what it means to be a migrant mother, we must continue to search for more examples of nonnormative mothers and matrifocal voices that share their stories of migration. Fiction provides a space for academics to explore diverse representations of matricentric feminism from around the world. Additional research must be done to document this mother wave of matrifocal voices from other countries with varied destination countries as well. Because this study is comparative in nature, it invites further explorations of works of literature from diverse countries so that we may observe where similarities and differences exist in our definitions of migrant mothering and matricentric feminism. Our world will continue to produce new generations, and this offspring will continue to cross and recross borders. It is in our best interest to understand these concepts of matricentric feminist mothering and migration to work towards a more empathetic and humane way of life. By doing this, we will contribute to the wave of matricentric feminism that continues to grow.

Endnotes

1. This novel was originally written in Catalán and translated to Spanish by Rosa María Prats. It has not yet been translated into English; therefore, the English translations are my own.
2. It is also noteworthy that El Hachmi's previous novel *La filla estranjera* (2015) tells a similar story from the point of view of the daughter character. Therefore, the author began thinking from the daughter's point of view and then transitioned to telling the story from the mother's perspective.
3. A video of this process can be seen at the following link: https://med.stanford.edu/newborns/professional-education/breastfeeding/early-initiation-of-breastfeeding.html.
4. Other books that explore this topic are *Contra los hijos* (2018) by Lina Meruane, *Childfree by Choice* (2019) by Amy Blackstone, and *La hija*

única (2020) by Guadalupe Nettel.

5. For further reading on how anxiety is prompted by the way society treats mothers in the United States see, *Ordinary Insanity* (2020) by Sarah Menkedick.

Works Cited

Álvarez, Julia. *Afterlife*. Algonquin Books of Chapel Hill, 2020.

Blackstone, Amy. *Childfree by Choice: The Movement Redefining Family and Creating a New Age of Independence*. Dutton, 2019.

Brown, Ivana. "Ambivalence, Maternal." *Encyclopedia of Motherhood. Vol. 1*. Edited by Andrea O'Reilly. Sage Publications, 2010, pp. 50–52.

Collins, Patricia Hill. "The Meaning of Motherhood in Black Culture and Mother-Daughter Relationships." *Maternal Theory: Essential Readings*. Edited by Andrea O'Reilly. Demeter Press, 2007, pp. 274–89.

Daly, Brenda O., and Maureen T. Reddy. *Narrating Mothers: Theorizing Maternal Subjectivities*. University of Tennessee Press, 1991.

El Hachmi, Najat. *La filla estrangera/La hija extranjera*. Translated by Rosa M. Prats, Editorial Planeta, 2015.

El Hachmi. Najat. *Mare de llet i mel. /Madre de leche y miel*. Translated by Rosa M. Prats. Editorial Planeta, 2018.

Garbes, Angela. *Essential Labor: Mothering as Social Change*. Harper Wave, 2022.

Gluck, Sherna Berger, and Daphne Patai. *Women's Words: The Feminist Practice of Oral History*. Routledge, 1991.

Green, Fiona. "Feminist Mothering." *The Routledge Companion to Motherhood*. Routledge, 2020, pp. 36–50.

Green, Fiona. "Practising Matricentric Feminist Mothering." *Journal of the Motherhood Initiative*, vol. 10, Spring/Fall 2019, pp. 83–99.

Knott, Sarah. *Mother Is a Verb: An Unconventional History*. Farrar, Straus and Giroux, 2019.

Lewis, Emilie. "Voluntarily Childless Women." *The Routledge Companion to Motherhood*. Edited by Lynn O'Brien Hallstein et al. Routledge, 2020, pp. 122–130.

Luiselli, Valeria. *Lost Children Archive: A Novel*. Alfred A. Knopf, 2019.

Maushart, Susan. "Faking Motherhood: The Mask Revealed." *Maternal Theory: Essential Readings*. Edited by Andrea O'Reilly. Demeter Press, 2007, pp. 460–81.

Menkedick, Sarah. *Ordinary Insanity*. Pantheon, 2020.

Meruane, Line. *Contra los hijos*. Random House, 2018.

Nettel, Guadalupe. *La hija única*. Anagrama, 2020.

O'Reilly, Andrea. "Feminist Mothering." *Maternal Theory: Essential Readings*. Edited by Andrea O'Reilly. Demeter Press, 2007, pp. 792–821.

O'Reilly, Andrea. "Maternal Theory: Patriarchal Motherhood and Empowered Mothering." *The Routledge Companion to Motherhood*. Edited by Lynn O'Brien Hallstein et al. Routledge, 2020, pp. 19–35.

O'Reilly, Andrea. "Matricentric Feminism: A Feminism for Mothers." *Journal of the Motherhood Initiative*, vol. 10, Spring/Fall 2019, pp. 13–26.

Oster, Emily. "End the Plague of Secret Parenting." *The Atlantic*, 21 May 2019, https://www.theatlantic.com/ideas/archive/2019/05/normalize-parenthood-workplacedont-hide-it/589822/. Accessed 13 July 2024.

Parker, Rozsika. *Torn in Two: Maternal Ambivalence*. Virago Press, 1995.

Podnieks, Elizabeth. "Matrifocal Voices in Literature." *The Routledge Companion to Motherhood*. Edited by Lynn O'Brien Hallstein et al. Routledge, 2020, pp. 176–190.

Rich, Adrienne. *Of Woman Born: Motherhood as Experience and Institution*. Norton, 1976.

Thurer, Shari. *The Myths of Motherhood: How Culture Reinvents the Good Mother*. Houghton Mifflin, 1994.

Verny, Thomas R, and Pamela Weintraub. *Tomorrow's Baby: The Art and Science of Parenting from Conception through Infancy*. Simon & Schuster, 2002.

16.

Matricentric Art: A Philosophy of Maternal Work through the Act of Creativity

Anna M. Hennessey

In the early 2000s, new art about pregnancy, birth, and mothering began to flourish, spreading across the internet through image sharing and online galleries, as well as on the ground in small gallery exhibitions. With a few exceptions, many of the artists who created this work are still not widely known. However, their art is increasingly recognized within communities devoted to birth and mothering around the globe, and there is a growth of interest in the work on its artistic merits alone. Using Andrea O'Reilly's theory of matricentric feminism, this chapter examines how this rise in artistic production of images related to mothering in the twenty-first century correlates with the emergence of new models of feminism and a philosophy of maternal work through the act of creativity. Matricentric art has created a visual space for collective understandings that mothering in all its forms is a means of empowerment for many women from around the globe. The chapter also looks at the rise of birth justice movements developed by and for women of colour, low-income women, and other marginalized people. In certain cases, women and others are using art and imagery related to birth and mothering to defend against reproductive oppressions based on the inequalities of race, class, gender, and sexuality.

A new generation of feminists, matricentric feminists are celebrating the work and experiences of mothers. O'Reilly, a Canadian scholar of feminist theory and motherhood studies, developed the concept of matricentric feminism in her 2016 book, *Matricentric Feminism: Theory, Activism, and Practice*. The book also provides extensive data on the way that the field of women's studies has historically marginalized the topic of mothering. Looking at the treatment of mothering in such contexts as National Women's Studies Association conference panels, top feminist journals—such as *Signs, Frontiers, Women's Studies Quarterly, Feminist Studies,* and *Gender and Society*—and gender and women's studies textbooks and syllabi, O'Reilly found that in the decade preceding publication of her book, between 1 to less than 3 per cent of the content was devoted to the topic of mothering (O'Reilly 197).[1] As O'Reilly notes, "Given that 80 percent of women become mothers in their lifetime, there is an evident disconnect between the minimal representation of motherhood in academic feminism and the actual lives of most women" (O'Reilly 197).

For many women, though certainly not for all of them, mothering in all its forms, including those of adoptive and foster parenting, and inclusive of the experiences of pregnancy and birth, is a major part of identity and life itself. Traditional liberal feminism, in both its academic and popular forms, has often viewed reverence for these acts of mothering as negatively related to a patriarchal understanding of women's identities. Furthermore, this form of feminism casts women who identify with the experiences of pregnancy and birth as bound to their reproductive capacities, describing such identification as the problem of biological or gender essentialism. Matricentric feminism, in its respect for the rich diversity of mothering experiences, including the experiences of those who give birth, as well as those who do not give birth or mother in the traditional sense, provides feminists with a positive and intersectional model of feminism that includes ample space for discourse on mothering, pregnancy, and birth.

Contemporary artists play an important role in this discussion, showing through their creative acts how mothering is a source of empowerment for many, including for artists who are mothers or parents.

Art and Creation in a Philosophy of Maternal Work

In the twenty-first century, a rapid increase in the numbers and kinds of images related to birth and mothering has taken place in the art world. These matricentric artworks are important representations correlating with the emergence of a philosophy of maternal work through the act of creativity. Artists have begun to express the transformative process taking place in how their work about mothering is a means of empowerment for them and for others.

In "Neo-Maternalism: Contemporary Artists' Approach to Motherhood," an article written for *The Brooklyn Rail* in 2008, contemporary artist Sharon Butler examines the way that the topic of mothering has been overlooked, dismissed, negated, and rejected as serious matter for artistic representation along the history of twentieth-century feminist art. She then shifts her focus to describe a new phenomenon in this area of art, which is how contemporary artists have begun to integrate maternal experiences into their work:

> Some contemporary artists, in fiercely honest work, apprehend the entire messy process of creation, birth, and childrearing as raw material for their art practice.... In a contemporary context, the complex processes and emotions involved in raising children could certainly provide rich material for practitioners of relational aesthetics with post-studio practices. (Butler)

Butler contends that the very acts of mothering and childrearing are not just mundane parts of everyday life but also have the capacity to influence and integrate with artistic production: "Such artists' collaborative, expansive approach to their art, and their reluctance to embrace the hermeticism of previous generations, suggest that peak creativity and the embrace of worldly responsibility are no longer considered mutually exclusive. Raising a family and making art can, in fact, become one seamless activity" (Butler). Butler also explains how certain twentieth-century artists—such as Elizabeth Murray, a painter, and Sally Mann, a photographer—have depicted children in their own work and influenced Butler's own understanding of representing the maternal subject. Murray and Mann did not represent maternity as a submissive act dominated by patriarchy but rather as an act marked by high energy and controversial imagery. Butler emphasizes this type of energy in the maternal experience: "Birth and childrearing do not automatically turn women into retrogressive panderers to small-minded conventions." Some of the artists she mentions who integrate mothering and art making include Catherine Opie, Jenny Saville, and Jennifer Wroblewski.

Similarly, contemporary Canadian artist Kate Hansen created her *Madonna and Child Project* between 2007 and 2011 to capture the life energy and interaction between mothers and their children. Hansen's *Krista and Colum* (Fig. 1) is one of the images from the collection. Writing about the production of her artwork following the births of her children, Hansen describes a phenomenon similar to that described by Butler—a period of increased and not decreased creativity in conjunction with the events of birth and mothering:

> After the birth of my son in 2007 I felt an incredible energy and drive to make art. Contrary to the popular belief that art making is one of the things that falls to the wayside after the birth of children, in my case I felt inspired and compelled by my experience of childbirth and motherhood. It was almost as though the creative act of making another human being awoke a creative drive in me (Hansen).

As opposed to stifling her work or drive, which in this case pertain to artistic productivity, the events of birth and mothering stimulated Hansen's creativity and ability to work.

Hansen's affirmation that the maternal is a powerful source of creativity and work drive serves as one of many contemporary matricentric voices questioning statements that birth and mothering are oppressive for women. In her essay, "Motherhood: The Annihilation of Women," the final chapter of a highly influential if not canonical book in feminist theory, *Mothering: Essays in Feminist Theory*, women's and gender studies scholar Jeffner Allen asserts that mothering is dangerous for women: "Motherhood is dangerous to women because it continues the structure within which females must be women and mothers and, conversely, because it denies to females the creation of a subjectivity and world that is open and free" (315). But Kate Hansen, similar to Sharon Butler, finds that the acts of birth and mothering actually broadened her world, opening up possibilities for the expression of subjectivity. None of this is to say that becoming a mother does not entail work, but as Hansen explains, mothering also has the capacity to shift a person's perception of time:

"I also found that the time limitations involved in caring for an infant forced me to be more disciplined in my art making. I would eke out hours here and there when my son was sleeping to continue my portraits. After my daughter was born in 2008, I had determined to form a series of mother and child portraits and accompany them with birth stories written by each subject."

Figure 1. *Krista and Colum,* conte crayon and goldleaf on paper. Copyright 2010, Kate Hansen, printed with permission.

Not only did Hansen not abandon artmaking following the births of her children, but she also witnessed how mothering brought a flourishing of new artistic energy and creativity into her work and life. Hansen's perspective reflects a strong contemporary voice of matricentric feminism that diverges from the dominant viewpoints of academic and neoliberal feminists.

Although the lives of most women and other parents change significantly after a child's birth or entry into the home, comments such as Hansen's and Butler's suggest a philosophy of maternal work: These experiences also can empower mothers, bringing new energy and vitality both to their work and to their creative selves. For some, the connection between mothering and feminism is profound, and more discussion of this power could embolden the feminist movement, not weaken it.

The Impact of Neoliberal Feminism and Capitalism on Mothering

In addition to academic feminists, mainstream feminists have had a profound impact on opinions and policies related to birth and mothering. Capitalism is inextricable from many of the critiques emerging within this sphere. In France, Elisabeth Badinter has written prolifically on the topic of mothering. She is one of the most recognized French intellectual figures today, and her work is widely read in France and abroad. Badinter is a vocal critic of various parenting movements. She is especially bothered by the concept of maternal instinct, which she thinks is a socially constructed myth.

In her work, *Le Conflit: la femme et la mere,* written in 2010 (translated in 2012 by Adriana Hunter as *The Conflict: How Modern Motherhood Undermines the Status of Women*), Badinter critiques various women-led parenting groups, such as La Leche League, an American organization devoted to the promotion of breastfeeding. But as several writers have noted, it is difficult to separate Badinter's criticism from her corporate endeavours. In her 2011 piece on Badinter for *The New Yorker,* for example, Jane Kramer notes the glaring capitalist motives Badinter has for opposing these groups, pointing to Badinter's corporate ties.[2] Badinter is one of France's wealthiest citizens and the billionaire shareowner of Publicis, the giant French advertising and public relations company. The company is known for promoting and advertising synthetic diapers and powdered milk formula. Nevertheless, Badinter is a highly influential figure in France who has been able to brand herself first and foremost as a university professor, an intellectual, and a feminist philosopher. Her ideas are relevant to how popular discussions of mothering and feminism affect mothering more broadly.

Sheryl Sandberg is perhaps even more influential than Badinter in mainstream feminism. The American has greatly influenced how mothering is viewed around the globe, especially in the United States. While not an academic herself, academic circles discuss Sandberg, the former chief operating officer at Facebook. She is also referenced in academic books and conference talks. The main thesis of her wildly popular 2013 book, *Lean In: Women, Work, and the Will to Lead,* is that women can achieve a balance in their lives, having both a high-powered career and a family.

In my 2018 book, *Imagery, Ritual, and Birth,* I discuss problems with Sandberg's ideology at length. Sandberg assumes that when women "lean back," the decision comes from a belief that they will not be able to juggle their careers with raising children. She undermines both the possibility that in some cases, leaning back may have to do with a strong desire to mother, and the possibility that mothering may enhance a person's work qualities or qualities as a leader. Although she is careful not to assert it outright, Sandberg diminishes the work of mothering by suggesting that women in the workforce should prioritize career advancement and think about becoming a mother later in life.

Facebook, where Sandberg worked, was one of the first companies to promote egg freezing in its employee benefits packages, encouraging employees to postpone pregnancy and mothering. Such policies indicate that mothering is less important or relevant than career advancement. In this context of popular feminism, the topic of mothering is again relegated to something lesser and not worthy of as much discussion, as well as other topics, such as corporate success and higher salary.

Writing in *Signs,* feminist theorist Catherine Rottenberg emphasizes that Sandberg's ideology represents a rise of neoliberal feminism in the US, one that has more to do with market values and individual liberation than it does with collective justice. [3] Rottenberg explains how such a balance is only attainable for the top one percent, those women who can outsource the reproductive and carework necessary when they decide to have children. Promoting this neoliberal ideology has a deep impact on the values of middle-class women (Rottenberg). Furthermore, beyond its reach with upper- and middle-class women, neoliberal feminism has its greatest impact on society's most underprivileged women. As Rottenberg explains, the work of mothering, as well as that of reproduction itself, is diminished and increasingly outsourced to these more marginalized and disposable women.

This capitalist brand of feminism is not concerned with improving the lives of women as a whole, especially not the world's less privileged women. Rather, it is construed for those at the top, who can use other women to do the work of mothering, and in the case of surrogacy, the work of pregnancy and birth as well, such that individual career goals are reached.

By discussing the corporate promotion of egg freezing for Silicon Valley employees, as well as the practices of "womb renting" and hiring nanny caregivers to take care of children already born, Rottenberg's work provides evidence that for certain segments of society, birth and mothering are treated as hassles that should be postponed until a woman has first secured her career aspirations. Sandberg was the main corporate proponent behind the promotion of egg freezing in Facebook's employee benefits package, and the company added the procedure to the package in 2014, one year after Sandberg publicized *Lean In* (Alter). Thus, her neoliberal feminist ideology has already had actual implications on policy in the real world.

Matricentric Art and Social Justice

Mothering and birth are sites of power for many women, and these experiences can be potent in the context of healing and justice for the most marginalized women. Matricentric art and poetry connected to these experiences help to mark and make sacred these life events, bringing people together and increasing community awareness for those who are marginalized, underrepresented, or harmed within the context of the medical establishment.

In the US, a wealthy nation, infant and maternal death rates remain high, and most new parents receive no paid time off after childbirth and adoption. The medicalization of birth is at an all-time high in the US and worldwide, even though the World Health Organization and other important institutions continue to recommend against it. This situation is especially alarming for Black women, who die three times as often as white women during childbirth in the US, as well as for Black infants, who die at a rate more than twice that of white infants (Belluz; Effiong).

The issue of maternal healthcare in the US is therefore especially dire. Academic and neoliberal feminists have avoided the topics of mothering and birth. In some cases, they have also criticized the sociology of reproduction, which has meticulously tracked the global increase in medicalized birth and its dangers to women. Their treatment of birth and mothering in these ways is a disservice to marginalized women, many of whom are subjected to this medicalization and do not receive proper care within the medical establishment.

Similarly, scientific research has shown the profound effect prenatal care and early parent-child relationships have on children's physical, social, emotional, and psychological development (Karoly et al.; Verny

1987). On a primary level, the architecture of a child's brain is significantly affected by social experiences with parents and caregivers during the first three years of life (Zigler et al.). This evidence shows that mothering and parenting should be of central interest to all concerned with individual cultivation and the bettering of society. Matricentric feminism understands the central role that caregivers play in our world, as well as the importance of acknowledging social justice and histories of violence against marginalized communities and mothers.

In *Medical Apartheid*, medical ethicist Harriett Washington shows how the history of the medical establishment in the US, a white establishment, has historically harmed Black women in the context of birth. She finds evidence of destructive procedures related to birth that are not widely discussed within the sphere of traditional feminism. One of the more well-known examples is that of François Marie Prévost, the Louisiana surgeon who brought the caesarean section to the American medical community in 1820 (Washington 106 and Oparah 10). The doctor first conducted numerous experiments of this procedure on enslaved Black women, many of whom lost their lives or were deeply injured, or whose children's lives were lost during the experimentation. Although this experimentation is in the past, traces of the same type of harm continue to the present day, connected to the fact that higher maternal mortality and infant death rates exist for Black people than they do for any other race in the US. Black women and their families continue to encounter a system of birth that is particularly dangerous for them.

Resistance to the medical establishment is growing within the Black community, and matricentric art is an important piece of this resistance. The Birth Justice Movement—a movement developed by and for women of colour and including midwives, doulas, scholars, and artists—is, for example, reclaiming the knowledge that maternal bodies are sacred and powerful entities. Julia Chinyere Oparah's 2016 publication, *Birthing Justice: Black Women, Pregnancy, and Childbirth*, is an important contribution to matricentric feminism and academic and popular feminisms more broadly, providing foundational scholarship on the Birth Justice Movement. As some writers within the movement explain, establishing an understanding that birth is a sacred and powerful moment for women and other birthing people is part of how marginalized individuals and communities find healing (Hennessey 2018, 199–206). Art, creation, and liberation are part of this healing process.

This theme of liberation and healing through matricentric art emerges in "The First Cut Is the Deepest: A Mother-Daughter Conversation about Birth, Justice, Healing, and Love," a joint interview in Oparah's *Birthing Justice* with Pauline Ann McKenzie-Day and her daughter, Alexis Pauline Gumbs, both of whom are involved in community projects and scholarship. The mother-daughter team writes about the connection between a reclamation of the sacred in birth and the broader theme of justice for marginalized people:

> Being born and giving birth are important moments of our liberation. In a Western society that does not yet respect and honor the full brilliance, self-determination, and spiritual power of Black women, the oppressive tendencies of the medical-industrial complex violate the sacredness of birth.... We have decided to become part of a movement of women of color reclaiming the power to protect and honor sacred birth experiences. (qtd, in Oparah 145)

As part of reclaiming the sacred in birth, Gumbs uses matricentric poetry in birth rituals, providing those who are pregnant with praise poems as they approach birth. McKenzie-Day acknowledges the role that poetry plays in the ritual of birth:

> It's so exciting to envision you helping birthing women to open a spiritual passageway. I can envision you writing a poem for everyone who is going to give birth that we are working with and having that poem resonating with them before the baby is born and during the process of birth. (qtd. in Oparah 154)

Gumbs responds to her mother, commenting on the interconnectedness of the poem, something that is most often written, made material, and verbalized. The poem, a matricentric artifact, is part of the ritual of birth or even acts as a ritual in itself, she claims, and it is through that artifact that people connect to power and justice. Writing and poetic expression are an artistic means through which birth and mothering become understood as sacred, regardless of whether that sacred form is of a religious or humanistic nature.

Born to parents who immigrated from Haiti, artist Anoa Kanu is a Harlem-based water-media artist. She is also a registered nurse and a certified lactation consultant, and some of her artwork pertains to the theme of birth. Her work references the sacredness and empowerment of pregnancy and birth, as well as how birth is connected to themes of justice for women, especially marginalized women. In Kanu's *Girl in Bamboo Earrings* (Fig. 2), the main figure squats amid lush vegetation, supported by warm brown bamboo shoots behind her. Cradling her belly, the woman's arms and hands arch down and draw the viewer's attention to the soft swirl of a crowning baby at her vulva. She remains serene during this process of birth and emergence, her facial expression focused and calm. The painting emphasizes the squatting position, an ideal manner of using gravity as a natural aid in delivering one's baby. Unassisted in the birth, the main figure also reminds others who are pregnant that they are part of a long lineage of women who have birthed before.

In our correspondence, Kanu describes the making of this matricentric image, and her words about its creation and meaning are powerful in her understanding of how the theme of justice is integral to her work. Kanu verbalizes the empowerment of the marginalized and a person's ability to transcend space and time during the birth event. This explanation of birth is not related to an experience of the mundane world but of one inspired by a sense of awe, timelessness, and the sacred:

> I am a painter, but I also work in women's health with new mothers and babies in an urban environment. I see a lot of beauty, new life, beginnings. But I also see a lot of disempowerment, young women not knowing their rights, what questions to ask or that they could even ask.
>
> When I imagined this image in my mind's eye, I saw a young woman, birthing for the first time, knowing she was capable, transcending space and time. She is protected and is able to tap into her elemental self and ancestral memory. She transforms through the birth process into a new being, a more fully empowered version of herself. (Kanu)

Figure 2. *Girl in Bamboo Earrings,* watercolour. Copyright 2016, Anoa Kanu, All Rights Reserved.

For Kanu, when a labouring woman is provided a safe environment where she can go into a deeper place and realize birth as a timeless, sacred event, her body's processes have a better chance of unfolding. In this space of birth, the woman is transformed, empowered, and liberated. Kanu's work, while pertinent in the context of how sacred images of birth are important for marginalized women, is also significant to an understanding of matricentric feminism.

In "Refusing Delinquency, Reclaiming Power: Indigenous Women and Childbirth," Claire Dion Fletcher, an Indigenous registered midwife, and Cheryllee Bourgeois, midwife and expert in Indigenous midwifery, discuss the interaction of knowledge and ritual, this time in the historical contexts of Indigenous nations living and practising in North America, as well as in the context of art about pregnancy, birth, and mothering created by contemporary Indigenous artists. Looking at colonial imagery, narratives, and histories, Fletcher and Bourgeois provide evidence that Indigenous knowledge and practice around birth and labour were dismissed during the eighteenth and nineteenth centuries (Fletcher and Bourgeois 159). Yet they also reveal a reclaiming of this knowledge and an assertion that Indigenous people have not disappeared or been destroyed. This process of reclaiming makes itself manifest in the artwork of contemporary Indigenous artists: "Contemporary art that depicts positive images of pregnancy and birth, drawing from cultural symbolism and realistic representations, not only contradicts the notion that Indigenous women and people have disappeared from North America but also celebrates and honours the roles of women that colonizers have tried so violently to destroy" (Fletcher and Bourgeois 165). Expressed in matricentric art, knowledge of birth promotes the understanding that Indigenous traditions of birth, including its ceremonies and rituals, are legitimate forms of knowledge connected to Indigenous cosmologies (169). Fletcher and Bourgeois find that, in Toronto, Indigenous-led midwifery initiatives have established projects geared towards serving both Indigenous and non-Indigenous women and sharing traditional birth knowledge and practices, including ritualistic practices, within the birth community (168–69).

Damien Leggett, a Canadian artist and trans man, addresses themes of birth, mothering, and empowerment in his work. In *Freebirth of Amara* (Fig. 3), Leggett depicts the emergence of a crowning baby. At the centre of the composition rests the image of an eye, representing a sacred chakra within the body. Commonly depicted in non-Western images, chakras correspond to the powerful and sacred centres of the body, which together regulate its functioning. When Leggett was transitioning in 2011, he explained to me the meaning of the work and the transformative powers of birth as a rite of passage: "Freebirth of Amara ... is exactly what it was inspired by. This is a woman who is surrounded by fire and helping spirits, but she is ultimately alone. This is a moment of transformation; having only herself to rely on, this woman has pushed past fear, passed through many emotions to ultimately find herself free of attachment ... she just is, in this moment" (Leggett).

Figure 3. *Freebirth of Amara,* ink and watercolour. Copyright 2011, Damien Leggett, Printed with permission.

Explaining his background with childbirth, Leggett describes the importance of birth and parenting in his own life:

> I have been working in the realm of birth for almost ten years, advocating for the right of women and infants to dignity in their birth experiences. I have apprenticed with birth here in Canada, as well as in Central America. I am in the process of transitioning to a male body but honor the feminine in everything around me, including my Self. I am a single father of three amazing children who have shown me who I truly am. (Leggett)

Mothering intersects with everyone, not just women, and is inclusive of transgender communities. O'Reilly's *Matricentric Feminism* emphasizes this point, explaining how queering motherhood also acts to destabilize patriarchal motherhood (100).

Matricentric Art in Pop Culture and Museums

In early 2017, photos and videos of Beyoncé Knowles splashed across popular magazines and the internet to announce the American singer's second pregnancy, this time with twins. Shot by Ethiopian American photographer Awol Erizku, the photos depict Beyoncé as what some have interpreted to be a Madonna, goddess, or Venus figure (Grady). In a few of the photos, flowers frame the singer's body or rest at her feet, and she is seated against a blue sky. In others, she appears reclined or standing with a yellow background, again surrounded by flowers and foliage, a bust of Nefertiti at her side. Shortly after appearing in these photos, the singer performed at the Grammy Awards, appearing as a pregnant goddess in golden attire and crown. Paying tribute to African spirituality, Beyoncé used the event to show through her body the imagery of Oshun, an orisha, or deity, from the Yoruba religious tradition (Kuo).[4]

After the birth of Beyoncé's children, additional photos emerged, again shot by Erizku, in which the singer is seen standing and holding her twins. With hair down, leg bent, and a blue veil flowing from her head, Beyoncé stands in front of a large flower arrangement, the sea and blue sky in the background. Like the portraits of her pregnancy, this portrait is reminiscent of both the Virgin Mary and Botticelli's Venus (Grady). The photographer hybridizes a variety of figures (goddess, African deity, Madonna figure, etc.), and the meanings of the images emerge not as succinct resacralizations of an original object but as matricentric celebrations of the artist's own body as a pregnant woman or as a mother.

While glorifying the artist, which is also inseparable from the business of capitalist American moneymaking, these photos act to penetrate the public mind; they showcase pregnancy, birth, and mothering, presenting these events as empowering moments in life.[5] Infused with religious imagery, the works tap into the sensibilities of the religious viewer. Yet even the nonreligious viewer can understand the religious references of these works and be in awe without religious sentiment at the birth event.

The widespread sharing, acceptance, and celebration of Beyoncé's pregnancy and maternity photos point to a shift in public perception about birth. When Annie Leibovitz's now famous photograph of a nude and pregnant Demi Moore appeared on the cover of *Vanity Fair* in 1991, the image at first set off a major backlash, with many stores either refusing to sell it or treating the image as pornography and covering it up for sale (Tavani). Controversial at the time of its publication, the picture of Moore today acts as a symbol of maternal empowerment. Since the early twenty-first century, an increasing number of actresses, athletes, and other public figures have appeared in magazines, usually in the nude, to show what their bodies look like during pregnancy. In the meantime, many painters and other artists have begun to depict pregnancy and mothering, as well as the actual event of birth, signifying to viewers that these events are empowering as opposed to disdainful, disgusting, or a sign of fragility.

Known for her large-scale figurative paintings of nude women, Jenny Saville is a contemporary British artist who began to explore themes of maternity after becoming a mother herself. During the first decade of the 2000s, Saville sketched and painted several pieces related to the theme of mothers and children in which she depicts herself holding her two infant sons. Influenced in part by Leonardo da Vinci's monumental Renaissance cartoon of Saint Anne and Saint John the Baptist, Saville's massive works show her seated naked and grasping the two babies on her lap, both of whom are also naked and squirm from her. As in Saville's other works, the charcoal lines of her sketches and colours of her paintings produce a frenetic dynamism in *The Mothers*. Through this dynamism, the artist captures the physicality, emotionality, and phenomenology of what it is to be a mother of young children. The religious references in the work, however, are fused with a representation of Saville and her children, making sacred the nonreligious bodies of the artist as a mother with her children.

Using her matricentric art, Saville has broken through the closed culture of high-end museums. Her paintings emphasize and celebrate the physicality required when mothering. There is nothing patriarchal about Saville's images. Her painted figures are massive celebrations of maternal work. As O'Reilly explains in *Matricentric Feminism*, feminist mothering is the primary practice of matricentric feminism. Saville and other artists like her are using their artwork to highlight a narrative of motherhood that counters patriarchal motherhood.

Conclusion

This chapter has explored how the rise of matricentric art in the twenty-first century represents a philosophy of maternal work through creativity. Through its various images, matricentric art is inclusive of mothering in all its forms and is a means of empowerment for many. The chapter has also looked at how matricentric art is a powerful means of healing, empowerment, and growth, especially for marginalized women. Traditional and neoliberal forms of feminism have contributed to the marginalization of mothering as a topic worthy of discussion in academic discourse and more broadly. Breaking into the spheres of pop culture and the high-end work of museums, matricentric art is now spreading, celebrating the work and diversity of maternal experiences and representing an integral piece to matricentric feminism.

Endnotes

1. See pages 192–197 for the data breakdown.
2. "No one [in the media] except the satirical weekly *Le Canard Enchaîné*, a *Marianne* critic, and a couple of Green Party bloggers even mentioned the connection between Badinter and Publicis, which represents Procter & Gamble (Pampers) and Nestlé (powdered milk)—though Badinter herself told *Der Spiegel* that she got the idea for the book, in 1998, when France not only enforced an E.U. directive banning advertisements for powdered milk but also stopped the distribution of free samples in maternity wards" (Kramer).
3. Rottenberg had previously explained in an article for *Cultural Studies* that Sandberg is a figure who represents the emergence of neoliberal feminism in the US.
4. For a discussion of Beyoncé's broader use of African spirituality in her work, see Rutledge Emerald.
5. bell hooks addresses some of the issues of capitalism in Beyoncé's work, specifically as occurs in the context of the artist's visual album, *Lemonade*.

Works Cited

Allen, Jeffner. "Motherhood: The Annihilation of Women." *Mothering: Essays in Feminist Theory*. Edited by Joyce Trebilcot Totowa. Rowman & Allanheld, 1984, pp. 315–30.

Alter, Charlotte. "Sheryl Sandberg Explains Why Facebook Covers Egg-Freezing." *Time*, 24 Apr. 2015, http://time.com/3835233/sheryl-sandberg-explains-why-facebook-covers-egg-freezing/. Accessed 11 July 2024.

Badinter, Elisabeth. *Le Conflit: la femme et la mere*. Flammarion Lettres, 2010.

Badinter, Elisabeth. *The Conflict: How Modern Motherhood Undermines the Status of Women*. Translated by Adriana Hunter. Metropolitan Books, 2012.

Belluz, Julia. "Black Moms Die in Childbirth 3 Times as Often as White Moms." *Vox*, 3 July, 2017, https://www.vox.com/health-care/2017/7/3/15886892/black-white-moms-die-childbirth-north-carolina-less. Accessed 11 July 2024.

Butler, Sharon. "Neo-Maternalism: Contemporary Artists' Approach to Motherhood." *TheBrooklyn Rail: Critical Perspectives on Arts, Politics, and Culture*, 12 Dec. 2008, https://brooklynrail.org/2008/12/artseen/neo-maternalism-contemporary-artists-approach-to-motherhood. Accessed 15 March 2014.

Effiong, Utibe, et al., "Infant Mortality among Black Babies." *The University of Michigan School of Public Health Blog*, 29 Oct. 2020, https://sph.umich.edu/pursuit/2020posts/infant-mortality-among-black-babies.html. Accessed 11 July 2024.

Fletcher, Claire Dion, and Cheryllee Bourgeois. "Refusing Delinquency, Reclaiming Power: Indigenous Women and Childbirth." *Natal Signs: Cultural Representations of Pregnancy, Birth and Parenting*. Edited by Nadya Burton. Demeter Press, 2015, pp. 153–71.

Grady, Constance. "Decoding the Artistic References in Beyoncé's Gorgeous Birth Announcement for Her Twins," *Vox*, 14 July 2017, https://www.vox.com/culture/2017/7/14/15971588/beyonce-twins-birth-announcement-madonna-venus. Accessed 11 July 2024.

Hansen, Kate. "Madonna and Child Project: Portraits and Birth Stories." *Kate Hansen*, http://www.katehansen.ca/madonna-and-child-project.html. Accessed 22 April 2012.

Hennessey, Anna. *Imagery, Ritual, and Birth: Ontology Between the Sacred and the Secular.* Lexington Books (an imprint of Rowman & Littlefield), 2018.

hooks, bell. "Moving Beyond Pain." *bell hooks Institute Blog*, 9 May 2016, http://www.bellhooksinstitute.com/blog/2016/5/9/moving-beyond-pain. Accessed 11 July 2024.

Kanu, Anoa. Email with author. Sept. and Oct., 2016.

Karoly, Lynn A., et al. *Investing in Our Children: What We Know and Don't Know About the Costs and Benefits of Early Childhood Interventions.* RAND Corporation, 1998.

Kramer, Jane. "Against Nature: Elisabeth Badinter's Contrarian Feminism." *The New Yorker*, 25 July 2011, http://www.newyorker.com/magazine/2011/07/25/against-nature. Accessed 11 July 2024.

Kuo, Lily. "At the Grammys, Beyoncé Paid an Epic Tribute to African Diaspora Spirituality." *Reuters*, 13 Feb. 2017, https://qz.com/908973/at-the-grammys-beyonce-paid-an-epic-tribute-to-afro-diaspora-spirituality/. Accessed 11 July 2024.

Leggett, Damien. Email to author. 17 Dec. 2011.

Oparah, Julia Chinyere, and Alicia D. Bonaparte, eds. *Birthing Justice: Black Women, Pregnancy, and Childbirth.* Routledge, 2016.

O'Reilly, Andrea. *Matricentric Feminism: Theory, Activism, and Practice.* Demeter Press, 2016.

Rottenberg, Catherine. "Neoliberal Feminism and the Future of Human Capital." *Signs: Journal of Women in Culture and Society* 42.2, 2017, pp. 329–348.

Rottenberg, Catherine. "The Rise of Neoliberal Feminism." *Cultural Studies*, vol. 18, Nov. 2013, pp. 1–20.

Rutledge, Emerald. "African Spirituality and the Power of Religious Reclamation." *Black Perspectives*, 9 Oct. 2017, http://www.aaihs.org/african-spirituality-and-the-power-of-religious-reclamation/. Accessed 11 July 2024.

Sandberg, Sheryl. *Lean In: Women, Work, and the Will to Lead.* Knopf, 2013.

Tavani, Andrew. "1991 Vanity Fair Cover Featuring Pregnant Demi Moore Named One of Most Influential Images of all Time." *New York Times*, 18 Nov. 2016, http://nytlive.nytimes.com/womenintheworld

/2016/11/18/1991-vanity-fair-cover-featuring-pregnant-demi-moore-named-1-of-most-influential-images-of-all-time/. Accessed 25 July 2017.

Verny, Thomas. *Pre- And Perinatal Psychology: An Introduction*. Human Sciences Press, 1987.

Washington, Harriet. *Medical Apartheid,* Doubleday, 2006.

Zigler, Edward F., et al. *The First Three Years and Beyond: Brain Development and Social Policy.* Yale University Press, 2002.

17.

Commoning the Maternal: Matricentric Feminism and the Motherworks Festival

Jodie Hawkes and Pete Phillips

With the blinders of today's dominant ideologies ... it is difficult to see the common, even though it is all around us
—Michael Hardt and Antonio Negri viii.

Introduction

It's a grey, drizzled morning outside Cambridge Junction (United Kingdom) as audience members (mostly mothers) step over Jodie as they enter the building. Jodie is lying prone on the floor on a costume shop red carpet, camouflaged by her red dress, exhausted and undignified. Jodie is playing at being Kate Middleton. Her *Playing Kate* performance persona layers the image of the Princess of Wales with her own maternal identity—both visible, disrupting one another, a visual tussle between classed maternal identities. Pete holds the royal baby (a roll of turf wrapped in Jodie and Pete's own baby's hospital blanket, a hand-me-down that Pete himself was once wrapped in over forty years ago) and an umbrella to protect the baby from the rain. Pete's playing the butler/aide/personal assistant; he's there to help.

This chapter argues that class is an often overlooked and marginalized feature of maternal performance. Through reflecting on Search Party's

Playing Kate: Disruptions and Confrontations, we aim to articulate how this performative interruption to public space foregrounds class within the maternal commons. The chapter begins by arguing that *Playing Kate* enacts a performance of commoning, which is a distinct category of Andrea O'Reilly's concept of queering of motherhood—a disruption or confrontation of normative mothering through the foregrounding of class. The chapter then discusses commoning and the maternal performance commons, articulating how the commoning performed by *Playing Kate* articulates the absence of class within the Motherworks festival as an important example of a maternal commons and the field of maternal performance more broadly.

Figure 1. *Playing Kate: Disruptions and Confrontations* (2019). Photo credit Zoe Manders.

Playing Kate: Disruptions and Confrontations, performed at the Motherworks festival, was one of a number of live performances called *Playing Kate* by live art duo Search Party.[1] During the festival, Jodie and Pete performed various actions and interventions in the spaces between other artworks and performances—as the audience arrives, queuing for the theatre, and in the café during breaks in the program. In this chapter, we reflect on two of these performative interventions to articulate what we are calling a "commoning" of maternal performance. We reflect on two distinct features of commoning. First, we examine the category of queering and add to O'Reilly's strategies for challenging normative mothering within matricentric feminism, elevating class (the commoner) as an often unseen leftover of maternal discourse. Second, we explore how this commoning draws on the commons as a shared resource—a relational, social framework—to consider performance as a strategy to keep the maternal commons in movement.

The Motherworks festival was a day-long festival of maternal performance commissioned by Cambridge Junction as part of their Vision Mixers program and produced by independent producer Ruth Dudman. Several wider events under the umbrella of Motherworks also took place, funded by Arts Council England and The Big Lottery Community Fund, in partnership with Arts and Minds, The Place, and Fertility Fest at The Barbican. The festival included marginalized representations of the maternal and made visible the lived realities of motherhood. Inclusion and access were central. Maternal performances included perspectives on infertility, neurodiverse parenting, and maternal mental health.

The festival was part of a recent surge in visible maternal art practice and maternal performance in the UK. The field of maternal performance has been expanding rapidly and projects that support artists who are mothers have increased dramatically since our first baby in 2009. Despite significant contributions to understanding motherhood and maternal performance, little academic writing and performance work address maternal performance and the working-class mother. After sustained research on what Lena Šimić calls "maternal performance" leading up to our performance at the festival, we began to question whether class remained a leftover from academic and performance discourse on the maternal. That is not to say that class is not discussed within maternal performance in the UK or that it is actively and explicitly ignored; rather, discourse on maternal performance offering a specific focus on class is far less prominent. Excellent notable exceptions include performances *MUVAHOOD* by Libby Liburd and *CHAV* by Kelly Green, both of which explore single motherhood within a UK context. Šimić and Emily Underwood-Lee in their most recent publication on maternal performance acknowledge this gap: "We note that the majority of artists we write about in this book are white, cis-gendered, academically and economically privileged, and do not present as disabled" (14). Our aim at the festival was to foreground class as an often overlooked and marginalized area of study within maternal performance.

By combining three threads of research—matricentric feminism, class politics, and the performance of persona—we focussed on the term "common" and its various definitions. *Playing Kate* is contextualized by three distinct connotations of common: (in)common, common(er), and common(ing). We argue that the intersections between these various terms highlight multiple ideas on class, persona, and maternal performance, which can be examined about one another. The performance addresses ideas (in)common through the notion of normative motherhood and the violent neoliberal rhetoric of the (middle-class) maternal ideal. O'Reilly's work on matricentric feminism examines and studies normative motherhood to question its prevalence and dominance and how it oppresses mothers. She offers ten principles of normative motherhood: essentialization, privatization, individualization, naturalization, normalization, idealization, biologicalization, expertization, intensification and depoliticalization (*Matricentric Feminism* 10). These principles exclude nonnormative mothering, including the working-class mother. We also connected to the term "common" through its use as a British slang word meaning to lack taste, manners, or education, often associated with the figure of the common(er) (a derogatory classed term). Finally, we also connected the term to the idea of the common(s) (i.e., resources available to all) and specifically the social relations of common(ing).

Commoning as Queering: Disrupting and Confronting Normative Mothering

Despite little research into maternal performance and the working-class mother, a significant body of research explores the working-class mother within social, cultural, and media studies (Jenson; Skeggs, *Formations*; Tyler "Chav Mum"; McRobbie). Beverley Skeggs and Helen Wood note: "Since the ancient Greeks, the term 'class' has operated to include and exclude, to mark through classification and materialise inequalities, in an effort to organise and constitute understandings of value" (8). Skeggs considers class in relation to academic discourse and how certain voices are excluded (*Class*). Drawing from "ordinary everyday experience" (Walkerdine para. 9), *Playing Kate* aligns with discourses of class as it is felt and experienced as a "structure of feeling" (Beswick, "Feeling" 268) as opposed to a way of categorizing people economically and socially.

Playing Kate: Disruptions and Confrontations aims to encounter (confront) and interrupt (disrupt) multiple inferences and understandings of the term "common(s)." These ideas of encounter (Ettinger) and interruption (Baraitser, *Maternal Encounters*) are often drawn on within maternal performance discourse (Šimić and Underwood-Lee) though often without a specific class perspective or classed feeling. Our work shifts from these familiar terms of encounter and interruption to confrontation and disruption to articulate these ideas more precisely from a class perspective and to convey the feeling when class is brought into the foreground. During the festival, we performed disruptions in the communal spaces inside and outside the venue at Cambridge Junction. We considered these communal spaces in relation to "common space" (Stavrides 2), which Stavros Stavrides asserts "is a set of spatial relations produced by commoning practices." The interconnected disruptions all employed the *Playing Kate* persona and the presence of a turf baby (made of grass and soil).

Figure 2. *Playing Kate: Disruptions and Confrontations* (2019). Photo credit Zoe Manders.

Playing Kate is an "indeterminate persona" (Clancy) created by Search Party and performed by Jodie, drawing from our analysis of Kate the Princess of Wales as a maternal media object (MMO) (Hawkes, "Who?"). We argue that Kate as a MMO works to enclose other maternal identities and is an example of how normative motherhood (O'Reilly) is perpetuated and reproduced. Drawing from Jodie's own "social location" (O'Reilly) and through comparisons and differences to MMO Kate, we examine Kate as a maternal figure through the lens of performance, as we position Kate as a performer of class ideology. David Cole uses the term "political layering" (5) to describe how Kate as a media object can be understood. Similarly, we consider the Playing Kate persona as a complex layering of class politics. Through examining Kate's "indeterminate persona" (Clancy), we created Jodie's maternal performance persona—Playing Kate—as a type of maternal activism rejecting the normative motherhood produced by MMO Kate. Placed between Kate (the apparent commoner done good) and the maternal performance artist (Jodie), the Playing Kate persona confronts and disrupts representations of maternal experience as produced by MMO Kate.

At the festival, we used the Playing Kate persona to introduce the notion of commoning as a type of queering of maternal performance (O'Reilly)—that is, in its attempt to disrupt normative motherhood, the persona foregrounds and places a confrontation with class. O'Reilly notes how motherhood is a "cultural practice that is continuously redesigned" (56) depending on the sociopolitical context. In this way as motherhood shifts and changes across time and space, O'Reilly observes that "there is no essential or universal experience of motherhood" (56). She writes:

> Patriarchal motherhood has become the official meaning of motherhood, and as such, it marginalizes and renders illegitimate alternative practices of mothering. As a normative discourse, it polices all women's mothering and results in the pathologizing of those women who do not or cannot perform normative motherhood. Finally, the patriarchal institution of motherhood, as a normative discourse, restrains women's power to challenge and change the oppressiveness of their motherhood experience. (58)

Playing Kate: Disruptions and Confrontations draws from O'Reilly's matricentric feminism as a strategy for resistance, empowerment, and agency, approaching "mothering as a practice and not as a fixed, stable, and essentialist identity" (26). The performance held the intersectional view that it is impossible to separate class in relation to the (maternal) self and society and that these terms depend on one another to create identities. Patricia Hill Collins and Sirma Bilge argue that only through an intersectional approach can one understand how power relations "are intertwined and mutually constructing" (7). Intersectionality is a vital lens when considering the maternal experience and how varying combinations of class, gender, race, ability/disability, and age position mothers differently from one another. O'Reilly describes resistance to the process of normalization by "outlaw mothers" (19) as queering motherhood: "To queer motherhood is to re-think, re-shape, re-establish notions and practices of [normative] motherhood"' (19). For O'Reilly, queering strategies arise from the "social location of the mother" (20) in which they are empowered; these distinct strategies of resistance (while not including all mothers) do make possible "a multitude of maternal identities" (21).

In queering the normative motherhood produced by the MMO Kate, we could define Jodie's queering strategy in our performance work from her social location, a strategy we define as "commoning maternal performance." We argue commoning motherhood in this way, like queering, is a strategy to disrupt normative mothering but one which foregrounds class as a distinct position. Commoning maternal performance at the festival combined spatial strategies, persona, and maternal time foreground the leftovers and left out (commoners) from maternal performance and disrupt normative motherhood as presented by MMO Kate.

Playing Kate: Disruptions and Confrontations draws from Lisa Baraitser's theories of interruption, not as a strategy to understand maternal subjectivity but as a strategy of making, performing, and queering (commoning) maternal performance. Baraitser refers to interruptions as "a seemingly endless series of 'micro-blows' ... as breaches, tears or puncturings to the mother's durational experiences bringing her back 'again and again' into the realm of the immediate, the present, the here-and-now of the child or infant's demand" (*Maternal Encounters* 68). Our disruptions intended to "break the duration of the festival and demand class was brought into the 'realm of the immediate, the present, the here-and-now" (68) of the festival. Our series of disruptions produced confrontations with class at several points throughout the day, which built upon Baraitser's articulation of the conflicting dynamics of maternal time, the relationality of endurance and interruption, and the tension between movement and being stuck. The Playing Kate persona embraced maternal time, returning during breaks in the festival program. Baraitser writes of the maternal "I want to wander off the subject, and yet the subject returns, again and again" ("Communality" 119). *Playing Kate: Disruptions and Confrontations* used Baraitser's notion of "maternal time" to disrupt and return to class; the persona made it the subject "again and again," resonating with Valerie Walkerdine's response to Valerie Hey's essay "Getting Over It." Hey and Walkerdine discuss class and the use of autobiographical practices in academia in relation to the disparaging notion that one should just "get over it," (the marginalisation of class) as if drawing from the self and class should be something hidden, forgotten, or outside of proper discourse. Walkerdine describes how "getting over it" has been part of a bigger practice in erasing classed histories and an attempt to ignore historical inequalities. Walkerdine also describes the derogatory idea that class can be spotted, and Katie Beswick (*Social Housing*) similarly describes how one's self-identification with class is often different from how others identify someone's class. Writing on natality and performance, Adele Senior notes: "We might, therefore, think of appearance in performance not necessarily as *seeing* the other's uniqueness but feeling, hearing, smelling, tasting and being moved by them in such a way that echoes something of the moment of that first meeting common to birth" (44).

During the festival, we play with these complex ideas; Jodie's body is spotted around the space, and the audience smells, tastes, hears, and feels the Playing Kate persona bringing class into the foreground and keeping it the subject. By placing the Playing Kate persona around the common space, we create multiple spatial strategies of disruption, which involve "getting in the way" (unable to avoid or ignore the subject), "being at a distance" (foregrounding being on the outside of the commons, seen through the window), "encroaching and expanding" (taking up and taking back space in the commons), "up close" (confronting the subject) and "among" (an example of a hopeful alternative).

For example, the first disruption begins outside the venue where we wait for the audience of (m)others to arrive in the pouring rain. We play with distance, intimacy, and access, waving to the ticketless, unsuspecting passersby (new commoners) and disrupting the audience's passage as they arrive at the festival. Pete is visible in all the disruptions: acting as an aide, staying on the sidelines, and holding the (turf) baby (making visible the invisible structures allowing MMO Kate to perform so effortlessly). This disruption confronts the audience as they arrive; it exists outside of the festival's timeframe, starting before the festival officially began. It is already taking the festival off topic by disrupting the usual proceedings. Outside the venue, a long red carpet is rolled out, first by Pete and is later pushed out from between Jodie's legs.

The image has several meanings. From between her legs, Jodie births (rolls out) menstrual blood, leaking along the pavement in a theatrical spectacle of birth. The image references the privileges she holds as a white, academic, and artist in a Western context, MMO Kate's royal reproductive privileges and the privilege of bodies able to step through the doors and into the intellectual and creative maternal performance commons. It is an opportunity to foreground the invisibility of some mothers over others. Alternatively, it is also an act celebrating and valuing the attending mothers, offering these often marginalized bodies a red carpet and honouring them as important people.

During the red carpet performance, Jodie shuffles, crawls, slides, lies, and hides her body along the carpet. There is no other way to get in the building but to step over, step on, or step around her and no way to ignore, her unclassy spectacle, which is intentionally foregrounded. But her presence is also a reminder of MMO Kate acting as an obstruction into other maternal worlds. Beswick offers specific examples of how theatre spaces still enact classed and racist practices of exclusion ("Feeling").

Our performance outside of the doors offers a performative response to Beswick's question "How do people *feel welcome* here?" (271). Beswick notes:

> Creating spaces of hospitality, which also give way to the potential of ownership and leadership for working-class people, is essential if we are to overcome the underrepresentation of the working-class in funded arts spaces. "How do people *feel welcome* here?" is the central question that institutions seeking to address working-class disadvantage must ask and answer as they make decisions towards inclusion in cultural production. (271)

Impromptu audience members observe this strange but familiar persona from the street; ticketed audience members once inside view through the large glass windows, a gathering of dry, warm, mothers together, inside, smirking, Jodie outside, separated by ideas of performing badly, performing inappropriately, tastelessly. Often, Jodie glances into the window at the mothers, making contact, wanting to join them, wanting them to join her outside in the dirt, a mother outside of the maternal performance commons. Nobody does.

After a while, Jodie becomes hidden under the carpet, only a leg poking out, perhaps trying to hide from the normative maternal ideal but unable to, perhaps being hidden by oppressive structures (MMO Kate) or perhaps as a forgotten afterthought, the left-over mother. In the final series of actions, Jodie crawls or slids herself along the red carpet towards the doors, mirroring the effort and difficulty many mothers experience in the labours of commoning. Jodie's costume is soaked, her mascara runs down her cheeks, and the wig hair becomes heavy, foregrounding the unclassy resemblance of MMO Kate and the enclosures of the maternal performance commons.

Figure 3. *Playing Kate: Disruptions and Confrontations* (2019). Photo credit Zoe Manders.

By the time the festival officially begins, Jodie scoops up the soaking and heavy carpet and drags it over her shoulders and through the festival doors into the cafe, like a long encumbered royal gown (enforced burden). Pete carries the (turf) baby. While still in a dishevelled state, Jodie, along with Pete, greet the audience inside queueing for the first performance. We shake their hands, say hello, and show them our newborn (soiled) dirty baby. Some coo and play along at the absurd spectacle of a grassy baby; others are more startled by the soaking wet presence and the dirty mound of grass and soil that Jodie clutched tightly wrapped in our son's first baby blanket and try to ignore her completely. The persona creates an uncomfortable engagement playing on middle-class embarrassment bound in classed stigmatization of taste and respectability, and the classed rules and regulations of the spaces our performance disrupts are no longer viewed behind the glass, or stepped over, but up close, unavoidable. The doors to the theatre close as they make their way inside. Jodie is left alone with the turf baby as the doors shut in her face.

Commoning and the Maternal Performance Commons

When the audience arrives at the common space (foyer) for a break, we bring in more grass and dirt (something we commonly share) for our next disruption in the hope of creating a common land and foregrounding the idea of enclosure. During the tea break, Jodie is among the other mothers on a small square of grass while she soothes the turf baby. She sings a lullaby to shush the baby (representing land/nation) and drinks tea just like the other mothers but at a distance (not like them) is confined to a grassy gated estate.

Pete brings over a sign bearing the word "private" and sticks it into Jodie's small square of grass. Jodie's shushing lullaby to the land can be read as the way MMO Kate worked to pacify any sense of revolting (protesting) against neoliberal enclosures of normative motherhood. Jodie instructs Pete across the foyer to bring more turf, which he does from a replication version of the royal pram, which is heaped with turf. As he brings more turf over on a silver platter, the grassy island begins to grow, encroach and fill all the communal space in the bar/foyer of Cambridge Junction. Audience members have to step over and around Jodie's expanding island, squeeze up on the sofas, and make room, she is stealing the common space back from under their feet.

Figure 4. *Playing Kate: Disruptions and Confrontations* (2019). Photo credit Zoe Manders.

The Playing Kate persona responds to the multiple (often invisible) practices of enclosure by Kate MMO and maternal performance (Šimić) in which class has often been a leftover. Imogen Tyler's (*Revolting Subjects*) definition of a maternal commons as involving disparate acts of maternal resistance in response to neoliberalism is relevant here. But it is useful to consider how the term "commons" has shifted and changed. Guido Ruivenkamp and Andy Hilton discuss theoretical perspectives on the "discourse of the common" (1), which is continuously intertwined with understandings of enclosure. Although the term "commons" was originally theorized concerning land access and the sharing and managing of natural resources and then immaterial resources, such as information and knowledge, Ruivenkamp and Hilton consider the more recent inclusion of the commons as "relational social frameworks" (1).

Massimiliano Mollona, building on Massimo De Angelis, echoes this inclusion of social frameworks, noting how "commons" as a term now includes three meanings: "(1) a pool of natural and/or human resources, (2) a community of people with reciprocal and sharing relations and (3) acts of working together towards the reproduction of the community" (9). For Mollona, it is the coming together of all these elements that makes the definition of a "real commons" (9). Ruivenkamp and Hilton assert that the inclusion of relational social frameworks as a dimension of commons has shifted the focus from the term "common" to "commoning," which works 'to denote the continuous making and remaking—the re(production)—of the commons through shared practices" (1). For Angelis commoning is "the living force of their reproduction, sense making and development" (247).

These ideas relate to Silva Federici's bringing together of feminist thought and the politics of the commons (which Tyler draws from, too), in which the production and equalities of commoning have often been overlooked. Federici discusses the ongoing exploitation of reproductive work and unpaid domestic labour by capitalist structures. Federici reminds us that women through their reproductive labour have been most affected by the privatization of the commons; women have depended on and defended natural resources the most. For Federici, rethinking the commons must begin with acknowledging and working from the collective struggles of reproductive work. Angelis asserts that these collective shifts towards the term "commoning" rather than "commons" resists the hopelessness and powerlessness of dominant neoliberal ideas that there is no alternative.

Commoning reminds us that there are in fact many alternatives, as there have been throughout history. It highlights how the commons are entwined with the practices, relations, and social arrangements of commoners, a process ignored, devalued, and made invisible by capitalist enclosures. As neoliberal capital expands and transforms, Angelis suggests commoning, too, has to expand and shift as "a deep wave of new enclosures" (239) in neoliberalism emerges—enclosures that engulf and claim the commons for its own purposes.

Commoning works to disrupt the enclosures of neoliberal capital and, as Stavrides asserts, is "a set of practices and relations that hint towards a different kind of social values and priorities" (264). Normative mothering can be closely tied to neoliberal ideologies. Jacqueline Rose comments that for mothers it is "as if the props of neoliberalism were the most that mothers can aspire to, the highest form of social belonging and agency they can expect" (17). At the Motherworks festival, the Playing Kate persona keeps the maternal commons in movement (Stavrides) by foregrounding this common gap in maternal performance, namely class. We developed an understanding of persona as a disruption, drawing from

Baraitser's idea of "maternal time" ("Commonality") as a performative strategy in the intervention of shared (common) space, since we positioned the Playing Kate persona as a confrontation with class—a commoning of the maternal. We brought together an intersectional strategy based on integrating O'Reilly's ideas of queering and class. The Playing Kate disruptions through commoning maternal performance offer tiny openings in the maternal performance commons of the Motherworks festival. As Stavrides notes, commoning is connected "with processes of opening" (3); it is therefore a useful strategy to further resist enclosure.

Figure 5. *Playing Kate: Disruptions and Confrontations* (2019). Photo credit Zoe Manders.

Later in the day, we occupy the upstairs foyer and erect a cardboard children's colour-in-palace (playhouse) during another festival break. Inside the playhouse, there is a small lamp, and music plays. There is also a patchwork blanket Jodie's mom made when she became pregnant. Pete waits outside with the turf baby rocking it in the big, impractical and noisy second-hand pram, which we earlier struggled to carry up the Junction Cambridge staircase. On the front of the house is written "Mum's House Croydon," and a silver platter of crayons lies waiting. Jodie fits her body inside the house and begins to cover the inside with classed maternal anecdotes. Occasionally, another mother squeezes herself in through the small doorway and joins her. Reading as she writes, as Jodie moves her body to cover the doorway, there is no way out but to sit and dwell. When no one is in the house with her, Jodie can be seen peeking out of the small windows and watching the other moms enjoying themselves. Not many people want to come in; they are on a break and want to relax and spend time chatting and socializing.

Somehow in the process of making this disruption, we forget that children at the festival may want to come inside the playhouse, and we're embarrassed to have overlooked this. We have set up a playhouse that the children can't really come in because there are now some complex things written over the walls that are inappropriate for them to read. We have an awkward conversation with a mother whose son wants to come in; we're making it harder for her by saying he should stay out. In our attempts to foreground class, we have created another enclosure. Our mistake reminds us of how ingrained neoliberal structures are, and we are confronted with the complexities of navigating and negotiating with others (this time the excluded kids). After a while, we leave the playhouse for a break, and when we come back the playhouse has been completely scrawled over inside and out by the children. They have made themselves visible; Jodie's words merge with theirs in bright red Crayola.

The Motherworks festival is a fleeting commons, one offering ongoing social relations of friendship, kindness, solidarity, and intellectual and emotional traces across time. Angelis reminds us how the commons are continually in process and are social systems that vary in size and shape. Maternal commons, by the very nature of the maternal, demand to operate in different configurations of time and against neoliberal parameters of scale as success. Angelis reiterates how commons relate to other commons and how they relate to capital and the state. They do not exist outside of capitalism but, as Mollona notes, have found ways for autonomy and self-organization within. Even brief, temporary commons can still be defined as commons. For Angelis, the binary thinking of separating commons and capital is a false assertion.

Our performance and others at the festival were far from utopian, but they aim to at its core hold a "radical openness for the other" (Mollona 137). For Mollona, the commons are not possible without this. Our value or common good was the sharing of diverse strategies, experiences, vocabularies, and practices of care—ideas brought about through our shared desire for noncapitalist notions of productivity and our different connection and struggles with normative motherhood. Mollona notes that the commons are created through "diversity, not identity and by different people with common interests and needs" (149). In our attempts at commoning, we tried to expose the commons as being too small and too inclusive, yet Mollona notes that commons "are not 'for everybody'"—as states are supposed to be—but "among everybody." They are spaces of socialization, of unity in difference and of shared vulnerability" (149).

While we worried about the private and the public nature of this tiny community, the commons operated as neither private nor public but in the "fluid thresholds between" (Mollona 148). We fumbled in our attempts to define the parameters of what we were doing, but we were doing it: We were building a commons. We were commoning, as commons are always in negotiation, being built and remade: "unfinished and open—not as islands but as relational spaces that enable conflict, cooperation and negotiation" (148). Mollona, referencing Stavrides's work on commoning, describes how commons continuously transform, asserting that they are "worlds in movement" (9). Although the Motherworks festival was a tiny, a fleeting act of commoning, perhaps even a failure in its inability to be a "real commons" (Mollona 9), it foregrounded the importance and value of being among others in commonality and difference.

Discourses on commoning are useful in relation to class. As Mollona notes: "Commoning is a form of doing from below, of sharing and cooperating in situations of precariousness. It is how the poor, the working-class, the disenfranchised, and those living at the margins of capitalism or in non-capitalist zones make their lives anew-all day, everyday" (164). Mollona's assertion resonates with Emmanouela Mandalaki and Marianna Fotaki's provocation of a "relational embodied ethics of the commons"(745). Feminist thought can foreground the commons through the vulnerability of bodies and particular shared "embodied interactions" and "corporeal concerns" (745) rather than abstract ethical positions. This resonates with Federici's and Baraitser's assertations, who both query the assumption that a feminist and maternal commons do not imply that the burden of the commons is left to those in vulnerable positions, as Angelis reminds us commons are always entwined with capital (our time and labour).

In this way, the commons can "reproduce their resource systems and communities based on recognition of their actual corporeal vulnerabilities, which drives reciprocity and embodied relationality with the other" (745). Mandalaki and Fotaki argue this may counter some of the ongoing failures of the commons, such as its unsustainability. The Motherworks festival involved practices of commoning that considered the reproductive labour of its commoners (i.e., the mother artists). In O'Reilly's terms, it considered the social location of those who queered motherwork. As Stavrides notes, "Commoning practices importantly produces new relations between people. They encourage creative encounters and negotiations" (2). Like the fluid movement of commons, Mollona defines art as "knowledge in movement" (168). Motherworks festival was an opportunity to engage in a maternal performance commons, for Mollona, an art commons is "a way of doing, knowing and relating to the other that sustains a non-alienated and good life" (165–66).

Of course, this visibility does not imply innovation. The Motherworks festival as a type of maternal art/commons was not unique, but as commons occur across time (as does the maternal), they relate and are layered with the traces of intergenerational maternal commoning and wider practices of maternal commons. Tyler affirms the way in which women through "common forms of 'maternal politics'" (*Revolting Subjects* 106) have mobilized and resisted against the effects of neoliberalism. Tyler uses the example of naked protest as a means to identify acts of resistance by women who would usually be classed as waste populations. Tyler refers to specific examples of naked protests having taken place at Yarl's Wood detention centre and by mothers in the Niger Delta region. Tyler appears to suggest how smaller acts are interconnected in the shaping of a wider maternal commons and "recognising what we share, what we have in common, is also a political act" (23).

The field of maternal performance and Tyler's wider understanding of the maternal commons (which is not limited to art) share with O'Reilly a revolt against accepted, normalized, marginalized, d-valued, oppressed, abject, and commodified positions of maternal experience brought about through patriarchal and capitalist states. Performing at the Motherworks festival was the methodology of our '"common forms of 'maternal politics'" (Tyler, *Revolting Subjects* 106); performance was used as a common methodology to present other maternal identities, subjectivities, and bodies that were then shared with an audience (i.e., the new commoners) through political performance acts of resistance and visibility.

Although commons often create their own enclosures and autonomy, they must find ways to remain open (to new commoners and ideas). Stavrides notes, "Participating in a common world is often connected to practices of securing the limits of this world and to practices that reproduce separation" (31). Ruud Kaulingfreks and Femke Kaulingfreks remind us of the coexistence of the shared world; they note "everything that exists always exists together with something else" (300). Thinking from a common and commoning perspective allows us to create maternal performance as always opening out.

As the nature of commoning is a process of "making and remaking" (Ruivenkamp and Hilton 1), Rebecca Solnit reminds us of the need to vocalize and celebrate examples from recent and past history to remember how change has been made possible and to borrow (and develop) from these (sometimes tiny) practices. In a similar way, Elena Marchevska and Valerie Walkerdine assert that maternal art practice is often developed through intergenerational dialogue between maternal artists, demonstrating the importance and potential found in connecting histories and the present. Vocalizing maternal strategies of commoning, like this example of the Motherworks festival to share and learn from, is essential to future commoning and extends O'Reilly's strategy for queering within matricentric feminism. Our small opening sits within O'Reilly's matricentric feminism and as Tyler (*Revolting Subjects*) suggests, these distinct queerings are part of a wider common practice. One could argue a commons in movement, or matricentric feminism, always involves leftovers, the things needed to make and remake (Ruivenkamp and Hilton 1).

O'Reilly offers insight into motherhood's complex and difficult relationship with feminism, arguing that matricentric feminism offers an opportunity to foreground the often-ignored experiences and identities of those who associate as a mother. Some might argue that dividing feminism into smaller and smaller groups weakens the movement and strengthens neoliberalism and by implication class struggle in general. However, when we view matricentric feminism in relation to contemporary theories of commoning, we can understand O'Reilly's mother-centred feminism not as an enclosed branch of feminism or as a diminishing separating off but as a way of listening to the needs and precarities of commoners. In this way matricentric feminism can open feminism out, as commons are "worlds in movement" (Mollona 9). For O'Reilly, matricentric feminism can move "beyond gender towards resistant and inclusive mothering" (10). In this way, matricentric feminism remains both open but also specific to the demands and experiences of the maternal. It is through different forms of queering, used in further fractional strategies of resistance, that O'Reilly notes "a multitude of maternal identities, diverse family formations, and a variety of motherhood practices" (20–21) is possible. Our intention here in queering the normative motherhood produced by MMO Kate and that excludes class from the field of maternal performance (Šimić) is to define another queering strategy from our own "social location" (O'Reilly 31), a strategy which we call commoning (opening out to the commoner). We argue commoning motherhood, like queering, is a strategy to disrupt normative mothering but one which foregrounds class as a distinct position. We hope that the very nature of Tyler's wider term "maternal commons" (*Revolting Subjects*) might also work to bridge a gap that keeps all of these queerings as distinct strategies.

Endnotes

1. For images of the performance, we direct the reader to the video and photographic documentation of *Playing Kate: Disruptions and Confrontations* (2019) on the Search Party website http://searchpartyperformance.org.uk/project/playing-kate/. Accessed 12 July 2024.

Works Cited

Angelis, Massimo de. "Grounding Social Revolution: Elements for a Systems Theory of Commoning." *Perspectives on Commoning: Autonomist Principles and Practices*. Edited by Guido Ruivenkamp and Andy Hilton. Bloomsbury Publishing, 2017, pp. 213–55.

Baraitser, Lisa. "Communality across Time: Responding to Encounters with Maternal Encounters: The Ethics of Interruption." *Studies in Gender and Sexuality*, vol. 13, no. 2, 2012, pp. 117–22.

Baraitser, Lisa. *Maternal Encounters: The Ethics of Interruption*. Routledge, 2009.

Beswick, Katie. *Social Housing in Performance: The English Council Estate on and off Stage*. Methuen Drama, 2019.

Beswick, Katie. "Feeling Working Class: Affective Class Identification and Its Implications for Overcoming Inequality." *Studies in Theatre and Performance*, vol. 40, no. 3, 2020, pp. 265–74.

Clancy, Laura. *Running the Family Firm: How the Monarchy Manages Its Image and Our Money.* Manchester University Press, 2021.

Cole, David R. *Capitalised Education.* Zero Books, 2014.

Collins, Patricia Hill, and Bilge, Sirma. *Intersectionality.* Polity Press, 2016.

Ettinger, Bracha L. *The Matrixial Borderspace.* University of Minnesota Press, 2006.

Federici, Silva. *Re-enchanting the World: Feminism and the Politics of the Commons.* PM Press, 2018.

Green, Kelly. *CHAV.* Directed by Kelly Green, 2020.

Hardt, Michael, and Antonio Negri. *Commonwealth.* Harvard University Press, 2009.

Hawkes, Jodie. *Playing Kate: Disruptions and Confrontations.* Directed by Jodie Hawkes, Search Party, 2019, Cambridge Junction.

Hey, Valerie. "'Getting Over It?' Reflections on the Melancholia of Reclassified Identities." *Gender and Education*, vol. 18, no. 3, 2006, pp. 295–308.

Kaulingfreks, Ruud, and Femke Kaulingfreks. "The Square as the Place of the Commons." *Perspectives of Commoning: Autonomist Principles and Practices.* Edited by Guido Ruivenkamp, Guido and Andy Hilton. Zed Books, 2017, pp. 291–324.

Liburd, Libby. *MUVAHOOD.* Directed by Julie Addy, 2017.

Mandalaki, Emmanouela, and Marianna Fotaki. "The Bodies of the Commons: Towards a Relational Embodied Ethics of the Commons." *Journal of Business Ethics*, vol. 166, no. 4, 2020, pp. 745–60.

Marchevska, Elena, and Valerie Walkerdine, eds. *The Maternal in Creative Work.* Routledge, 2020.

McRobbie, Angela. "Notes on 'What Not to Wear' and Post-Feminist Symbolic Violence." *Feminism after Bourdieu.* Edited by Lisa Adkins and Beverley Skeggs. Blackwell Publishing, 2004, pp. 97–109.

Mollona, Massimiliano. *Art/commons: Anthropology Beyond Capitalism.* Bloomsbury Publishing, 2021.

O'Reilly, Andrea. *Matricentric Feminism: Theory, Activism, Practice.* Demeter Press, 2021.

Rose, Jacqueline. *Mothers.* Faber and Faber, 2018.

Ruivenkamp, Guido, and Andy Hilton, eds. *Perspectives on Commoning: Autonomist Principles and Practices.* Bloomsbury Publishing, 2017.

Senior, Adele. "With the Maternal." *Performance Research*, vol. 23, no. 4–5, 2018, pp. 40–44.

Šimić, Lena. "Encountering Performing (M)Others: Feminist Maternal Practice in Contemporary Performance." *Contemporary Theatre Review*, vol. 28, no. 3, 2018, pp. 401–12.

Šimić, Lena, and Emily Underwood-Lee. *Maternal Performance: Feminist Relations.* Palgrave Macmillan, 2021.

Skeggs, Beverley. *Class, Self, Culture.* Psychology Press, 2004.

Skeggs, Beverley. *Formations of Class & Gender.* SAGE Publications, 1997.

Skeggs, Beverley, and Helen Wood. *Reality Television and Class.* Palgrave, 2011.

Solnit, Rebecca. *Hope in the Dark: The Untold History of People Power.* Canongate Books, 2004.

Stavrides, Stavros. *Common Space: The City as Commons.* Bloomsbury Publishing, 2016.

Tyler, Imogen. "Chav Mum Chav Scum." *Feminist Media Studies*, vol. 8, no. 1, 2008, pp. 17–34.

Tyler, Imogen. *Revolting Subjects: Social Abjection and Resistance in Neoliberal Britain.* Zed Books Ltd, 2013.

Walkerdine, Valerie. "Coming to Know." *Rhizomes: Cultural Studies in Emerging Knowledge*, no. 27, 2014, http://www.rhizomes.net/issue27/walkerdine/index.html. Accessd 12 July 2024.

18.

The Last American Housewife

Martha Joy Rose

We're at the end of an era. I witnessed its collapse.
I'm here to tell the tale. I am the last American Housewife.
—Martha Joy Rose

Introduction

This chapter provides an autoethnographic and a historical account of the motherhood movement's evolution, highlighting its successes and setbacks. It argues that in the face of ongoing challenges to women's autonomy and choice, matricentric feminism is more necessary than ever. By drawing on personal experiences, academic scholarship, and literary texts, this chapter demonstrates the continued relevance of matricentric feminism as a significant means of advancing women's rights and promoting gender equality. I also argue for a more comprehensive understanding of the herstory of women's movements. I provide a brief and succinct overview of some of the important actors in the American women's movement and investigate other distinct motherhood practices outside of mainstream culture. Matricentric feminism emphasizes the importance of feminism focussing on the already oppressed category of woman and mother. This call, by Andrea O'Reilly and others, cites the need for a distinctive feminism for and about mothers—one that moves "beyond gender and towards resistant and inclusive mothering" (O'Reilly

10). This is a call that honours carework, the sacredness of birth, and gives social value to mothering (O'Reilly 15). It may also be interpreted as a call for collaborative mothering—a type of mothering that goes beyond the nuclear paradigm and is situated outside patriarchal constructions.

In her book *Matricentric Feminism*, O'Reilly echoes the call of Adrienne Rich and others to "dismantle patriarchal motherhood" and argues that "empowerment of the mother must be the primary aim of feminist mothering" (O'Reilly 208). Nonnormative, feminist mothering embraces the "five A's of empowered mothering: agency, autonomy, authenticity, authority, and advocacy/activism" (O'Reilly 11). She specifically calls for us to embrace the term "mother" as a verb, which according to Sara Ruddick (and O'Reilly) enforces an inclusive perspective that anyone who dedicates themselves to mothering can indeed be called a mother (O'Reilly 11). *Matricentric Feminism* argues for a specific category within feminism that interrogates these many subjects. Yet universities and dominant normative constructions of family have not adopted these insights, nor has the gender parity issue been addressed.

No hordes of liberators are coming. It is us—the mothers, the women, queer people, and anyone who suffers under patriarchy—who must liberate ourselves and then continue the ongoing work of mothering and motherhood outside patriarchal constructions. Examples of movements, conferences, collectives and collaborations are elucidated in this chapter and other books, within the Demeter catalogue and beyond. These evolutions are ongoing and require continual review, energy, clarity, and action, as well as education and the commitment of a core group of dedicated persons willing to produce knowledge that is not hierarchically constructed, grounded in principles of respect and care, and embedded in places and spaces that others can access.

To that end, my work in this chapter, and my work in general, aims to highlight the progress of the last four waves of the American women's movement. I am interested in both the personal and social perspectives. The term "housewife," which I employ in the title of this chapter, is a term I leveraged when I first set off to make changes in my own life after a catastrophic postnatal illness, which was sandwiched within the framework of an oppressive and unsustainable marriage. I find the phrase "last American housewife" especially salient twenty-six years after I used this term (with all its laden insinuendo) to create a feminist music project called *Housewives on Prozac* in the late nineties. But first, I want to situate myself at the beginning of the current contemporary feminist mothers' movement as it has exerted itself collectively first in the 1990s and through its crescendo around 2010, when I endeavored to create and participate in a unique community of creative women. After that, my focus turns to the historical context of contemporary motherhood as it has been interpreted by the founding mothers of sociology, with an eye on contemporary theorists from several disciplines. I take into account several watermarks for the ongoing, changing waves of feminism and matrifocal feminism using works from these founding sociologists of Western thought—all of whom were women and some of whom were mothers—and then connect the first, second, and third wave ideas and action to the origins of the twenty-first-century motherhood movement of the fourth wave. Finally, I examine the relevance and importance of matricentric feminism in the contemporary context of today's culture and how we might best incorporate it into our lives.

I highlight new language and fresh approaches for contemporary activism that are less oppositional and more collaboratively constructed. Specifically, I aim to focus on inclusive, compassion-based language and programming willing to bypass binary definitions. This must be done with a keen eye on recognizing ongoing patriarchal constructions, which are, in some cases, immutable. We must work to invest in new activities, partnerships, and highly inclusive organizations to connect more individuals to work towards an empowered future. Although the past is beyond reconciliation, it is potentially mendable, even with the marks and wounds it has assembled. Although I do not pretend to have a one-size-fits-all solution to the problem of patriarchy or to reconcile the goals of various feminist movements, I have experienced the revolutionary power of words, art, scholarship, and community. I have also participated in and guided collaborations to heal the harms inflicted by a largely man-made society on its inhabitants. Therefore, a theory that counters oppression with compassion, hate with kindness, hierarchy with equality (to the best of our ability), and conformity with personal autonomy might provide some liberation from our confounding cultural conundrum.

Background

My feminist journey began in the 1990s when I played in a band that used art and music for social change. The Housewives on Prozac band, formed in 1997, countered the values of middle-aged suburban life and motherhood with a sense of comedic irony. Several years into that project, at the onset of the twenty-first century, I organized the large-scale festival series Mamapalooza to better reach a broader population with a message of empowerment for women with a special emphasis on mothers.

This ongoing involvement in the motherhood movement has been unabating—first in the capacity of a musician, then as a concert promoter, and finally, as an archivist and activist serving as the founder and director of the Museum of Motherhood (MoM). The journey has not been easy, but it has been the theme of my adult life. In 2003, the idea for the MoM was born, and then I immersed myself in matricentric feminist conferences, which framed the study of motherhood as a truly academic enterprise. To this end, I applied to graduate school where I earned a master's degree in a self-designed major in mother studies organized through the sociology and women's studies departments at CUNY in New York City. Those activities were followed by five years of adjunct teaching. I have been riding this wave of the modern motherhood movement for over twenty-six years. Many of the issues framing the women's movement over the last 250 years in the United States (US) are still at play in our social systems. Patriarchal constructions remain. Threats to women's ability to make decisions over their bodies, along with rampant misogyny jeopardizing equality and economic disparities impeding the next generation. At the same time, other epic changes have occurred in terms of who can birth, how those who give birth identify, and how gender-fluid definitions counter widely held assumptions about mothers, fathers, and children. In the face of multiple shifts and obstacles, amid muddy waters, now is the time to raise the volume and leverage action on behalf of feminists everywhere. The question remains: How best to do that?

The most under-studied, under-appreciated, and visually absent narrative from the annals of museums, art galleries, and schools are the voices of women who are mothers. Once I had children, it quickly became obvious that the voices of women who held procreative and caregiving roles had no audible presence on the radio waves or at the performance venues I'd once frequented as a professional musician. To that end, my attention quickly turned to devoting energy, money, art, scholarship, and time, to closing the gap on invisibility as it pertains to the legacy of mothers—or, now as the term is sometimes referenced, m/others, emphasizing the significance of relational status. Within these dynamic and evolving progressive states, I situate myself and the MoM as legacy keepers, which to some extent includes archiving the progress of women's and mothers' movements, activities, research, art, history, and science.

My personal story has been shaped by three major factors: art, illness, and motherhood, coupled with the inherent norms and conventions that have arisen out of the latter role. I was raised to be a good wife. My parents poured all their well-intentioned energy into making me agreeable, attractive, and helpful. These qualities set me up to be a more than adequate homemaker, which I practised for the duration of a seventeen-year marriage. Twelve years into that marriage I was diagnosed with a chronic and potentially terminal illness, which caused me to reflect on the aspects of my life that were healthy and those that were not. I loved being a mother. That area of my life required little interrogation. The marriage, however, and the manner in which both wifedom and motherhood were determined to be performed, was fundamentally destructive to my health and my sense of wellbeing. The performative demands, overarching surveillance, and level of expectation were exhausting. These expectations were embedded into the heteronormative marital conventions I initially embraced and eventually succumbed to. I had, over time, relinquished my sense of self and purpose for the qualities of agreeableness, acquiescence, and beauty. In my efforts to be an effective and attractive partner and caregiver, I became subsumed and eventually subservient. After the devastating diagnosis of SLE and renal failure, I spent the next several years undergoing chemotherapy, meditating from the bed to which I was relegated, and dreaming of the creative projects I'd begin as soon as I was well enough. Some of the earliest lyrics and music I wrote in the nineties reflect the desperation I felt.

Watch out! Stand back!
Here she comes! It's a mom attack
Spatula anxiety
Virtual sobriety
Responsible insanity
We tear our hair
Because we care
But today's the day we crack
("Eat Your Damn Spaghetti" excerpt, song by Joy Rose Housewives)

The first full-on project I embraced as soon as I was well enough to manage outside the hospital and home was the formation of the Housewives on Prozac band. Housewives reflected the sense of irony, bittersweet anguish, and humour I felt in my everyday life and my recently reinvigorated music career. Surrounded by children and kitchen chaos, barely out of chemotherapy, I posed with another local homemaker for our first photo shoot only months into starting rehearsals. In only a few months, we had an interview in the *New York Times*, titled "Band Sings about What It's Like to Raise a Family in the Nineties" and other multiple gigs. The children were eight, six, four, and three. The musical enterprise was life affirming in the deepest sense. The band also leveraged a well-intentioned poke at the status quo of which I had become an unwitting part. By breaking through the banality of suburban life, picking up a pink guitar at the age of forty, after children, and then leveraging music to push back at middle age while targeting a sense of thwarted restlessness felt by those stuck amid their own smug comfort, I employed the tools that brought me my greatest joy as a youth—the power of a microphone, a sharp lyric, and tonal integrity. I was alive and truly honed to the fact that I had survived something terrible, and I wanted to thrive. I affirmed that others should thrive as well. I shared this testimony with anyone who would listen and at every venue we performed. As a self-declared "housewife," I set myself and others up to appreciate the paradoxical irony of the bouffant blonde mom clutching a mic (not a martini) as she attempts to break free.

Joy Rose with Beth Rudd and children posing for Housewives on Prozac Band photo, NY 1997aAA

I employed the term "Housewives (on Prozac)" as a commentary about the trapped nature of the ever-smiling, ever-pleasant woman who unconditionally supports everyone around her, appears immutably unfrazzled at all times and operates seamlessly by well-tuned devices and environment which she manages like a domestic queen. The term "housewife" is still used today, sometimes in earnest but mostly in recognition of a bygone era when women stayed home to manage the babies and domicile while husbands went to work to earn a living. Generally applied to white women of a certain socioeconomic standing, the word is laden with implications of the delicate, if not perky, elaborately coiffed woman standing next to her new dishwasher, emotionally checked out of any meaningful civic social-change exercises. That being said, women of colour, including Nicki Minaj, have embraced the "housewife" persona in photo shoots and articles, while the term is still employed in popular television with shows like *The Housewives of Orange County*, to name one of many. We know now that this is an impossible persona, long liberated by the likes of Betty Friedan and others. After my illness, I declared that I wanted to be the last American housewife. Unfortunately, we know

now that I have not been the last housewife. I have been one of many who still find themselves laden with the embedded limitations of the housewife ideology that continue to haunt our collective unconscious and crop up in alarming ways.

Historical Context of the Motherhood Movement

Women have always pushed back. They have created communities, found their voices through collaborative activities, and engaged in activism, scholarship, and theoretical meaning making. A variety of texts situate women's movements and mothers' movements at different periods. Indeed, there have been many movements, large and small, around the world and throughout history. The difficulty with many of these movements is they are erased or made invisible or nearly impossible to access. Some statistics state that "only 3% of American history textbooks are about women" (Pereze 1). So if the feminist, labour, temperance, and civil rights movements were all women empowered, then let us acknowledge that women have gathered and wielded influence albeit often within the boundaries of what might be considered acceptable behaviour. A recent lecture in 2023 by colleague Paul Ivey at the Museum of Fine Art in St. Petersburg, FL titled "Women Build Museums" certifies the presence of women and mothers concerned with a civil society engaged in the consistent betterment of their neighbourhoods, cities, and states throughout the eighteenth and nineteenth centuries.

So then, here, we may ask ourselves, what constitutes a movement? What distinguishes a mothers' movement? And, also, how do we more widely disseminate knowledge of our foremothers? My expertise and focus for this chapter begins during the first-wave feminist movement alongside the suffragettes in the US. Many of the first-wave women spoke and wrote not only of their subjugated place in society but also of their status as wives and mothers, which, in some cases, elevated their standing and in others diminished it. The same is also true for the second and third waves of the feminist movement and is also true for many today.

The American women's movement has been championed first through the theories and activism of the first wave. This identifiable movement was followed by the second, third, and fourth wave of activists we now call feminists. Although these waves have no hard ending or beginning, there are arbitrary dates that help to frame initiatives into identifiable periods for situating timelines. Beginning in the early 1800s, suffragists argued for abolition, the right to vote, and women's equality. Colonial laws of coverture, long-established in parts of medieval Europe and then reaffirmed in the New World, ensured that married or common-law wives' legal identities belonged to their husbands, leaving them with little to no rights, including rights to children or property, which translated into civic and social constraints. Feminists in tentative leadership positions, as much as a woman could lead in colonial America, made assertions on behalf of "ladies" as a whole. Abigail Adams (Letters to her husband, 1776), Judith Sargent Murray ("On the Equality of the Sexes," 1790), Mary Wollstonecraft (*A Vindication of the Rights of Woman*, 1792), and Phillis Wheatley (*Poems on Various Subjects, Religious and Moral*, 1773) questioned women's status in print in the late seventeen hundreds. Then, sixty years after the US Constitution and seventy years after the Declaration of Independence, in 1848, a group of feminist thinkers, including Cady Stanton, declared "to hold these truths to be self-evident, that all men *and women* are created equal" (Stanton et al. 1). Of her many grievances, she writes: "He [mankind] has endeavoured, in every way that he could, to destroy her confidence in her own powers, to lessen her self-respect, and to make her willing to lead a dependent and abject life" (Stanton et al. 1).

Stanton's Declaration of Sentiments is a radical alteration of the original Declaration of Independence, which omits any mention of women. Following the speech, Stanton and other organizers of the first Women's Rights Convention solicited signatures in Seneca Falls, NY, to further their full human rights, thus collectively engaging a bubbling surge of activism we still recall today. Although it is impossible to know the exact connections formed during these movements, we do have testimony, letters, and publications that form the bedrock of what we now recognize as the early women's movement, including the copresenter of the document, Susan B. Anthony, and the sixty-eight women and thirty-two men signatories (Stanton et al.).

Three years after the Seneca Falls Convention, free slave Sojourner Truth argued to a large crowd in Akron, Ohio, that women should be treated similarly to men in her speech titled "Ain't I a Woman." This was one of many women's conventions happening around the country. There was reportedly a large crowd in attendance and the dissemination and continuation of similar assertions united the cause, although not all perspectives completely aligned. Of note, is the fact that Stanton and

Truth, as well as many others in this founding movement, were mothers, and some were wives, entrenched in the associated activities as well as activism. Advocacy like theirs shape a shared and complimentary socially constructed theory about women's place in the world. They acknowledged themselves (obviously in different capacities) as being legally and practically subservient citizens, engaged in the continuing beat of what would become a seventy-year struggle for equal citizenry, which has commenced in multiple capacities to this day.

Since aspects of the struggle remain unresolved; here, I argue that the analysis of society by these women and their views of people's place in it still hold relevance and establish foundations of not just a feminist history (or *her*story) but a sociology imagined by women. Movements within the context of sociology and the social sciences, including their assessments regarding said society, establish a timeline of developing thought regarding women's lives that is its own unique body of women-centred knowledge. Countering the consistent erasure of women from the canons of significant texts and general bodies of knowledge relegates such information to women's studies departments and feminist studies departments in university settings when the study of these theories and movements should be taught in mainstream classes.

Women have always been involved in creating perspectives and opinions about the society in which they live. What then constitutes a body of activist or theoretical knowledge if those activities have historically taken place in the marketplace, sewing circles, or church gatherings of yesteryear? Because the world has always been inhabited by women, even if their voices have been less audible, we must apply our methodology leniently to trace a timeline of these loosely constructed clusters of knowledge. We must trace the viewpoints and perspectives of women's intellectual pursuits collectively and individually by acting like detectives, since the annals of Western thought and government have largely been crafted by men. Women's perspectives have mostly been interpreted in art, scholarship, psychology, and science through the male lens. Amid the first wave of suffragists, a rising group of women began developing social theory during a movement that continues to impact us today. Applying the idea of a women's movement or a mother's movement, we might begin with Harriet Martineau's writings, which contributed to the methodology of social science at its inception (she was the mother of sociology), and followed by her *her*storical counterparts: Jane Addams (the mother of social work); Charlotte Perkins Gilman (analyst of sexual-economics in the context of marriage); Ida B. Wells-Barnett (working mother, married suffragist, and antilynching advocate), Sojourner Truth (who was first a mother and who also argued for equality concerning gender and race inequities), and Cady Stanton (a mother and wife advocating for women's equality), to name a few. Effective sociological parallels are drawn between Martineau, Addams, Gilman, and Wells-Barnett in the powerful work of Patricia Madoo Lengermann and Jill Niebrugge-Brantley in their pivotal text *The Women Founders: Sociology and Social Theory 1830-1930*. These women all shared their first-wave feminist, suffragette, and abolitionist perspectives by writing, speaking, teaching, and creating activism focussed on a greater women's movement that included the betterment of society as well as the legitimization of women's voices in all things, and in some cases, they also knew one another, even if remotely, and collectively formed an early mother's movement.

Second-wave feminists followed WWII, and after large swaths of American women left wartime activities, factory jobs, and hard times behind for the greatest economic boom in the US, with the rising middle class identified by sociologist C. Wright Mills. This period is foreshadowed by thought-leader Jessie Bernard who began groundbreaking feminist work on *American Family Behavior* (1942), which examines mainstream gender inequity in marriage, arguing essentially that marriage was beneficial to men but not to women. Other important works included Simone de Beauvoir's *The Second Sex* (1949) and Betty Friedan's *The Feminist Mystique* (1963), which critique the image of the contented wife and mother who followed blithely in the footsteps of the all-knowing husband-father. Each work examines the social structures implicitly embedded in the fabric of lived experiences.

I am greatly simplifying great bodies of theoretical work that set the stage for second-wave feminists' work on behalf of women's bodily autonomy, equality in the workplace, antisexist and antiracist policies, as well as for the ongoing civil rights movements focused on the wellbeing and equality of Black and brown people. Throughout these movements, women and mothers united in marches, activism, protests, and scholarship and championed different causes with sometimes divergent and differing agendas. Each rise of activism set the stage for subsequent waves. By the time third-wave feminists began working through theory, philosophy, psychology, and activism, big changes were underway.

The third wave rolled in with a thunderous clap. After the preceding movements, beginning in the late 1970s and early 1980s through the 1990s, women began to identify their place in a world not just defined by gender but by motherhood, queer identity, intersectionality, race, socioeconomic status, disability, immigration standing, and other standpoints. This fracturing of previous incarnations of the women's movements smashed dominant assumptions promoted by white women who held the majority standing and more prominent positions of power. The scholarship of feminist articulations which included philosophers and psychologists in the second wave with Adrienne Rich (*Of Woman Born*, 1976), Phyllis Chesler (*With Child*, 1979), evolved to include sociologists, including Dorothy Smith (*The Everyday as Problematic*, 1987), Barbara Katz Rothman (*Recreating Motherhood*, 1990), and Patricia Hill Collins (*Black Feminist Thought*, 1990), to name a few. Of course, there are more. So many more. Each work speaks to women's perspectives and lived experiences. The authors embrace concepts of motherhood and examine the social systems we inhabit. Specifically, each of these women confronted the institution of motherhood and how labouring individuals must be liberated from the normative constraints of motherhood—literally and figuratively. Rich's position is clear from the onset. Part one of her text is aptly titled "Patriarchal Power and Maternal Outrage" (Rich 25). Chesler, who marvels at the miracle of synchronicity and the body during the birth of her first and only child, brings us into the experience with the eyes of a poet and social scientist. This book follows on the heels of her best seller, *Women and Madness* (1972), which skillfully dissects the collective patriarchal loathing of women who deviate from the norm. With the early formation of a burgeoning mother-made scholarship in full swing, the sociologists stepped in with their astute dissemination of the shape of the world as we know it. Barbara Katz Rothman defines the constraints of the patriarchy within our family structures (30); Smith argues for inclusion of the perspective of women (and mothers) in institutions as well as the everyday experience (Smith 46, 88); Collins sets the stage for a new and more expansive sociological theory that tells the stories of historically marginalized Black Americans. She argues that Black women in the US have produced social thought designed to oppose oppression, which can take the form of poetry, music, essays, and the like (Collins 9). This bold new third wave sets itself apart as theoretical assertions about mothers' place in the world and articulates new dimensionality and depth, paving the way for matricentric feminism.

In summary, the *her*story of American women's movements has included the first, second, and third waves of feminism. The first-wave suffragettes argued for women's vote, autonomy, and abolition in the 1800s through 1920. This is not a hard stop but rather an arbitrary date we collectively assign to this period, using the ratification of voting rights as the marker for success. From the 1960s through the 1970s, second-wave feminists pushed back at the inequity of the sexes, and the artificial constraints of the middle-class housewife (among other things), arguing for rights to bodily autonomy, birth control, salary equity, and access. In the third wave, queer rights and recognition, lesbian motherhood, intersectionality, patriarchy, and ongoing issues continued to be expanded upon (1980s–2000). Within the rise of third-wave feminism, some feminist theorists and activists began paving the way towards a matrifocal and matricentric movement (though those terms would come later).

By the time we entered the twenty-first-century mothers' movement and the fourth wave, the internet had begun to facilitate initiatives for connection through the web. Beginning in the 1990s, the seeds sown by multiple organizations that aimed to focus on mothers' issues within the feminist paradigm were disseminated widely. The rise of mothers' voices in theory, literature, the arts, and media was precipitous and documented. Andrea O'Reilly uses the term "matricentric" to define and describe a mother-centred mode of feminism, which this chapter sees as a defining aspect of this fourth-wave movement.

The fourth wave has been fuelled by the connectivity and collaborations shaped by the internet and how people use websites, blogs, articles, and information. Feminist/activist campaigns founded by women and focussing on issues that affect women include the following: The Vagina Monologues and V-Day (Eve Ensler 1996 and 1998, respectively), #MeToo (Tarana Burke, 2006), World Breastfeeding Week (World Health Organization, 2010), Slut Walk (International, including Amber Rose, 2011), Free the Nipple (Linda Esco, film by the same name, 2012), Black Lives Matter (Alicia Garza, Patrisse Cullors, and Opal Tometi, 2013).

Figure 1. Photo of the author visiting Andrea O'Reilly and team at an ARM Conference circa 2004.

It was during this period—after my children were born in 1989, 1991, 1993 and 1994—that I too began to find my voice. In early 2001, my energies turned to focus on a woman-made, mother-inspired performing arts movement, which was made manifest through Mamapalooza, a festival seeking to establish entertainment, education, and business opportunities for those raising children. Our first festival in 2002 took place in New York City after the success of the Housewives band. We encouraged others as they also picked up instruments for visibility and change. Word spread; performance venues were levied, and women's centres and cultural and parks departments collaborated. Within two years, we were performing to crowds of thousands at multiple locations, with mother-made art and music sprouting up across the US. It was not long after these first heady gatherings that I had the opportunity to attend one of the early Association for Research on Mothering (ARM) conferences in Toronto at the urging of Alana Ruben Free, a writer and friend who served with me as the editorial consultant for the *Mom Egg* literary zine.

Because I was an outsider, unfamiliar with academia and academic conferences, and because my mind was spongy and fertile after years of infirmity after the illness that kept me sequestered, and in no small part because I was beginning to see myself at a critical intersection of my life, as a newly single mother, I was able to perceive, in the company of these great thinkers, and with profound clarity, the vital need for feminism in all aspects of life. More specifically, I could see the need for matricentric feminism as it was embodied through the conferences I attended. I suddenly saw women's history as critical to institutional education and wanted everyone to have access to the same information I had so recently discovered. Every cell in my body called out to pull the curtain back on a legacy of knowledge that felt like a first peek at real illumination. I needed this. I recognized that others needed it, too. I felt incredible passion and excitement. The idea of matricentric feminism became my new love language. It was imperative to connect, collect, and share this information. I regarded these new academic cohorts and all those associated with the work as essential. I worked to promote this as loudly and boldly as my platform would allow. Although some leaders focussed on scholarship, others focussed on health care, equity in the workplace, media depictions, and visibility. Some continued grassroots efforts and to that end, the Mamapalooza Festival, which had been working with Madre, Code Pink, Planned Parenthood, and others, aligned itself meaningfully with Andrea O'Reilly, the Westchester Womens' Center, and the Women's Media Center to name a few.

In 2008, I brought a film crew back to the third Toronto conference I'd attended only a few short years before and videotaped leaders from the motherhood movement to capture some of the excitement as it existed in those days. It was astonishingly thrilling to connect with scholars, activists, and artists concerned with amplifying the voices of women who were mothers. Friendships were formed, and partnerships were made. *The Twenty-First Century Motherhood Movement* and the *Encyclopedia of Motherhood* were just two of the collections that came out edited by Andrea O'Reilly and others in which I was able to participate. I continued attending the conferences for many years. We were making waves. Distinct waves. Waves that continued to reverberate. Mother waves. Matricentric feminism was expanding in theory, practice, and action. However, deeper questions remain. How has a matricentric feminism that addresses the unique needs of mothers, gained traction in the public domain? Have women been liberated within their homes, marriages, and motherhood?

Figure 2. Photo ARM Conference Poster 2008.

Has equality of the sexes penetrated the pervasive patriarchal construction of our civic and personal realms? I think the answer is obvious: yes and no. Although the word "feminism" was the word of the year in 2017, according to Merriam Webster, following the Women's March on Washington, the rise in consciousness was preceded by perhaps the most patriarchal figure in recent politics, Donald Trump and his pack of white supremacist, sexist, and misogynist cronies. So even as the #MeToo movement gained traction, and the word "feminism" gained in popularity, the reek of patriarchy persisted and still persists. Feminists have argued for equality, from their earliest beginnings, which is a long and wide stick with no obvious beginning and no obvious end for measurement. Have women got the vote? Yes. Has the Equal Rights Amendment been ratified? No. Have women gained traction towards the right to equal pay? Yes. Are women still discriminated against based on pregnancy? Yes. Do women have ongoing access to reproductive choice? Not always. Has racism in the world and within women's movements been eradicated? No. Have mothers amplified their voices, theories, and practices within the civic realm? Somewhat. The lists go on and on.

Even as victories seem to appear on the horizon, the tide of self-sabotage, ignorance, and patriarchy persist. Certainly, the rise of the relatively recent TradWive culture is an alarming development. TradWives (traditional wives) on social media and in the news embrace a lifestyle that encourages a matrimonial state of dependence. They embody a nostalgic reach for a time that never actually existed in the manner that it has been portrayed in history. The traditional values they aspire to embody are a lifestyle perpetuated in a climate of capitalist consumerism and sexual submission. This identity is largely lost on the population who doesn't understand the extent to which this persona was mostly a media campaign meant to keep women in their middle-class white homes in post-war US during a manufacturing boom. These intersecting initiatives of beauty, perceived simplicity, and compliance are relevant in today's fractured world of changing identity. It is as reactive as it is unimaginative. For me, the choice to hit back hard at the housewife identity was an attempt to root out the legacy in all its retro, self-indulgent glory. Matriarchal feminism calls to each of us to access and inhabit the parameters of personal autonomy, personal power, and choice as it emerges free from predetermined constraints of a surveilled, economically disadvantaged, and morally corrupt state of dependency, acquiescence, and subservience.

Conclusion: The Revolution Is Ongoing

Women who have spent their scholarship and activism analyzing gender, class, sexuality, and race inequality and advocating for social reforms have always existed, as have multiple movements. The waves of progress are not fixed. They are a product of human actions, evidenced by how our lives have been affected by grand social processes. We have made great progress and little progress at all. We live in a world rife with unfairness, difficulty, hardship, and inequity, occasionally balanced by wonderful acts of courage, gorgeous miracles, and great kindness. But regarding women and matricentric feminism, there is still so much work to do. O'Reilly argues for matricentric feminism, a feminism that "explores mothers' experiences and desires which continue to be marginalized as compared to non-mothers" (O'Reilly 9). For there to be marginalization, there must be a dominant narrative. In the case of feminism, we are talking about the feminist theories (and experiences) in mainstream university texts that have gained traction. O'Reilly argues for something else—for women who are mothers to be recognized as a distinct human category in a world that doesn't want to acknowledge their very real needs and experiences. This is a lot to ask. It might not be impossible to expect equity, yet some argue we may never get there. According to Marcie Bianco, author of *Breaking Free: The Lie of Equality and the Feminist Fight for Freedom*, those dreaming of gender equality will have to wait another three hundred years. The article quotes Bianco as stating that "billionaires will land on Mars before we achieve gender equality." Bianco argues that including women in institutions that are "supremacist and capitalist, created by men, for men [and that] were established to preserve the status quo cannot ever transform women's lives for the better." She argues for freedom and defines it as the "process of self-creation and world-building rooted in accountability and care, because freedom is collectively—not individually—realized and experienced." Bianco acknowledges that we are never equal. Each of our freedoms is distinct and different based on our situations. This perspective is akin to intersectionality in the sense that discrimination happens within an imbalanced system based on race, gender, ability, immigration status, etc. In a life and system that are inherently unequal, how could we hope to find equality? Within patriarchy, how could women hope to find habitable spaces? Perhaps we cannot? Since we all come to feminism with differing circumstances, abilities, backgrounds, and experiences, equality might be an illusion. However, within each of our situations, is it possible to create autonomy and self-governance over our own lives if indeed we have enough freedom to do that.

The ideas of the five A's—agency, autonomy, authenticity, authority, and advocacy/activism coupled with economic, psychological, social, and geographic factors—are useful for understanding and situating a person's sense of wellbeing, purpose, connection, and accomplishment. Additionally, cultivating familiarity with our shared social movements aids in furthering our argument for the importance of matricentric feminism. Making women's history (*her*story) part of mainstream vernacular is essential. Since Betty Freidan uttered the words "the problem that has no name," with a focus on wives' second-class status and enormous social malaise, some have ignored the call. Women's issues are top and centre of the media cycle, yet pushback from conservative agendas, as well as feminist scholars themselves, can be discouraging. As I argue, we have indeed named the problem. We have named it again and again. We know these ongoing problems, as they have been articulated. Most of us have experienced the problems as they present themselves theoretically and in the everyday world. Those include misogyny, sexism, racism, patriarchy, homo/transphobia, binary thinking, etc. Restating the problems as they have been defined does not solve the problem. We need more creative solutions. Some exist and are ongoing, including Demeter Press, *JMI*, *JourMS*, MER, the Museum of Motherhood, IAMAS, MomsRising, the Procreate Project, the Mother Art Prize, Spilt Milk Gallery, residencies in art and motherhood around the world, as well as university access and accessible coursework (and so many more, too long to list here). All demonstrate progress even amid the current right-leaning legislative attacks on women's access to healthcare, autonomy, and bodily rights. Let's celebrate the small chorus of consistent voices who continue to champion the mother movement as it exists today while labouring on towards the imagined goal of some semblance of a more balanced, more just, more equitable society.

For me, by killing off the housewife, I have liberated myself, but the process of destruction is limited. I've grown tired of the "smash the patriarchy" rant because of its long-term ineffectuality. The rant and the rage aimed at the patriarchy is like a bouncing rubber ball. It doesn't stick. However, I do believe it is possible to build new boats on which to float. O'Reilly, and others within a feminist circle of scholars. are still pushing for "inclusion in academic feminism" within the university setting (O'Reilly 225). Of course, this is a mandatory priority. We must address our "larger and pervasive feminist discomfort with all things maternal" (O'Reilly 227). We must confront our deep and utter embedded contempt for all things mother, encouraged by a society that values production, material gains, and shiny surface objects over the messiness of procreation and the reality that our procreators are at the center of this endeavour. One need look no further than recent healthcare statistics on maternal morbidity in the US for evidence of our deep and abiding indifference. Our collective societal loathing of mothers, of feminist ideals, and of women in general can and should be countered through creativity, inclusion, love, and collaboration. By prioritizing values that put our voices in audible positions of access, it is possible to create channels undermining mainstream archetypes. In the words of Serena Williams, "The success of every woman should be the inspiration to another. We should raise each other up. Make sure you're very courageous: be strong, be extremely kind, and above all be humble (qtd. in Lo 3). We do the kind of living we aspire to by finding courageous examples throughout *her*story that inspire and lift us. We empower and create organizations that seek to examine their own patriarchal tendencies. We must be willing to go beyond the limitations of the patriarchal construction of our current world to embody liberation. The box within a box is that thing that keeps us within the male gaze under the thumb of someone else's mandates and remains in the clutches of negativity and hierarchy.

By focussing every day, in every possible way, on the inherent value of every being and by creating new streams of support (like this book) and collaboration outside dominant systems, we may hope to invent a movement that starts on the inside and spreads outwards. I believe that this is an inside job. Matricentric feminism is a living breathing body of measure, which continues to evolve each time an author puts word to page, action to activism, and life to more equitable, compassionate, and accessible portals of education, care, and media. Following that flow, from our past to our present, while inclusively identifying our future and practicing those values in tangible ways is the path forward.

Finally, as stated at the beginning of this chapter, it was my personal choice to put a metaphorical dagger into the heart of the contrived and socially constructed woman at the centre of the housewife ideology. I did this to save my life. Others may choose different reasons. However, there is no human being, in the long run, who benefits from a less liberated, less just, less realized life. Matricentric feminism's fourth wave surge is the legacy of the collective women's movements, as they now appear in historical as well as contemporary texts and art. We must provide wide access to them. These are the initiatives from which we might all rise and surge forward in an unprecedented collective that is simultaneously embodied internally through knowledge and values as well as externally (in practice and places) towards a personal and collective journey of autonomy and emancipation. Ever onwards!

Works Cited

"Abigail Adams." *National Parks Service*, U.S. Department of the Interior, www.nps.gov/wori/learn/historyculture/abigail-adams.htm#:~:text=Do%20not%20put%20such%20unlimited,have%20no%20voice%20or%20Representation.%E2%80%. Accessed 13 July 2024.

Adams, Abigail. "Abigail Adams to John Adams, 31 March 1776." *National Archives and Records Administration,*. Accessed 13 July 2024.

Bernard, Jessie Shirley. *American Family Behavior.* Harper and Brothers Publishers, 1942.

Beauvoir, Simone de. *The Second Sex.* Translated by H. M. Parshley. Penguin, 1972.

Beauvoir, Simone de. "The Second Sex." Translated by H. M. Parshley, *The Second Sex by Simone de Beauvoir 1949.* Marxist Internet Archive, 2005, www.marxists.org/reference/subject/ethics/de-beauvoir/2nd-sex/. Accessed 13 July 2024.

Bianco, Marcie. "Opinion: For Women, It's Past Time to Give Up the Ghost of Equality." *CNN*, 6 May 2023, www.cnn.com/2023/05/06/opinions/equal-rights-amendment-equality-impossible-bianco/index.html. Accessed 13 July 2024.

Black Lives Matter. "Black Lives Matter: A Herstory of the #blacklivesmatter Movement by Alicia Garza." *Black Lives Matter: A Herstory of the #BlackLivesMatter Movement by Alicia Garza | School of Medicine Anti-Racist Coalition | Stanford University*, blacklivesmatter.stanford.edu/2020/10/26/herstory-of-blm.html. Accessed 13 July 2024.

Burke, Tarana. "Me Too Is a Movement, Not a Moment." *Tarana Burke: Me Too Is a Movement, Not a Moment | TED Talk*, 2006, www.ted.com/

talks/tarana_burke_me_too_is_a_movement_not_a_moment. Accessed 13 July 2024.

Chesler, Phyllis. *With Child: A Diary of Motherhood*. Lawrence Hill Books, 2018.

Collins, Patricia Hill. *Black Feminist Thought: Knowledge, Consciousness, and the Politics of Empowerment*. Routledge, Taylor & Francis Group, 2015.

Ensler, Eve, and Gloria Steinem. *The Vagina Monologues*. Virago Press, 2001.

Friedan, Betty. *The Feminine Mystique*. W.W. Norton & Company, 2013.

Hershenson, Roberta. "Band Sings about What It's like to Raise a Family in the 90s." *The New York Times*, 9 Nov. 1997, www.nytimes.com/1997/11/09/nyregion/band-sings-about-what-it-s-like-to-raise-a-family-in-the-90-s.html. Accessed 13 July 2024.

Ivey, Paul. "Women Build Museums: Dr. Paul Ivey." *Museum of Fine Arts, St Petersburg*, 18 Apr. 2023, mfastpete.org/event/women-build-museums/.

Kay, Yana. "Nicki Minaj Changes from Housewife to Golden Goddess on Dazed Magazine Cover." *Daily Mail Online*, 12 Sept. 2014, www.dailymail.co.uk/tvshowbiz/article-2751253/Naughty-nice-Nicki-Minaj-changes-demure-housewife-golden-goddess-graces-double-cover-Dazed-magazine.html. Accessed 13 July 2024.

Lange, Allison. "Rights in the Early Republic." *History of U.S. Woman's Suffrage*, 2015, www.crusadeforthevote.org/early-republic. Accessed 13 July 2024.

Lengermann, Patricia M., and Jill Niebrugge-Brantley. *The Women Founders: Sociology and Social Theory, 1830-1930: A Text/Reader.* Waveland Press, Inc., 2007.

Lo, Danica. "The Best Advice Ever from Madeleine Albright, Iman, Billie Jean King, and Serena Williams." *Glamour*, 10 Nov. 2015, www.glamour.com/story/best-advice-women-ever. Accessed 13 July 2024.

Merriam Webster. "Word of the Year 2017—Feminism." *Merriam-Webster*, Merriam-Webster, 2017, www.merriam-webster.com/wordplay/word-of-the-year-2017-feminism.

"Mamapalooza 2022." *The Motherhood Foundation*, 2022, https://mamapalooza.wordpress.com. Accessed 30 August, 2023.

Mills, Charles W. *White Collar the American Middle Classes.* Oxford University Press, 1953.

Munar, Ana Maria. "Dancing between Anger and Love: Reflections on Feminist Activism." *Dancing between Anger and Love: Reflections on Feminist Activism | Ephemeral Journal,* Feb. 2019, ephemerajournal.org/contribution/dancing-between-anger-and-love-reflections-feminist-activism. Accessed 13 July 2024.

O'Reilly, Andrea, ed. *Encyclopedia of Motherhood.* Sage Press, 2010.

O'Reilly, Andrea. *From Motherhood to Mothering: The Legacy of Adrienne Rich's Of Woman Born.* State University of New York Press, 2004. *Project MUSE,* https://doi.org/10.1353/book4871. Accessed July 13, 2024.

O'Reilly, Andrea, ed. *Maternal Theory: Essential Readings.* Demeter Press, 2007.

O'Reilly, Andrea. *Matricentric Feminism: Theory, Activism, Practice.* Demeter Press, 2021.

O'Reilly, Andrea. "Matricentric Feminism: A Feminism for Mothers". *Journal of the Motherhood Initiative for Research and Community Involvement,* vol. 10, no. 1/2, Dec. 2019, https://jarm.journals.yorku.ca/index.php/jarm/article/view/40551.

Perez, Rachel Lee. "'A Womanless History': The Importance of Including Women in the Historical Narrative." *Ms. Magazine,* 25 Aug. 2022, msmagazine.com/2022/08/25/women-history-textbooks/. Accessed 13 July 2024.

Proctor, Devin. "The #tradwife persona and the rise of radicalized domesticity." *Persona Studies,* vol. 8, no. 2, 2023, pp. 7–26, https://doi.org/10.21153/psj2022vol8no2art1645.

Sargent, Judith. "Judith Sargent Murray's 'On the Equality of the Sexes.'" 1790. *The Public Domain Review,* Feb 2022, publicdomainreview.org/collection/equality-of-the-sexes/. Accessed 15 August 2023.

Smith, Dorothy E. *The Everyday World as Problematic: A Feminist Sociology.* Northeastern University Press, 1987.

Stanton, Cady. "Declaration of Sentiments." 1848. *National Parks Service,* U.S. Department of the Interior, Feb. 2022, www.nps.gov/wori/learn/historyculture/declaration-of-sentiments.htm. Accessed 13 July 2024.

Triggs, Ariana, et al. "What Is a 'Trad Wife'? These Controversial Women Are Drawing Attention—and Opinions." *USA Today*, Gannett Satellite Information Network, 31 July 2023, www.usatoday.com/story/life/health-wellness/2023/07/14/trad-wife-meaning-controversy/ 70407456007/. Accessed 13 July 2024.

Rich, Adrienne. *Of Woman Born*. Virago, 1976.

Rothman, Barbara Katz. *Recreating Motherhood*. W. W. Norton & Company, 1990.

Truth, Sojourner. "'Sojourner Truth: Ain't I a Woman?' 1851." *National Parks Service*, US Department of the Interior, 17 Nov. 2017, www.nps.gov/articles/sojourner-truth.htm. Accessed 13 July 2024.

Wheatley, Phillis. "Poems on Various Subjects, Religious and Moral." 1772. *A Spotlight on a Primary Source by Phillis Wheatley*, The Gilder Lehrman Institute of American history, 2013, www.gilderlehrman.org/history-resources/spotlight-primary-source/phillis-wheatley%E2%80%99s-poem-tyranny-and-slavery-1772. Accessed 13 July 2024.

Wollstonecraft, Mary. "Vindication of the Rights of Woman" *Renascence Editions*, core.ac.uk/download/pdf/36679668.pdf. Accessed 13 July 2024.

"World Breastfeeding Week 2023." *World Health Organization*, World Health Organization, 2023, www.who.int/campaigns/world-breastfeeding-week/2023. Accessed 13 July 2024.

19.

Riding the Wave Rather than Waving Off: The Academic Study of Religions and Matricentric Feminism

Florence Pasche Guignard and Pascale F. Engelmajer

This chapter discusses the impact of motherhood studies, maternal theory, and matricentric feminism on religious studies, an academic field allegedly more traditional and conservative than women, gender, sexuality, and feminist studies. We explore the emergence of a maternal turn in our academic field, drawing on our personal and collective experiences and reflecting on our continued monitoring of new publications related to the study of mothers, motherhood, and mothering at the intersection with religion and spirituality. Drawing from our organization of and participation in academic events in the past ten years, we describe how this turn is manifested in both theory and academic practice and offer insights into its development.

As coauthors, we are part of an international group of mother scholars contributing to the field of religious studies and belonging to various cultural or spiritual traditions, or none. While this situates our collective positionality, discussing our personal beliefs and values or our religious identities (or lack thereof) is beyond the scope of this chapter and irrelevant to our point. Although we each have other engagements relevant to feminism, in this chapter, we focus on how we are developing an academic praxis of matricentric feminism in various aspects of our scholarship, particularly research, publications, dissemination (symposiums, conferences, panels, etc.) and, to a lesser extent, teaching.

The core group of this informal international network in academia started in 2015 when two of us (Florence Pasche Guignard and Giulia Pedrucci) met at the International Association for the History of Religions conference. Since then, the core group has expanded with two more scholars (Sucharita Sarkar and Pascale Engelmajer),and we consolidated our bilateral or multilateral collaborations through mutual invitations and coauthored publications (for instance, Pasche Guignard and Pedrucci; see the short bios at the end of this volume for more details).[1]

Our preferred methodologies and types of data vary, ranging from archaeological artifacts to social media posts and various types of literature. Our locations also have different degrees of privilege, from tenured to assistant or associate professors or contingent faculty, working in or at the margins of academic institutions in the United States, Canada, Italy, Germany, and India. We may have differing opinions on a range of issues, including the nature and scope of religious studies or feminism, but as coauthors we are committed to engaging in productive and respectful dialogue and to working together towards the advancement of scholarship on mothers, motherhood, and religion. Our common ground lies in our contributions to the field of religious studies, as well as in the intersection of our identities as mothers and women, which have significantly affected our academic careers. Furthermore, we have chosen to focus our work on a topic neglected in our discipline, bringing it to the forefront.

We start with defining religious studies, the academic field from which we draw our contributions and perspectives. After noting how religious studies effectively navigated the gender-critical turn in the 1980s through the influence of women's studies, we contend that the field could now benefit from motherhood studies and matricentric feminism in a similar way. Like a surfer who rides a wave as it builds and moves forward, the phrase "riding the wave" is used to describe taking advantage of a trend or opportunity that is gaining momentum, such as the rise of motherhood studies and matricentric feminism in recent decades.

This metaphor implies that success in riding the wave requires skill, appropriate timing, and a willingness to take risks and move with the flow of events. We provide examples of initiatives that helped establish dedicated spaces within academia for studying mothers, motherhood, and mothering in relation to religion and spirituality. We reflect on the limitations and challenges we met while highlighting our success in establishing motherhood and religions as a distinct topic within the broader field of gender and religions, specifically within the most prominent scholarly society in religious studies in North America. Additionally, we emphasize our commitment to international, collaborative, and comparative approaches in our work.

Our focus in this chapter is on our roles as scholars, although we recognize that applying matricentric feminism to our own lives, outside of academia, has been integral to reaching our current positions. Our purpose is to share with readers unfamiliar with religious studies yet familiar with motherhood studies how we see a wave of matricentric feminism being realized and enacted in theory and in our academic practice, in diverse ways at micro and macro levels. We contend that the ripple effects of matricentric feminism are not limited to fields closely related to motherhood or gender studies, but that the impact of the wave of matricentric feminism is extensive and visible even in disciplines like religious studies, which due to their origins may seem least likely to adopt feminist matricentric perspectives.

What Is Religious Studies?

As a discipline in the humanities and social sciences, the academic study of religions, also known as religious studies, explores the nature, beliefs, practices, and cultural expressions of religions from a multidisciplinary and comparative perspective. Religious studies seeks to understand religion as a human phenomenon that has shaped societies, cultures, and individuals throughout history and across the world. Scholars of religion investigate sacred texts and narratives (literary and oral traditions), systems of beliefs, and practices, such as rituals, of different religious traditions and consider the various factors that shape them in the social, historical, and cultural contexts in which religions emerge and evolve. They draw on methods and insights from a range of academic disciplines—such as anthropology, history, sociology, philosophy, psychology, and theology—to study the multifaceted dimensions of religion. In addition to exploring religious traditions, religious studies also examines the role of religion (and secularism) in contemporary societies and its impact on various social issues, including the relationship between religion and politics, gender, race, and identity, among other topics. As scholars of religion, we generally adopt a critical and objective stance in our research and work from an analytical and comparative perspective.

The academic study of religions does not promote or reject any particular worldview or assess truth claims expressed by those who belong to these traditions. Although our academic field is closely related to that of theology—and sometimes aggregated with it (or philosophy) in the same faculties or departments—and despite large overlaps in the interests and in some of the methodologies we prefer, it nevertheless remains distinct from it. Theology tends to focus on a particular religious tradition or belief system and is often based on a set of religious doctrines and scriptures. Many theologians teach from a faith-based perspective (Catholic, Protestant, Muslim, Jewish, Vaishnava, etc.) and seek to understand religion as a way of experiencing and knowing the divine.

Although both religious studies and theology explore the nature and role of religion, they differ in their approach, scope, and objectives. Religious studies constitutes a multidisciplinary and comparative field seeking to understand religion as a human, social, and cultural phenomenon, whereas theology focusses on understanding the nature of the divine and religious beliefs, generally from a faith-based perspective (see, for example, McCutcheon "What Is the Academic Study of Religion").

Just like one does not need to be a mother to contribute to motherhood studies, in the same way, religious studies scholars may or may not self-identify with a particular tradition. What matters most is an awareness of our own biases and assumptions: We seek to minimize their influence while also considering ethical issues in conducting research, especially in contemporary contexts and while working with groups or individuals that are vulnerable, marginalized, or constitute religious minorities.

Debates on methods, positionality, and public engagement in the academic study of religions are ongoing (MisirHiralall et al.). The feminist notion of positionality has challenged the idea that knowledge is objective and universal, recognizing that it is produced from a particular standpoint and shaped by an individual's social identity and experiences. The tension remains between those who claim that scholars of religions should be "critics not caretakers" (McCutcheon, *Critics*) and those who engage their scholarship publicly to the service of particular religious institutions or other actors (e.g., faith-based or secular nongovernmental organizations or governments). Notions of public, engaged, or participative scholarship have integrated the field but are not as common and accepted as they may be in other disciplines, such as feminist studies.

When comparing the place of motherhood studies and religious studies in academia, one immediately notices that the former has largely been shaped by mother scholars in North America and other anglophone contexts over the past three decades. In contrast, the latter emerged as an academic field in European universities during the late nineteenth century, marked by imperialism and colonialism, and was influenced by male scholars who often perceived themselves as superior to women, non-Europeans, and non-Christians. Our work aims to integrate the best aspects of religious studies and matricentric feminism. Drawing upon the rich tradition of critical and comparative inquiry and interdisciplinary approaches in religious studies, including the postcolonial, gender-critical, and positionality-aware "turns," we believe that matricentric feminism can offer valuable insights into the study of both contemporary and historical religious contexts and issues.

Studying Mothers in Religious Studies

Providing an extensive state of the literature is beyond the scope of this chapter, and such a review (up to 2017) can be found in Pasche Guignard ("The Academic Study" 61–88). Furthermore, her 2020 contribution, "Religions and Mothers," to *The Routledge Companion to Motherhood* features a list of key topics and references. Collectively, as part of the project Beyond Mother Goddesses: New Directions for International Scholarship on Motherhood in Religious Studies, the coauthors and their collaborators created a bibliography of publications relevant to the topic.

It is revealing that even the second, revised, 2005 edition of the *Encyclopedia of Religion*, the most important and extensive reference work in religious studies, among its 2,750 original entries and approximately six hundred entirely new articles, features an entry on monkeys but none on mothers. This typical omission highlights that although there is an emerging and even burgeoning scholarship on mothers, motherhood, mothering and religions still face a "triple-blind" that matricentric feminism may help us overcome. Our expression, "triple obliviousness," is inspired by Ursula King's term (one of the pioneers in the study of religion and gender).[2] King argued the following in the 1990s:

> Gender studies are beginning to make an impact on the contemporary study of religion and are setting new research agendas for religious studies. However [despite several successfully negotiated "gender-critical turns" since the 1960s], this is a slow process, and the profoundly transformative effect of a basic paradigm shift has so far been less noticeable in religious studies than in other areas of the humanities. (King, "Introduction: Gender and the Study of Religion" 3–4)

In 2005, King called out the continuing "double blindness" characterizing the study of gender and religion: on the one hand, most contemporary gender studies, whether in the humanities, social sciences or natural sciences, remain extraordinarily "religion-blind"; on the other hand, many studies in religion continue to be profoundly "gender-blind" (King, "General Introduction: Gender-Critical Turns in the Study of Religion." 1–2; also see Lee's review of major contributions to the field, and Juschka 37). We argue that this "double blindness" is now superseded, and the insights drawn from feminist and gender studies are now well integrated into the field. The *Journal of Feminist Studies in Religion* (based at the University of Indiana) was founded in 1985 and *Religion and Gender* (published by Brill) started in 2011. Most programs in religious studies include at least one course focussing on women or gender. Even colleagues, most of them men, who are the least likely to engage with feminist theory or gender studies can no longer ignore the topic, at least in their teaching (for instance, in general courses on key transversal topics, such as myth, ritual, sainthood, or in introductions to a specific tradition). Recent introductory textbooks (Geaves), key terms or key concepts books (Boyarin; Olson), and general handbooks and companions to religious studies by academic publishers and university presses (Strenski) contain sections on gender and religion. Our examples here (and there are many others) are limited to publications in English, but our international perspectives allow us to observe similar trends in French, German, and Italian scholarship.

A quick survey of those texts, however, shows that despite the wealth of scholarship on gender and religion, motherhood is rarely studied. In the past decade, the focus has shifted towards gender and sex rather than gender and women, or women and mothers. The words "mother," "maternal," or "motherhood" are rarely mentioned, and more inclusive words such as "parent" or "parenting" are not frequent either (see Lofton as a recent exception). Keyword searches for "gender" in prestigious and classical journals in our field, yield hundreds of results but only a few dozen for "mother" (and the related words already mentioned). Academic conferences feature papers, sessions, or even recurring units on gender and religion. For instance, the American Academy of Religion (AAR), the most important scholarly society for the academic study of religion in North America, includes a Lesbian Feminisms and Religion Unit and a Queer Studies in Religion Unit, which reflect its commitment to inclusivity and nondiscrimination, in line with its code of conduct. We discuss below our collective efforts to advance the study of motherhood, mothering, and mothers through establishing an exploratory session at the AAR, which, we hope, might become a new permanent unit. But first, we must account for the triple obliviousness we mentioned.

The first element of this triple obliviousness is that religious traditions and academics who study them rarely recognize mothers or the maternal as central issues, or, when they do, they never do so explicitly. Relatively few scholars of religions have examined motherhood or mothers and even fewer mothering. Most fall into what Andrea O'Reilly denounces as the "failure to take into account the important difference between the institution of motherhood and women's experiences of mothering" (O'Reilly 21). Motherhood is not only a patriarchal institution but a religious one as well, in the sense that normative religious discourses may contribute to reinforcing patriarchal aspects of the lives of mothers, whether they identify with a religion or not. Motherhood is taken for granted while it remains a contested site for religious institutions. Other religious discourses, though, may have the potential to call attention to the experience of women (and others who do not identify as such while engaging in motherwork).

Second, perspectives in gender and feminist studies participate in this triple obliviousness. Until recently, both religion and motherhood were often identified mainly as factors of oppression for women and thus dismissed as irrelevant. As noted by O'Reilly, "Motherhood ... is the unfinished business of feminism" (13). She and others have already explained the "'disavowal of motherhood' in academic feminism" (20) and "the marginalization of motherhood in feminist thought" (Kawash 972).

Mainstream feminist research has shown a tremendous disinterest, if not a complete disdain, for religion and motherhood. This is even more obvious in the context of francophone feminist studies, due to a predominant Beauvoirian perspective that viewed not only religion but also motherhood in a very negative light as a source of women's servitude (Beauvoir 97, 222) and saw it only as an oppressive patriarchal institution. Through our work and collective efforts, we strive to close this gap by bringing matricentric feminism alongside other intellectually responsible epistemologies to explore this previously overlooked but crucial subject.

The third strand in the triple obliviousness is associated with and results from the first and second strands: Motherhood is still mostly neglected in the now extensive scholarship on women, gender, and religion. Most research focusses on women who do not conform to the religiously sanctioned script of marriage and motherhood. These are special or extraordinary figures—martyrs, saints, nuns, priestesses, or poetesses—a minority of whom are presented as mothers. Most papers and panels on women and religion at the AAR, which frequently discuss women's religious agency, often ignore the distinction between mothering and motherhood and rarely consider mothering as a potential site of religious agency for women. (It is noteworthy that whereas the AAR has the Death, Dying, and Beyond Unit it has none on birth and birthing). The religious experiences of women (and others who do not identify as women) as mothers have also not been sufficiently discussed in this regard.

Access to contraception and abortion, religious agency, and subordination remain key issues for feminist research in religious studies. Still, it is necessary to examine further what happens after giving birth, to women who are childless by choice or by circumstance, and to other forms of mothering not tied to biology, such as adoption, othermothering, communal mothering, families with several maternal figures (e.g. polygynous marriages in religious contexts), and spiritual mothering (inside and outside of religious institutions and traditions).

We build on previous work, grounded in religious studies, and recognize that both the institution of motherhood and the mothering experience are shaped and influenced by religious beliefs, discourses, texts, and practices. Whenever source materials are sufficient, we strive to bring mothers' voices to the centre. Collectively, we aim to bring together scholars seeking to apply matricentric feminist perspectives to religious studies to create new paths for research. We anticipate that these will lead beyond the study of normative discourses on motherhood and other-than-human maternal figures (e.g., mother goddesses, maternal figures in myth, and mothers of founders of religions or saints considered as mere sacred vessels). We are encouraged by seeing that neighbouring disciplines, such as theology and philosophy, have already integrated this maternal turn to some extent. Theologians, thealogians, or even "motherlogians" might be ahead of religious studies scholars in this regard, probably due to the centrality of Mary as a key maternal figure in Christianity and its theologies or due to the influence of African American and womanist theologians who tend to be more aware of the centrality of motherhood in religion because of their particular positionality. These scholars and thinkers have brought rich contributions to the field (e.g., Bischoff et al.; Buckhanon Crowder; Jacob; Kirk-Duggan and Pippin) but these are focussed on Christianity, whereas we, as scholars of religions, strive for broader and necessarily comparative perspectives.

The reception of studies on religion and spirituality in motherhood studies would deserve another chapter of its own. Here we will only note that there is openness to study religion and spirituality at the intersection with motherhood, although the topic remains marginal compared to others such as politics, arts, literature, or sports. Motherhood studies scholars recently started considering religion either as a decisive vector in enforcing traditional or conservative gender norms but also as a possible path to empowerment, not only spiritual but also social. Several edited volumes published by Demeter Press (Kerry and Epp Buller; Jordan and Alexandre; Pappano and Olwan; Reimer; Salla Dieng and O'Reilly) provide spaces for mothers to speak from within their tradition, which is important.

Unlike the *Encyclopedia of Religion*, which has no entry on motherhood, the *Encyclopedia of Motherhood* features several articles on religion (see Harper, for the main one; see Pasche Guignard, "The Academic" 76–77 for comments on the other entries that include perspectives on religions other than Christianity or contexts of the global minority). Yet comparative and critical approaches do not seem prominent in motherhood studies. These have a strong potential to help identify what is common to the patriarchal institution of motherhood across cultures and religions and what can be singled out as particular to specific worldviews or theologies.

Bringing in Matricentric Feminist Perspectives

In this section, we explain how we get inspired by and apply matricentric feminism to our field of religious studies. We address several of the points of what O'Reilly sees as "central and governing principles and aims of matricentric feminism" (18) in her article "Matricentric Feminism: A Feminism for Mothers." We acknowledge leaving out of the discussion the aspects of social justice and activism present in O'Reilly's definition, mostly due to the prevailing stance on positionality in religious studies as an academic field (see above, the mention of ongoing debates). Like O'Reilly's, our perspective "asserts that the topic of mothers, mothering, and motherhood is deserving of serious and sustained scholarly inquiry" (18). As discussed above, this has not been the case until recently in religious studies.

Most religious traditions would have no qualms regarding "mothering as work that is important and valuable to society" (O'Reilly 18), despite their tendency to also consider such work either as natural, divinely ordained, or both. To counter these ideas, as scholars, whenever relevant, and especially when studying contemporary (as opposed to past) religious contexts, we insist on the second part of this normative proposal by O'Reilly: "The essential task of mothering is not, and should not be, the sole responsibility and duty of mothers" (18). The history of religions provides examples of not just myths or fantasies of communal parenting or mothering but actual experiments, for better or for worse, in terms of results (for instance, kibbutzim in the Israeli context, large polygamist families, or the many orphanages run by nuns, monks, or priests, Catholic or Buddhist).

Building upon earlier proposals by scholars of religions, such as Susan Starr Sered's *Priestess, Mother, Sacred Sister: Religions Dominated by Women*, our perspective, echoing O'Reilly's, "contests, challenges, and counters the patriarchal oppressive institution of motherhood and seeks to imagine and implement a maternal identity and practice that is empowering to mothers" (18). Although most religious institutions continue to promote a patriarchal view of motherhood and reinforce the institution, there are ways in which mothers find empowering stances from within their religious traditions, worldviews, philosophies, or other spiritual practices that they reclaim or shape into their own (see examples studied by Duncan and Hennessey).

Although we cannot address here the aspects of social justice and activism mentioned by O'Reilly, we agree that focusing on mothers in religion may contribute "to correct[ing] the child centredness that defines much of the scholarship ... on motherhood" (18). Just as she suggests, we strive to "develop research ... from the experience and the perspective of mothers" (18) and not just the concern about children. The latter is present in many religious discourses (in terms of ensuring the wellbeing of children and especially of orphans and disadvantaged children, or in the patriarchal notion that a male child is more desirable or more of a blessing than a female one).

By refocussing on the experiences of mothers or of any type of religious women as mothers and seeing them as central, we shift the focus away from normative constructions that discourses, produced by a literate male elite in most cases, often engage in. For instance, if we consider the propensity to have many children, clerics imposing sexual norms and mandatory procreation on women is different from women valuing their fertility or reclaiming for themselves and celebrating their powers of reproduction, including through narratives and rituals. Similarly, the words (real or mythical) of a childless woman engaging in prayers or ritual practices to become pregnant or a mother expressing gratitude for a safe delivery may be tainted by patriarchal norms but expressed in a maternal voice.

In the historical study of religion, it is difficult to retrieve mothers' voices from the past (Pasche Guignard, "The Academic" 63). We read their experience between the lines of the texts of the elite dead men. As historians of religions, we do not have the luxury of just tossing out such materials, as biased as they may be. The voices of women that have been preserved through time are rarely those of mothers, and those who were mothers and close enough to the elite to have their thoughts preserved rarely discussed their experiences, including religious ones.

Furthermore, we fully agree with O'Reilly that a matricentric perspective "understands mothering and motherhood to be culturally determined and variable, and is committed to exploring the diversity of maternal experience across race, class, culture, ethnicity, sexuality, ability, age, and geographical location" (18). To this list, we add religion as a determining factor, often—though not always—at the intersection of these other factors listed by O'Reilly, quoted above. In the case of South Asian traditions, for instance, although there are many common challenges for mothers in the same cultural spaces, some issues are particular to specific religious observances. Although Hindu, Sikh, and Muslim mothers may face racism, especially when they are part of minorities in Western societies, or colourism, only observant Sikh mothers have to deal with the demand to maintain kes (uncut hair) of their sons as part of upholding a distinct identity and obeying a command framed as religious. Moreover, Hindu mothers in South Asia may encounter more pressure around the notion of preference for sons over daughters than Muslim mothers.[3]

Finally, and still following O'Reilly, our perspective also "endeavours to establish maternal theory and motherhood studies as an autonomous, independent, and legitimate scholarly discipline" (18). The existence of motherhood studies as an independent discipline strengthens the legitimacy of scholars from other disciplines borrowing some of the key tenets of maternal theory and applying them through interdisciplinary approaches.

Advancing the Study of This Topic in Our Academic and Professional Organization

Our collaborative efforts in organizing events and publishing on motherhood and religion, thus granting the topic more exposure within our field, culminated in our proposal for an Exploratory Session, which AAR approved for its 2023 Annual Meeting. Acceptance of such proposals requires going through a competitive selection process. We must show that there will be enough scholarly interest to sustain participation through three consecutive years before we can apply for a permanent unit. Although we, the coauthors, served in leadership roles, this was a collective endeavour shaped by a feminist and collaborative perspective that involved a dozen scholars who contributed to and provided feedback on multiple drafts of the proposal.

The need for a dedicated Unit on Religion and Motherhood is borne out of the interest in and support for the activities we have organized at the AAR since 2019, following many earlier informal conversations. In 2019, the Comparative Studies in Religion Unit sponsored Motherhood and Mothering across Religious Traditions: A Comparative Roundtable with seven presenters and a respondent (most of whom are still part of this core group). Attended by nearly twenty participants, it established the basis for future collaborations. In 2020, Pascale Engelmajer and

Florence Pasche Guignard organized the preconference workshop Motherhood and Religion: A Comparative, Interdisciplinary, Matricentric Feminist Approach, attended online by over thirty scholars (from students to full professors), and specialists in several religious traditions. In the same year, Engelmajer (United States), Pasche Guignard (Canada), Giulia Pedrucci (Italy), and Sucharita Sarkar (India) successfully applied for the AAR Collaborative International Research Grant (CIRG). Through 2021, collaborating online, we completed the AAR CIRG-funded research project Beyond Mother Goddesses: New Directions for International Scholarship on Motherhood in Religious Studies. Pedrucci and Sarkar presented the results at the AAR 2021 annual meeting online during a follow-up workshop, attended by over twenty participants, one-third of whom had participated in 2020. In 2022, the Women's Scholars Network of the International Association for the History of Religion invited the AAR-CIRG team to present the project at one of its webinars, thus giving the project international exposure. At the 2022 AAR Annual Meeting, a third workshop on Consolidating Matricentric Perspectives was held. Enthusiastic feedback and active support from the participants for a new AAR Unit on Religion and Motherhood constituted our main motivation to propose an Exploratory Session, which was accepted for the 2023 Annual Meeting.

Limitations and Mitigations

Much remains to be explored about motherhood in religious studies, and scholars have blind spots that only time will reveal. As mentioned above, sacred narratives provide fertile grounds to explore family structures and kinship systems, including some in which figures who are not female or feminine birth or nurture children and sometimes engage collectively in motherwork. For instance, in Greek myths, Zeus gives birth through his head to his daughter Athena after swallowing Metis, his lover. He also carries to term, in his thigh, his son Dionysus after striking Semele, another lover, with his thunderbolt. Athena is born as an adult goddess, and Dionysus is swiftly whisked away to be cared for by the nymphs. Reproduction within what is presented as a sexual binary is prevalent in most narratives, yet several extraordinary tales feature alternative modes of reproduction with or without bodies or even genitals.

So far, though, these explorations of reproduction and motherwork beyond binaries are limited to myth and are rarely reflected in the study of social realities in religious contexts. We might hypothesize that the low number of parents who identify as queer, trans, non-binary, or in any way other than male and female and who simultaneously claim a religious or spiritual identity is a reason why this is not a point of entry for such topics in religious studies. Exploring queer mothering and child-rearing practices that step out of normative definitions would allow disentangling the concepts of "parent," "mother," and "woman" that religious discourses tend to conflate. Another hypothesis as to why, for now, the few studies on mothers and religions focus on more traditional (or even conservative) forms of mothering and motherhood is because religious studies scholars identifying as 2SLGBTQ+ have their own dedicated scholarly spaces, associations, and units, such as those mentioned above. Issues around parenting or mothering do not appear as prominent or urgent to be discussed at the intersection with religion. This might account, at least partially, for why most contributors and attendees to the events we facilitated are cisgender women and self-identify as such.

In the same way that, from the perspective of the academic study of religions, one does not need to be a member of a specific tradition to study it, similarly, one does not need to identify as a mother to contribute to motherhood studies. There were a few men participants or attendees at our roundtables and workshops, and we interviewed three male authors (out of twelve interviewees) for the Beyond Mother Goddesses project. The only requirement to participate in the AAR pre-conference workshops we organized was to have an interest in the study of motherhood, mothering, mothers, or maternal figures.

Riding the Wave Rather Than Waving Off

Based on a systematic review of literature, personal knowledge of our field, our experiences, and collaborative initiatives, the material presented in this chapter provides compelling evidence that scholars in religious studies are embracing matricentric feminism. Despite their potential for cross-fertilization, scholars of motherhood and religion have yet to fully tap into the interdisciplinary opportunities between these two fields. As scholars primarily engaged in religious studies, we believe that such initiatives will continue to thrive. Readers with a focus on motherhood and gender studies can benefit from exploring recent and forthcoming scholarship in religious studies examining the topic of motherhood from a matricentric perspective or engaging with it centrally.

In the past decade, as coauthors or coorganizers of academic events, collaboratively, we have raised our voices within our field. We did so more as scholars than as mothers and rarely identified as mother-scholars, although, increasingly, we have recognized that both identities are often impossible to disentangle completely. The origin of our interest in such topics is located more in our maternal than our religious or spiritual experiences. The members of our core group of scholars hold different sets of personal beliefs and values, and those are intentionally set aside when we collaborate: We do not practise interreligious dialogue, although we welcome colleagues who do so at our events. In contrast, what brings us to our common scholarly interest is our experiences of becoming mothers and engaging in motherwork while contributing to the academic sphere. In various cultural, religious, national, and institutional backgrounds, we experimented with similar situations, first as mothers and, sometimes, also as women.

For us, the notion that "maternity matters more than gender" (O'Reilly 14) rings true. We raised our voices as scholars, we carved out a subfield of our own thanks to the inspiration we gained from matricentric feminism and motherhood studies. Yet, as mothers, we rarely shared our stories, probably because our field still frowns upon disclosing too much of the personal. This might contrast with other disciplinary fields, in which acknowledging that "the personal is political" is emphasized more than in religious studies and in which people first speak of their own stories and struggles and then turn these into valid academic inquiries. Strategically, we started by restating the importance of the topic in relation to religion, without bringing our respective stories to the forefront, which, in our own contexts, would have been counterproductive. Anecdotes about who was caring for our children while we organized or attended conferences internationally were shared at coffee breaks.

Although we may not have been as vocal for matricentric feminism as colleagues in other fields, we believe that we made waves, albeit quiet ones. Through the events we organized, we created significant change, at least for ourselves and for those who accepted our invitation, including early-career scholars and those who identify with categories that remain underrepresented in our field and in its scholarly associations, such as 2SLGBTQ+, BIPOC, or, more generally, mothers.

Through our publications and organization of and contributions to scientific events, we draw attention to the gaps and inequalities we observe in society and, particularly, in religious institutions, in representations, including religious ones (myth, hagiography, other sacred narratives), and in the expectations placed by normative religious discourses on women who are mothers or not. By focussing on mothers, motherhood, and mothering, we also became more aware of how women and others who combine religious and maternal activism may be marginalized by some strands of feminism, particularly in some francophone contexts, which cannot admit that observant religious women can have agency and make their own choices.

In other words, just like in other fields of the humanities and social sciences, with the perspective of matricentric feminism, we connect, network, and continue building inclusive scholarly communities. We also resist feminist discourses that exclude religion as a topic of study other than under the angle of oppression, and even worse, that exclude religious women and mothers from sharing their stories and perspectives. We demonstrate the relevance of the focussed intersection of motherhood and religion, beyond the more general and now well-recognized interest for gender and religion. We seek and obtain our own academic spaces at the highest level in scholarly societies to foster excellence in scholarship. Sometimes, too, we defy clueless colleagues and contemptuous anonymous peer reviewers who visibly have no expertise in these topics.

As remote from gender and feminist studies or from motherhood studies as the academic study of religions may seem, we can nevertheless observe the ripple effects of the wave of matricentric feminism. Our progress in fully integrating useful aspects of maternal theory in religious studies may take years or even decades, but it has started. Even just ten years ago, we would not have believed that such progress was possible. By coming together through interdisciplinarity and comparative perspectives, we are better at negotiating the maternal turn in our field at the international level. Whether or not we succeed in establishing an official space for discussing such issues at one of our largest scholarly society, at different universities, in our courses, in our publications, and at various academic events, in the forthcoming years, we will continue monitoring the impact of the wave of matricentric feminism and benefiting from it.

Endnotes

1. The authors thank Giulia Pedrucci and Sucharita Sarkar for their feedback on this chapter that accounts for some of our collaborative work over the years, for which we are also grateful.
2. We use "obliviousness" as "blindness" may refer negatively to a situation of disability.
3. See the contributions in Sangha and Gonsalves for more on mothers in South Asia and the diaspora and on the influence of Hindu, Sikh, and Muslim traditions on their mothering.

Works Cited

Beauvoir, Simone de. *Le deuxième sexe. Les faits et les mythes.* Gallimard, 1949.

Bischoff, Claire, et al. *Parenting as Spiritual Practice and Source for Theology: Mothering Matters.* Palgrave Macmillan, 2017.

Boyarin, Daniel. "Gender." *Critical Terms for Religious Studies.* Edited by Mark C. Taylor. University of Chicago Press, 1998, pp. 117–35.

Buckhanon Crowder, Stephanie R. *When Momma Speaks: the Bible and Motherhood from a Womanist Perspective.* John Knox Press, 2016.

Duncan, Ann W. *Sacred Pregnancy: Birth, Motherhood, and the Quest for Spiritual Community.* Fortress Press, 2023.

Fast, Kerry, and Rachel Epp Buller, eds. *Mothering Mennonite.* Demeter Press, 2013.

Geaves, Ron. "Religion and Gender." *The Study of Religion: An Introduction to Key Ideas and Methods.* Edited by George D. Chryssides and Ron Geaves. Bloomsbury, 2013, pp. 275–302.

Harper, Susan. "Religion and Mothering." *Encyclopedia of Motherhood.* Edited by Andrea O'Reilly. Sage, 2010, pp. 1056–61.

Hennessey, Anna M. *Imagery, Ritual, and Birth: Ontology between the Sacred and the Secular.* Lexington Books, 2018.

Jacob, Sharon. *Reading Mary Alongside Indian Surrogate Mothers: Violent Love, Oppressive Liberation, and Infancy Narratives.* Palgrave Macmillan, 2015.

Jordan, Nané, and Chandra Alexandre, eds. *Pagan, Goddess, Mother.* Demeter Press, 2021.

Juschka, Darlene. "Feminism and Gender Theory." *The Oxford Handbook of the Study of Religion*. Edited by Michael Stausberg and Steven Engler. Oxford University Press, 2016, pp. 137–49.

Kawash, Samira. "New Directions in Motherhood Studies." *Signs*, vol. 36, no. 4, 2011, pp. 969–1003.

King, Ursula. "General Introduction: Gender-Critical Turns in the Study of Religion." *Gender, Religion, and Diversity. Cross Cultural Perspectives*. Edited by Ursula King and Tina Beattie. Continuum, 2005, pp. 1–10.

King, Ursula. "Introduction: Gender and the Study of Religion." *Religion and Gender*. Edited by Ursula King. Blackwell, 1995, pp. 1–38.

Kirk-Duggan, Cheryl A., and Tina Pippin, eds. *Mother Goose, Mother Jones, Mommie Dearest: Biblical Mothers and Their Children*. Society of Biblical Literature, 2009.

Lee, Becky. "Gender-critical Studies in Religious Studies," *Method & Theory in the Study of Religion*, vol. 16, no. 4, 2004, pp. 386–97.

Lofton, Kathryn. "Religion and the Authority in American Parenting." *Journal of the American Academy of Religion*, vol. 84, no. 2, 2016, pp. 806–41.

McCutcheon, Russell T. "What is the Academic Study of Religion?" Department of Religious Studies, University of Alabama, 2017, https://religion.ua.edu/wp-content/uploads/2017/07/mccutchintrohandout.pdf. Accessed 16 July 2024.

McCutcheon, Russell T. *Critics Not Caretakers: Redescribing the Public Study of Religion*. SUNY Press, 2001.

MisirHiralall, Sabrina, et al., eds. *Religious Studies Scholars as Public Intellectuals*. Routledge, 2018.

Olson, Carl. *Religious Studies: The Key Concepts*. Routledge, 2011.

O'Reilly, Andrea. "Matricentric Feminism: A Feminism for Mothers," *Journal of the Motherhood Initiative*, vol. 10, no 1–2, 2018, pp. 13–26.

Pappano, M. Aziza, and Dana M. Olwan, eds. *Muslim Mothering: Local and Global Histories, Theories, and Practices*. Demeter Press, 2016.

Pasche Guignard, Florence. "Religions and Mothers". *Routledge Companion to Motherhood*. Edited by Lynn O'Brien Hallstein, et al. Routledge, 2020, pp. 156–64.

Pasche Guignard, Florence. "The Academic Study of Religions and Mothering, Motherhood and Mothers". *Maternità e Politeismi—Motherhood(s) and Polytheisms*. Edited by Florence Pasche Guignard et al. Pàtron, 2017, pp. 61–88.

Pasche Guignard, Florence, and Giulia Pedrucci. "Motherhood(s) and Polytheisms: Epistemological and Methodological Reflections on the Study of Religions, Gender, and Women," *Numen*, vol. 65, no 4, 2018, pp. 404–34.

Reimer, Vanessa. *Angels on Earth: Mothering, Religion, and Spirituality*. Demeter Press, 2016.

Rich, Adrienne. *Of Woman Born: Motherhood as Experience and Institution*. Norton & Co., 1976.

Ruddick, Sara. *Maternal Thinking: Toward a Politics of Peace*. Beacon Press, 1989.

Salla Dieng, Rama, and Andrea O'Reilly, eds. *Feminist Parenting: Perspectives from Africa and Beyond*. Demeter Press, 2020.

Sangha, Jasjit K., and Tahira Gonsalves, eds. *South Asian Mothering: Negotiating Culture, Family and Selfhood*. Demeter Press, 2013.

Sered, Susan Starr. *Priestess, Mother, Sacred Sister: Religions Dominated by Women*. Oxford University Press, 1996.

Strenski, Ivan. "Sex and Gender." *The Wiley Blackwell Companion to the Study of Religion*. Edited by Robert A. Segal and Nickolas P. Roubekas. Wiley, 2021, pp. 429–39.

Notes on Contributors

Editors

Fiona Joy Green, PhD, (she/her/hers) is a cisgender straight mother who believes in the power of revolutionary feminist motherwork and matricentric feminism. She's a white settler and holds the position of professor in the Department of Women's and Gender Studies at the University of Winnipeg, located on the original lands of the Anishinaabeg, Anisininewuk, Dakota Oyate, and Denesuline, in the National Homeland of the Red River Métis, and on Treaty 1 Territory. Dr. Green is interested in the agency of children and mothers, in gender identities, and in the ability of feminist matroreform and feminist motherlines to contribute to feminist parenting, feminist theorizing, and feminist praxis. She is the sole author of *Practicing Feminist Mothering* (ARP) and co-editor of seven books (Demeter Press) addressing feminist parenting or maternal pedagogies.

Andrea O'Reilly, PhD, is a full professor in the School of Gender, Sexuality, and Women's Studies at York University, founder/editor-in-chief of the *Journal of the Motherhood Initiative* and publisher of Demeter Press. She is coeditor/editor of thirty-plus books, including *Feminist Parenting: Perspectives from Africa and Beyond* (2020), *Mothers, Mothering, and COVID-19: Dispatches from a Pandemic* (2021), *Maternal Theory, The 2nd Edition* (2021), *Monstrous Mothers: Troubling Tropes* (2021), *Maternal Regret: Resistances, Renunciations, and Reflections* (2022), *Normative Motherhood: Representations, Regulations, and Reclamations* (2023), and *Coming into Being: Mothers on Finding and Realizing Feminism* (2023). She is the editor of the *Encyclopedia on Motherhood* (2010) and coeditor of the *Routledge*

Companion to Motherhood (2019). She is the author of *Toni Morrison and Motherhood: A Politics of the Heart* (2004), *Rocking the Cradle: Thoughts on Motherhood, Feminism, and the Possibility of Empowered Mothering* (2006), and *Matricentric Feminism: Theory, Activism, and Practice, The 2nd Edition* (2021). She is twice the recipient of York University's Professor of the Year Award for teaching excellence and is the 2019 recipient of the Status of Women and Equity Award of Distinction from OCUFA (Ontario Confederation of University Faculty Associations). She has received more than 1.5 million dollars in grant funding for her research projects including two current ones: Older Young Mothers in Canada, and Mothers and Returning to "Normal": The Impact of the Pandemic on Mothering and Families.

Contributors

Daniele Bobb is a Caribbean scholar whose research interests include gender and development, social policies, mothering, and work. In addition to publishing around gender and education and gender and sexuality, she coauthored the book *Marginalized Groups in the Caribbean: Gender, Policy and Society*. Dr. Bobb sits on several committees and faculty boards. She is steadfast in her devotion to the work for gender equity and enhancing the quality of life for all.

Sophie Brock is a sociologist and mother living in Sydney, Australia. Sophie's work explores how motherhood is socially constructed and individually experienced. She works independently developing online courses for mothers and mother-supporting professionals who want to learn about the sociology of motherhood. She hosts *The Good Enough Mother* podcast, holding conversations with those passionate about advocating for social, cultural, and institutional change to support mothers, families, and communities better.

Alexis Carrion, MA, is a fifth-year doctoral candidate in Temple University's sociology department. She hopes to combat inequity in higher education through research and advocacy. Her research focusses on eliminating the challenges to degree completion experienced by nontraditional student populations. Her current research focusses on mothers who pursue credentials in higher education and the institutional barriers preventing them from achieving their academic goals.

Andrea DeKeseredy is a PhD student in the sociology department at the University of Alberta. Her research explores gender, work and family.

Pascale F. Engelmajer is a professor of religious studies at Carroll University. Her books include *Women in Pāli Buddhism: Walking the Spiritual Path in Mutual Dependence* (Routledge), *Buddhism* (Hodder & Stoughton), and *365 Ways to Live Mindfully* (John Murray). Her recent work focusses on motherhood in Buddhist texts. One of her latest publications on mothers and mothering is "Like a Mother Her Only Child: Mothering in the Pāli Canon," *Open Theology*, vol. 6, 2020, pp. 88–103.

Veronica Frigeni PhD, is a Visiting Scholar in Gender Studies at CEU in Vienna. Previously she was an affiliated researcher at the Amsterdam School for Cultural Analysis and a Visiting Scholar in Italian at the University of Cambridge. She has contributed chapters on Italian literature, reproductive justice, and trauma. She serves on the editorial board of the *Critical Gender Studies Journal*.

Katie B. Garner, PhD, focusses on motherhood, childcare, and labour equity via her PhD in English and is the executive director of IAMAS. Katie is currently writing *The Illusion of Choice*, which incorporates interviews with 100 US mothers. In addition to publishing with a myriad academic outlets, Katie has been consulted for or appeared in releases by the Center for Public Integrity, *Chicago Tribune*, Fast Company, *Nature*, NPR, and numerous podcasts. She is the mother of three human children and two furry ones.

Zaje A. T. Harrell, PhD, is a health psychologist with a passion for feminist theory and praxis. She holds a joint doctorate in psychology and women's studies, with expertise in coping, mental health, social identity, and community. She descends from the activist, justice-seeking tradition of Black clubwomen. Zaje owns a consulting practice and is a married Black feminist mother of three children, ages fourteen, eleven, and nine. They live in greater Baltimore Maryland.

Jodie Hawkes is an artist-researcher and senior lecturer in theatre at the University of Chichester. Jodie's research focusses on maternal performance, feminism, class politics, and activist practice. Jodie is a fellow of the Higher Education Academy. Jodie's artistic practice is undertaken in collaboration with Dr. Pete Phillips as the live art duo Search Party. Search Party's work is driven by practice and research and engages in collaborative strategies for performance-making and thinking.

Anna M. Hennessey, PhD, is a visiting scholar at the Graduate Theological Union in Berkeley, California. Her research is at the intersection of art, philosophy, religion, and birth. She is the author of *Imagery, Ritual, and Birth* (2018), an academic book, and has written numerous articles, book chapters, and essays about birth and mothering. Hennessey lives in San Francisco, California, with her husband and two children. For more information about her work, see annahennessey.com.

Bailey Higgins lives in Northeastern Pennsylvania with her husband and daughters. She earned a doctorate in social work from Kutztown University. She is passionate about social justice topics that impact mothers, such as access to child care, paid leave from employment, mental health, and overall wellness. She currently is employed as a case manager but hopes to one day join the rank of social work faculty to share her wisdom with budding social workers.

Dr. Nicole Dezrea Jenkins is an Assistant Professor in the Department of Sociology and Criminology at Howard University and a current Harvard University Faculty Fellow. She received her Doctoral degree from the University of Nevada Las Vegas in the Department of Sociology and holds an M.A. in Sociology from the same institution. In 2013, she earned an A.A. in Criminal Justice after serving six years of active duty in the United States Air Force as Military Police. Dr. Jenkins teaches undergraduate and graduate courses in Ethnography, Theory, Poverty, and the Black Community. As a qualitative researcher and urban ethnographer, she incorporates intersectional and critical feminist frameworks into her research, centering on the experiences of women in the African Diaspora. Her current book project, under contract with Princeton University Press and tentatively titled *CROWNed: Black Women's Entanglement with U.S. Institutions*, is based on two years of ethnographic research in a Las Vegas African hair braiding salon. This research delves into the complexities of Black women's identity-making and examines how perceptions of nationhood and Black womanhood can hinder this process. She leads the Global Crowns research project, expanding the discourse on natural hair discussions worldwide, and serves as faculty advisor for the Mothers of the Mecca Research Initiative, focusing on the experiences of student-parents at Howard University.

Sheree Mack is a Creatrix, she who makes with a practice which manifests through poetry, storytelling, image, and the unfolding histories of Black people. Sheree engages audiences around Black feminism, grief and healing, ecology and nature, as well as identity and memory. Sheree advocates for Black women's voices, facilitating national and international creative workshops and retreats in the landscape, encouraging and supporting women on their journey of remembrance back to their bodies and authentic selves. This journey is supported and recognized by Mother Nature.

Abigail L. Palko is the inaugural director of the Residential Commons Program at Colgate University, where she leads community efforts to nurture intellectual engagement and a sense of belonging through living-learning communities. Her scholarship focuses on literary/cultural representations of mothering and motherhood, especially the ways women writers depict the complexities of maternal practices labelled monstrous. Her monograph *Imagining Motherhood in Contemporary Irish and Caribbean Literature* (Palgrave Macmillan) examines abortion and queer mothering in contemporary novels; she is coeditor of *Monstrous Mothers: Troubling Tropes*; and *Mothers, Mothering, and Globalization* (all from Demeter Press), and *Feminist Responses to the Neoliberalization of the University: From Surviving to Thriving* (Lexington Books).

Michelann Parr is a white, able-bodied, cisgender woman, mother, daughter, sister, and scholar. She is the proud mother of three (plus one) children, one of whom would identify her as a radical feminist. She has two grandchildren who benefit from her later-years wisdom. Michelann is full professor in the Schulich School of Education at Nipissing University. Recent and upcoming edited collections include *Writing Mothers: Narrative Acts of Care, Redemption, and Transformation*; *Mothering Outside the Lines: Tales of Boundary Busting Mamas;* and *The Pain Mothers Must Never Expose: Confronting the Silences of Maternal Life.*

Florence Pasche Guignard is an assistant professor in religious studies at the Faculty of Theology and Religious Studies at the Université Laval (Quebec City). Her research explores issues at the intersection of religion with gender, ritual, embodiment, and digital and material cultures. She brings her interdisciplinary scholarship into conversation with anthropology, ritual studies, media studies, gender studies, and women's studies. Most of her recent publications explore motherhood and religion. More information is on her website: fpg.bio.

Pete Phillips is an artist-researcher and senior lecturer based at the University of Chichester. Pete's research includes the performativity of sport, collaborative duos, and ecological thinking. Pete's artistic practice is undertaken in collaboration with Dr Jodie Hawkes as the live art duo Search Party. Their work has been performed in venues and festivals in the UK and internationally. Jodie and Pete's current collaborative research project examines the performance and politics of care-making.

Martha Joy Rose is a writer, community organizer, and museum founder. Her work has been published across blogs and academic journals. She founded the Museum of Motherhood (MoM) in 2003. She currently lives in St. Petersburg, Florida, where she oversees the ongoing development of MoM.

Carolina Toscano has a PhD in Comparative Literature from the University of Washington. She teaches writing instruction and literature at the Saint Louis University Madrid Campus. She studies feminist maternal theory and migration in contemporary literature and film from Spain, Latin America, and the US.

Else Werring is a doctoral research fellow in Literature at the University of Oslo. She is currently working on the monograph *Swimming Against Plato: Timely Meditations on (m)Otherhood in Jeanette Winterson and Rachel Cusk.*

Nicole Willey is a professor of English and the associate director of the Center for Teaching and Learning at Kent State University. She writes about mothers, mentoring, and academe, and her most recent books are the co-edited collections *Motherhood Memoirs: Mothers Creating/Writing Lives* and *Feminist Fathering/Fathering Feminists: New Definitions and Directions*. She lives in New Philadelphia, Ohio, with her family.

Deepest appreciation to
Demeter's monthly Donors

DEMETER

Daughters

Brent & Heather Beal
Carole Trainor
Khin May Kyawt
Tatjana Takseva
Debbie Byrd
Tanya Cassidy
Myrel Chernick
Marcella Gemelli
Donna Lee, In Memory of Dee Stark, RN, LNHA,
Trailblazer for Women, Women's Rights Advocate
Catherine Cheleen-Mosqueda

Sisters

Fiona Green
Paul Chu
Amber Kinser
Nicole Willey

Mother

Mildred Bennett Walker (Trainor)

Grandmother

Tina Powell